DAILY LIVES OF

Civilians in Wartime Latin America

Recent Titles in
the Greenwood Press "Daily Life Through History" Series

Immigrant America, 1870–1920
June Granatir Alexander

Along the Mississippi
George S. Pabis

Immigrant America, 1820–1870
James M. Bergquist

Pre-Columbian Native America
Clarissa W. Confer

Post-Cold War
Stephen A. Bourque

The New Testament
James W. Ermatinger

The Hellenistic Age: From Alexander to Cleopatra
James Allan Evans

Imperial Russia
Greta Bucher

The Greenwood Encyclopedia of Daily Life in America, Four Volumes
Randall M. Miller, general editor

Civilians in Wartime Twentieth-Century Europe
Nicholas Atkin, editor

Ancient Egyptians, Revised Edition
Bob Brier and Hoyt Hobbs

DAILY LIVES OF

Civilians in Wartime Latin America

From the Wars of Independence to the Central American Civil Wars

EDITED BY PEDRO SANTONI

The Greenwood Press "Daily Life Through History Series"
Daily Life of Civilians during Wartime
David S. Heidler and Jeanne T. Heidler, Series Editors

GREENWOOD PRESS
Westport, Connecticut • London

Library of Congress Cataloging-in-Publication Data

Daily lives of civilians in wartime Latin America: from the wars of
independence to the Central American civil wars / edited by Pedro Santoni.
  p. cm. — (The Greenwood Press "Daily life through history" series,
ISSN 1080–4749)
  Includes bibliographical references and index.
  ISBN-13: 978–0–313–33594–5 (alk. paper)
  1. Latin America—Social life and customs. 2. War and society—Latin America.
  3. Latin America—History, Military. I. Santoni, Pedro. II. Series.
  F1408.3.D35 2008
  980—dc22   2008019220

British Library Cataloguing in Publication Data is available.

Library of Congress Catalog Card Number: 2008019220
ISBN: 978–0–313–33594–5
ISSN: 1080–4749

First published in 2008

Greenwood Press, 88 Post Road West, Westport, CT 06881
An imprint of Greenwood Publishing Group, Inc.
www.greenwood.com

Printed in the United States of America

The paper used in this book complies with the
Permanent Paper Standard issued by the National
Information Standards Organization (Z39.48–1984).

10 9 8 7 6 5 4 3 2 1

Contents

Series Foreword

Few scenes are as poignant as that of civilian refugees torn from their homes and put to plodding flight along dusty roads, carrying their possessions in crude bundles and makeshift carts. We have all seen the images. Before photography, paintings and crude drawings told the story, but despite the media, the same sense of the awful emerges from these striking portrayals: the pace of the flight is agonizingly slow; the numbers are sobering and usually arrayed in single file along the edges of byways that stretch to the horizon. The men appear hunched and beaten, the women haggard, the children strangely old, and usually the wide-eyed look of fear has been replaced by one of bone-grinding weariness. They likely stagger through country redolent of the odor of smoke and death as heavy guns mutter in the distance. It always seems to be raining on these people, or snowing, and it is either brutally cold or oppressively hot. In the past, clattering hooves would send them skittering away from the path of cavalry; more recently, whirring engines of motorized convoys push them from the road. Aside from becoming casualties, civilians who become refugees experience the most devastating impact of war, for they truly become orphans of the storm, lacking the barest necessities of food and clothing except for what they can carry and eventually what they can steal.

The volumes in this series seek to illuminate that extreme example of the civilian experience in wartime and more, for those on distant home fronts also can make remarkable sacrifices, whether through their labors to support the war effort or by enduring the absence of loved ones far from home and in great peril. And war can impinge on indigenous populations in eccentric ways. Stories of a medieval world in which a farmer fearful about his crops could prevail on armies to fight elsewhere are possibly exaggerated, the product of nostalgia for a chivalric code that most likely did not hold much sway during a coarse and vicious time. In any period and at any place, the fundamental reality of war is that organized violence is no less brutal for its being structured by strategy and tactics. The advent of total war might have been signaled by the famous *levée en masse* of the French Revolution, but that development was more a culmination of a trend than an innovation away from more pacific times. In short, all wars have assailed and will assail civilians in one way or another to a greater or lesser degree. The Thirty Years' War displaced populations just as the American Revolution saw settlements preyed upon, houses razed, and farms pillaged. Modern codes of conduct adopted by both international consent and embraced by the armies of the civilized world have heightened awareness about the sanctity of civilians and have improved vigilance about violations of that sanctity, but in the end such codes will never guarantee immunity from the rage of battle or the rigors of war.

In this series, accomplished scholars have recruited prescient colleagues to write essays that reveal both the universal civilian experience in wartime and aspects of it made unique by time and place. Readers will discover in these pages the other side of warfare, one that is never placid, even if far removed from the scenes of fighting. As these talented authors show, the shifting expectations of governments markedly transformed the civilian wartime experience from virtual non-involvement in early modern times to the twentieth century's expectation of sacrifice, exertion, and contribution. Finally, as the Western powers have come full circle by asking virtually no sacrifice from civilians at all, they have stumbled upon the peculiar result that diminishing deprivation during a war can increase civilian dissent against it.

Moreover, the geographical and chronological span of these books is broad and encompassing to reveal the unique perspectives of how war affects people whether they are separated by hemispheres or centuries, people who are distinct by way of different cultures yet similar because of their common humanity. As readers will see, days on a home front far from battle usually become a surreal routine of the ordinary existing in tandem with the extraordinary, a situation in which hours of waiting and expectation become blurred against the backdrop of normal tasks and everyday events. That situation is a constant, whether for a village in Asia or Africa, or Europe or the Americas.

Consequently, these books confirm that the human condition always produces the similar as well the singular, a paradox that war tends to amplify. Every war is much like another, but no war is really the same as any other. All places are much alike, but no place is wholly separable from its matchless identity. The civilian experience in war mirrors these verities. We are certain that readers will find in these books a vivid illumination of those truths.

David S. Heidler and Jeanne T. Heidler
Series Editors

Preface

The purpose of *Daily Lives of Civilians in Wartime Latin America* is to explore the experiences faced by those who are not active members of the military during times of war. It observes the profound legacies that nine periods of war have left on Latin America's civilian population from the first part of the nineteenth century to the end of the twentieth century. The chapters in this book examine many types of warfare in Latin America, including domestic war, international conflict, and state-sponsored terror. Despite these often terrifying upheavals, the complexity and resilience of civilian life in the midst of Latin America's tumultuous development shines through.

Arranged in chronological order, the 10 chapters are written by distinguished scholars of Latin American history, two of whom have lived as civilians through the wars and bloodshed they describe. The first chapter, "Two Centuries of War in Latin America: An Overview," serves as my summation of this book's motivating purpose, and provides helpful background to its finely authored contributions. The second chapter, "Death, Destiny, and the Daily Chores: Everyday Life in Spanish America during the Wars of Independence, 1808–1826" by Karen Racine, is set during the region's struggle against Spanish colonial rule. Her essay discusses the wars' impact on a wide array of topics that include popular and elite forms of entertainment, street life, gender, race, and economic affairs such as the collection of tariffs and wartime profiteering.

My contribution to this volume, "The Civilian Experience in Mexico during the War with the United States, 1846–1848," describes the conflict's impact on the everyday life of residents of Mexico. The chapter examines the interaction between U.S. troops and Mexican civilians, the impact of military operations on people in several towns and cities, the relationship between the government and its citizens as Mexico went about securing money and men to support the war, the consequences of collaboration with the enemy, and the effect of war on everyday social activities.

The next essay, "Civilians and Civil War in Nineteenth-Century Mexico: Mexico City and the War of the Reform, 1858–1861," by Daniel S. Haworth, takes place in the aftermath of the so-called 1854 Ayutla Revolt. The rebellion forced General Antonio López de Santa Anna into exile in mid-1855, and allowed liberal leaders to usher in the period known as the *Reforma* (Reform) (1855–1876). During this era the reformers attempted to modernize Mexico by instituting profound changes in the country's politics and economic structures, but their efforts started a violent cycle of political strife that lasted for more than 20 years and led to immense human suffering.

The essay by Vitor Izecksohn and Peter M. Beattie, "The Brazilian Home Front during the War of the Triple Alliance, 1864–1870," looks at the Brazilian civilian experience on the home front during its conflict against Paraguay. According to the authors, the scale of the struggle was so unlike most wars that had confronted the Brazilian state since independence in 1822. As a result, the efforts of the constitutional monarchy led by Pedro II to raise troops encountered several roadblocks that were unknown before. These obstacles placed numerous strains on the traditional social hierarchies of race, age, and gender, and also led to problems with traditional ways of conducting politics at the local and regional level.

"Civilians and the War of the Pacific, 1879–1884," by Bruce W. Farcau, describes the effects on civilians of the other major international conflict in South America in the late 1800s. Hostilities meant that a significant part of the male populations of all three participating countries, Chile, Bolivia, and Peru, had to endure military service. Furthermore, the war thrust women into roles such as serving along with the army as laundresses, medics, and caterers. Women also provided companionship to the troops and occasionally fought on the battlefield. The conflict caused significant damage to the Peruvian economy because most of the war took place on its soil.

The chapter by John Lear, "'¡*No Vamos a la Revolución!*' Civilians as *Revolucionarios* and *Revolucionados* in the 1910 Mexican Revolution," examines how the Mexican people took part in and lived through the revolutionary decade of 1910, and in so examining, identifies three major (and sometimes overlapping) groups or categories—those who shared the same social background and objectives of the rebel groups, those who did not associate with any of the insurgents and simply tried to survive as the violence disrupted their everyday lives, and those who left their homes either for urban areas or for the United States.

Gillian McGillivray's chapter, "Reading Revolution from Below: Cuba 1933," shows how urban and rural workers proved instrumental in bringing about the ouster of President Gerardo Machado's repressive regime in 1933. McGillivray focuses her piece on the revolution in Havana, but she pays close attention to sugar workers in the countryside as well. She demonstrates that the workers' actions and the ensuing unrest raised the specter of social warfare, and led Fulgencio Batista to seize power in 1934. Nonetheless, the experience of 1933 allowed the Cuban masses to subsequently pressure governments for better working conditions and political participation.

Margaret Power elaborates on military governments in her chapter "Repression and Resistance, Hatred and Hope: Civilian Life during the Military Dictatorships in the Southern Cone, 1964–1990," which pays particular attention to Chile under General Augusto Pinochet. In addition to describing her own experiences in Chile during the dictatorship, she explains the domestic and international context that allowed the armed forces to seize power, how the dictatorships controlled public affairs and affected everyday civilian life, why men and women supported or opposed military regimes, and the legacies of military rule. Power reminds us that violence has a psychological dimension, one that decisively shapes not only the political environment, but also social relations.

Arturo Arias's chapter, "And the Storm Raged On: The Daily Experience of Terror during the Central American Civil Wars, 1966–1996," takes readers inside the world of these vicious struggles, with a particular focus on the terror that military regimes and death squads inflicted on Guatemalans. Arias is a widely acclaimed professor of literature and author, probably best known for the 1979 novel *After the Bombs*, which captures the essence of everyday life in Guatemala following the 1954 U.S. Central Intelligence Agency-led covert operation known as PBSUCCESS. Arias's intense tone in this piece emanates from his personal investment in the subject. A native of Guatemala, Arias lived through many of the experiences he relates in his powerful, emotionally charged essay.

The book closes with a glossary to help the reader better understand some of the people, concepts, events, and places discussed in the chapters. An annotated bibliography, divided by chapter topics, guides the user to more resources that will help build a better understanding of the lives of Latin American civilians during wartime, and a comprehensive index is included as well.

Acknowledgments

Because a book is a collaborative endeavor, I would like to thank those individuals whose hard work made this volume possible. First and foremost I am indebted to David Heidler, who invited me to take on this project. I hope that the final product meets his expectations. The help of Greenwood's very own Mike Hermann and Anne Thompson proved invaluable. Anne in particular went above and beyond the call of duty as she not only read the entire manuscript, but also tracked down many photographs that appear in the book. I am grateful for the assistance of David Nimri, the wizard of California State University, San Bernardino's Information Technology Department. Thanks to his immense know-how of computers I was able to include the lithograph of Celedonio Jarauta in my essay on the U.S.-Mexican War, as well as the two lithographs of Mexico City in Daniel S. Haworth's chapter. I found the latter images thanks to the help of my good friend in Mexico City, Helia Emma Bonilla Reyna; Helia also put me in touch with María José Esparza, who kindly sent a photograph she had taken of the lithograph about the Battle of Tacubaya that also appears in Haworth's chapter.

In Peru the generous spirit of another dear friend, Judy Yong, as well as of Captain José Carlos Perales Wong and Colonel Manuel Ríos Lavagna, the Director of Museums for the Peruvian army, merits my appreciation. Their efforts allowed me to enhance Bruce

Farcau's essay with a reproduction of Ramón Muñiz's 1888 painting, "*El Repase,*" which is located at the *Museo del Ejército Real Felipe* in the port city of Callao. The comments made by three contributors— Haworth, Margaret Power, and Gillian McGillivray—as well as by my fellow historians of Mexico Paul Vanderwood and Shannon Baker-Tuller, greatly improved the two chapters I authored for this volume. Last, but certainly not least, I am indebted to each and every contributor. They all patiently endured my suggestions on how to revise their essays. I know that my pleas must have proved burdensome, but in the end I can only hope that they are pleased with the end result.

Timeline

1808	Napoleon Bonaparte invades Spain, forces Charles IV and his son Ferdinand to abdicate, and installs his brother Joseph as king. Creole juntas that seek autonomy emerge in Spanish America
1810	Struggle for independence begins in Spanish America with revolts in Mexico, Venezuela, Argentina, Chile, and Colombia
1811	Independence of Paraguay
1814	Ferdinand VII assumes Spanish throne, restores absolutist rule, and repeals 1812 Cádiz Constitution
1816–1818	Independence of Argentina and Chile
1820	Rebellion in Spanish port of Cádiz by Lieutenant Colonel Rafael del Riego forces Ferdinand VII to restore 1812 Cádiz constitution
1821	Independence of Mexico, Central America, Venezuela, and Colombia
1822	Brazil gains independence from Portugal and becomes a constitutional monarchy

1824–1825	Peru and Bolivia gain their independence
1836	Texas declares its independence from Mexico
1841	Pedro II is crowned emperor of Brazil
1845	U.S. annexation of Texas
1846	Skirmish in disputed territory leads to U.S.-Mexican War
1847	U.S. General Winfield Scott lands with U.S. expeditionary army in Mexico's east coast, and marches inland to capture Mexico City
1848	The Treaty of Guadalupe Hidalgo brings to an end war between Mexico and the United States, and strips the former of half its territory
1854–1855	Ayutla Revolution (Mexico) ends dictatorial rule of General Antonio López de Santa Anna and launches the *Reforma*
1857	Conservative Mexican General Félix Zuloaga stages a coup in December that shuts down Congress and revokes a recently issued constitution
1858	General Zuloaga declares himself president; this marks the beginning of the War of the Reform/Three Years' War in Mexico
1859	Conservative leaders in Mexico appoint General Miguel Miramón to replace Zuloaga as chief executive
1860	Liberal army defeats Miramón at the Battle of Calpulalpan on December 22. Within two weeks Liberal president Benito Juárez arrives in Mexico City, bringing the War of the Reform/Three Years' War to a close
1864–1870	Paraguayan strongman Francisco Solano López seizes Brazilian vessel, effectively beginning the War of the Triple Alliance (Brazil, Argentina, and Uruguay versus Paraguay)
1868–1878	First Cuban War (Ten Years' War) for independence from Spain

1869	Paraguayan-organized armed resistance to the Allied assault ends
1870	Brazilian troops surround and kill Solano López. The War of the Triple Alliance ends with a Brazilian victory
1876–1911	Porfirio Díaz rules Mexico
1879–1884	War of the Pacific (Chile versus Peru and Bolivia) for control of nitrate-rich lands begins. When the war ends, Chile has increased its territory by one-third
1881	Chilean troops sack and occupy Lima
1889	Military rebellion in Brazil forces Pedro II to abdicate. The country becomes a republic
1895	Second War for Cuban independence
1898	United States intervenes in Cuba's Second War for independence; ensuing peace treaty ends conflict between the United States and Spain, and transfers Cuba's sovereignty to the former
1899	U.S. military occupation of Cuba begins
1901	U.S. Congress adopts the so-called Platt Amendment, which for all practical purposes makes a Cuba a U.S. protectorate
1902	U.S. military occupation of Cuba ends. This event begins Cuba's life as a sovereign nation
1903	United States signs three treaties with Cuba—including a Reciprocity Treaty—to insure informal control over island's affairs
1910	Francisco Madero rebels against Díaz, and launches the Mexican Revolution
1917	Mexico adopts a new constitution; the charter sets forth the goals for the Revolution
1920	General Alvaro Obregón becomes president of Mexico, and the military phase of the 1910 Revolution comes to an end
1924–1933	Gerardo Machado rules as president of Cuba

1927–1933	Nicaragua's Augusto César Sandino leads insurrection against U.S. forces
1928	National Revolutionary Party (later the *Partido Revolucionario Institucional*, or PRI) established in Mexico. Start of one-party rule
1933	U.S. President Franklin Delano Roosevelt institutes the Good Neighbor Policy; its keystone is nonintervention
	Cuban Revolution of 1933 ousts Machado, and brings to power Ramón Grau San Martín, who enacts numerous social, economic, and political reforms
1934	Fulgencio Batista, with assistance from U.S. ambassador, overthrows Grau San Martín government. Batista stands as the dominant figure in Cuban politics until 1959
1937–1979	The Somoza family rules Nicaragua
1952	Guatemalan president Jacobo Arbenz issues Decree 900. The law, as it promotes agrarian reform, also threatens the property owned by the United Fruit Company, a large U.S. corporation
1954	The U.S. Central Intelligence Agency (CIA) puts into effect Operation PBSUCCESS to overthrow President Arbenz
1959	Fidel Castro seizes power in Cuba. Castro's victory inspires guerrilla insurgencies throughout Latin America
1960	Cuba and the Soviet Union reestablish diplomatic relations
1960–1973	Guerrilla movement emerges in Guatemala
1961	U.S. President John F. Kennedy launches the Alliance for Progress
	At Punta del Este, Uruguay, foreign ministers from Latin America and the United States establish specific goals for Alliance for Progress
1964	Military in Brazil seize power

1967	Ernesto "Che" Guevara is killed in Bolivia as he attempts to spark a continent-wide guerrilla uprising
1970	Salvador Allende is elected president of Chile
1973	General Augusto Pinochet leads Chilean military in coup. The takeover deposes Allende, who dies in the presidential palace
1976	Argentina's military takes power and launches so-called "Dirty War"
	Formation of the Mothers of the May Day Plaza (*Madres de la Plaza de Mayo*) in Argentina. Their struggle for human rights stirs women elsewhere in Latin America to fight for the same cause
1979	Sandinista rebels overthrow Somoza dictatorship. The Sandinista Revolution begins
1980	Farabundo Martí National Liberation Front (FMLN) is created in El Salvador
1981	Approximately 1,000 civilians, including women and children, are massacred by the Atlacatl Battalion in El Salvador in the towns of El Mozote, La Joya, Cerro Pando, Ranchería, Los Toriles, and Jocote Amarillo
1982	Argentina's military invades Falklands/Malvinas islands, but is defeated by Great Britain. Military government collapses as a result
	General Efraín Ríos Montt seizes power in Guatemala. His regime becomes notorious for human rights violations
1985	Civilian rule restored to Brazil
1988	Chile's General Pinochet loses plebiscite, paving the way for the return of civilian rule
1990	Sandinista president Daniel Ortega loses elections to Violeta Chamorro; Sandinista Revolution comes to an end
1992	Salvadoran government signs agreement with guerrillas to end civil war

1996	Peace agreement between the government and the guerrillas ends Guatemalan civil war
1998	General Pinochet is arrested in Great Britain on charges of human rights violations
2006	General Pinochet dies in Santiago, Chile. He receives a military funeral, but not a state funeral as his supporters desired

ONE

Two Centuries of War in Latin America: An Overview

Pedro Santoni

Of all the scourges to hit Latin America since the late 1970s, none has weakened its social fabric as much as *el narcotráfico* (drug trafficking). While the consequences of the drug trade have particularly harmed Colombia, a country with a history of widespread violence, the carnage engendered by the war on drugs during the latter part of the twentieth century reached unprecedented heights because it "progressively invaded all spheres of [Colombia's] public and private life." Drug trafficking, as one author recently put it, has transformed that country into a near replica of Germany during the destructive Thirty Years' War (1618–1648). Both nations were "overrun by private armies and opportunistic soldiers of fortune," and consequently became "plundered land[s] full of displaced and desperate people."[1] Statistics bear out this assessment. As of 2004 in Colombia more than 20,000 guerrillas, 250,000 army and police, and at least 10,000 members of right-wing paramilitary death squads had waged war against each other, and by 2006 the conflict had driven more than 3 million people (a disproportionate number of which are Afro-Colombians) from their homes. In comparative terms, only the African nation of Sudan had more internally displaced persons in its midst.[2]

Most scholars trace the roots of this bloodshed to the assassination of popular Liberal presidential hopeful José Eliécer Gaitán in

Bogotá on April 9, 1948. His death provoked an immense urban riot, the so-called *Bogotazo*, wherein the city's poor lynched the suspected killer and went on a rampage, destroying government and religious buildings, as well as other symbols of authority, perceived oppression, and power.[3] The fighting then spread through the countryside in a "nightmarish period of bloodletting so empty of meaning" that claimed the lives of at least 200,000 peasants from 1948 to 1966.[4] During this era, commonly known *La Violencia*, opposing political parties organized paramilitary death squads and armed guerrillas with the intent not just to "kill the enemy but to wipe it from the earth completely." To that end sympathizers from both sides committed unspeakable acts of violence that included bayoneting babies, raping women in front of family members, and mutilating men and women alike.[5]

La Violencia gave way during the 1960s to guerrilla warfare as young Colombians intent on duplicating the experience of the 1959 Cuban Revolution in their homeland formed several insurgent groups. Although within 20 years the guerrilla movement found itself in dire straits, the rebel groups that managed to survive showed renewed vigor during the 1980s partly as a result of Colombia's emerging role as the main purveyor of cocaine to the United States. By 1978, according to Drug Enforcement Agency estimates, 85 percent of all cocaine sold in the United States came from Colombia. The expansion of the cocaine trade, as well as its value (an approximate U.S. $4 billion a year) allowed guerrilla groups like the *Fuerzas Armadas Revolucionarias de Colombia* (FARC, or Revolutionary Armed Forces of Colombia) to charge the recently emerged cartels that dominated drug trafficking a 10 percent tax to protect coca fields and processing plants.[6]

Countering the guerrillas and the drug traffickers—who became increasingly reliant on the use of bribes, intimidation, and violence to eliminate or silence those who opposed their power—was the Colombian military as well as a growing number of paramilitary groups who in 1997 coalesced into an organization known as *Autodefensas Unidas de Colombia* (AUC, or United Self-Defense Groups of Colombia).[7] This volatile mix nearly wrecked the Colombian political system in the 1990s as the country descended into a "deadly cycle of violence and counter-violence. Guerrillas kidnapped and assassinated candidates, blew up police stations, and sought to disrupt elections. Paramilitary rightist death squads responded in kind and worse . . . Human rights violations and politically inspired murders in Colombia exceeded levels in the worst military dictatorships in South America. . . . Peasants, businessmen, labor leaders, politicians, judges—indeed, virtually anyone—could be victimized by a society at war with itself." Conditions in Colombia had not improved by 2004, at which time the United Nations' undersecretary for humanitarian affairs characterized the situation as "by far the biggest humanitarian catastrophe in the Western Hemisphere."[8]

The U.S. media—as illustrated by the following stories taken from major metropolitan newspapers like the *Los Angeles Times* and *The New York Times*—has reported extensively about the ways the war on drugs continues to intrude into the everyday lives of Colombians of all ages, genders, and social classes in a variety of locales. Buenaventura, home to 300,000 people and Colombia's most important urban center on the Pacific coast, became the country's deadliest city in 2006; the 408 murders registered there gave the port city a homicide rate of 144 per 100,000 inhabitants, which greatly exceeded that of Bogotá and Medellín. The levels of violence have forced public figures to forego even the most basic forms of recreation. Cielo Gónzalez, the mayor of Neiva in southern Colombia, lamented early in the spring of 2007 that she could no longer "do any of the simple things . . . [she] used to do, like jog in the mornings, go to the hairdresser, parties, or the movies." Having survived two attempts on her life since her election to the post in late 2003, Gónzalez began to travel in the country's most heavily armored sport utility vehicle (SUV) accompanied by a security escort of 10 armed bodyguards. Innocent civilians have paid an even higher price for the war due to the increased reliance on land mines by all combatants. According to the International Campaign to Ban Landmines, in 2003 Colombia ranked third in the world—behind Afghanistan and Cambodia—in terms of casualties. An illiterate farmer named Luis Alfonso Quintero, a resident of Aquitania, a remote village in Antioquía state located 90 miles off the main highway via a rutted dirt road, became his town's first civilian mine victim. One day that June, as Quintero headed down a path he had taken to harvest some crops just 24 hours before, he stepped on a mine and lost his left leg; because the explosion also injured his right leg Quintero might never walk again.[9]

The war on drugs that has wreaked havoc on Colombia and its people (and present-day Mexico as well) is but the latest chapter in the history of warfare in Latin America since the achievement of independence from Spain and Portugal in the 1820s. The advent of political freedom from European powers did not bring peace to the region; during the nineteenth century 44 international wars and foreign invasions, as well as numerous civil wars, ravaged Latin America and left it "with a deserved reputation as chaotic, violent, and authoritarian."[10] Warfare remained a constant in Latin America during the next 100 years—as evidenced, for instance, by the 1910 Mexican Revolution, the so-called "Dirty Wars" that unsettled Latin America's Southern Cone beginning in 1964, and the conflicts that ravaged Central America in the 1980s. These and other struggles did much to uphold the validity of Robert Holden's assessment of the twentieth century as "humanity's golden age of killing, both in the monumental scale and the astonishing inventiveness of the planning, organization, financing, execution, and legitimization of killing."[11]

CIVILIANS' DAILY LIVES IN NINE EPISODES OF WAR

The essays that appear in these pages bring together fresh efforts to address the deep imprints that nine episodes of war have left on Latin America's civilian population during the last 200 years. They complement works such as René de la Pedraja's *Wars of Latin America, 1899–1941,* and Miguel A. Centeno's two-volume edited set entitled *Warfare in Latin America.*[12] Both books tackled this same subject and appeared in print during the time that this volume was conceived, written, and edited. Readers of this work, however, need to understand two issues to clarify the impact of war on the everyday affairs of Latin Americans across different countries and time periods. The first involves the meaning of "civilian" in the context of Latin American warfare. As currently defined in the United States, the term denotes anyone who is not a member of the standing army or its reserves. This idea does not hold true in Latin America, where combatants can include members of the standing army, state or local militias, and insurgents who are otherwise indistinguishable from the general population. Essays in this collection, then, equate *civilian* with *noncombatant.* Second, because the chapters in this book address the manifold nature of warfare in Latin America—domestic war, international conflict, and state-sponsored terror—readers will appreciate the complexity and resilience of civilian life in the midst of Latin America's tumultuous development.

The second essay, "Death, Destiny, and the Daily Chores: Everyday Life in Spanish America during the Wars of Independence, 1808–1826," by Karen Racine, is set during the region's struggle against Spanish colonial rule. Until recently, historians of the wars that erupted in the wake of the 1808 French occupation of Spain placed the great national heroes of the conflicts, men like Venezuela's Simón Bolívar, Argentina's José de San Martín, and Mexico's Miguel Hidalgo y Costilla, to name but three, in a pantheon of glory.[13] Contemporary views of the process of independence are more complex, however, and shy away from such adulation. A vivid and popular expression of this reassessment is the 1989 novel by Colombian Nobel Prize laureate Gabriel García Márquez, *The General in his Labyrinth*. Set in 1830, the book chronicles the last two weeks of Bolívar's life as he journeyed downstream along Colombia's Magdalena River en route to exile, and depicts him as a disillusioned man nursing his lost dream of a united continent. A new collection of essays about Bolívar, as well as one recent article and two biographies of the independence leader, also steer clear of hagiography. Of the latter, the book penned by the preeminent British scholar John Lynch aims to "integrate Bolívar more closely into the new research" of Spanish American independence.[14]

Scholars engaged in this agenda are paying less attention to the economic, political, and ideological causes and effects of the conflicts for independence, and are instead producing "new and compelling interpretations about the nature of the insurgencies, counterinsurgencies, rebellions, guerrilla movements, civil wars, revolutions, riots, banditry, and other forms of disorder that helped to engender the new nations."[15] Notable among these works is Eric Van Young's account of the insurrection against Spanish rule in Mexico. Popular insurgency between 1810 and 1821, he contents, attempted to defend communal identity against "forces of change both internal and external, rather than to achieve the observed outcome of the political struggle, the consolidation of independence from Spain."[16] Historians who study the period have also begun to closely scrutinize categories like race, class, and gender. For example, Aline Helg examined the role of the lower classes in Colombia's Caribbean region, particularly those of African descent, in that country's independence movement, while Sarah C. Chambers has shed light on how the transition to independence severely limited the political and social freedoms of women in the Peruvian city of Arequipa.[17]

Racine's essay on civilian life during the wars of independence builds on these trends as it discusses the wars' impact on a wide array of topics that include popular and elite forms of entertainment, street life, gender, race, and economic affairs like the collection of tariffs and wartime profiteering. Her panoramic view of the liberation movements' effects on these endeavors goes a long way toward demonstrating how the larger processes of securing independence from Spanish rule and setting up nation-states affected the everyday life of men, women, and children in the region, and shows how people tried to maintain a measure of control over daily life amidst the chaos and bedlam wrought by war.

In the decades that followed independence, Latin American leaders attempted to build stable and prosperous nations, but political chaos, economic dislocation, and social hatreds made the process difficult. These seemingly interminable convulsions particularly affected Mexico and made it easier for the United States, which had long coveted Texas, to annex the former Mexican province in 1845. Relations between both nations steadily deteriorated from that point on, culminating in the outbreak of war late in the spring of 1846. Within two years U.S. armies not only held much of northern Mexico, but they also had marched east from the port city of Veracruz and occupied the national capital. The conflict came to an end early in 1848 when negotiators from both countries hammered out a peace settlement—the Treaty of Guadalupe Hidalgo—that stripped Mexico of half its territory.

To this day—and in stark contrast to the United States, where the war is no more than an afterthought in the public imagination—reverberations from the conflict remain deeply embedded in the Mexican psyche. The two-year struggle, according to Mexican historian Miguel Soto, left a "wound [that] never really healed," and the abrasion has since manifested itself in a "virulent, almost pathological, Yankeephobia" that still drives Mexican nationalism.[18] Ill feelings toward the United States surface in a variety of settings (particularly during periods of domestic crisis), and affect bilateral relations with regard to issues such as immigration, water resources, and the war on drugs. The antipathy materializes on the soccer field as well, where the United States and Mexico compete in "the most heated international rivalry in North American sports." When the U.S. soccer team faced Mexico in a qualifying match for the 2004 Olympics, Mexican fans shouted "Osama [bin Laden]! Osama [bin Laden]!" Another recent manifestation of Mexican hostility took place during the 2007 Miss Universe pageant when the Mexico City audience booed Miss U.S.A. in what many would consider not a "simple matter of bad manners toward a guest, but an upwelling of national angst."[19]

Such unsympathetic sentiments have not deterred historians, particularly since the 1996 sesquicentennial of the commencement of armed hostilities, from reinterpreting the issues around which the conflict revolved and exploring as well neglected aspects of the war. Two collections of essays, one by Laura Herrera Serna and the other by Josefina Zoraida Vázquez, have examined the war's impact on Mexico's regions. Their approach has provided a much-needed counterbalance to the focus on the war from the viewpoint of central Mexico and the nation's capital, a position borne out by one of the most common monikers that Mexicans use to refer to the conflict. The term *"Guerra del '47"* (War of [18]47), by limiting itself to the year that Mexico City fell to the U.S. army, infers that all other events were irrelevant. In addition, scholars have shed light on the war's cultural dimensions. They have probed into ways that Mexican statesmen manufactured heroic symbols and figures, and subsequently negotiated their public memory, in order to bolster the country's self-esteem and national spirit in the aftermath of war. Historians have also chronicled the activities of three other little-known protagonists of the conflict—the heretofore-shadowy guerrillas who roamed the countryside and resisted both the foreign invaders and the Mexican state, the so-called "masses" of Mexico City, who in mid-September 1847 staged a three-day riot against General Winfield Scott and the U.S. expeditionary army, and the Indians that raided northern Mexico during the 1830s and 1840s—so as to illustrate their vital role in the U.S.-Mexican War.[20]

My chapter, "The Civilian Experience in Mexico during the War with the United States, 1846–1848," touches on various aspects of the conflict's impact on the everyday life of residents of Mexico. The chapter examines the interaction between U.S. troops (officers as well as rank-and-file soldiers) and Mexican civilians, the impact of conventional military operations on residents of several major population centers, the relationship between the Mexican state and its citizens as the former sought to raise money and men to support the war effort, the consequences of collaborating with the enemy, and the ways in which the war affected everyday social activities. These wartime developments had an ambiguous effect on civilian life. On the one hand they exposed deep political, economic, and social insecurities, and exacerbated as well anxieties about national survival, but they also created opportunities for civilians to more fully participate in Mexican public affairs in the near future.

"Civilians and Civil War in Nineteenth-Century Mexico: Mexico City and the War of the Reform, 1858–1861," by Daniel S. Haworth, is an essay that focuses on a common nineteenth-century Latin American phenomenon—civil wars and *pronunciamientos* (revolts).

Earlier accounts considered these episodes as nothing but "pur-
poseless tragedies" largely manufactured by "the blind obedience
of individual soldiers to a charismatic leader," but recent research
has challenged these interpretations. Historians have argued that
the origins and impact of these internal disputes were more complex than previously thought, that such conflicts were inherent to
Latin America's political culture, and that their participants often
understood the wars' ideological context.[21] One scholar has further
suggested, with regard to the rebellions that erupted in Mexico
during the so-called Age of Santa Anna (1821–1855), that these upheavals did not significantly destabilize the country because they
only affected a small number of its residents. Of the 12 uprisings
that had a crucial effect on national politics during that era only two
involved large-scale fighting on a national scale.[22]

One of the rebellions that had nationwide consequences for Mexico provides the historical background for Haworth's essay. The so-
called Ayutla Revolt erupted early in 1854 in the southern Mexican
state of Guerrero as a reaction to the project of General Antonio
López de Santa Anna and Conservative politicians to crush federalism, states' rights, and regional autonomy. The rebellion's steady
expansion throughout the country forced Santa Anna into exile in
August 1855, and enabled Liberal leaders to usher in the period
known as the *Reforma* (Reform) (1855–1876). Intent on modernizing
Mexico by eliminating all remnants of the Spanish colonial legacy
from its political and economic structures, the victors' endeavors
triggered a more violent cycle of political strife that launched the
country's "most profound crisis of the nineteenth century," one that
lasted for more than 20 years and produced "human suffering on
a scale unequaled since the ravages of disease had decimated the
Indian population in the sixteenth century."[23]

Some of that destruction occurred during the civil war commonly
known as either the War of the Reform or the Three Years' War
(1858–1861). As Liberals and Conservatives took to the battlefield to
settle their differences and impose their vision for Mexico's future,
they caused great damage in the nation's heartland, where most of
the fighting took place. The U.S. consul in Veracruz reported in 1859,
for example, that "haciendas were abandoned, ranchos deserted,
and villages pillaged and sacked." In the mountainous regions of
the central state of Puebla, the Three Years' War amplified daily tensions as it unleashed a "novel and disturbing pattern of political assassinations, atrocities, and retaliatory plunderings" that deepened
"traditional enmities and rivalries between neighboring towns."[24]

Such devastation, however, did not dramatically impact the daily lives of many Mexicans elsewhere in the country. Although Liberals and Conservatives relied on conscription to swell the ranks of their armies, the total number of men under arms never surpassed 25,000 (out of a total population of 8 million). Haworth's examination of everyday life in Mexico City during the War of the Reform underscores this idea. He shows that the civilian population of the nation's capital hardly experienced the fury and the destructiveness unleashed by that bitter conflict. For the most part residents of Mexico City went about their daily activities untouched by wartime violence. The major constraints that war imposed on them concerned taxation and press censorship, and this was partly due, as Haworth puts it, to the fact that "Conservative regimes depended on the capital for their survival and so worked to preserve an orderly status quo." This finding reinforces the idea that the War of the Reform was "not a popular war in either sense of the word. The great mass of people neither approved of it nor enlisted in it. It was a war between the ruling minorities."[25]

Like Mexico, the nascent republics of South America experienced both domestic unrest and international war during the nineteenth century, and two chapters in this book address the impact on civilians of the latter type of conflict. The essay by Vitor Izecksohn and Peter M. Beattie, "The Brazilian Home Front during the War of the Triple Alliance, 1864–1870," is set during the conflict that pitted Brazil, Argentina, and Uruguay against Paraguay. This war, the most prolonged in the region since the 1820s, holds a more prominent place in Paraguay's iconography than in the symbols and sites associated with the conflict in the other belligerent nations. Nonetheless, the War of the Triple Alliance is as significant to South American history as the civil war of 1861–1865 is to the United States. The conflict also represents, within the annals of Latin America, a "unique case of total mobilization" comparable to some European struggles of the past century,[26] and historians have begun to reassess some long-standing assumptions about the war.

One such reevaluation, the extent of Paraguayan population losses during the war, recently provoked a spirited debate among scholars of the conflict. Conventional wisdom holds that the War of the Triple Alliance cost Paraguay half of its prewar population of 400,000.[27] After analyzing a number of sources that included Paraguayan censuses and household structures in 1988, Vera Linn Reber concluded that such casualties had been "enormously exaggerated," and that a more accurate assessment would place the losses somewhere between 8 and 17.8 percent of its population.[28] Two years later Thomas L. Whigham and Barbara Potthast challenged Reber's interpretation because her position, in their opinion, "lacked a strong foundation," and involved "serious methodological and empirical difficulties."[29] But thanks to a fortuitous turn of events, by 1999 the debate apparently came to an end when a Paraguayan military officer accidentally found a national census from 1870 at the *Ministerio de Defensa Nacional* (National Defense Ministry). Whigham's and Potthast's analysis of its data led them to assert that previous references to the percentages of Paraguayans who died or were displaced by the war had to be discarded; they came up with a much higher estimate that ranged between 60 and 69 percent.[30]

Other publications have reexamined various topics or shed light on new issues about the War of the Triple Alliance. In 2002 Whigham and Chris Leuchers reconsidered the factors that led to war and reassessed the role of Paraguayan strongman Francisco Solano López in the conflict. Solano López comes off as a more positive and complex personality than usual; he was not simply a "vainglorious tyrant who sought war in a futile effort to make himself emperor of South America."[31] The Paraguayan ruler is also the subject of a new scholarly biography by James Schofield Saeger.[32] Most pertinent to the theme of this volume is the collection of essays edited by Hendrik Kraay and Whigham, *I Die with My Country: Perspectives on the Paraguayan War, 1864–1870.* Published in 2005, this work consists of 10 articles that "look beneath the political, military, and diplomatic questions that have dominated scholarship" on the war, and instead focuses on trying to "understand how men and women saw this conflict and how it shaped them and their societies."[33] Two of the pieces look closely at the war's effects on Paraguay's economy, population, and women, while five essays discuss home-front activities (e.g., draft resistance, challenge to racial hierarchies) in Brazil, Uruguay, and Argentina.

Izecksohn's and Beattie's chapter, which is enhanced by a number of vivid caricatures from the era, adds to these findings as it looks at the Brazilian civilian experience on the home front. They argue that the scale of War of the Triple Alliance bore little resemblance to most conflicts that had confronted the Brazilian state since independence in 1822, and consequently the efforts of the constitutional monarchy led by Pedro II to raise troops not only encountered several roadblocks, but also placed numerous strains on traditional social hierarchies—of race, age, and gender—and on time-honored ways of conducting politics at the local and regional levels. Forced conscription, moreover, had significant long-term consequences because it became a formidable stumbling block to military recruitment reform that government officials could not solve until the 1910s.

A chapter by Bruce W. Farcau, "Civilians and the War of the Pacific, 1879–1884," describes the effects on civilians of the other major international conflict in South America in the late 1800s. This war, which set Chile against Peru and Bolivia, to this day holds a prominent place in the memories of the participating nations. Residents of Chile, the triumphant party in the conflict, look upon the War of the Pacific with utmost reverence. They regard the names of the war's martyrs and heroes "with respect and pride," and the yearly May 21 commemoration of the 1879 Battle of Iquique, in which Captain Arturo Pratt died heroically as he and his men attempted to board a Peruvian warship, brings forth "what at times seems a frenzy of nationalism" as "Chileans of all classes momentarily forget their problems and vicariously relive Chile's past."[34] For Peru the war consolidated anti-Chilean sentiments that date back at least to the 1820s, and which to this day emerge periodically over issues like maritime boundaries and the production of pisco, a grape liquor that Peruvians consider part of their own cultural heritage.[35] Notwithstanding these sources of tension, Chilean leaders have recently tried to improve relations with Peru. In March 2007 the state-owned television company TVN indefinitely postponed the airing of *Epopeya* (Epic), a series about the War of the Pacific, and eight months later Chile returned to Peru 3,778 books that soldiers took from its national library after capturing Lima in 1881.[36] For Bolivia, on the other hand, the conflict resembles "a Greek tragedy" largely because the country lost its coastal provinces, and the lack of direct access to the Pacific Ocean has remained the "most intransigent of Bolivia's international problems."[37]

Elsewhere, however, the War of the Pacific remains a relatively little known conflict. William F. Sater, the U.S. academic who has written most extensively about the confrontation, recently noted that in many ways the war was "just one more of the countless blood baths that characterized the nineteenth century," and "perhaps for that reason . . . many scholars never heard of [it] . . . or . . . the few who may vaguely recall it confuse [it] with the Pacific theater of the Second World War." Yet the historical significance of the conflict belies the apparent historical amnesia that surrounds it. For example, the amphibious operations launched by Chile can provide

many valuable insights for students of naval warfare. Of more relevance for this volume's focus, hostilities meant that a significant
part of the male populations of all three participating countries had
to endure military service. The most recent estimate puts these figures at 44,000–45,000 for Chile, and at least 10,000 for Bolivia and
30,000 for Peru. The war also thrust women into a variety of roles in
the contending armies that included serving as laundresses, medics, dispensers of beneficence, and caterers; women also provided
companionship to the troops and occasionally fought on the battlefield. Finally, the conflict caused significant damage to the Peruvian
economy because most of the war took place on its soil. Much of its
coastal infrastructure was destroyed when Chilean admiral Patricio
Lynch launched a series of punitive raids on the coast north of Lima
during the early fall of 1880.[38]

Farcau's essay showcases these and other effects of the conflict on
the civilian populations of the contending nations. It corroborates
the revisionist viewpoint that has challenged Heraclio Bonilla's interpretation of Peru's dismal showing in the War of the Pacific; he
attributed the Peruvian defeat to the fact that its population that
"had no interest in defending the national territory and no notion of
what that meant." Farcau briefly expounds on what recent research
has suggested—that the conflict presented Andean peasants with
"the possibility of participating in an emerging multiethnic, multiclass, nationalist coalition."[39] In this way, for Peru at least, the War of
the Pacific continued a social development begun a century before
by the Túpac Amaru rebellion (1780–1784), a revolt against Spanish
rule that split indigenous Andeans into rebel and loyalist factions.[40]
Yet the War of the Pacific also marked the decline of armed confrontation between Latin American countries. Aside from a recent and
quickly concluded border skirmish between Peru and Ecuador, the
final episode of international war in South America came with the
Chaco War (1933–1936) between Bolivia and Paraguay.[41] The twentieth century would otherwise perpetuate the nineteenth-century
pattern of internal conflict, or civil war.

Indeed, the early twentieth century witnessed the eruption of
bloody political revolutions with far-reaching programs for political, social, and economic change in various countries throughout
the world, including Mexico. The 1910 Revolution, as this seminal
event in Latin American history has come to be known, has attracted a great deal of scholarly attention. Over the years historians
have vigorously debated its causes, character, goals, and legacy, as
well as the matter of whether in fact the events of 1910 did or did

not constitute a revolution. Despite the lack of general agreement about these issues, the 1910 Revolution gave a semblance of legitimacy to the political system that ruled Mexico between 1929 and 2000, as both the state and the once-dominant party known as the *Partido Revolucionario Institucional* (PRI) billed themselves as "the culmination and continuation of the Mexican Revolution."[42] While the popularity of the PRI has certainly diminished, as evidenced by its losses in the 2000 and 2006 presidential elections, one could still well argue that Friedrich Katz's 1998 observation remains true today—that the 1910 Revolution still enjoys "enormous legitimacy in its own people's eyes." As Katz noted, in the former Soviet Union "Leningrad has been renamed St. Petersburg, and in China, students questioned Mao's revolution on Tiananmen Square . . . [but] no one in Mexico is thinking of renaming the streets that bear the names of [Pancho] Villa or of other revolutionary heroes. In fact, not only the official government party but one of the main opposition parties and a newly emerged guerrilla movement in Chiapas [the *Ejército Zapatista de Liberación Nacional* (Zapatista National Liberation Army)] all claim to be legitimate heirs of the revolutionaries of 1910–20."[43]

The authority that postrevolutionary Mexican governments enjoyed for much of the twentieth century, however, cannot obscure the fact that the armed phase of the Revolution nearly tore the country apart. As contending factions battled for political supremacy between 1910 and 1920, Mexico endured "the bloodiest conflict ever witnessed in the Western Hemisphere, and, until the recent years of the carnage in Cambodia . . . the most violent revolutionary struggle ever fought in terms of the proportion of population lost: in 1910 Mexico counted a population of only 14.5 million people, and as many as 1.5 million Mexicans lost their lives over the next decade." In addition, thousands of Mexicans fled the violence into the United States, never to return. The impact of the death toll and the displacement became evident in the 1920 census, which showed that "eight thousand villages had completely disappeared from the map of Mexico as a direct result of the revolution."[44] Such brutal realities were vividly captured by Mariano Azuela in his novel *The Underdogs*. First published in 1915, the fictional account closely follows the actions of Demetrio Macías, an ambitious revolutionary leader loosely allied with Villa's army in northern Mexico. Through Macías and other characters, Azuela showed all the imperfections that for him characterized both the revolution and the men and women who fell into its maelstrom—the destruction, looting, cynicism, and brutality.[45]

The chapter by John Lear, "'¡No vamos a la Revolución!' Civilians as *Revolucionarios* and *Revolucionados* in the 1910 Mexican Revolution," nicely complements Azuela's portrayal of the human cost of the events of 1910. Lear's essay examines how the Mexican people took part in and lived through the revolutionary decade of 1910, and in so doing identifies three major (and sometimes overlapping) groups or categories—those who shared the same social background and objectives of the rebel groups, those who did not associate with any of the insurgents and simply tried to survive as the violence disrupted their everyday lives, and those who left their homes either for urban areas or for the United States. Lear's contribution to this volume thus shifts the focus of attention away from major revolutionary leaders to the nameless civilians who both endured and helped shape the outcome of the Revolution, and who in recent times, as he puts it, have regained "the central role in local and national affairs, and became once again subjects worthy of the attention of historians."

Just as events in Mexico between 1910 and 1920 threw thousands of persons into the revolutionary fray, the Cuban revolutionary experience during the twentieth century—which culminated in Fidel Castro's 1959 overthrow of the Fulgencio Batista regime—also affected, as well as mobilized, large numbers of men, women, and children of all races and ages. One episode in this sequence, the so-called 1933 Revolution, largely succeeded because "the intensity of popular protest had reached unprecedented levels."[46] Indeed, by early 1933 university students, urban and rural workers, and others had moved to the forefront of public affairs, and in August of that year they removed from power an individual many Cubans had come to loathe, President Gerardo Machado. The forces that had opposed Machado then installed a short-lived government, which espoused a nationalist, reformist program that defied long-standing U.S. political and economic interests. This agenda prompted U.S. ambassador Sumner Welles early in 1934 to strike a deal with Batista that not only led to the government's downfall, but also thrust the future strongman into the political spotlight for the next 25 years.[47]

As with most of Cuban history prior to the Revolution of 1959, however, the events that comprised the 1933 Revolution are "lost in the historical mists." The reason for that amnesia is clearly illustrated by one scholar's recent visit to Cuba's *Museo de la Revolución* (Museum of the Revolution), where an elaborate exhibit showcased the ills inflicted on the island between 1933 and 1959, and in so doing left the "the impression that everything was made right by the [1959 Castro] revolution." Since the end of the Cold War, however, scholars of Cuba have taken steps to remedy this situation by reexamining the country's early twentieth century history. For example, Julia E. Sweig's recent work about the role that the urban underground played in insuring Castro's victory over Batista makes clear her intent to overturn the mythic stature of 1959. "Of course"—she noted—"that year was a watershed-year in Cuban twentieth-century history. But almost all the individual and institutional actors on the Cuban political stage in the late 1950s were consciously playing out a drama that in fact began during the Wars of Independence against Spain and the American intervention in 1898, and continued in the 1930s during the antidictatorial struggle to rid the country of President Gerardo Machado."[48]

The massive popular mobilization that played a key role in the ouster of Machado did have its roots in the island's nineteenth-century struggle to end Spanish colonial rule. Cuba's first war of independence, otherwise known as the Ten Years' War (1868–1878), marked the beginning of a nationalist insurgency that sought to build a country where racial equality and social justice would flourish. These goals insured that numerous blacks, mulattos, and women joined the struggle against Spain. Popular mobilization continued throughout the *Guerra Chiquita,* or Little War (1879–1880), and the Second War of Independence (1895–1898), by which time tens of thousands of men and women had joined the so-called Liberation Army, "a multiracial fighting force that was integrated at all ranks."[49]

While recent research suggests that the Second War of Independence may not have been as popular as previously thought,[50] the Cuban masses did continue to mobilize even after the struggle against Spain came to an end. When U.S. military officials and Cuban administrators, as well as the influx of many Spanish immigrants, blocked the efforts of Afro-Cubans to participate in the public affairs of the new republic early in the twentieth century, many joined the *Partido Independiente de Color* (Independent Party of Color) as a means of demanding "full equality for Afro-Cubans, proportional representation in public service, and social reform." Cuban elites, however, believed the party threatened the new order, so they issued legislation to outlaw it in 1910; then, when party leaders organized an armed protest in the province of Oriente two years later in an effort to lift the ban, the Cuban army massacred the demonstrators and for all intents and purposes destroyed the

Partido Independiente de Color.[51] But such brutality did not end the mass mobilization of Afro-Cubans, as they joined the short-lived Veterans' and Patriots' Movement in the early 1920s. More importantly, by 1933 members of the middle and working classes were actively engaged in social protests, and in "generating their own political and social responses to changing circumstances." Their efforts culminated with the triumph of the Revolution of 1933.[52]

As Gillian McGillivray's chapter "Reading Revolution from Below: Cuba 1933" demonstrates, the events of 1933 in Cuba did indeed spur thousands of the island's lower classes into action. McGillivray focuses her piece on the revolution in the city of Havana, but she pays close attention to sugar workers in the countryside as well. Her emphasis on the latter is important because not only were most Cuban cities small in comparison to those of other nations in Europe, North, and South America, but also 80 percent of the economy was based on sugar. As a result, a vast number of Cubans lived in sugar mill communities near the cane fields and mills, and they too played a key role in the events of 1933. McGillivray argues that civilians, emboldened by the revolutionary fervor, claimed— and in many cases won—more social and political rights in 1933. Their victory proved short-lived, however, and they would have to join Castro two decades later to reclaim these rights when Batista seized power in 1952 and rolled back many of the accomplishments of 1933.

The 1959 Cuban Revolution also had a dramatic impact beyond the Caribbean island. According to the internationally acclaimed Peruvian novelist Mario Vargas Llosa, Castro's victory enabled the Latin American Left to believe for the first time ever "that revolution was something possible in our countries. Until then the idea of revolution was romantic and remote to us, something we took more as an academic idea that could never become a reality in countries like ours."[53] Indeed, Castro's victory provided the "youth of the world with an example of how to bring about change," and there was no more powerful symbol in the campaign to spread revolution through the hemisphere than the Argentine doctor-turned-revolutionary Ernesto "Che" Guevara. In October 1967 Guevara died at the hands of Bolivia's military while trying to establish a springboard there for a continent-wide uprising, but "something in his premature death," as Jorge Castañeda noted, "rejuvenated him, completing his assimilation by the generation that followed his own." Indeed, news of Guevara's demise was "like a drug to the educated youth of Argentina." When students from *El Colegio*

Nacional de Buenos Aires (Buenos Aires National High School) met for their 30-year reunion in 2003, one of them reminisced that in 1967 Gloria Kehoe, then 14 years old, had "started doing laps around her neighborhood park, walking briskly around swings and slides where she had played as a girl" because "she was in training to become a guerrilla."[54]

For U.S. government officials and Latin American elites, however, the 1959 Cuban Revolution represented a serious threat, especially after Castro consolidated his hold on power and turned to the Soviet Union for assistance. U.S. policymakers dramatically expanded military spending throughout the hemisphere to combat the threat of communist insurrection, and Latin America's armed forces, which U.S. leaders needed as partners, used U.S. assistance to displace reformist civilian regimes and set up military dictatorships intent on eradicating those they considered subversives and their sympathizers. As a result, during the 1970s and 1980s Latin America felt the effects of "an unprecedented wave of political repression and a severe crisis of human rights." Not only did thousands of individuals disappear (*desaparecidos* in Spanish), but also the word became a euphemism to signify "a method of killing that left no trace of the victims." The oppressors subjected many others to unimaginable acts. For example, female prisoners at a detention center in the Chilean capital city of Santiago known as La Venda Sexy were, according to reports, routinely raped by a German shepherd dog. Countless men and women had to flee their countries to save their lives. In Chile the military dictatorship made exile its "centerpiece . . . for gaining and retaining control of the country," and as a result nearly 200,000 Chileans—about 2 percent of the population—had no choice but to run away to foreign soil.[55]

The legacy of the state-directed political violence that became part of everyday life in the Southern Cone, however, remains a deeply controversial matter for residents of the affected countries. On one hand, by the early 1980s the military's hold on power had begun to weaken, and their loss of control allowed an emboldened civil society to expose the hideous acts that the dictatorships had either committed or facilitated. Numerous novels, feature films, and investigative works of journalism put on view the military's atrocities to a wider public.[56] Many civilians have demanded and continue to seek legal redress for the actions of those individuals and institutions that held power or positions of influence during the "Dirty Wars." A recently revealed case involved Christian Federico von Wernich, a Catholic priest in Argentina who worked as a police informant for that country's military junta (1976–1983). In October 2007 von Wernich became the first cleric convicted of human rights abuses for his actions—"coauthor" in 7 murders, 42 kidnappings, and 31 cases of torture. In addition to extracting information from individuals whom the military had apprehended, von Wernich offered spiritual comfort to a provincial police chief who ran a network of secret detention centers and to officers who participated in the so-called "flights of death," wherein drugged prisoners were tossed alive from special flights into the ocean.[57]

Many others, however, still endeavor to protect the authors of the violent incidents perpetrated during the "Dirty Wars," as illustrated by what transpired in Chile following General Augusto Pinochet's death on December 10, 2006. While President Michelle Bachelet (a political prisoner in the 1970s) refused to give the deceased general a state funeral, she could not prevent the army from burying him with full honors. Several speakers at the funeral eloquently praised Pinochet. His eldest daughter remarked that the September 11, 1973 coup where he seized power had also brought "the flame of liberty" to Chile, while one of Pinochet's former ministers credited him "for restoring private property, opening the economy to the outside world, stimulating exports, privatizing pensions, and other free market initiatives." At the same time, the president of the Pinochet Foundation, an organization in Santiago that upholds his legacy, justified "the former dictator's political policies, noting that he died without ever being convicted of any crimes." Then, approximately two weeks after the interment, Pinochet's closest associates continued their effort to portray him as a "victim of a vengeful leftist cabal" when they published a six-page farewell letter from Pinochet to all Chileans. In the missive the deceased dictator contended that he acted as he had in September 1973 to prevent an unrelenting civil war that the Left had intended to launch.[58]

But these issues remain highly contentious, as illustrated by the story of two young men whose families were on opposite sides of the political spectrum. At the wake for General Pinochet the grandson of General Carlos Prats walked up to the coffin and "deliberately, calmly spat on the dictator's face as he lay there in full regalia."[59] General Prats had resigned as commander-in-chief of the Chilean army in August 1973, an action that removed the last obstacle to the military coup. One year later agents of Pinochet's secret police set a car bomb in downtown Buenos Aires, Argentina, that took the life of Prat and his wife. Then, one of Pinochet's grandsons (a captain in the Chilean army) made an unscheduled appearance during the funeral. He defied military regulations that barred officers from publicly discussing politics, and delivered a speech that praised his grandfather's decision to "take down the Marxist model that sought to impose its totalitarian model." His words drew the most applause of the orations read on that occasion.[60] These two incidents lend much weight to one scholar's recent assessment of Chile following the death of Pinochet. While the dictator's demise "has created pressure to leave that past behind, as a nation Chile has yet to arrive at a true point of national closure."[61]

Margaret Power further elaborates on these issues and on the military regimes' inner workings in her chapter, "Repression and Resistance, Hatred and Hope: Civilian Life during the Military Dictatorships in the Southern Cone, 1964–1990," which pays particular attention to Chile under General Pinochet. In addition to reminiscing about her experiences in Chile during the dictatorship, she explains what domestic and international context allowed the armed forces to seize power, how the dictatorships controlled public affairs and affected everyday civilian life, why men and women supported or opposed military regimes, and the legacies of military rule. Violence, Power reminds us, has a psychological dimension, one that decisively shapes not only the political environment, but also social relations.

At about the same time that military dictatorships in the Southern Cone exacted an emotional and physical toll on the daily lives of many residents, the people of Central America encountered "the bloodiest, most violent, and most destructive" epoch in the region's history since the Spanish conquest.[62] Scholars have obsessed over Central America's troubles. One observer has calculated that the civil war in El Salvador "stimulated an outpouring of academic research that probably exceeded the total volume of English-language works on El Salvador from independence until the outbreak of the civil war in 1979."[63] While academics certainly took notice of this and the other conflicts that ravaged Central America, their effects barely registered a blip among the U.S. general public. Even as the U.S. government attempted to influence the outcome of these wars, leading to the televised spectacle in 1987 of the Iran-*contra* scandal in which Congress investigated U.S. involvement in an illegal scheme to supply weapons to Nicaragua's U.S.-backed *contra* rebels, "public opinion polls . . . showed that the majority of the American people never grasped" whether Washington backed the government or the rebels in El Salvador or Nicaragua. Fewer still knew what the warfare in Guatemala was all about.[64]

These conflicts, however, took a heavy toll on the fabric of everyday life in Central America. The wars in Nicaragua and El Salvador took the lives of more than 90,000 people, and by the time that Guatemala's four-decade-long civil war ended in 1996 the state had killed 200,000 men, women, and children.[65] Numbers alone, however, fail to do justice to the pain and suffering that these individuals endured. Consider, for example, what transpired in December 1981 when El Salvador's elite Atlacatl Battalion slaughtered nearly 700 residents of the village of El Mozote and the nearby hamlets in the mountains near the border with Honduras. Rufina Amaya (perhaps the only person who emerged from that event with "her wits about her, [and] a clear memory of what took place,") recalled her husband's failed attempt to escape the village during this bloody episode. After they shot him the soldiers strode to where he and another man lay "gasping on the ground, and, unsheathing their machetes, they bent over them, grasped their hair, jerked their heads back sharply, and beheaded them with strong blows to the back of their necks."[66]

The civil wars that ravaged Central America also thrust unwilling civilians into the midst of conflict. During the November 1989 Farabundo Martí National Liberation Front (FMLN) offensive on the capital city of San Salvador, FMLN guerrillas forced residents of at least one outlying neighborhood "to dig trenches for them, [and] then refused them permission to leave the area of combat."[67] Just as war disrupted the lives of adult civilians, it also had a pervasive effect on children. The recent feature film *Innocent Voices* (2004) shows that by the mid-1980s the government of El Salvador was forcibly recruiting children as young as age 12 to fight the guerrillas. In Nicaragua the conflict between the *contras* and the Sandinista government had similar effects on civilians. The Sandinistas had to dedicate over 50 percent of the national budget to defense spending, which led them to neglect the social and economic reforms they had begun to introduce after seizing power in 1979.[68] They also had to rebuild a conventional army to fight the *contras*, and many middle-class Nicaraguans fled the country to protect their teenage children from military service. This development meant that "forced conscription was used almost exclusively against working-class and peasant youth, sometimes against boys who were not yet draft age."[69]

Arturo Arias's chapter, "And the Storm Raged On: The Daily Experience of Terror during the Central American Civil Wars, 1966–1996," takes readers inside the world of these vicious struggles, with a particular focus on the terror that military regimes and death squads inflicted on Guatemalans. A widely acclaimed professor of literature and author probably best known for the 1979 novel *After the Bombs*—which captures the essence of everyday life in Guatemala following the 1954 U.S. Central Intelligence Agency-led covert operation known as PBSUCCESS—Arias's piece is underlain by an intense tone in large part because he is personally invested in the subject. As a native of Guatemala, Arias lived through many of the experiences he relates in his powerful, emotionally charged essay. In doing so Arias lays bare the "one keynote" that remains "the taproot of Guatemalan history"—its "culture of fear," the fact that "violence, torture, and death" remain to a large extent the final arbiters of that society.[70]

HOPES FOR THE FUTURE

While many essays in this volume pay a great deal of attention to the detrimental consequences of war on everyday life, one needs to remember that amidst the chaos and destruction, hope for a brighter, more peaceful future remains. Recent events in Colombia bear out

A Colombian soldier guards a pile of weapons to be destroyed in Sogamoso, Colombia, December 14, 2007. Most weapons were handed over by right-wing paramilitary groups as part of a 2003 peace agreement with the government. (AP Photo/Fernando Vergara)

these expectations. More than 15 years ago the city of Medellín, home to approximately 2 million residents, earned the title of the world's deadliest city with 381 homicides per 100,000 inhabitants partly because it housed the cocaine cartel headed by the notorious kingpin Pablo Escobar. As of mid-summer of 2007, and despite a host of critics, an unconventional mayor named Sergio Fajardo had dramatically transformed the city's image by turning it into "a showcase for new educational and architectural projects." His philosophy can be summed up in one sentence—"our most beautiful buildings must be in our poorest areas"—and such an endeavor stands on a hill in the sprawling slum of Santo Domingo Savio. There, in the Biblioteca España Park, one can find "a hulking rectangular structure that looks not unlike some medieval citadel and includes a library, auditorium, Internet rooms, day care center, and an art gallery." Another promising sign surfaced in mid-December 2007 when former paramilitaries and their victims gathered in the city of Sogamoso to witness the destruction of a cache of weapons that weighed 60 tons. The armaments were dumped into a giant caldron, and authorities will use the melted steel to create sculptures that will be auctioned off to raise money for victims of the conflict. The final episode that bodes well for the future took place early in February 2008 as thousands of men, women, and children marched in cities across Colombia and the world to condemn the FARC's practice of abducting civilians as hostages.[71] Wars, indeed, plant an assortment of seeds among civilian populations, and these developments serve as a reminder of the determination and inherent optimism of everyday life in Latin America, out of which arises a peaceful alternative to two centuries of war.

NOTES

1. The first quote comes from Gonzalo Sánchez G., "Introduction: Problems of Violence, Prospects for Peace," in *Violence in Colombia, 1990–2000: Waging War and Negotiating Peace*, eds. Charles Bergquist, Ricardo Peñarada, and Gonzalo Sánchez G. (Wilmington, DE: Scholarly Resources, 2001), 1; the second appears in W. John Green, "Guerrillas, Soldiers, Paramilitaries, Assassins, Narcos, and Gringos: The Unhappy Prospects for Peace and Democracy in Colombia," *Latin American Research Review* 40:2 (June 2005), 138.

2. Steven Dudley, *Walking Ghosts: Murder and Guerrilla Politics in Colombia* (New York: Routledge, 2004), 2; and "Afro-Colombians Driven off Land in Cocaine War," *Los Angeles Times*, January 4, 2006. The matter of domestic refugees is more fully treated in Aviva Chomsky, "The

Logic of Displacement: Afro-Colombians and the War in Colombia," in *Beyond Slavery: The Multilayered Legacy of Africans in Latin America and the Caribbean*, ed. Darién J. Davis (Lanham, MD: Rowman & Littlefield, 2007), 171–198.

3. Herbert Braun, *The Assassination of Gaitán: Public Life and Urban Violence in Colombia* (Madison: The University of Wisconsin Press, 1985), 134–135, and 155–166.

4. Mark Bowden, *Killing Pablo: The Hunt for the World's Greatest Outlaw* (New York: Penguin Books, 2001), 11.

5. Dudley, *Walking Ghosts*, 6–7; and Bowden, *Killing Pablo*, 14. Other violent conflicts with parallels to *La Violencia* include those fought between Catholics and Protestants in Northern Ireland, between the Hutu and the Tutsi in Rwanda, and between Serbs and Croats in the Balkans. Mary Roldán, *Blood and Fire: La Violencia in Antioquía* (Durham, NC: Duke University Press, 2002), 318, n. 19.

6. Stephen J. Randall, *Colombia and the United States: Hegemony and Interdependence* (Athens: University of Georgia Press, 1992), 248; Mary Roldán, "Colombia: Cocaine and the 'Miracle' of Modernity in Medellín," in *Cocaine: Global Histories*, ed. Paul Gootenberg (New York: Routledge, 1999), 167–171; and E. Bradford Burns and Julie A. Charlip, *Latin America: An Interpretive History*, 8th ed. (Upper Saddle River, NJ: Pearson Education, 2007), 300.

7. Harvey F. Kline and Vanessa Joan Gray, "Colombia: A Resilient Political System with Intransigent Problems," in *Latin American Politics and Development*, 6th ed., eds. Howard J. Wiarda and Harvey F. Kline (Boulder, CO: Westview Press, 2007), 222–225.

8. The first quote is taken from Che Guevara, *Guerrilla Warfare*, 3rd ed., with revised and updated introduction and case studies by Brian Loveman and Thomas M. Davies, Jr. (Wilmington, DE: Scholarly Resources, 1997), 259; the quote from the United Nations' representative appears in Jan Knippers Black, "Colombia's Split Level Realities," in *Latin America: Its Problems and Its Promise*, 4th ed., ed. Jan Knippers Black (Cambridge: Westview Press, 2005), 403.

9. This paragraph draws upon material from "Cocaine Wars Make Port Colombia's Deadliest City," *The New York Times*, May 22, 2007; "Fear is a Way of Life for Colombian Mayor," *Los Angeles Times*, March 31, 2007; and "Use of Land Mines Spreading in Colombia," *Los Angeles Times*, May 29, 2005.

10. Cheryl E. Martin and Mark Wasserman, *Latin America and Its People* (New York: Pearson Education, 2005), 273–274; the quote is from Brian Loveman, *For la Patria: Politics and the Armed Forces in Latin America* (Wilmington, DE: Scholarly Resources, 1999), 58.

11. Robert Holden, *Armies without Nations: Public Violence and State Formation in Central America, 1821–1960* (New York: Oxford University Press, 2004), 10.

12. De la Pedraja's book was published in Jefferson, North Carolina, by McFarland & Company in 2006; the publisher for Centeno's 2007 work is Ashgate, located in Burlington, Vermont.

13. Christon I. Archer, "Preface," in *The Wars of Independence in Spanish America*, ed. Christon I. Archer (Wilmington, DE: Scholarly Resources, 2000), xi.

14. The publications mentioned in the text are *Simón Bolívar: Essays on the Life and Legacy of the Liberator*, eds. Lester D. Langley and David Bushnell (Lanham, MD: Rowman & Littlefield, 2008); John Chasteen, "Simón Bolívar: Man and Myth," in *Heroes & Hero Cults in Latin America*, eds. Samuel Brunk and Ben Fallaw (Austin: University of Texas Press, 2006), 21–39; David Bushnell, *Simón Bolívar: Liberation and Disappointment* (New York: Pearson Longman, 2004); and John Lynch, *Simón Bolívar: A Life* (New Haven, CT: Yale University Press, 2006). The quote is from Lynch, *Simón Bolívar*, xiii.

15. Archer, "Preface," in *The Wars of Independence*, xii.

16. Eric Van Young, *The Other Rebellion: Popular Violence, Ideology, and the Mexican Struggle for Independence, 1810–1821* (Stanford: Stanford University Press, 2001), 496.

17. Aline Helg, *Liberty and Equality in Caribbean Colombia, 1770–1835* (Chapel Hill: University of North Carolina Press, 2004); and Sarah C. Chambers, *From Subjects to Citizens: Honor, Gender, and Politics in Arequipa, Peru, 1780–1854* (State College: Pennsylvania State University Press, 1999).

18. Soto is quoted in Tim Weiner, "Of Gringos and Old Grudges: This Land is Their Land," *The New York Times*, January 9, 2004; the other quote is taken from Michael C. Meyer, William L. Sherman, and Susan M. Deeds, *The Course of Mexican History*, 8th ed. (New York: Oxford University Press, 2003), 304.

19. The quotes are from Grant Wahl, "Yes, Hard Feelings," *Sports Illustrated*, March 28, 2005; and "Why They Booed Her in Mexico," *The New York Times*, June 3, 2007.

20. See *México en guerra (1846–1848): Perspectivas regionales*, ed. Laura Herrera Serna (Mexico City: Consejo Nacional para la Cultura y las Artes, 1997); *México al tiempo de su guerra con Estados Unidos (1846–1848)*, coord. Josefina Zoraida Vázquez (Mexico City: Secretaría de Relaciones Exteriores, El Colegio de México, y Fondo de Cultura Económica, 1997); Enrique Plascencia de la Parra, "Conmemoración de la hazaña épica de los Niños Héroes: Su origen, desarrollo y simbolismos," *Historia Mexicana* 45:2 (October–December 1995), 241–279; Pedro Santoni, "Where Did the Other Heroes Go? Exalting the *'Polko'* National Guard Battalions in Nineteenth-Century Mexico," *Journal of Latin American Studies* 34:4 (November 2002), 807–844; Irving W. Levinson, *Wars within War: Mexican Guerrillas, Domestic Elites, and the United States of America, 1846–1848* (Fort Worth: Texas Christian University Press, 2005); Luis Fernando Granados, *Sueñan las piedras: Alzamiento ocurrido en la ciudad de México, 14, 15, y 16 de septiembre de 1847*

(Mexico City: Ediciones Era, 2003); and Brian DeLay, "Independent Indians and the U.S.-Mexican War," *The American Historical Review* 112:1 (February 2007), 35–68.

21. Rebecca Earle, introduction to *Rumours of War: Civil Conflict in Nineteenth-Century Latin America,* ed. Rebecca Earle (London: Institute of Latin American Studies, University of London, 2000), 3.

22. Will Fowler, "Civil Conflict in Independent Mexico, 1821–1857: An Overview," in Earle, *Rumours of War,* 52–54.

23. Peter Guardino, *Peasants, Politics, and the Formation of Mexico's National State: Guerrero, 1800–1857* (Stanford: Stanford University Press, 1996), 180, 185; the quotes are in Richard N. Sinkin, *The Mexican Reform, 1855–1876: A Study in Liberal Nation-Building* (Austin: University of Texas Press, 1979), 3.

24. The quotes in this paragraph appear in Mark Wasserman, *Everyday Life and Politics in Nineteenth Century Mexico: Men, Women, and War* (Albuquerque: University of New Mexico Press, 2000), 34; and Guy P. Thompson and David G. LaFrance, *Patriotism, Politics, and Popular Liberalism in Nineteenth-Century Mexico: Juan Francisco Lucas and the Puebla Sierra* (Wilmington, DE: Scholarly Resources, 1999), 68–69.

25. The material and quotes in this paragraph come from Enrique Krause, *Mexico, Biography of Power: A History of Modern Mexico, 1810–1996* (New York: HarperCollins, 1997), 170.

26. Thomas L. Whigham's *The Paraguayan War, Volume 1, Causes and Early Conduct* (Lincoln: University of Nebraska Press, 2002), xiv; and Miguel Angel Centeno, *Blood and Debt: War and the Nation-State in Latin America* (State College: Pennsylvania State University Press, 2002), 198–202; the quote comes from Centeno, *Blood and Debt,* 260.

27. Loveman, *For la Patria,* 50.

28. Vera Linn Reber, "The Demographics of Paraguay: A Reinterpretation of the Great War, 1864–1870," *Hispanic American Historical Review* 68:2 (May 1988), 290, 307.

29. Thomas L. Whigham and Barbara Potthast, "Some Strong Reservations: A Critique of Vera Linn Reber's 'The Demographics of Paraguay: A Reinterpretation of the Great War,'" *Hispanic American Historical Review* 70:4 (May 1990), 667.

30. Thomas L. Whigham and Barbara Potthast, "The Paraguayan Rosetta Stone: New Insights into the Demographics of the Paraguayan War, 1864–1870," *Latin American Research Review* 34:1 (1999), 179, 185.

31. Whigham, *The Paraguayan War,* and Chris Leuchars, *To the Bitter End: Paraguay and the War of the Triple Alliance* (Westport, CT: Greenwood, 2002). A review of both books by Peter H. Wilson appears in *War in History* 12:1 (January 2005), 102–105. The quoted phrase is in 104.

32. James Schofield Saeger, *Francisco Solano López and the Ruination of Paraguay: Honor and Egocentrism* (Lanham, MD: Rowman & Littlefield, 2007).

33. Hendrik Kraay and Thomas L. Whigham, "Introduction: War, Politics, and Society in South America, 1820s–60s," in *I Die with My Country: Perspectives on the Paraguayan War, 1864–1870,* eds. Hendrik Kraay and Thomas L. Whigham (Lincoln: University of Nebraska Press, 2005), 2.

34. Frederick M. Nunn, *The Military in Chilean History: Essays on Civil-Military Relations 1810–1973* (Albuquerque: University of New Mexico Press, 1976), 69, 314, n. 6.

35. "Peru Sues Chile in Boundary Feud," *Los Angeles Times,* January 17, 2008; and "Something's Fishy in Peru," *Los Angeles Times,* August 31, 2007.

36. "Chilean TV War Series Suspended," March 13, 2007, in http://news.bbc.co.uk/go/pr/fr/-/2/hi/americas/6445347.stm, and "Chile Returns Looted Peru Books," November 7, 2007, at http://news.bbc.co.uk/go/pr/fr/-/1/hi/world/americas/7082436.stm. Clips from *Epopeya* can be found on the popular Web site http://www.youtube.com/.

37. Herbert S. Klein, *Bolivia: The Evolution of a Multi-Ethnic Society,* 2nd ed. (New York: Oxford University Press, 1992), 144, 149. For an eyewitness account of the yearly March 23 "march to the sea" staged by citizens in Bolivia's capital of La Paz, see Bruce W. Farcau, *The Ten Cents' War: Chile, Peru, and Bolivia in the War of the Pacific, 1879–1884* (Westport, CT: Praeger, 2000), 1.

38. This paragraph draws upon the ideas of William F. Sater, *Andean Tragedy: Fighting the War of the Pacific, 1879–1884* (Lincoln: University of Nebraska Press, 2007), 21–23, 75–84, and 262; Paz Larrain Mira, "Mujeres tras la huella de los soldados," *Historia* 33 (2000), 227–261; and Centeno, *Blood and Debt,* 58. The quote appears in Sater, *Andean Tragedy,* 1.

39. Florencia E. Mallon, *Peasant and Nation: The Making of Postcolonial Mexico and Peru* (Berkeley: University of California Press, 1995), 1–2, and 328.

40. The Túpac Amaru Rebellion has been exhaustively studied. A succinct discussion of the historical literature opens an insightful treatment of the rebellion's progress and social context in David T. Garrett, "His Majesty's Most Loyal Vassals: The Indian Nobility and Túpac Amaru," *Hispanic American Historical Review* 84:4 (November 2004), 575–617; see also Ward Stavig, *The World of Túpac Amaru: Conflict, Community, and Identity in Colonial Peru* (Lincoln: University of Nebraska Press, 1999).

41. Bruce Farcau has also written about this conflict. See his *The Chaco War: Bolivia and Paraguay, 1932–1935* (Westport, CT: Praeger, 1996). Early in March 2008 another border incident threatened to erupt in war as the Colombian government infringed Ecuador's sovereignty when it sent troops into that country to kill a Colombian guerrilla leader. The raid led to a major diplomatic crisis between both countries, and involved Venezuela as well. Efforts by the Organization of American States helped defuse the crisis. "Crisis at Colombia Border Spills into Diplomatic Realm," "Colombia Is Flash Point in Chávez's Feud with U.S.," and "Take a Deep Breath," *The New York Times,* March 4, 5, and 6, 2008.

42. Thomas Benjamin, *La Revolución: Mexico's Great Revolution as Memory, Myth, and History* (Austin: University of Texas Press, 2000), 23. For an examination of the interpretive approaches to the 1910 Revolution, see Gilbert M. Joseph and Daniel Nugent, "Popular Culture and State Formation in Mexico," in *Everyday Forms of State Formation: Revolution and the Negotiation of Rule in Modern Mexico*, eds. Gilbert M. Joseph and Daniel Nugent (Durham, NC: Duke University Press, 1994), 3–23.

43. Friedrich Katz, *The Life and Times of Pancho Villa* (Stanford: Stanford University Press, 1998), xiii–xiv.

44. Judith Adler Hellman, *Mexican Lives* (New York: The New Press, 1999), 48–49.

45. Mariano Azuela, *The Underdogs* (Prospect Heights, IL: Waveland Press, 2002).

46. Robert Whitney, *State and Revolution in Cuba: Mass Mobilization and Political Change, 1920–1940* (Chapel Hill: University of North Carolina Press, 2001), 1–2.

47. Frank Argote-Freyre, *Fulgencio Batista: From Revolutionary to Strongman* (New Brunswick, NJ: Rutgers University Press, 2006), 35, 93, 96, and 102; and Marifeli Pérez-Stable, *The Cuban Revolution: Origins, Course, and Legacy*, 2nd ed. (New York: Oxford University Press, 1999), 40–42.

48. The first two quotes in this paragraph appear in Argote-Freyre, *Fulgencio Batista,* ix, xiv; the citation from Julia E. Sweig is from her *Inside the Cuban Revolution: Fidel Castro and the Urban Underground* (Cambridge: Harvard University Press, 2002), 2.

49. Ada Ferrer, *Insurgent Cuba: Race, Nation, and Revolution, 1868–1898* (Chapel Hill: University of North Carolina Press, 1999), 3. For a detailed look at the role women played in these struggles, see Teresa Prados-Torreira, *Mambisas: Rebel Women in Nineteenth-Century Cuba* (Gainesville: University Press of Florida, 2005).

50. This issue, as well as the effects of Spanish General Valeriano Weyler's reconcentration policy, is further discussed in John Lawrence Tone's *War and Genocide in Cuba, 1895–1898* (Chapel Hill: University of North Carolina Press, 2006).

51. Aline Helg, *Our Rightful Share: The Afro-Cuban Struggle for Equality, 1886–1912* (Chapel Hill: University of North Carolina Press, 1995), 3. Chapters 6 and 7 of this book (pages 162–226) provide an in-depth discussion of these events.

52. Whitney, *State and Revolution in Cuba,* 31–35, and 82. Two other recent essays about the events of 1933 are Philip Dur and Christopher Gilcrease, "US Diplomacy and the Downfall of a Cuban Dictator: Machado in 1933," *Journal of Latin American Studies* 34:2 (2001), 255–282; and Anthony Kapcia, "The Siege of the Hotel Nacional, Cuba, 1933: A Reassessment," *Journal of Latin American Studies* 34:2 (2001), 283–309.

53. Jorge G. Castañeda, *Utopia Unarmed: The Latin American Left After the Cold War* (New York: Vintage, 1992), 68. The author offers a useful

definition of the six groups that comprised the Latin American Left in pages 19–23.

54. For the ideas and quotes in this paragraph, see Anthony DePalma, *The Man who Invented Fidel: Castro, Cuba, and Herbert L. Matthews of the New York Times* (New York: Public Affairs, 2006), 148; Jorge G. Castañeda, *Compañero: The Life and Death of Che Guevara* (New York: Alfred A. Knopf, 1997), 393; and "Revolution Was One of Their 3 Rs," *Los Angeles Times*, December 6, 2003.

55. Quotes and material in this paragraph come from J. Patrice McSherry, "Operation Condor as a Hemispheric 'Counterterror' Organization," in *When States Kill: Latin America, the U.S., and Technologies of Terror*, eds. Cecilia Menjívar and Néstor Rodríguez (Austin: University of Texas Press, 2005), 29; Steve J. Stern, *Remembering Pinochet's Chile: On the Eve of London 1998* (Durham, NC: Duke University Press, 2004), xxiii; Thomas C. Wright, *State Terrorism in Latin America: Chile, Argentina, and International Human Rights* (Lanham, MD: Rowman & Littlefield, 2007), xi, 30; Teresa A. Meade, "Holding the Junta Accountable: Chile's *Sitios de Memoria* and the History of Torture, Disappearance, and Death," *Radical History Review* 79 (2001), 134, n. 14; and Thomas C. Wright and Rody Oñate, *Flight from Chile: Voices of Exile* (Albuquerque: University of New Mexico Press, 1998), 8. Various articles in the July 2007 issue of *Latin American Perspectives* shed additional insight on exile in Latin America during the "Dirty Wars."

56. Among the many novels that deal with this issue, the following two are particularly insightful—Isabel Allende's *Of Love and Shadows* (New York: Alfred A. Knopf, 1987), and Gerardo di Masso's *The Shadow by the Door* (Willimantic, CT: Curbstone Press, 1985). Nonfictional works include Patricia Verdugo's *Chile, Pinochet, and the Caravan of Death* (Coral Gables, FL: North-South Center Press, University of Miami, 2001), and Adolfo Scilingo's *Confessions of an Argentine Dirty Warrior: A Firsthand Account of Atrocity* (New York: The New Press, 2005). A pair of noteworthy films are Roman Polanski's *Death and the Maiden* (1994) and Gaston Biraben's *Cautiva* (2003).

57. "Priest's Conviction Awakens Old Ghosts," *Los Angeles Times*, October 21, 2007.

58. The quote from Pinochet's daughter appears in "Pinochet Is Given a Full Military Send-off," *Los Angeles Times*, December 13, 2006; all other quotes and information are from "After Death, a Campaign to Praise Pinochet," *The New York Times*, December 27, 2006.

59. "Spitting on a Dead Man," *Los Angeles Times*, December 17, 2006.

60. "Pinochet Is Given a Full Military Send-off," *Los Angeles Times*, December 13, 2006.

61. Peter Kornbluth, "Introduction," in Marjorie Agosín, *Tapestries of Hope, Threads of Love: The Arpillera Movement in Chile*, 2nd ed. (Lanham, MD: Rowman & Littlefield, 2008), 3. Another matter that in the future will likely affect Pinochet's legacy is his shady financial dealings. At the time

of his death investigators had discovered that Pinochet held more than $28 million in secret bank accounts abroad, most of which were located in the United States ("The Dexterous Dictator," *The New York Times*, December 11, 2006). He also built a 55,000-book private library valued at nearly $2.9 million. See Cristóbal Peña's article on this topic in "Exclusivo: Viaje al fondo de la biblioteca de Pinochet," Centro de Investigación e Información Periodística, http://ciperchile.cl./2007/12/06/exclusivo-viaje-al-fondo-de-la-biblio.

62. Walter La Feber, *Inevitable Revolutions: The United States in Central America*, 2nd revised and expanded edition (New York: Norton, 1993), 362.

63. T. David Mason, "The Civil War in El Salvador: A Recent Analysis," *Latin American Research Review* 34:3 (1999), 180.

64. Clifford Krauss, *Inside Central America: Its People, Politics, and History* (New York: Summit Books, 1991), 15.

65. Greg Grandin, *The Last Colonial Massacre: Latin America in the Cold War* (Chicago: University of Chicago Press, 2004), 3.

66. Anaya's quote is in "Shedding Light on Humanity's Dark Side: The Outspoken Survivor of Slaughter," *The Washington Post*, March 14, 2007; and the second appears in Mark Danner, *The Massacre at El Mozote* (New York: Vintage, 1994), 69.

67. Krauss, *Inside Central America*, 106.

68. Forest Colburn, *My Car in Managua* (Austin: University of Texas Press, 1991), 126.

69. Matilde Zimmerman, *Sandinista: Carlos Fonseca and the Nicaraguan Revolution* (Durham, NC: Duke University Press, 2000), 224.

70. Piero Gleijeses, "Afterword: The Culture of Fear," in Nick Cullather, *Secret History: The CIA's Classified Account of Its Operations in Guatemala, 1952–1954*, 2nd ed. (Stanford: Stanford University Press, 2006), xxiii.

71. This paragraph draws upon material from "Medellín's Nonconformist Mayor Turns Blight to Beauty," *Los Angeles Times*, July 15, 2007; "In Colombia, Forging Peace with Old Arms," *Los Angeles Times*, December 15, 2007; "60 Tons of Weapons Destroyed in Colombia," *The Seattle Times*, December 16, 2007; and "Colombians Protest Rebel Kidnappings," *Los Angeles Times*, February 5, 2008.

TWO

Death, Destiny, and the Daily Chores: Everyday Life in Spanish America during the Wars of Independence, 1808–1826

Karen Racine

Our country is wherever we are well off.

—John Milton

The wars of independence in Spanish America (1808–1826) intruded on everyday life in innumerable ways. Men and women of all ages found themselves subject to periodic conscription and forced levies, wanton destruction of villages and displacement of undesirable categories of people, distortions in the economy, and altered demands from newly reconstituted and ever-changing governing authorities. At the same time, smaller but no-less-significant struggles played out in the daily lives of individual families and communities. Any war for independence turns a person's mind and body into a contested site, a place where the new order seeks to establish itself. And so it was for residents of Spanish America, whose understanding of racial categories, class status, gender roles, and national identity were challenged during the nearly two decades of the protracted struggle to break free from Spain. Yet somehow, while generals and soldiers tried to settle the larger questions of national destiny on the battlefield, daily life went on. After all, someone still had to do the dishes. Children were born and had to be fed. The sick and dying had to be nursed. People fell in and out of love. Small businesses persevered the best they could. Crops needed to be harvested, and animals tended. Indeed, Spanish Americans clung to their normal routines as the best way to preserve their health, their sanity, their families, and their communities during a time of tremendous up-heaval and sacrifice. Their destinies might have been decided amid deaths on the battlefield, but daily chores kept those on the home front occupied.

EVENTS LEADING TO INDEPENDENCE

The events that led to Spanish American independence proceeded differently throughout the hemisphere, although the basic issues and debates were similar everywhere.[1] There had been mounting discontent, particularly among indigenous people in Mexico and the Andes and the more liberal Creole merchant families of port cities like Caracas and Buenos Aires, the bitter results of a century of reform led by Spain's Bourbon monarchs that had intended to centralize the empire and make it more profitable for the motherland. Then, a constitutional crisis arose as a result of the so-called 1808 Bayona Capitulation, an event in which Napoleon Bonaparte invaded Spain, took the royal family hostage (or, depending on one's political stance, the traitors Charles IV and his son Ferdinand VII voluntarily went into French exile and thus abandoned their heroic nation), and swiftly installed his brother Joseph on the Spanish throne. According to tradition dating back to the thirteenth-century legal code known as the *Siete Partidas,* if a Spanish monarch became disabled or threatened, governing power temporarily devolved upon local *cabildos* (town councils), which would rule until central authority could be reestablished. A *junta* (governing committee) emerged in Seville and began issuing calls to citizens in Spain and in America to join the patriotic cause and resist the French. The relevance of this rhetoric was not lost on disaffected elite Spanish Americans, some of whom had started to view the Bourbons as tyrants and who now possessed a legal avenue to seize power and govern themselves.

The ruling *juntas* that consequently sprang up across Spanish America proved especially energetic and reform-minded in the most recently settled parts of the empire (e.g., modern-day Argentina and Venezuela), where economic life depended on trade more than agriculture and where elite Creoles felt least threatened by large indigenous or African populations. By mid-1810 important *juntas* had constituted themselves in Quito, Caracas, and Buenos Aires. Although they professed to be holding power until Ferdinand VII, *el Deseado* (the Desired One), returned, more radical elements in America always considered the *juntas* to be a stopover on the way to full republican independence.

Events in other parts of the region, however, took a different turn. While Peru remained quiet owing to its large indigenous population, recent history of violent revolt, and deeply entrenched colonial authority, the other center of Spanish royal power—Mexico—experienced intermittent bouts of revolt and repression. In September 1810 an iconoclastic parish priest named Miguel Hidalgo called for an end to bad government, begged protection from the Virgin of Guadalupe, and ordered death to the *gachupines* (European Spaniards) when he issued the *Grito de Dolores* (Cry from Dolores). The proclamation sparked a revolt that spread quickly and included tens of thousands of indigenous, mixed race, and lower class people. Mexican urban Creole elites had initially shared Hidalgo's desire for more local autonomy, economic diversification, freedom of the press, and other pro-American reforms, but they became frightened by the nature of Hidalgo's movement and threw their weight behind the colonial establishment. After Hidalgo's capture and execution by colonial authorities in 1811, his supporters, led by José María Morelos, retreated to the country's southern and western provinces and began a guerrilla campaign against the old order. They also initiated a patriot congress at Chilpancingo in 1813 that declared independence and one year later issued a constitution at Apatzingán. This remarkably liberal document outlawed racial distinctions, made provisions for land reform, free trade, and a free press, abolished slavery, and established equality before the law. Shortly afterward, with Ferdinand restored to the Spanish throne, Mexican royalists captured Morelos, hauled him back to the capital for trial, and executed him for heresy and treason on December 22, 1815. The patriot resistance scattered and continued its struggle under the joint leadership of Vicente Guerrero and Guadalupe Victoria.

Meanwhile, citizens in Argentina and Chile faced a similar challenge from the newly strengthened royalists after a brief period of autonomous rule. In 1812, the Spanish *Consejo de Regencia* (which had replaced Seville's *Junta Suprema* in 1810) issued the Cádiz constitution, a pronouncedly liberal charter that attempted to redress some of the Americans' grievances. When Napoleon Bonaparte went into exile in 1814, however, Ferdinand VII reoccupied the Spanish throne and immediately demanded that his wayward colonies return to the royal fold. Their refusal to comply led him to send forces across the Atlantic to coerce their obedience, and consequently events in South America took on the form of a war for independence (which included aspects of a civil war as well). In Argentina, José de San Martín organized the famous Army of the Andes, which received notable contributions from women, Afro-Argentines, and the rural common folk. He and his troops mounted a spectacular surprise attack on Spanish forces in Chile by crossing the Andes on foot and winning decisive battles at Chacabuco (February 12, 1817) and Maipo (April 5, 1818). With his ally Bernardo O'Higgins in control of Chile, San Martín then turned his attention northward to the center of royal power in Peru and enlisted British Admiral Thomas Dundonald, Lord Cochrane, to create a Chilean navy for the expedition.

At the same time, Simón Bolívar, the most renowned of all Spanish American independence leaders, headed the fight against the royalists in northern South America. In 1813, one year after the demise of the short-lived First Venezuelan Republic, he declared an all-out "War to the Death" in which he promised that all Spaniards would be killed or driven from America's shores. Bolívar joined forces with José Antonio Páez, the *llanero* (cowboy, or plainsman) chieftain, and engaged in a vicious struggle against equally bloodthirsty royalist troops led by Pablo Morillo. Tales of unimaginable torture and violence from this era resound in contemporary travel accounts, newspapers, and memoirs; pregnant women were sliced open, babies were dashed against walls, entire towns were burnt, and taunting letters written in captives' blood were sent to the other side. Bolívar and his troops moved westward and southward, and with the aid of British and Irish Legions and funds from Haitian President Alexandre Pétion they scored important victories at Boyacá (August 7, 1819), Carabobo (June 24, 1821), and Pichincha (May 24, 1822). Bolívar then met San Martín, who had by that time captured Lima and was pressing northward and eastward, at Guayaquil in late July 1822. Following the meeting, the Argentine general removed himself from the theater of operations and took his young orphaned daughter to exile in Europe, leaving Bolívar to secure the final decisive patriot victories at Junín (August 6, 1824) and Ayacucho (December 9, 1824). Although skirmishes continued for several years afterward while border disputes were hashed out and the old viceroyalties splintered into the smaller nations of today, South American independence was assured by 1826 when Bolívar issued his famous Bolivian Constitution and called a Pan-American Congress at Panama.

Simón Bolívar's monument in the city of La Paz, Bolivia. (AP Photo/Dado Galdieri).

Events in Spain finally pushed Mexico away from the royalist camp. In January 1820 a military officer named Rafael Riego forced the recalcitrant Ferdinand VII to accept the 1812 Cádiz constitution. Now more fearful of the implications of a liberal regime in Spain, Mexican Creole elites preemptively rallied around a royalist military officer named Agustín de Iturbide, whose February 1821 Plan of Iguala promised to uphold the Catholic religion, the independence of Mexico within the Spanish cultural orbit, and the unity between Europeans and Americans. Iturbide's plan gained adherents throughout Mexico, and he and his troops entered Mexico City faced only by slight opposition on September 27, 1821. Thus, within a short period of time, and with relatively little bloodshed, Iturbide had managed to pull off Mexican independence.

LIFE DURING WARTIME

Although reliable statistics are difficult to come by, the wars of independence dramatically altered demographic conditions throughout Spanish America. The number of residents in urban areas swelled as desperate people fled turmoil in the countryside for the relative safety of the cities. Mexico City's population exploded from 137,000 in 1800 to over 169,000 in 1811, an increase of 19 percent in just one decade that made it the fifth largest city in the world. Moreover, during the first six years of the guerrilla struggle that followed Hidalgo's revolt more than 600,000 Mexicans died from war, disease, famine, and unsanitary conditions, a staggering number considering that one estimate put the entire population of the colony at just 8 million in 1822.[2] The numbers were equally dramatic in South America. Venezuela's population of 825,000 at the start of the wars in 1810 had fallen to 651,000 when most of the fighting was finished in 1825.[3] In Potosí, the formerly wealthy mining capital of Peru, the population had been 24,000 in 1780, but a decade of vicious warfare reduced its size to a ghostly 9,000 by 1827.[4] Elsewhere in the Andes, the 1824 census in La Paz, Bolivia recorded a population of 28,000 people, 46.5 percent of whom were under the age of 20. The census also found an "excessively low number of men" between ages 15 and 25, as well as a disproportionately high number of single women of marriageable age.[5]

Disease, Injury, and Crime

Epidemic disease accompanied tired and hungry armies wherever they went and inflicted great casualties on the civilian populations in their wake. Yellow fever, for example, raged across Northern South America throughout the 1810s, with serious outbreaks in 1817 and 1819.[6] The summer of 1818 proved particularly deadly in Peru as an earthquake, a flood, and unseasonably hot temperatures combined to devastate the region. The government gazette detailed the precarious health conditions in Lima, which included widespread diarrhea, cholera, tertian fever, and a highly contagious influenza.

Viceroy Joaquín de la Pezuela commissioned agents to survey the area and devise recommendations to arrest the spread of disease; he was all too aware that the royalists' failure to defend the citizens' health could undermine their claim to their allegiance, making microbes the patriots' most valuable ally.[7]

Spanish Americans not only had to protect themselves from natural elements and virulent contagion, but they also had to guard against the predatory natures of unscrupulous fellow citizens who sought to take advantage of their desperation. Newspapers from the era contained numerous notices to the public that offered miracle cures or advertised the services of various medical practitioners, not all of whom were honest or well-intentioned. Shops in Lima offered "boxes of select surgical instruments that have just arrived from Europe." The city's Royal Medical Academy offered a prize to Dr. José Manuel Valdés for "his useful public works on behalf of humanity," and Dr. Joaquín Solano concocted an emetic of tartar to treat influenza. In Mexico City, a professor of surgery named José Miguel Múñoz invented an artificial leg and applied for a patent for 10 years' exclusive manufacture so that he could profit from an increased wartime demand for prosthetics.[8] One J. B. Vignaux appeared in Caracas in 1811 claiming to be the "former surgeon mayor of the military hospital of armies in Italy and Egypt," trained in "the art of curing," and willing to make house calls and treat everyone regardless of their status (for a fee, of course).[9] European travelers never failed to comment on the inferior standard of professional medicine practiced in Spanish America, and lamented the pain and suffering caused by the plague of quacks who preyed on poor and unsuspecting patients.[10] On the other hand, the critiques by Europeans and some elite Spanish Americans of many of the traditional medical practices of *curanderos* (indigenous folk healers) were often erroneous, as they were based on their unfamiliarity with those methods—which in fact usually worked. In any case, there is no doubt that wherever human misery arose those who sought to profit from others' pain quickly appeared.[11]

Insects and other natural pests also brought much suffering to soldiers and civilians throughout the region. Ravenous mosquitoes devoured the forces camped along the Caribbean coasts of Colombia and Venezuela, regularly depleting their ranks with dengue fever and malaria. Chiggers were another constant companion that caused discomfort and infection. Richard Bache, an American traveler in Colombia in 1823, was disgusted to discover three nests of chiggers in his elbow, each the size of a pea, despite his best efforts to remain insect-free; he extracted them and applied hot ashes to cauterize the wound. George Flinter, an Irishman who bitterly opposed the patriot cause, reported seeing many people whose limbs had been destroyed by untreated chigger infestations.[12] Head lice were commonplace, and spread easily wherever linens were not washed regularly and cramped conditions kept dirty bodies in close contact. Goiters, a tumor-like growth of the thyroid gland caused by a lack of iodine in the diet, were observed throughout South America during the independence era, from Mendoza in Argentina all the way to Honda in Colombia. Similarly, elephantiasis, a grotesque swelling of the trunk and legs caused by an infected lymph system, was prevalent in Colombia, and afflicted persons frequently crawled along the road while dragging their monstrously bloated appendages behind them.[13] The parade of human misfortune increased the number of beggars and cripples who positioned themselves in the plazas of the towns and at crossroads in the countryside, "displaying their deformities to excite compassion."[14]

Personal security became a serious and daily concern throughout Spanish America during the wars of independence. Despite the absence of trustworthy data to determine whether petty crime rates rose at that time, government edicts, travel accounts, newspaper articles, and private correspondence all regularly referred to the proliferation of robberies, murders, kidnappings, and property crimes. One thing is certain: wherever the authorities were distracted by rebellions, or whenever ill-paid, undisciplined royalist or patriot troops rolled through town, civilians suffered. A resident of Valparaiso, Chile noted fearfully in 1823 that a night in that port city rarely passed without a murder, the favorite method being a stab in the unfortunate victim's loins.[15] No one was exempt from the criminal depredations of bandits; women living alone on rural haciendas were ideal targets. For example, in 1819, Lady Cochrane, whose husband British Admiral Thomas Dundonald, Lord Cochrane, commanded the Chilean navy, was frightened out of her wits when a "ruffian" broke into their country house at Quillote and threatened her with a stiletto.[16] In Curicó, a young lady named Trinidad Salcedo fled from her home and hid in the bushes for days when the infamous robber Pincheyro attacked; according to local legend the traumatized girl never smiled again.[17]

Bandits also lay in wait along the highways and transportation routes, particularly in the mountain passes of the Chilean, Peruvian, and Colombian Andes, and along the route from Veracruz to Mexico City. One observer writing in Peru in 1823 noted that "every traveler we met on the road was armed with a brace of pistols in the holsters of his saddle, and with a sabre by his side."[18] Local custom in Colombia required that victims murdered by robbers along the roads not be buried but rather that each passerby place one stone upon him/her until the body was covered. Although the practice may sound ghoulish, this highly visible and participatory collective interment served—in the days before rapid and reliable communication was available—as an early warning system for travelers making their way along a particular route.[19] On the Callao Road from Lima to the coast Peruvian royalist sympathizers regularly cut communications, stripping travelers of their clothes, horses, money, jewelry, and weapons, intentionally posing as Chileans patriots and "blacks from Rio de la Plata" to create further suspicion and instability.[20]

Government Controls of Civilian Life

Colonial authorities throughout Spanish America regularly tried to brand patriot forces as bandits, thieves, robbers, and common criminals, and issued dozens of edicts. While such pronouncements ostensibly intended to enhance personal security, the larger goal was to shut down the patriots' freedom of movement. In January 1816, after identifying "a group of malcontents" whose egotistical crimes were damaging the "common cause and public security," the royalist captain-general of Chile, Francisco Casimiro Marcó del Pont, ordered that no one be allowed to leave Santiago or other cities without his express and explicit consent; anyone who disobeyed the order would have their goods confiscated, receive 50 lashes, and spend 10 years in the local *presidio* (jail). Shortly thereafter, Marcó del Pont issued regulations for a Tribunal of Vigilance and Public Security that would meet for two hours each day, including holidays, to prevent "meetings of suspicious persons," solicit informants, monitor public behavior for signs of disloyalty, and impose fines and other punishments on patriot-criminals.[21] This tactic, common throughout Spanish America during the independence period, signified imperial desperation and weakness rather than strength. In Mexico, for example, after the initial specter of the Hidalgo revolt awakened colonial authorities to the unseen dangers of sedition, Viceroy Francisco Xavier Venegas and Brigadier General Félix María Calleja jointly demanded that rural residents hand over all machetes, knives, firearms, and powder to their agents, and decreed that no individuals could leave their towns without official permission.[22]

The September 1820 actions of Peruvian viceroy Joaquín de la Pezuela mirrored those of Venegas. He described patriot troops that approached Lima as naked and unpaid hordes who hoped to "satisfy themselves with riches" through forced contributions, violent exactions, and pillage, and he forbade anyone to leave town without an urgent motive and a special passport. Any male between the ages of 18 and 45 who contravened this order would be jailed for two years. Furthermore, all residents had to provide authorities with a tally of their horses, beasts of burden, and carts; failure to do so meant that they forfeited any claim to compensation if their property was seized.[23] The tactic reflected not just a struggle between royalists and patriots, but also a contest between levels of government vying for more power and control. For example, soldiers in the imperial service in Mexico City often scuffled with night watchmen patrolling the streets on behalf of the *cabildo*. In one notorious incident in June 1815, the night watchmen stopped a bunch of rambunctious troops and asked them to state their business, to which the soldiers called them "a bunch of bastards" and said they were out "screwing people."[24]

One's definition of criminality during wartime depends on one's political sympathies. Royalist authorities were quick to brand patriots and patriot supporters as bandits and pirates, yet they themselves regularly confiscated their subjects' property to help defray the costs of putting down the insurrections. As in theaters of war everywhere, Spanish American citizens who were just trying to go about their daily business likely did not appreciate the distinction drawn between royalists and patriots, or governments and criminals, when it came to the greed, rapaciousness, and attacks on a family's meager property practiced by members of all four categories. Indeed, a major feature of daily life in Spanish America during the wars of independence was the constant levying of taxes or forced contributions to support the military campaigns. Both royalists and patriots regularly helped themselves to the people's property to advance their cause and used similar justifications for doing so.

The two sides employed forced levies not just out of desperation or convenience, but also as a targeted method of political retribution. Royalist officials in La Paz in 1809 confiscated the haciendas and movable property of suspected patriot sympathizers Gregorio and Victoria García Lacunza, who they subsequently charged with "high treason." In 1815 Peruvian Viceroy Pezuela imposed a monthly levy on each of the region's towns determined by its size, ability to pay, and reputation for loyalty; La Paz residents had to produce 25,000 pesos per month, Oruro owed 6,000, while Potosí had to come up with a whopping 45,000 pesos monthly at a time when the mining economy had gone bust.[25] One year later, in Venezuela, royalist general Pablo Morillo demanded 200,000 pesos from the citizens of Caracas when he entered the city to fund his campaign against Bolívar.[26] As late as 1823 royalist officials were still stripping the homes of La Paz residents of the last vestiges of their metal wealth or personal goods, forcing them to hand over 160,000 pesos to fund the increasingly futile struggle against the patriots.

By the same token, the patriots themselves regularly demanded that opponents hand over their fortunes, and quickly cracked down on any sign of grumbling or discontent. For example, when San Martín's expeditionary army left Chile in 1820 to liberate Peru, Santiago's wealthy elite and its bishop attempted to stage a coup against Bernardo O'Higgins, who managed to cling to power and then unleashed the retributive powers of the new state upon them. Conspirators had their property seized, their slaves freed, and their colonial titles invalidated, then were themselves packed off to domestic exile in Melipilla and Mendoza. During the summer of 1822 Bernardo Monteagudo, Peru's Secretary of State and Foreign Relations under San Martín, acted similarly, extracting vast amounts of cash, jewels, and property from his political opponents in Lima, and exiling anyone who dared to protest his self-interested actions.[27] Venezuelan military chieftain José Antonio Páez habitually liked to toy with the citizenry when bored. He would descend upon the best houses in town "as if invited" and watch in amusement as the owners desperately tried to throw together a suitably lavish meal on short notice; if Páez judged the food insufficient (which was often), the house would be sacked.[28]

The New Republican Order

Many residents of Spanish America first encountered the emerging new republican order when a smelly band of ill-clad soldiers appeared at their doorstep, thrusting out a paper from the leaders authorizing them to take anything they wanted in service of the national effort. The notes usually closed by expressing appreciation for the set-upon person's patriotism, a flowery sentence which was considered to be payment in full for their losses. Between 1819 and 1821 "officers of the Republic" rode throughout Venezuela and Colombia using their warrants to seize boats, crew members, horses, food, textiles, and anything else that caught their eye.[29] Government agents confiscated the best house in each town to use as their quarters and to lodge travelers, diplomats, entrepreneurs, or other helpful types who might be visiting the region. The general expectation seems to have been that a person traveling on official business could expect to be lodged and fed at no charge by any citizen he met on his way. There is ample evidence, however, that locals felt confident enough of their rights to demand that they be shown documentation if their goods were to be appropriated. For example, when in 1823 a patriot guide in Pativilca, Peru, demanded that a peasant supply corn for their "horses of state," the man agreed only on the condition that the foreigner display his credentials and a signed authority; the guide's embarrassed British officer quickly offered to pay for the confiscated produce.[30]

The common folk probably felt the presence of the new republican governments even more intensely as these regimes established new customs houses and toll booths (provided that they could be staffed). The roads leading to and from Chile's busy port town of Valparaiso, for example, had toll gates placed on them each Sunday to extract small sums from merchants and muleteers, although officials were always careful to explain that the money collected would be used for road repairs. Even far inland at Pamplona, Colombia, travelers expressed their surprise at the omnipresence of customs officers who attempted to tax goods being taken from one region to another. Notions of the larger national body would take much longer to gain meaning among the populace following the wars. Quite likely, any subtle distinctions between bandits, petty thieves, and official government agents from a remote city were lost on the harassed, taxed, burdened populations during the anarchy of wartime.

Military commanders and government bureaucrats who regularly used their positions to demand support from the public for official purposes were no less quick to use their newfound power to shore up their own personal finances. Corruption, sweetheart deals, lucrative no-bid contracts, and excessive compensation are hallmarks of wartime, and all formed part of daily life in Spanish America during the wars of independence. In the name of security against patriot brigands, Mexican royalists created monopoly supply zones in the 1810s and made huge profits for themselves.[31] *Llanero* (plainsmen) fighters placed no value on the land title scrip they received as compensation for their service, allowing their savvier leader Páez to build up his own vast personal fortune by buying the bits of paper from his men for very small sums. Venezuelan Admiral Luis Brión applied for, and received, the exclusive right to operate steamboats on the Orinoco River after he and his friends won the war.[32] Chilean merchant family networks also took advantage of the independence era's general confusion to buttress their own economic position. Antonio José de Irisarri married into the elite Larraín family, went to London as a diplomatic envoy, and proceeded to negotiate a disastrous loan for Chile that paid him a handsome fee and landed him in an English court in 1825. Other overseas agents—Francisco Antonio Zea for Colombia, Manuel José Hurtado for Mexico, and Juan García del Rio and James Paroissien for Peru—similarly contracted personally lucrative but nationally harmful loans in London. It seemed as if everyone, and not just those in power, tried to cash in on wartime profiteering. Contemporary newspapers were filled with accounts of financial exploitation and artificial shortages; for example, the government of Peru blamed the "excessive price" being charged for soap on "the scandalous abuse of so many monopolists."[33] In highly unstable and war-torn Venezuela, the scene of some of the continent's most vicious fighting, interest rates sometimes soared to 15 percent per month during the independence period.[34]

Celebrations and Entertainment

Despite the ubiquity of shady characters that were out for a quick profit, many others shared in the collective joy with celebratory processions and late-night fiestas. Traditional Catholic feast days and secular imperial holidays such as the arrival of a new viceroy or the king's birthday were celebrated in places where colonial authorities held on longest. Several days of public festivities, including illuminations and the erection of a triumphal arch of laurel leaves and olive branches, marked the July 1816 entry of Viceroy Pezuela into Lima, although it is hard to interpret what was meant by the "expressive silence" of the American men who turned out to watch. Four months later *limeños* celebrated Charles IV's birthday with a lavish party and a play performed in the best theater.[35] When the businesslike English Lord Cochrane arrived at Valparaiso, Chile, to assume his post, officials met him with "a variety of fêtes . . . prolonged for so many days as to amount to a waste of time."[36] Likewise, Simón Bolívar was the frequent object of patriotic processions. He enjoyed being welcomed into a liberated city through a triumphal arch by virginal girls dressed in white and throwing flowers in his path (although the bitter royalist George

Flinter later claimed that the Liberator was secretly hated by all).[37] When Bolívar entered Caracas on August 4, 1813, its balconies were decorated with flower garlands, music played and candles stood lit in every window at night, and a grand ball was held in his honor. Wherever he went, the approach was the same—the townspeople would hear an artillery discharge, bells ringing, and the sound of a regimental band, all indicating that they had about an hour before the Liberator would appear.[38]

Indeed, pomp and circumstance mattered greatly to both patriots and royalists. In Angostura, where the patriots had their headquarters in 1818 and 1819, General Mariano Montilla arranged for a huge symbolic celebration of the eighth anniversary of the 1810 Venezuelan declaration of independence, complete with an indigenous dance that portrayed, oddly and inaccurately, the Aztec Emperor Moctezuma's struggle against Hernán Cortés and the Spanish conquistadors in Mexico. He planted a coconut tree in the central plaza as a local stand-in for the Jacobin-style tree of liberty, paraded his troops to church to receive benediction, handed out alcohol freely, and ordered a symbolic eight rounds of cannon fire.[39] When Iturbide and his army marched into Mexico City on September 27, 1821, they headed straight for the cathedral, where Archbishop Pedro José de Fonte greeted them with a solemn *Te Deum* and a celebratory mass.[40] Having just cleared the Venezuelan province of Coro of royalist holdouts, patriot leader Carlos Soublette held a civilian and military parade on St. Simon's Day (October 28, 1822) that brought 10,000 people into the central plaza to enjoy bullfights, artillery salvos, and an evening ball, to listen to toasts and speeches praising the new order, and to delight in the houses decorated in the national colors of red, blue, and yellow.[41] The extensive fiestas held in Lima in April and May 1823 under the flags of Argentina, Chile, Colombia, and Peru further made visible the fraternal success of Spanish American patriots. People dressed in national colors danced in the streets, and many proudly wore medals from San Martín's new Order of the Sun.[42] Similar celebrations marked the daily lives of Spanish American everywhere, particularly in the late 1810s and 1820s as the patriots' ultimate victory became apparent and the populace grew increasingly certain of who would control their daily lives and destinies.

Nevertheless, because it was wartime many of the games that passed for entertainment reflected the coarseness of the population and the general taste for violence and blood sports. In 1816, for example, Peruvian royalists held a special bullfight as a benefit to raise money for the Concordia regiment; the sport remained popular well into the nineteenth century despite several attempts by republican authorities to ban it as the remnant of an uncivilized colonial mentality.[43] Residents of Spanish America also passionately followed cockfighting, and when prize birds met for a match the whole town dressed up and came out to watch. British travelers remarked upon the game with a mixture of horror and fascination, noting that it appeared to be the national pastime everywhere they went. It seemed as though all Spanish American men raised fighting cocks, hinting at a not-so-subtle link between blood sports and masculine identity.[44] Indeed, skill and bravado seemed to characterize much of the games Spanish American men played in their leisure time. Wild pig hunting was a favorite activity in Colombia, all the more popular because it displayed one's marksmanship and also brought food to the table. Cattle roping in the great plains of Argentina and Northern Mexico served the same function.

Others found their game of choice indoors at the billiard table or among decks of cards, and when mixed with alcohol such diversions often led to violence and financial ruin. The inability of colonial authorities to effectively enforce the royal monopoly on playing cards gave rise to a thriving black market, and card games of all sorts flourished in saloons, private homes, and plazas. Spanish American officers particularly enjoyed *monte* and apparently were willing to play for days on end, staking their last dollar on the hopes that the perfect hand would come through.[45] Soldiers and unemployed men gambled and drank their leisure time away, and knife fights or brawls frequently ensued.[46] Games could be invented out of anything, and violence was often part of the fun. In Bogotá, bored patriot troops came up with a game called *golpes* (knocks) in which they used three flat stones with marks on one side and guessed what combination would come up when tossed; if the player was wrong, he would get his knuckles smacked. Billiard tables popped up throughout Venezuela during the independence period, typically in taverns operated by French merchants. Several of the era's military and political leaders, including Carlos Soublette and Manuel Valdés, apparently became devoted to the sport while based in patriot headquarters on Margarita Island.[47]

Popular theater—religious performances, operas, traveling theater troupes, puppet shows, dances, and concerts—also thrived during the wars for independence, occasionally serving as a propaganda venue but more often simply providing refuge and delight to a war-weary population. Nonetheless, fictional heroes and villains in these performances started to present a new ethos, identifying the patriotic values of the emerging order and bringing newly created citizens of all ranks and races together in previously unimaginable ways. Many plays, for example, had stock indigenous or Afro-American characters, some of whom were buffoonish and subservient but who increasingly joined center stage as heroic protagonists. At the same time the composition of the audiences became more mixed; members of all classes paid differing ticket prices and regularly attended performances at Mexico City's *Teatro Principal.* Even so, private attitudes toward issues of race and class changed more gradually than public policy. For example, the prominent Mexican journalist José Joaquín Fernández de Lizardi divided theater-goers into three general classes: the enlightened, the ignorant, and the stupid.[48] Similarly, in 1824 a grumpy Lorenzo Justiniano Araujo surveyed the *Teatro Principal* and complained about the "excesses that are committed by the spectators who occupy the *cazuela* (space reserved for women) at night," meaning their shouts of insolence, raucous behavior, and likely things more scandalous than that.[49] Even worse, audiences at the city's main institution of high culture usually had to hold their noses to reduce the "emanations" coming from the attached bathrooms.[50] But, like everything else during the wars for independence, the show nevertheless went on.

Where Spanish Americans of all socioeconomic classes relished any chance to escape their troubles at the many venues for entertainment and recreation, the ambitious figures who hoped to lead them saw opportunities to build support. The creation of an elevated national culture of performance proved important to royalists and patriots throughout Spanish America, all of whom understood both its didactic function and its ability to convey their political message to a largely illiterate population. In 1817 an impoverished troupe of actors at Mexico City's *Teatro Coliseo* started a collective organization to pay their wages; their first fundraiser was a musical that celebrated the capture and execution of patriot hero Francisco Javier Mina, who had launched an ill-fated, pro-independence invasion at Soto la Marina earlier in the year.[51] Other troupes also gauged the political temperament of their audiences and calibrated their shows' content accordingly. In royalist Peru that same year a Lima company put on a performance called "Charlotte Corday, the Most Royalist Heroine who aided France." The show reenacted the life and early death of the young woman who in 1793 tried to save her country from further damage from the regicidal, godless republican Jacobins by assassinating their leader, Jean-Paul Marat, in his bathtub.[52]

Music was also an ever-present feature of daily life in Spanish America during the wars for independence. From the loftiest European-style sonatas to the homeliest guitar-picking, songs could be heard everywhere. In Caracas the music of Haydn, Pleyel, and Mozart entertained the townspeople during the short-lived First Republic (1810–1812). Ten years later, an operatic version of Virgil's epic *The Aeneid* graced the same city, even if foreigners found it "miserably performed."[53] An Italian opera company featuring the lovely Carolina Griloni performed in the port city of Callao, Peru, in 1816 as part of a South American tour that included venues in Argentina and Brazil.[54] Other less formal and more spontaneous performances were more common, however. Families and neighbors gathered together in the evening to tell stories and dance. One traveler in the tiny village of Pinto, Colombia, stayed with a pro-independence Spanish family whose daughter was a "music-mad hoyden" who played "an old cracked guitar, upon which she accompanies her own delightful warblings." In Arecife, Argentina, the owner of a *pulpería* (bar) amused his patrons with a guitar, causing one to note that "almost all peasants play that instrument."[55] Other instruments were more particularly associated with certain races—drums and maracas, for example, often signified African heritage, while flutes and tambourines implied indigenous ethnicity.[56]

Wartime Poverty and Destruction

The presence of games, music, and merriment lightened the daily lives of Spanish Americans, a much-needed distraction from the poverty and destruction that the wars brought. Capital flight was a huge problem, inflation ran rampant, and food shortages were compounded by drought, fires, earthquakes, and neglect. Residents of Cartagena quite literally ran out of food during Pablo Morillo's siege of the city in 1815, and they began to consume their household pets out of desperation; one horrified observer recorded that a cat sold for as much as $8 and a bigger dog for $20.[57] When an opposing army approached, merchants were desperate to sell their goods at any price or to find horses and carts to get them out of town before their shops could be raided.[58] Mexican mining output declined significantly, from 25 million pesos in 1810 to 10 million per year every year until 1815, and Querétaro's textile industries fell off by

70 percent. By 1821, the Mexican treasury had barely 6,000 pesos left in its central account.[59] Indeed, the macroeconomic impact of the independence era was complex; areas like the port of Buenos Aires benefited from unrestricted international trade in some aspects but also suffered from the loss of inland markets in Upper Peru (today Bolivia). Grain that would have gone to Peru was diverted to the much smaller Chilean market instead and left many small producers scrambling to find buyers for their crops. In the Andes, evidence suggests that family-based barter relations among indigenous people increased during this period as commercial markets dissolved.[60] All regional economies suffered from some type of distortion in the early decades of the nineteenth century. It seems clear, however, the general standard of living dropped during the wars of independence, and that everyone had to work harder or hustle more shamelessly just to stay alive.

People tried their best to maintain their homes and towns under the most difficult of circumstances. A large and growing urban area like Mexico City struggled then as it does today to keep up with demands for clean water and waste removal. There was open sewage on the streets, and garbage sometimes piled high enough to block the roadways.[61] Rubbish also filled the town square in Angostura, Colombia, and its wells were "rendered nauseous and unwholesome by the putrid human carcasses thrown into them at the time when the city was besieged." Rural people frequently shared living quarters with their domestic animals: cats, dogs, pigs, parrots, goats, and the occasional monkey.[62]

Moreover, earthquakes damaged the buildings of many cities and towns. The 1812 tremor in northern South America was particularly devastating, and its effects remained visible for more than a decade across Venezuela and Colombia because the wartime violence, capital flight, and labor disruptions made it impossible to reconstruct. Half of Caracas remained in ruins 10 years later, its cathedral drowning in a decade's worth of rubbish and rubble. Mérida's cathedral was also destroyed, and the town of Honda in Colombia remained nearly flattened under debris in 1820.[63] An earthquake in Chile badly damaged Valparaiso, but luckily many people were outside for their evening stroll, thus reducing the number of lives lost in collapsed buildings. The same tremor shook the town of Quillote, where residents fled into the square, "many of them kneeling and praying in a state of nudity."[64]

At the same time, some areas escaped destruction caused by warfare and natural disasters, and people continued to go about their daily lives in more pleasant environments. Caloto, Colombia, was described as a healthy town owing to a sea breeze, where the houses all had fruit and vegetable gardens. Along the Magdalena River, the village of Santa Anna was "neat and clean," and parts of the lovely colonial city of Mompox had tidy houses surrounded by trees and flowering shrubs, making it a pleasant stop for weary travelers.[65] Many towns continued to have their daily and weekly markets, with women selling whatever crops, goods, or crafts they had gathered up: flowers, fowl, textiles, fruit, vegetables, prepared foods like tacos or empanadas, alcohol, and medicines. Their clientele was largely female as well. In war zones in particular women often had to assume even more responsibility for the family's destiny, and expanded their range of daily chores and activities more openly into the public sphere.

It is difficult to draw any generalizations about the daily life of Spanish Americans during the wars for independence, as much depended on one's race, class, gender, region, and luck. Conditions varied dramatically over nearly 20 years, from Mexico to Tierra del Fuego. While patriot military and political leaders might have functioned in "an environment of unprecedented liberalism," fighting to change the destinies of millions, for most people "everyday concerns were focused on food and shelter, rather than issues of governance."[66] Although history books are more likely to record the momentous clashes on the battlefield, or the stirring orations pronounced by politicians and intellectuals, it was the slow but sure changes in the daily practices and beliefs of the common folk that gave meaning to independence over the long run. That process had started by 1826, but may yet be incomplete. For most Spanish Americans, whether resident in rural or urban areas, the terrible truth of the wartime era was that battles, disease, economic dislocation, crime, and predatory fellow citizens destabilized their lives and livelihoods for nearly two decades. Yet, in response, they claimed what autonomy and power they could for themselves and their communities, tended their homes and gardens, raised their children and buried their dead. Their political destinies could wait, but the daily chores could not.

NOTES

1. Among the best comprehensive surveys in English are: John Lynch, *The Spanish American Revolutions 1808–1826: Old and New World Origins* (Norman: University of Oklahoma Press, 1994); John Lynch, *Latin America: Between Colony and Nation: Selected Essays* (New York: Palgrave, 2001); Jaime E. Rodríguez O., *The Independence of Spanish America* (Cambridge: Cambridge

University Press, 1998); Jay Kinsbruner, *Independence in Spanish America: Civil Wars, Revolutions and Underdevelopment* (Albuquerque: University of New Mexico Press, 2000); and Victor Uribe-Urán, *State and Society in Spanish America during the Age of Revolution* (Wilmington, DE: Scholarly Resources, 2001).

2. Mark Wasserman, *Everyday Life and Politics in Nineteenth Century Mexico: Men, Women, and War* (Albuquerque: University of New Mexico Press, 2000), 37, 62; Simón Tadeo Ortiz de Ayala, *Resumen de la estadística del imperio mexicano en 1822* (Mexico City: Biblioteca Nacional y la UNAM, 1968), 18.

3. M-D Demélas and Y. Saint-Geours, *La vie quotidienne en Amérique du sud au temps de Bolívar 1809–1830* (Paris: Hachette, 1987), 166.

4. Erick Langer, "Indian Trade and Ethnic Economies in the Andes, 1780–1880," *Estudios interdisciplinarios de América Latina* 15:1 (January–June 2004), 5.

5. Alberto Crespo et al., *La vida cotidiana en La Paz durante la guerra de la independencia 1800–1825* (La Paz: Editorial de la Universidad Mayor de San Andrés, 1975), 42, 51–52.

6. *Recollections of a Service of Three Years During the War of Extermination in the Republics of Venezuela and Colombia* (London: Hunt and Clarke, 1828), 1:184; George Flinter, *A History of the Revolution of Caracas* (London: T. and J. Allman, 1819), 53.

7. The *Gaceta de Gobierno de Lima* has many references in the months of February to June 1818, including long articles in no. 18 (March 10, 1818), 137, and no. 19 (March 14, 1818), 141.

8. *Gaceta de Gobierno de Lima* no. 8 (January 29, 1817), 60, and no. 31 (May 8, 1817), 247.

9. "Aviso," *El Publicista de Venezuela*, no. 8 (August 22, 1811), 64.

10. *Recollections of Service*, 1:156.

11. David Sowell, *The Tale of the Healer Miguel Perdomo: Medicine, Ideologies and Power in the Nineteenth Century Andes* (Wilmington, DE: Scholarly Resources, 2001); also see the extended discussion in Rebecca Earle, "'A Grave for Europeans?': Disease, Death, and the Spanish-American Revolutions," *War in History* 3:4 (1996): 371–383.

12. Richard Bache, *Notes on Colombia Taken in the Years 1822–23* (Philadelphia: H. C. Carey, 1827), 212; Flinter, *History of the Revolution*, 132.

13. *Recollections of Service*, 2:157. Elephantiasis is sometimes known as San Lázaro's disease and is spread among humans by infected mosquitoes. It remains common in Africa and Brazil.

14. Bache, *Notes on Colombia*, 18.

15. Robert Proctor, *Narrative of a Journey Across the Cordillera of the Andes* (London: Archibald Constable, 1825), 109–110.

16. Thomas Dundonald, Lord Cochrane, *Narrative of the Liberation of Chile, Peru, and Brazil from Spanish and Portuguese Domination* (London: James Ridgway, 1859), 1:22.

17. Thomas Sutcliffe, *Sixteen Years in Chile and Peru* (London: Fisher, Son, 1841), 133.

18. Proctor, *Narrative*, 90–91.

19. *Recollections of Service*, 2:152–153.

20. Proctor, *Narrative*, 335.

21. Chile, Real Audiencia, "Bando" (January 12, 1816), broadside held at the John Carter Brown Library (hereafter cited as JCBL), bBB .C537 1816 6; Chile, Real Audiencia, "Reglamento del Tribunal" (January 17, 1816), JCBL, bBB .C537 1816 1 1-size; "Reglamento para los operaciones del tribunal de vigilancia y seguridad pública del reyno de Chile," *Gaceta del Gobierno de Lima* no. 38 (May 9, 1816), 295.

22. "Usando el Brigadier D. Félix Calleja en gefe el Exército que derroto en el Pueblo de Aculco a los insurgentes. . . ." (Mexico City: November 12, 1810); Venegas, *Habitantes de Nueva Galicia* (Mexico City: December 31, 1810), broadsides held at Mexico City's Centro de Estudios de Historia de México (CONDUMEX), Fondo I-2 L.G., f.706.

23. Pezuela, "Este Gobierno ha instruido al Público sin misterio ni reserva. . . ." (Lima: September 20, 1820), broadside 71–33 held at the JCBL.

24. Eric Van Young, "Islands in the Stream: Quiet Cities and Violent Countryside in the Mexican Independence Era," *Past and Present* 118 (February 1988), 138.

25. Crespo, *La vida cotidiana*, 168–169.

26. Flinter, *History of the Revolution*, 184.

27. Sutcliffe, *Sixteen Years*, 51, 58. Not surprisingly, Monteagudo was very unpopular and subsequently was assassinated on the streets of Lima in 1825. It should also be noted that the Spanish general Canterac also levied fines on *limeños* he deemed disloyal.

28. Bache, *Notes on Colombia*, 147.

29. *Recollections of Service*, 1:204.

30. Proctor, *Narrative*, 173.

31. Brian Hamnett, "The Economic and Social Dimension of the Revolution of Independence in Mexico 1800–1824," *Ibero-Amerikanisches Archiv* 6 (1980), 19.

32. Charles Griffin, "Economic and Social Aspects of the Era of the Spanish American Independence," *Hispanic American Historical Review* 29:2 (May 1949), 179, n. 33, and 184, n. 52. Páez authored his own justificatory *Autobiografía del general José Antonio Páez*, 2 vols. (New York: Imprenta de Hallet y Breen, 1869). Some of Brión's related entrepreneurial schemes are detailed in *Documentos del almirante Brión* (Caracas: Ediciones del Congreso de la República, 1982), and *Correspondencia entre el Libertador y el almirante Brión* (Caracas: Ediciones de la Presidencia de la República, 1984). Also see Mary Lowenthal Felstiner, "Kinship Politics in the Chilean Independence Movement," *Hispanic American Historical Review* 56:1 (February 1976), 68.

33. *Gaceta del gobierno de Lima*, no. 12 (February 10, 1816), 88.

34. Griffin, "Economic and Social Aspects," 182, n. 47.

35. *Gaceta del gobierno de Lima*, no. 55 (July 11, 1816), 429, no. 67 (July 18, 1816), 442, and no. 87 (November 9, 1816), 690.

36. Dundonald, *Narrative*, 1:3.

37. Flinter, *History of the Revolution*, 50.

38. W. J. Adam, *Journal of Voyages Across Marguaritta, Trinidad and Maturin* (Dublin: J. Jones, 1824), 120.

39. Gustavus Hippisley, *A Narrative of the Expedition to the Rivers Orinoco and Apuré in South America* (London: John Murray, 1819), 307–312; see also the many descriptions in *General de División Mariano Montilla: Homenaje en el bicentenario de su nacimiento 1782–1982*, vol. 2 (Caracas: Ediciones de la Presidencia de la República, 1982).

40. *Diario de Lupita, 1821*, ed. Rafael Estrada Michel (Mexico City: Planeta, 2000), 140.

41. A troubling development, however, was that attendance at the party was compulsory. Bache, *Notes on Colombia*, 48–49.

42. Proctor, *Narrative*, 116–117.

43. *Gaceta del gobierno de Lima*, no. 36 (May 4, 1816), and Proctor, *Narrative*, 248–249; for a discussion of bullfighting's fate in Mexico, see William H. Beezley, *Judas at the Jockey Club and Other Episodes of Porfirian Mexico*, 2nd ed. (Lincoln: University of Nebraska Press, 2004).

44. Bache, *Notes on Colombia*, 181; Proctor, *Narrative*, 200.

45. Karen Racine, "Rum, Recruitment and Revolution: Alcohol and the British and Irish Legion in Colombia's War for Independence, 1817–1823," *Irish Migration Studies in Latin America*, 4:2 (March 2006), 50.

46. *Campaigns and Cruises in Venezuela and New Granada from 1817 to 1830* (London: Longman and Co., 1831), 1:102.

47. Adam, *Journal*, 111.

48. "El Pensador Mexicano," in *El Sol*, May 3, 1824.

49. Lorenzo Justiniano Araujo, "Letter to the Editor," in *El Sol*, June 26, 1824.

50. Luis Reyes de la Maza, *El teatro en México durante la independencia, 1810–1839* (Mexico City: UNAM, Instituto de Investigaciones Estéticas, 1969), 20.

51. Reyes de la Maza, *El teatro en México*, 12–13.

52. *Gaceta del gobierno de Lima* no. 40 (June 7, 1817), 320.

53. *Mercurio Venezolano*, no. 1 (January 1811), 54–56; Bache, *Notes on Colombia*, 51.

54. *Gaceta del gobierno de Lima*, no. 17 (February 28, 1816), 128.

55. *Recollections of Service*, 1:217–218; Proctor, *Narrative*, 11.

56. See John Charles Chasteen, *National Rhythms, African Roots: The Deep History of Latin American Popular Dance* (Albuquerque: University of New Mexico Press, 2004).

57. H.L.V. Ducoudray-Holstein, *Memoirs of Simon Bolivar* (Boston: Goodrich, 1829), 197.

58. *Campaigns and Cruises*, 1:146.

59. Wasserman, *Everyday Life*, 63, 67.

60. Langer, "Indian Trade," 8.

61. Wasserman, *Everyday Life*, 35.

62. Hippisley, *Narrative*, 337, 340.

63. *Recollections of Service*, 1:142, 236; Bache, *Notes on Colombia*, 22, 36.

64. Sutcliffe, *Sixteen Years of Service*, 11–12; Proctor, *Narrative*, 107.

65. *Recollections of Service*, 1:220–221; *Campaigns and Cruises*, 1:208. Today Mompox is protected as a UNESCO (United Nations Educational, Scientific, and Cultural Organization) World Heritage Site.

66. The first quote is from Peter Blanchard, "The Language of Liberation: Slave Voices in the Wars of Independence," *Hispanic American Historical Review* 82:3 (August 2002), 501; the second appears in Wasserman, *Everyday Life*, 9.

THREE

The Civilian Experience in Mexico during the War with the United States, 1846–1848

Pedro Santoni

When the specter of war with the United States loomed over Mexico late in the spring of 1846 the country found itself ill prepared to fight back against its northern neighbor. The sense of euphoria and optimism held by many public-spirited Mexicans following independence from Spain in 1821 dissipated during the next quarter century as the transition from colony to nation-state proved more difficult than anticipated. Multiple factors fueled the chronic turmoil that afflicted the young nation. These included the country's near-bankrupt status, regional antagonisms between leaders of many peripheral regions and the Mexico City-based political elite, and bitter strife among four political factions—moderates (or *moderados*), radicals (or *puros*), *santanistas* (as adherents of General Antonio López de Santa Anna came to be known), and conservatives—as to the best way to construct a modern nation-state.[1] Such intractable domestic problems prevented the former Spanish colony from effectively defending its territorial sovereignty as it headed into a catastrophic fight with the United States.

When hostilities began, therefore, U.S. armies were able to march into Mexican territory and vanquish every opposing force that stood in their path. The Army of the West, commanded by General Stephen Kearney, took control of present-day New Mexico and California, and by early 1847 had put down two movements that sought to restore Mexican sovereignty—the Taos Revolt in the former and the uprising of the *californios* in the latter. Another U.S. army, led by Colonel Alexander Doniphan, struck at the state of Chihuahua and entered its capital city on March 2, 1847. Meanwhile, the main theater of the war in northern Mexico saw General Zachary Taylor's Army of Occupation soundly defeat Mexican defenders at the Battles of Palo Alto and Resaca de la Palma (fought in present-day Brownsville, Texas, on May 8 and 9, 1846), push inland across the Rio Grande and pummel the city of Monterrey (September 20–24, 1846), and fight the Mexican army to a standstill at the Battle of Buena Vista (February 22–23, 1847).

Despite such losses Mexican authorities showed no inclination to end the war, so by late October 1846 the U.S. government had decided to press the issue and invade Mexico's heartland. Early in March 1847 General Winfield Scott and his 10,000 man army landed south of the fortified city of Veracruz on Mexico's eastern coast, and by month's end he had ordered an artillery barrage that pounded the port city into submission. From that stronghold Scott led his troops approximately 250 miles inland to Mexico City in an undertaking that military authorities like the Duke of Wellington—who in 1815 had defeated Napoleon Bonaparte at the Battle of Waterloo—considered impossible. Scott, however, routed the Mexican army at the Battle of Cerro Gordo (April 18), captured the city of Puebla one month later, and prevailed in several encounters in and around the capital before capturing Mexico City that September. By the time a peace treaty had been signed and ratified in mid-1848, Mexico had lost more than half its land to its northern neighbor. Furthermore, its national psyche had been thoroughly traumatized. In the long run, the conflict shaped—some might say poisoned—Mexico's bilateral relations with its northern neighbor.

This synopsis of the war underscores why Mexico failed to offer a more stubborn resistance to the foreign threat and hints at the profound effects that the conflict had on Mexico's national development. Nonetheless, the ways in which the struggle impacted the daily lives of the country's nearly 7.5 million inhabitants remains an understudied subject. "Most of what little literature is available on the U.S.-Mexican War in English," as one of most recent books about the conflict states, "deals primarily with military matters," and that narrative comes "almost exclusively from the U.S. point of view."[2] Given the historiographical vacuum, as well as U.S. President James K. Polk's "avowed intention of waging a war that bore only lightly on Mexico's civilian population,"[3] this essay analyzes four aspects of the everyday life of residents of Mexico during the conflict (leaving out of the analysis what is today the U.S. Southwest and California) that at times intersect. The first illustrates how the presence of foreign armies on Mexican soil brought significant violence and destruction to Mexican civilians. The second concerns the relationship between the Mexican state and its citizens; the longstanding weaknesses of Mexico's government had nearly as much impact on Mexicans during the war as did the U.S. intervention. Third, the essay regards the ways Mexicans from all walks of life took advantage of the war, whether to demonstrate their patriotism or to improve their economic situation. Some Mexicans also collaborated with U.S. officials; many did so out of an earnest desire to minimize the disruption caused by the occupation, others out of political ambition. Fourth, the essay suggests that the U.S. incursion into Mexican territory did not dramatically disrupt the ebb and flow of daily activities. The chapter concludes with a brief look at some of the conflict's reverberations, and at the ways they continue to affect many civilians today.

WARTIME DEVASTATION AND PROFITEERING

When President Polk declared war on Mexico in May 1846 many young American males rushed to enroll in a type of militia labeled volunteers, one of the two corps that made up the U.S. military (the other being the regular professional army). These volunteers were youths eager for adventure and fame, and intent on avenging the deaths of the men who had defended the Alamo and had been executed at Goliad during the struggle for Texas independence 10 years earlier. As the conflict with Mexico progressed, the U.S. popular press highlighted the volunteers' activities because of the soldiers' ostensible high-mindedness and generosity of spirit toward residents of the enemy country. Stories about volunteers—nearly 59,000 served in the conflict—"protecting Mexican civilians from bandits, ministering to the enemy wounded left behind on the battlefields, defending villages against the depredations of Comanche and Apache Indians, intervening to shield helpless Mexicans from the oppressions of their own military and religious leadership" became common.[4] Rhetoric, however, belied reality, as the volunteers' reported magnanimity sharply contrasted with the depredations that they inflicted on Mexican civilians.

The havoc that Mexico's inhabitants endured at the hands of U.S. volunteers can be explained in part because these troops "encountered an alien terrain, people, religion, and culture," something that no earlier U.S. army had quite experienced. Unlike some officers, who came into contact with wealthy, elite Mexicans, most of the army's rank and file "formed their opinions of the Mexican people on the basis of their dealings with various merchants and citizens of the lower classes." U.S. soldiers, consequently, came to regard Mexicans generally "as being of a lower racial order." This debasement not only "served a military purpose in that the troops had less difficulty in taking the lives of enemy soldiers if they considered them to be subhuman," but also facilitated the execution of "crimes of varying magnitude against the civilian population." Indeed, the future U.S. President Ulysses S. Grant remarked that some volunteers in the town of Matamoros (on the Texas border below Brownsville) "seem[ed] to think it perfectly right to impose upon the people of a Conquered city to any extent, and even to murder them where the act can be covered in the dark. And how much they seem to enjoy acts of violence too!" Such assaults form part of what one historian recently characterized as the "hidden dirty war."[5]

In northern Mexico "no single group of [U.S.] volunteers was so universally condemned for its conduct toward civilians as were the Texans."[6] While Texas cavalry units—the so-called Rangers—played key military roles in the conflict, their rough treatment of civilians "earned them the epithet *los diablos Tejanos*—the Texan devils."[7] One of their most heinous actions, believed by one U.S. officer to have formed "part of a larger campaign of reprisal" unleashed by General Taylor, took place near Cerralvo, Nuevo León, in March 1847. Following a particularly brutal ambush on a U.S. wagon train that resulted in 12 casualties and 40 of 120 wagons missing or destroyed, a detachment of Rangers attacked a nearby village and killed two dozen civilians. Taylor launched what he characterized as a rigorous investigation "but said he was unable to identify the culprits. Witnesses to the massacre failed to come forward, 'being afraid that they might incur a similar fate,'"[8] so in the end the incident only had a satisfactory resolution for the Texans.

In sharp contrast with the behavior toward civilians exhibited by Taylor's troops stands the comportment that General Scott demanded of his men. He had learned from his inability to wage an effective guerrilla war against the Seminole Indians in the 1830s, as well as from the irregular partisan warfare and political disorder that doomed Napoleon Bonaparte's efforts to control Spain during the Peninsular War (1808–1814). Scott therefore made a concerted effort to mollify the populace, an approach that gave him a strategic advantage as he marched inland from Mexico's eastern coast to the capital in the spring and summer of 1847. He imposed martial law in those parts of Mexico under his control in an effort to enforce stability and order, win over local residents, and avoid a protracted insurgency. Although Scott had to abandon his pacification plan late in the war when President Polk, impatient because peace was not forthcoming, ordered him to exact contributions from the population to support the army, his policies toward Mexican civilians greatly contributed to his success in Mexico.[9]

Despite Scott's orders (and the disciplinary measures he instituted to insure their effectiveness), his men on occasion heaped abuse on the Mexican people. Some transgressions might even be considered a bit humorous, an example of which occurred on the outskirts of Mexico City following the August 20, 1847, Battle of Churubusco. When U.S. infantryman Frederick Zeh saw some of his comrades coming his way "loaded with chickens," he and other soldiers decided to look for more of those "precious birds." Despite thoroughly searching the houses the men did not find anything in the village of Churubusco, but all of the sudden they "heard the cackling of a hen in a kitchen—without being able to see her, however." The soldiers then put their ears against a "freshly laid wall oven, and . . . established with certainty that this was the chickens' temporary abode. At once we poked a hole in the oven and then removed a goodly number of birds, to the dismay of their owner."[10] It is doubtful that the affected Mexican civilian lodged a protest against the raiders.

The propaganda that preceded conventional military operations, and the fears of what might transpire during the impending assault, also had a profound effect on the daily lives of civilians in urban areas of Mexico. Consider, for example, what transpired during the two months that preceded the U.S. attack on Monterrey, the capital of the northern state of Nuevo León. Late in July 1846 the city's main newspaper, the *Semanario Político*, moved to shape public opinion about the invaders. It described U.S. soldiers as that country's "most immoral and wanton people" who had committed numerous "offenses against among Matamoros' residents, especially women." Articles like these, designed to stimulate some patriotic feelings, also likely raised fear and apprehension among city residents. Many of Monterrey's men took their families to nearby towns so they would be out of harm's way, and they did not return to defend the city once the U.S. onslaught became imminent despite being ordered to do so.[11]

The three-day battle for Monterrey provides further insights into the ways that combat affected Mexican civilians, particularly women. Journalists and historians have described how some city residents reacted during the heavy skirmishing that took place within the city itself. According to the prominent U.S. newspaper correspondent George Wilkins Kendall, on the afternoon of September 23 "many women were seen in the doorways and in the streets, and even where the battle was raging, freely offering our men oranges and other fruits. Frightened out of their senses, they yet seemed impressed with the belief that we were to conquer, and thus attempted to propitiate our protection and good will." Kendall also reported that some U.S. soldiers who in one house had to pick "an entrance through a wall of massive thickness" found many women in a state of alarm due to the "lying stories of the brutality of the Americans," and "it was with the greatest difficulty that they could be assured of their safety."[12]

Contrary to Kendall, whose judgment on this occasion likely lacked objectivity, Mexican historians have shown that not all females lost their nerve during the battle for Monterrey. One woman known as Dos Amades put on the uniform of a Mexican cavalry officer and led a charge against U.S. forces. According to the well-known essayist Guillermo Prieto, who also edited several of Mexico City's most important newspapers during the 1840s, an even better known instance of bravery took place during the late morning hours of September 23. At that time María Josefa Zozaya, "sublime as the heroines of Sparta and Rome, and beautiful as the tutelar deities of Grecian sculpture," gave out provisions to Mexican soldiers posted on a rooftop that overlooked the city's main plaza and exhorted "them to despise danger."[13] Later that afternoon, an anonymous Mexican woman (who may or not have been Zozaya) nursed wounded soldiers from both sides. Although a stray bullet apparently struck and killed her after she concluded her ministrations, U.S. soldiers recognized her courage the following day and buried her despite heavy gunfire in the area.[14]

The heroics of some Mexican women could not alter the reality that both the city's physical characteristics and the emotional state of its residents had changed for the worse by the time Monterrey's defenders surrendered to General Taylor on September 24. Prior to the war one Mexican pundit had described the city as "one of the most beautiful" in the entire country, while foreign travelers had characterized it as "one of the very few places [in Mexico] . . . that seemed to be thriving."[15] After three days of fighting, however,

"Monterrey's inhabitants were on the verge of panic" as the city had been transformed "into a cemetery. Unburied cadavers, dead and rotten animals, deserted streets, all gave a frightful aspect" to that metropolis. Their despair at the ghostly images of their hometown had to be immense because a "multitude of residents decided to abandon their homes and goods to the foreigners" as they followed Mexican army when it withdrew from the city on September 27.[16] Those who remained had to endure for nearly two more weeks (until their discharge) the depredations of Colonel John C. Hays' Regiment of Texas Rangers. As one U.S. eyewitness put it, these men committed rape, murder, and robbery in broad daylight, and they would have "burned the city had it not been for the fact that most houses were fireproof."[17]

The civilian population of Veracruz suffered an even worse fate at the hands of U.S. forces because they largely experienced hostilities in the form of a military bombardment. U.S. artillery opened fire on the city late in the afternoon of March 22, 1847; the barrage continued for 88 hours during which more than 6,500 solid shots and shells burst into Veracruz. Although the number of casualties—a

Third Day of the SIEGE OF MONTEREY. Sept. 23° 1846.

A lithograph by a U.S. company entitled "Third Day of the Siege of Monterey [sic], Sept. 23, 1846." lith. & pub. by Sarony & Major. Courtesy Library of Congress.

recent estimate put them at approximately 200, including soldiers and civilians—appears low given that the city had 15,000 inhabitants and 3,360 soldiers defended it, the attack exacted a heavy toll on Veracruz and its residents.[18] By the second day of bombardment meat and bread had become scarce, and "missiles fell everywhere . . . so that no place was safe, forcing families to be on a constant alert." Five shells burst into the Governor's Palace, according to the journalist Kendall, one of which "killed a woman and two children asleep in the kitchen." Clerics subsequently stopped calling on victims of the bombardment, a development that further discouraged the city's inhabitants and its defenders, and by March 26 the shelling had rendered many sidewalks useless for transit because countless balconies were coming apart. The artillery barrage particularly affected the city's urban poor. When U.S. infantryman Frederick Zeh toured Veracruz on March 30 he noted that "the wretched huts of the proletariat" had been "dashed to pieces by our breach batteries," but that "the wealthy inhabitants had protected their buildings with sandbags, and thus [had] suffered only slight losses."[19]

Scene in Vera Cruz during the bombardment, March 25, 1847. Lithograph by E. B. and E. C. Kellogg Firm. (Courtesy Library of Congress).

Despite the destruction, daily life for Veracruz's civilians returned to a semblance of normality shortly after the defenders capitulated on March 27. After paroling the soldiers who had guarded the city General Scott distributed food, reopened shops and markets (prohibiting their owners from charging excessive prices for goods), and organized work crews to remove debris from city streets. These and other measures "had a noticeable impact as the townspeople began to accept the American occupation with little resistance," but residents of Veracruz's hinterlands soon endured new tribulations. The discharged Mexican troops began to ransack "the poor and defenseless inhabitants of the interior without hindrance and without remorse. The officers lay hands upon every horse and every mule, without money and without price, and the unfortunate devil thus despoiled is kicked if he utters the most feeble demurrer. The house as well as the garden of the poor laborer is entered by gangs of unorganized soldiers, his family insulted and his substance carried off. If he utters one word of complaint—his treatment is still worse . . . Such is the present state of affairs throughout the country between Vera Cruz and the cities of Jalapa and Orizaba."[20]

Although cities like Monterrey and Veracruz suffered devastating damage, and their residents experienced firsthand the horrors of war, the conflict with the United States also provided Mexican civilians with numerous opportunities to turn a profit. As soon as U.S. soldiers crossed the Rio Grande they bought fresh fruit, vegetables, bread, milk (from cows as well as goats and donkeys), eggs, chickens, and locally produced alcoholic beverages from Mexican vendors, sometimes at high prices. Kendall, writing from aboard the steamer *Aid*, described one such scene in northern Mexico late in July 1846. He noted that "greedy boys, anxious to be possessors of bits and picayunes, have brought . . . peaches and watermelons on board, and find a ready market, while vendors of chickens and other notions are also reaping for them a rich harvest." In so doing the youngsters flouted Mexican authorities, who had "threatened [them] with punishment the most severe if they show[ed] favor or render[ed] assistance to the invading army." Women in particular also set up booths in U.S. army camps to sell broad-rimmed straw hats, clothing items, and keepsakes. Vendors in urban settings took advantage of U.S. soldiers in their midst as well. Markets in the city of Puebla, for example, remained open following its occupation by Scott's army in May 1847, which not only suggests that "the Mexicans did not fear the Americans but also that they liked their presence."[21]

The practice of engaging in commerce with the U.S. army extended to Mexican government officials and elites. Leaders from the city of China, located nearly 60 miles northeast of Monterrey, warned Nuevo León governor Francisco de Paula Morales in September 1847 that he would have a difficult time reasserting his authority because many other towns were "in connivance" with the invaders. They added that many "officials, instead of defending the fatherland, had 'behaved most selfishly . . . by trafficking with the enemy.' "[22] Jacobo Sánchez Navarro, a member of a prominent landowning family in the northern state of Coahuila, accepted the assurances of U.S. General John Wool that those Mexicans who cooperated with his army would be secure. Sánchez Navarro "declared his neutrality in the war, supplied whatever provisions the conquerors required, and soon established excellent relations with Wool himself." Such complicity allowed Sánchez Navarro (and other landowners who adopted a similar stance) to turn a profit and have U.S. soldiers protect their properties.[23]

The general upheaval created by war both hindered and benefited the so-called private money lenders known as _agiotistas_, who since late 1827 had regularly advanced money to the government at high interest rates (sometimes more than 300%). What happened to the Martínez del Río merchant family late in December 1845 illustrates the former. At that time General Mariano Paredes y Arrillaga overthrew the regime of General José Joaquín Herrera partly on the grounds that the latter had failed to adopt a belligerent policy against the United States; the coup meant that the Martínez del Ríos, who had spent six months trying to arrange a deal with Herrera to become the agents for tobacco bonds (many considered the tobacco monopoly Mexico's sole remaining productive revenue source), had to start negotiations anew. On the other hand, in 1847 Mexican officials leased the Guanajuato and the Mexico City mints to the British consul to Mexico, Ewen C. MacKintosh. Other _agiotistas_ acquired property cheaply or sold armaments. The _agiotistas'_ influence even extended to the peace negotiations with the United States. On August 20, 1847, the Mexican government appointed MacKintosh as one of its three representatives to the armistice talks. The _agiotistas_ also showed much interest in the anticipated monetary indemnity due Mexico from the Treaty of Guadalupe Hidalgo ($15 million) because that amount would facilitate payment of outstanding debts due to them.[24]

STATE AND CITIZEN

While a variety of individuals profited from the war, the fiscal demands that the Mexican state attempted to impose on its citizens to prosecute the conflict did not make a significant dent in their daily lives. The widespread suspicion with which civilians regarded government attempts to raise money played a role in this regard. Witness, for example, the fact that in October and December 1846 two groups of Mexico City residents wrote letters to the press requesting that the government publish information about its finances; before they made any further contributions to fight the war they wanted to know how the money was being spent.[25] The government also failed to extract significant amount of monies from the citizenry because it lacked the authority to make regional officials comply with the contributions it decreed. For instance, in December 1846 the governor of Guanajuato, a state whose mining wealth had made it a pillar of the colonial economy, claimed that his treasury was empty, and that he could neither cover his state's administrative expenses nor provide the national government with funds to carry out the war.[26] Then, when the national government decreed a forced loan in mid-June 1847 intended to raise one million pesos, entrepreneurs from the state of Jalisco protested because their share of 123,450 pesos, they claimed, was too high in light of previous payments they had made. Government authorities, they argued, "needed to take into account the population and the wealth of individual states in cases like this to insure that the loan's burden was equitably distributed."[27]

The historical record, nonetheless, also shows that many civilians selflessly contributed whatever their means allowed to help the government cope with the U.S. invasion. Jalisco state deputy Juan G. Mallén in the fall of 1846 donated his salary for the war effort, while another resident of that state, one Tomás Bravo, lamented that his financial situation prevented him from offering more than five pesos a month for that cause. Merchants from the city of Guadalajara raised 21,600 pesos in mid-November to help fund the state's *Segunda División Militar,* which marched to San Luis Potosí to join Santa Anna's army. Then, four months later, these businessmen collected 1,364 pesos to aid Mexican soldiers wounded at the Battle of Buena Vista. Those individuals who could not make a financial contribution to the war effort lent their assistance in other ways. In mid-November 1846, for example, the Jalisco state newspaper published the names of those who had collected 12 carbines, 54

horses, and 1,031 pesos. The largest donor on this occasion was Ignacio Vizcaíno, who put up 200 pesos. Most contributors, however,
were only able to give 1 peso, and those who lacked money volunteered as soldiers.[28]

The war also meant that the civilian population would have to
take up arms to defend the country against the invading U.S. forces,
and for many males that meant service in the regular, professional
army. Although the Mexican army had emerged from the wars of
independence against Spain as a powerful force in domestic politics, and consolidated its position as the "ultimate arbiter of the national will" in the early 1840s,[29] on the eve of war with the United
States the army still met its manpower needs through conscription
methods that placed a heavy burden on the country's poor. According to Waddy Thompson, who served as U.S. minister plenipoten-
tiary to Mexico in the early 1840s, military recruitment essentially
consisted of "sending out recruiting detachments into the mountains, where they hunt the Indians in their dens and caverns, and
bring them in chains to Mexico; there is scarcely a day that droves
of these miserable and more than half naked wretches are not seen
thus chained together and marching through the streets to the barracks, where they are scoured and then dressed in a uniform made
of linen cloth or of serge, and are occasionally drilled."[30]

Mexican military leaders had tried during the 1830s to improve
on this method of impressment by instituting an annual lottery that
limited potential recruits to single men and childless widowers
between the ages of 18 and 40 who met certain health and height
requirements, as well as through other enticements to make military service more attractive. But these efforts did not succeed, and
consequently the pattern of forcefully mustering members of the
lower classes into the ranks of the army remained intact at the time
of war with the United States.[31] On April 23, 1846, then-president
General Paredes y Arrillaga decreed that "all persons lacking visible means of support were to be arrested, tried, and mustered into
the army if convicted of vagrancy."[32] Then, as the war progressed
and national authorities required states to provide their quota of
troops for the regular army, officials had little choice but to rely on
force to meet their allocation. For example, recruits in the central-
western state of Michoacán late in 1846 and through the first half of
1847 were enlisted against their will and brought to the state capital
at Morelia. There they were temporarily imprisoned, and then tied
up so they would not desert before being sent to the front. Indeed,
the army that Santa Anna assembled to defend Mexico City late in

the summer of 1847 consisted of 22,000 men whom authorities had forcibly rounded up in the various states of the republic.[33]

While service in the regular army proved unpalatable for many civilians, a number of Mexicans organized as well as joined the partisan groups that the government created early in the spring of 1847 to wage guerrilla war against the United States. Public-spirited Mexicans had urged national authorities since the previous summer to rely on guerrilla warfare as a means of resisting the U.S. army, but the government only turned to this tactic late in April 1847 after the devastating defeat that Scott inflicted on General Santa Anna at the Battle of Cerro Gordo. With public morale abysmally low after the debacle, and with the road to the nation's capital wide open, Mexican authorities had little choice but to rely on guerrillas to strike at one of the U.S. army's most vulnerable points: the supply line along the Veracruz-Mexico City road that transported ammunition, money, and soldiers to General Scott.[34]

Mexican guerrilla units came to pose "a strategic danger to the occupiers." They attacked numerous U.S. supply convoys, stragglers, as well as U.S. forces stationed in strongholds throughout the country. They even may have killed more U.S. soldiers than those who fell in conventional battles (2,800 versus 1,556). But guerillas did much more than inflict casualties on the U.S. army and destroy property; they also disrupted many other activities. In June 1847, for example, General Scott bemoaned the fact that guerrillas prevented him from transporting Major General John Anthony Quitman from Puebla to the coast so he could assume a new command in northern Mexico.[35] That same month one member of Scott's army, Lieutenant Ralph W. Kirkham, complained about the difficulty of sending a letter to his wife home in the United States. As he put it, "I am afraid to trust the mails here for they are very uncertain with the murderous guerrillas which infest the road all the way from this city to Veracruz."[36]

Guerrilla activity, however, also had a detrimental effect on Mexican civilians. Two merchants in the town of Salinas Victoria, Nuevo León, claimed that irregular troops led by one Francisco Treviño had ransacked their businesses, while the mayor of Apodaca reported that guerrillas had assaulted and kidnapped his secretary. Guerrillas, moreover, frequently put Mexican civilians in a no-win situation, as landowners in Nuevo León found out. Refusal to collaborate with Mexican partisans meant they risked having their haciendas burnt because they would be regarded as unpatriotic. On the other hand, providing assistance to guerrillas might lead U.S.

troops to destroy their property. U.S. authorities also frequently made civilians pay for the damages caused by said partisan forces. For example, in response to a guerrilla attack near China, Nuevo León, U.S. officials forced the mayor to pay in kind for the 82 mules, 1 ox, 7 pigs, and 95 bushels of corn that guerrillas had taken from them. Likewise, when, in the state of Nuevo León in February 1847, irregular troops commanded by General José Urrea destroyed a fleet of nearly 150 U.S. wagons full of clothes and provisions and seized goods worth $96,000, U.S. General Zachary Taylor imposed an indemnity of $47,500 on towns in Nuevo León and Tamaulipas. Towns in the latter state, however, refused to pay.[37]

The so-called national guard also affected civilian life in Mexico during the war, although its impact varied in different regions. First established in the 1820s as a reserve force of citizen-soldiers to preserve domestic order and security, protect states' rights, and curb the army's political strength until civilian power could be consolidated, the country's postindependence turmoil derailed all attempts to turn the guard into an effective, nonpartisan military force on the eve of the 1846–1848 conflict. Subsequent reorganization efforts met countless obstacles. Legislation issued in mid-1845—after the United States annexed Texas—authorized the Mexican government to re-arm the national guard, but also made service voluntary and unremunerated. Consequently, by early September of that year only 37 men had registered for service in the city of Morelia, 27 in Zacatecas, less than 20 in Tampico, 3 in Guadalajara, 2 in Aguascalientes, and 1 in Puebla; no one had enrolled in Ciudad Victoria, Guanajuato, or San Luis Potosí. The pervasiveness of regionalism hindered another attempt to reorganize the national guard in the fall of 1846, as at that time many state governors, anxious to preserve local leadership and provincial autonomy, publicly protested when the federal government tried to take command of those forces.[38]

In addition to these arguments, and because the national guard blurred the distinction between a civilian and a military institution, on occasion state authorities emphasized the detrimental consequences that would befall the civilian aspect of their citizen-soldiers' lives should these men be mobilized. One such instance took place as U.S. troops advanced into Mexico's heartland in mid-1847; not even that threat induced authorities like Guanajuato's chief executive Lorenzo Arellano to call up the guardsmen in his state and provide military assistance to the central government. The governor raised a number of constitutional and political arguments to substantiate his objections: that according to the 1824 federal constitution (which had been reenacted in mid-September 1846), the Mexican president could not "dispose of the states' local militia without the consent of Congress, nor can Congress give it [such endorsement] unless it specifically states the number of men; but never in a vague and undetermined manner." The governor added that he needed the guard at home because without its support the state government would be incapable of resisting the "despotic power" of those individuals who threatened states' rights as well the marauding bandits who stole cattle and pillaged villages. Arellano concluded that Guanajuato's economy would be devastated if the national guard left the state because most guardsmen were married, had family, and had established themselves in agriculture, commerce, or mining.[39]

Reorganization of the national guard in the nation's capital, on the other hand, had a more profound impact on the wartime civilian experience and beyond, both because of its involvement in an internal rebellion and its efforts against the United States. The battalions that emerged in Mexico City in September 1846 divided themselves according to political loyalties and social class, and fought against each other for nearly one month during an uprising known as the *polkos'* rebellion that erupted on February 27, 1847.[40] In so doing they prevented the government from assisting in the defense of Veracruz against Scott's army, and also brought much chaos to daily life in the capital. Lucas Alamán, the country's most prominent Conservative statesman, noted that city residents found it extremely difficult to purchase many goods during the mayhem. The *puro*-controlled *Boletín de la Democracia* stated that *polko* rebels had forcefully conscripted onlookers and forced them to dig trenches as well. This newspaper and the Spanish minister in Mexico also pointed out that public safety had diminished as a result of the rebellion. The former held members of the *polkos'* regiments responsible for the deaths of many innocent bystanders, while the Spanish diplomat observed that lower-class guardsmen from the *puro* battalions "at all hours shot at any person who dressed with any propriety, and [they] often amused themselves by firing [their muskets] at the women and children who appeared on the rooftops or ventured out into the streets."[41]

Although the decision to fight a civil war in Mexico City instead of protecting the nation's sovereignty in Veracruz temporarily stigmatized those guardsmen who supported the *polko* rebellion, military imperatives in the early spring of 1847 prompted the government to make yet another effort to put the national guard on a solid footing. Mexican authorities thus issued a decree on April 9 that called on all males capable of bearing arms to help defend the country's independence against the United States. Article two of that piece of legislation empowered the government to issue the necessary by-laws to effectively organize the national guard.[42] Mexican leaders immediately moved to win the support of the capital's residents to fulfill that task. First, the editors of the *Diario del Gobierno de la República Mexicana* (the government's official mouthpiece) appealed to the patriotism of its readers and urged them to enroll in the military force. They claimed that the Mexican people had an obligation to punish its "detestable invaders." The editors further argued that practical reasons made enlistment in the guard a necessity; one did not become dexterous in the use of firearms over the course of a few days' training in the guard. They also indicated that serving in the national guard would not prevent an individual from earning a livelihood; many public employees, merchants, and artisans had belonged to this institution for the past several months and still worked.[43] The Mexico City *ayuntamiento* (town council) set up registers to expedite enrollment, which seems to have proceeded smoothly despite the absence of a reliable census of the city's inhabitants. As a result, on May 9 government officials and military leaders reviewed some 5,000 guardsmen, the majority of whom possessed arms.[44] Even so, not every resident of the capital eligible for guard service moved to fulfill that duty. On the day after the review *El Monitor Republicano* noted with delight that "the most respectable part of society had assembled without distinction, without partisan hatreds," but also lamented the presence of a "numerous crowd of spectators," including many able-bodied civilians, at the inspection.[45]

The attitude of the assembled bystanders in Mexico City on that spring afternoon attests to the civilian population's ambivalence towards the war itself. To that point the course of the war had proven disastrous for the Mexican republic, but, as with the many outbreaks of rebellion the country had experienced since independence, it directly affected only those in the path of the contending forces. Indeed, for those living outside the combat zone, life would have continued as normal. Some among those spectators may well have concluded that the war would soon end, and that the most prudent action was to wait, and hence to survive. Many were also likely well acquainted with the miseries of military service, which undercut the government's appeal to their patriotism. Finally, mounting losses had sapped public confidence in the country's political and military leadership. For all who fought, as so many did with self-less devotion to the national interest, there were others equally unwilling to follow ineffective leaders into a losing fight. These men might consider the mustering of the guard as a spectacle worth witnessing, to be sure, yet it could not stir the heart of the spectator convinced that risking life and limb would prove futile.

Others, however, shared the feelings of the essayist Guillermo Prieto, who observed that the capital's national guardsmen presented

a portrait full of sublime grandeur and bravery. Dignitaries, beggars, energetic youth, the elderly, boys carrying their ill father's cartridge belt, distinguished women carrying a basket with their son's medicines, each and everyone obeying a single sentiment: the fatherland; one aspiration: its glory; one divine object: its honor . . . And when looking upon those ranks . . . one's soul filled with pride.[46]

Indeed, the eventual entry of General Scott and the U.S. army into the Valley of Mexico in preparation for the final assault on Mexico City prompted many of the capital's residents to join the national guard. On the afternoon of August 9, 1847, some 10,000 militiamen marched to El Peñón, a fortified 450-foot hill that guarded the eastern approach to the capital. Scott's engineers, however, determined that a successful assault on the defenses at El Peñón would entail unacceptably heavy losses, so the U.S. commander found an alternate route to bypass the stronghold. Scott advanced around the edge of Mexico City's southernmost lake (Xochimilco) to the two principal highways that led into the capital. The maneuver forced Santa Anna to set up a new defensive line behind the Churubusco River, more or less five miles south of Mexico City. There and in subsequent battles for the capital, Mexico City's citizen-soldiers fought bravely, and demonstrated exemplary audacity, selflessness, and patriotism.[47]

One guardsman in particular, a tailor by the name of Lucas Balderas, demonstrated these qualities during the September 8, 1847, Battle of Molino del Rey. Balderas, who commanded the "Mina" national guard battalion, had sided with the forces that challenged the government during the *polkos'* rebellion. Although *puro* newspapers then portrayed him negatively—they alleged, for instance, that he had filled the ranks of his battalion with prisoners from the Acordada jail, and that he merely was the errand boy of the leading *moderado* politician—Balderas's actions in the defense of his homeland propelled him into the pantheon of national heroes. Shortly after hostilities commenced, Balderas—who had brushed aside his family's request that he not serve in the guard because he had arthritis—suffered a leg wound that bled profusely. Nonetheless, he led a cavalry charge to retake artillery pieces captured by U.S. forces. A cannon ball struck Balderas as he advanced, but he remained steadfast in his mission. Brandishing his sword, Balderas continued to fight on one knee until four of his men carried him from the battlefield to a nearby hut. There, as he expired in the arms of his son, Balderas inquired about the status of the battle. Hearing that Mexican forces had been defeated, he supposedly uttered: "My poor country!"[48]

But the bravery of men like Balderas could not reduce the uneasiness that residents of Mexico City had felt as Scott's men approached. Prieto's family left the capital on August 9, taking their furniture with them.[49] Ten days later, on the eve of the Battles of Padierna and Churubusco, a teenaged Antonio García Cubas, who went on to become one of his country's preeminent cartographers and geographers, walked into his mother's bedroom and found her praying with his sister; he then joined them to implore God for a Mexican victory.[50] Appeals like that of the Cubas family, however, failed to produce the desired results and led to even greater consternation. When the well-known Mexican politician José Fernando Ramírez appraised the public mood following the defeats of August 20, he noticed "a general lack of confidence, which is worse even than a lack of spirit." Another prominent Mexican public figure, Mariano Riva Palacio, wrote from his hacienda in Chalco, southeast of the capital, that "our infamy is being consummated . . . Poor Mexico! Paredes!! Paredes!! What is your responsibility [?] I cannot go on."[51] Three weeks later, with the final U.S. assault on Mexico City just a few days away, Ramírez remarked that the resonance of the city's church bells produced "feverish excitement in the streets and public squares . . . followed by the silence of desolation, because half the inhabitants crowd the rooftops to see what their fate may be, while the other half lock themselves indoors or rush to arms to prepare to defend themselves to the last."[52]

PATRIOTS AND COLLABORATORS IN MEXICO CITY

Besides the growing sense of uncertainty, daily life became increasingly more arduous for most residents of the capital and its hinterlands. When General Scott's aforementioned flanking operation forced Santa Anna to redeploy his troops, the Mexican general ordered the destruction of the village of Santa Marta, located in a grove on the roadside east of El Peñón. According to one contemporary observer, "the natives of the little population beheld all without a murmur, and bowed to this cruel fate."[53] In addition, from this moment on Santa Anna and other Mexican military leaders, who since May had repeatedly petitioned city authorities for men, supplies, and equipment to shore up the capital's defenses, intensified their requests. After August 10 more than 1,000 men worked on the fortifications, a dramatic increase from earlier requisitions that had averaged 200 to 300 civilian workers.[54] To comply with these demands, the Mexican government drove "the *léperos* [urban poor] . . . to work at the fortifications at the point of the bayonet."[55]

These conditions helped forge among the *léperos* a primitive form of class solidarity that turned them into active historical actors at this key juncture of the war. Not only did they attack on August 27 more than 100 unescorted U.S. wagon trains that came into Mexico City during an armistice to secure supplies, forcing them to withdraw, but during the next two weeks they also sacked a number of warehouses that provided rations to the U.S. army.[56] The urban poor's capacity for collective action became even more evident in mid-September during one of the conflict's most important, yet little-known episodes—the spontaneous and massive three-day riot led by Mexico City's masses against General Scott and the U.S. army. The stage for that insurrection had been set by midnight on September 13. Earlier that day, after taking Chapultepec Castle, the U.S. army had marched on the city and reached its western edge by nightfall after overcoming stiff Mexican resistance at the San Cosme and Belén *garitas* (gates). But rather than fight another day Santa Anna withdrew the Mexican army and the *ayuntamiento* disbanded the national guard, leaving the city defenseless. Bandits, moreover, had begun to loot the National Palace. The situation became even more volatile as dawn broke on September 14 when a multitude of poor Mexicans gathered in the central plaza (*Zócalo*) to observe U.S. forces hoist the Stars and Stripes. City residents only saw disheveled soldiers—the assembled crowd, according to Lieutenant Daniel Harvey Hill, gazed at them "as at wild animals"—not the invincible military machine described by several Mexican pundits as Scott and his troops had made their way inland.[57]

The uneasiness turned into violence within a few hours as the urban poor began to attack the occupying U.S. soldiers with stones (the governor of the Federal District had previously ordered that streets be unpaved, and that stones be amassed on rooftops), bottles, and other loose objects. The riot was centered in lower-class

neighborhoods, and most of its leaders were mid-level political activists like Francisco Próspero Pérez, a radical (*puro*) militant, or
individuals with much popular appeal such as Celedonio Jarauta,
a Spanish priest who also distinguished himself as a proficient
guerrilla commander in the state of Veracruz. Members of Mexico
City's upper and middle class not only abstained from taking an
active role in the events of September 14–16, but they also hung
foreign flags from their balconies of their homes in an attempt to
avoid the commotion. In the end, fearful that the confrontations
between the masses and the invaders might ignite a massive popular revolt, members of the *ayuntamiento* put class solidarity ahead
of national interest and opted not to support their fellow Mexicans.
They instead worked feverishly to restore public order.[58]

"El Padre Jarauta." Padre Celedonio Jarauta leading the Mex-
ican masses in their attack on Scott's troops. Antonio Garcia
Cubas, *El libro de mis recuerdos,* 7th ed. (Mexico City: Editorial
Patria, 1978 [1904]).

U.S. military leaders, acting in accordance with Mexican authorities, may have been able to subdue the rioters, but the occupation of Mexico City by the U.S. army thrust its residents into an uneasy situation, a time of wariness, uncertainty, and mixed emotions. In the minds of the population, any sense of relief that the fighting was over was infused with the bitterness of defeat. The city's clerics sought to capitalize on the prevailing animosity on September 19 when they attempted to cancel Sunday masses in order to incite the populace against the U.S. army. Given that U.S. flags flew over Mexico City's churches, the clerics hoped to persuade residents that the United States was responsible for their closure. General Quitman's prompt and forceful response, however, averted an uprising. He ordered the priests to open the churches and ring their bells; otherwise he would withhold U.S. protection and remove the flags.[59] The lingering ill will also provoked bloodshed, and within two weeks of the city's surrender organized military action had given way to numerous random acts of violence against U.S. troops. One contemporary Mexican observer wrote that "anyone who takes a walk through the streets or goes a short distance away from the center is a dead man," and, indeed, the assassination of lone U.S. soldiers became "a nightly occurrence."[60]

But the violence cut both ways, as city residents felt the wrath of U.S. forces. When Scott's troops made their way into Mexico City they seized Lucas Alamán's home, broke down its doors, destroyed furniture, and mounted a cannon on its roof.[61] U.S. soldiers burst into the convent of Santa Clara as well, where they ripped down planks and beams to build a fire before falling asleep.[62] One of the outstanding printers of nineteenth-century Mexico, Vicente García Torres, suffered a violent attack shortly after mid-October 1847 because of an article that appeared in *El Monitor Republicano*, a newspaper he had edited since 1846. The piece read as follows:

A certain young Mexican lady, of a frolicsome disposition and romantic inclinations—a good singer, and who, since the arrival of the Americans at San Angel, has become *familiar* with an officer of that army, will soon be annexed, like Texas, and passed over to American dominion. The censure of the fair sex of her own people has fallen heavily upon her.[63]

This item—if one takes the U.S. journalist Kendall at his word—was part of García Torres' strategy of "prevent[ing] all intercourse between the first families of the city and our officers"; he also had "used . . . the most insidious [means] to prevent the Mexican ladies from visiting the theaters and other places of public amusement."[64]

Although *El Monitor* published a retraction two days after the above item appeared in print, noting that such a "rumor . . . was entirely unfounded,"[65] the explanation failed to save García Torres. On October 23 an acquaintance of the young lady, Lieutenant William T. H. Brooks, gave the Mexican journalist "a terrible cowhiding." The thrashing pleased Kendall because it had wrought "summary and most just punishment" upon the culprit.[66]

In spite of the tensions generated by these and other events, the occupation of Mexico City also produced significant collaboration between U.S. military authorities and Mexican political leaders. The most famous incident of this partnership was the luncheon held January 29, 1848, on the outskirts of the capital at the present-day site of the *Desierto de los Leones* National Park, an event remembered as the *Brindis del Desierto*. The feast intended to honor several U.S. army officers who had completed a survey to establish the level of the lakes that surrounded the city. It is said that during the course of the afternoon a toast was offered calling for Mexico's annexation to the United States.[67] But collaboration with the enemy, or at least its very appearance, encouraged recriminations, as six months later *moderado* Minister of Foreign Relations Mariano Otero filed charges of treason before the Chamber of Deputies against *puro* loyalist Francisco Suárez Iriarte. Otero claimed that Suárez Iriarte, who between late December 1847 and early March 1848 headed the Mexico City *ayuntamiento*, had cooperated with enemy troops and worked to secure Mexico's annexation to the United States as well. The *moderado* national government, then headed by General José Joaquín Herrera, kept the accusation under wraps at that time to defuse any kind of controversy that might rip it apart. Suárez Iriarte's trial took place in March 1850, and the Chamber of Deputies upheld the indictment. Although the case never made it into the court system, Suárez Iriarte's life came to a tragic end. He was imprisoned for several months and became ill. Authorities then released him, but Suárez Iriarte died in his hacienda early the next year.[68]

Politicians, however, were not the only individuals whose relationship with U.S. officials came under close scrutiny. A number of artists who remained in the capital to act in the vibrant theater scene were branded as collaborators; clerics threatened them from their pulpits with excommunication because they performed for audiences that largely consisted of U.S. military personnel.[69] Mexico City's prostitutes were also closely watched as U.S. army officers and soldiers who desired female companionship sought out their services. That type of "repugnant interaction," as one newspaper moralized in mid-November, had grown so common that the "scandalous manner in which these fallen women sauntered through the city's central streets" had become an affront to public decency.[70] The prostitutes' subordinate social position—outcasts in a society that still cherished traditional values of honor and propriety, especially as they applied to women—made them especially vulnerable to irrational hostility, and this hostility is precisely what evinced itself as the U.S. occupation came to a close early in June 1848. At that time residents of Mexico City stoned and harassed a number of the women—known as *margaritas*—who they suspected had engaged in sexual relations with U.S. soldiers. In San Angel at the southern edge of the capital some of these ladies were *selladas* (branded, marked, and/or scarred) and had their hair cut off. While such violence suggests that the people who engaged in these reprisals viewed the activities of the prostitutes as treason, it also speaks to the way gender and class mediated the impact of the war on the individual (one only need contrast the treatment of the *margaritas* with that of the male, elite Suárez Iriarte).[71]

DIVERSIONS AND DAILY LIFE

Although war raged through many areas of the country between 1846 and 1848, most Mexican civilians remained attached to their customary diversions and did their best to commemorate them. Sometimes the U.S. occupation hardly disrupted the normal cycle of amusements. Not three weeks had passed since Monterrey's surrender late in September 1846 when a circus began to perform in that city,[72] and within that same time span of the U.S. army's entrance into Puebla the following May, Lieutenant Ralph Kirkham had gone to a bullfight. He also noted that the typical Sunday routine of the city's residents continued as if nothing had changed. People went to mass, and as the day moved into the evening they amused themselves by attending the theater or dancing at one of the city's most important recreational centers, the Tivoli Gardens. Kirkham's stay coincided with the June 24 festivities that honored Saint John the Baptist. The celebration had begun with the firing of rockets at 3 A.M. Churches remained open during the day, and by the afternoon he noticed young women "out in their coaches in the Alameda, and most of the young men were prancing about on their horses. Those who had neither coach nor horse put on their best clothes and smiling faces, and joined the crowd, for happy they were determined to be."[73]

In some cases, however, hostilities muted popular diversions. Clerical authorities in Puebla ordered the abbess of the convent of the Purísima Concepción to hold the traditional Christmas Eve mass in the afternoon, rather than at midnight, to avoid a potential disruption of public tranquility.[74] The occupation of Mexico City by the U.S. army led to a near-nationwide cancellation in September 1847 of one of the country's most important public celebrations, those that commemorated its independence from Spain.[75] Nearly two months later city authorities severely restricted the sale of food and liquor during the *Paseo de Todos los Santos* (The Feast of All Saints), a popular Catholic fiesta held in early November that commemorates the dead, in hopes of maintaining public order. According to *El Monitor Republicano,* the festivity thus turned out much "different from what it had been in previous years; the ladies did not show off the luxury of their jewels, and few or none visited the relics after leaving Mass in their plain dresses."[76] The *Paseo,* nonetheless, still proved colorful enough to impress at least one foreigner. U.S. Lieutenant Hill remarked that city streets were "crowded with a gay throng . . . and stands loaded with toys and sweet-meats" packed the Portales Market and the *Zócalo.*[77]

War with the United States may have constrained a number of popular festivities, but the conflict also introduced residents of Mexico to new types of eating and drinking establishments. In mid-June 1846 journalist Kendall noted that henceforth Matamoros was "to be decidedly an American city. Let things turn as they will—no matter when peace comes or upon what terms it comes—the Americans have got in here, now, have opened stores, coffee-houses, restaurants, billiard-rooms, hotels, and the like, have introduced ice and mint-juleps—a long step toward civilization—and their back tracks will never be discovered." Kendall's prophecy apparently came to fruition. When he visited Matamoros the following January Lieutenant Hill remarked that it was now "an American town in all but name. I saw more American than Mexican faces. It has improved since I last saw it [July 1846], for though there are still hundreds of grog-shops some of them have been replaced by excellent stores . . . [and] articles of luxury even are for sale."[78]

A similar process took place in Mexico City. Within one week of the fall of the Mexican capital Kendall commented that the city was "rapidly becoming Americanized." One English-speaking newspaper had just begun publication, another one was due to appear shortly, and everywhere one could "see such announcements as 'Union Hotel,' 'Mash and Milk at all Hours,' 'American Dry Goods,' 'United States Restaurant,' 'St. Charles Exchange,' 'Egg-Nogg and Mince Pies for Sale Here,' and other kindred notices to the passer-by as to where he can be served on home principles."[79] Indeed, at times a good many residents of Mexico City enjoyed the foreign influence, and responded enthusiastically (or curiously) to some of the entertainment staged by the newcomers. A multitude once gathered at the *La Gran Sociedad* tavern to witness

six Americans who had dyed their faces black . . . each sat on a chair . . . with a [musical] instrument, the most notable being half a horse's jaw with two little bells . . . and a bone that banged it . . . and with the triangle, the violin, the guitar, the castanets, and a small frame drum formed a harmonious cadence . . . the grotesque movements, the gesticulations, the songs, the foot tapping, the clinching they engaged in while dancing . . . made everyone laugh . . . [80]

In this case, however, the performance's appeal may not have been due to its foreign content. The show had a strong African influence— the heading of the article that described it read "The Blacks from Africa: Their Music, Songs, and Folk Dances"—and thus it resembled the *jarabe*, one of Mexico's most popular folk songs. The *jarabe* became a patriot symbol during the wars of independence against Spain, and was widely associated with mixed-blood culture.[81]

But not everyone perceived these amusements or the types of behavior that the newly established businesses encouraged in as positive a manner. Drinking ranked among the top vices of U.S. soldiers, and while some officers argued that the behavior of drunk U.S. troops indicated "a sort of virtue . . . a special energy [,] and intellect,"[82] a number of Mexicans believed that many of the new businesses only fostered that kind of appalling behavior. Writing late in September, José Fernando Ramírez bemoaned the behavior of U.S. troops in the Mexican capital. He had "never seen such sodden drunkenness, nor any more scandalous and impudent than the drunkenness that holds these men in its grip. Nor have I ever seen more unrestrained appetites. Every hour of the day, except during the evenings, when they are all drunk, one can find them eating everything they see."[83] As in most such circumstances, some welcomed, others detested, the invaders and their wares.

AFTERMATH

By the time that the U.S. flag came down at the Mexico City *Zócalo* on June 12, 1848, hundreds of Mexicans had experienced significant changes in their daily lives. The war exposed many to devastation that might have entailed the loss of their homes or other property, countless anxious moments, and untold human

suffering. For others the war had created opportunity—the potential to profit from the conflict, to defend the nation's sovereignty,
or to collaborate in myriad ways with the foreign interlopers. And
there were those for whom the conflict represented nothing but a
distant afterthought; either the ravages of the war did not directly
affect them, or they managed to avoid pleas from Mexican authorities that they somehow contribute to the defense of the homeland. In
any case, although the end of hostilities held the promise for many
civilians that life would return to normal, the effects of the war lin-
gered and deeply affected a number of key aspects of their lives.

The war heightened elite anxieties regarding national survival,
and a number of intellectuals published works that tried to explain
Mexico's military fiasco and obtain a better understanding of the
country's political and social ills.[84] These writings, however, did
not entirely dispel the elite's apprehensions. Some observers believed that the United States might attempt to take over their nation
at any moment; they were also alarmed by the possibility that the
wave of popular uprisings that spread across Europe in 1848, which
demanded radical social reforms and threatened to topple monar-
chies, might extend to Mexico.[85] These concerns prompted government officials to stage public ceremonies in Mexico City late in the
summer of 1848 and for some years beyond in an attempt to turn
Balderas and other ordinary Mexicans into patriotic icons and symbols of nationwide solidarity. But such efforts could not surmount
the tensions that afflicted Mexico. In September 1848, for example,
Mexicans again commemorated the anniversary of the movement
for independence from Spain, and on that occasion speakers tried
to determine what factors had led to the military debacle of 1847.
One year later, however, orators used the event, as some of their
predecessors had done in the past, to bitterly denounce their political opponents. Indeed, partisan hatreds grew increasingly bitter
and erupted in yet another round of civil strife in the mid-1850s.[86]

The war, on the other hand, provided rural Mexicans with preexisting political and economic grievances an excellent opportunity
to take up arms in defense of their rights. In 1847 peasants in the Sierra Gorda region, which overlaps the central states of Guanajuato,
Querétaro, and San Luis Potosí, joined their demands for less taxes
and land distribution to a call for continued resistance against the
U.S. occupation. At the same time Maya Indians in the Yucatán pen-
insula launched an uprising that ranks among the "most violent
episodes in the history of the western hemisphere, costing the lives
of some two-hundred thousand people in 1848 alone."[87] These two

may have been the most important and widespread peasant rebellions, but other significant disturbances erupted elsewhere. In January 1848, for example, Veracruz peasant leader Juan Nepomuceno
Llorente called for a national alliance of all agrarian rebels, and in
so doing "infused a patriotic, nationalistic spirit into what had been
a local class conflict."[88] The war also made it easier for rural Mexicans to demand the rights of citizenship from national authorities in
the future. The conflict prompted the governor of the southwestern
state of Oaxaca, Benito Juárez, to organize and train national guard
units in 1848, and these forces came to Juárez's defense during the
civil wars of the mid-nineteenth century and his struggles against
French intruders in the 1860s. The men who enrolled in the guard
used their military service to impress on national authorities their
contributions to the making of the Mexican nation, and thus secure
financial rights and educational opportunities.[89]

Finally, the struggle against the United States created what until
recently had been one of Mexico's most enduring symbols of national solidarity—the so-called *Niños Héroes* (Boy Heroes). The
legend asserts that six cadets from the national military academy
(*Colegio Militar*), who in September 1847 helped to defend Chapultepec Castle against the U.S. forces, chose to die rather than surrender
to their adversaries. One of the adolescents, Juan Escutia, reputedly
wrapped the Mexican flag around his body and jumped over the
battlements to his death.[90] Although the young boys lapsed from
the national historical memory for approximately 25 years, the patriotic euphoria that accompanied Mexico's victory over the French
invaders in 1867 set the groundwork for the cadets' subsequent
commemoration as national heroes. Beginning in 1871 and continuing throughout the twentieth century, a host of Mexican military organizations and government officials reworked the legend to fulfill
their own particular agendas.[91]

In 1992, however, Minister of Education Ernesto Zedillo authorized the revision of history textbooks for the nation's elementary
schools. The new books challenged official mythology and questioned, among other things, the authenticity of the legend of the
Niños Héroes. Although the effort did not succeed, as protests by
the army, politicians, and teachers led to the recall of nearly seven
million volumes,[92] just over a decade later the Mexican state engaged in another attempt to debunk the myth of the *Niños Héroes*.
In the summer of 2005 Mexico's National History Museum, which
is located in Chapultepec Castle and welcomes an average of 10,000
visitors a day (and even more on Sundays, when entrance is free),

finished a thorough reorganization of its permanent exhibits. The displays no longer showcased the country's most relevant historical events in chronological or sequential fashion, but rather in a thematic and conceptual manner. In keeping with the modification, museum officials removed from the main passageway those objects and ideas that did not conform to the new vision, including everything that referred to the *Niños Héroes* (such paraphernalia was taken to a small and rather unpretentious room). To further underscore the fresh outlook, one of the museum's curators, Víctor Manuel Ruíz, informed journalists that no young cadet leaped to his death with the Mexican flag wrapped around him.[93]

Members of Mexico's intellectual elite may have devoted much time and effort to rendering a more accurate (as they see it) and nuanced portrayal of their country's history, but such efforts do not mean that the public will forget the *Niños Héroes* or debunk the myth. Indeed, one could still well argue that Enrique Plasencia de la Parra's 1997 observation about the young cadets remains true today. Back then de la Parra noted that visitors to the *Niños Héroes* memorial in Mexico City's Chapultepec Park were likely to encounter a father regaling his children with his own version of the cadets' heroics. Such a story—in all likelihood historically inaccurate—will nonetheless pass on to the youngsters an insightful message and provide them with models worthy of imitation and respect.[94] As a result, while the resentments that emerged and crystallized in Mexico in the aftermath of the war with the United States are likely not to vanish, the memory of the *Niños Héroes* should also remain embedded in the Mexican popular imagination and remain a pervasive—and positive—influence on the everyday life of contemporary Mexicans.

NOTES

1. For a discussion of Mexico's major political groups and their stance on the issues that shaped this struggle, see Will Fowler, *Mexico in the Age of Proposals, 1821–1853* (Westport, CT: Greenwood, 1998).

2. Timothy J. Henderson, *A Glorious Defeat: Mexico and Its War with the United States* (New York: Hill & Wang, 2007), xvii.

3. Robert W. Johannsen, *To the Halls of the Montezumas: The Mexican War in the American Imagination* (New York: Oxford University Press, 1985), 32.

4. James M. McCaffrey, *Army of Manifest Destiny: The American Soldier in the Mexican War, 1846–1848* (New York: New York University Press, 1992), 33–34; Paul Foos, *A Short, Offhand, Killing Affair: Soldiers and Social Conflict during the Mexican-American War* (Chapel Hill: University

of North Carolina Press, 2002), 84; the quote is from Johannsen, *To the Halls*, 31.

5. McCaffrey, *Army of Manifest Destiny*, 66–67, 73–74, and 79; Grant is quoted in McCaffrey, *Army of Manifest Destiny*, 123; the final quote in the paragraph appears in Foos, *A Short, Offhand, Killing Affair*, 125.

6. McCaffrey, *Army of Manifest Destiny*, 125.

7. Benjamin Heber Johnson, *Revolution in Texas: How a Forgotten Rebellion and Its Bloody Suppression Turned Mexicans into Americans* (New Haven, CT: Yale University Press, 2003), 12.

8. Foos, *A Short, Offhand, Killing Affair*, 121–122.

9. Timothy D. Johnson, *Winfield Scott: The Quest for Military Glory* (Lawrence: University Press of Kansas, 1998), 165–170; Johannsen, *To the Halls*, 33.

10. Frederick Zeh, *An Immigrant Soldier in the Mexican War*, eds. William J. Orr and Robert Ryal Miller, trans. William J. Orr (College Station: Texas A&M Press, 1995), 71–72.

11. Miguel Angel González Quiroga, "Nuevo León ante la invasión norteamericana, 1846–1848," in Laura Herrera Serna, coord., *México en guerra (1846–1848): Perspectivas regionales* (Mexico City: Consejo Nacional para la Cultura y las Artes, 1997), 430–431. For a broader exploration of the ways Mexican elites portrayed U.S. invaders, and of the effects of such representations, see Malcolm Bruce Colcleugh, "War-Time Portraits of the Gringo: American Invaders and the Manufacture of Mexican Nationalism," *Journal of the Canadian Historical Association* 6 (1995), 81–101.

12. George Wilkins Kendall, *Dispatches from the Mexican War*, ed. Lawrence Delbert Cress (Norman: University of Oklahoma Press, 1999), 138–139.

13. Johannsen, *To the Halls*, 137; and Ramón Alcaraz et al., *The Other Side: or Notes for the History of the War between Mexico and the United States*, trans. Albert C. Ramsey (New York: Burt Franklin, 1970 [1850]), 76–77. The chapter in Alcaraz et al.'s book about the siege of Monterrey was authored by Prieto. Guillermo Prieto, *Memorias de mis tiempos* (Mexico City: Editorial Porrúa, 1985), 281–282. For a biographical sketch of Prieto's career see Richard N. Sinkin, *The Mexican Reform, 1855–1876: A Study in Liberal Nation-Building* (Austin: University of Texas Press, 1976), 49–50.

14. Gónzalez Quiroga, "Nuevo León ante la invasión," in Herrera Serna, *México en guerra (1846–1848)*, 442; and Johannsen, *To the Halls*, 138. For a synopsis of the varying tales concerning Zozaya, see Yolanda García Romero, "María Josefa Zozaya," in *The United States and Mexico at War: Nineteenth-Century Expansionism and Conflict*, ed. Donald F. Frazier (New York: Macmillan, 1998), 491.

15. The first quote is from Alcaraz et al., *The Other Side*, 65, and the second appears in Ruth R. Olivera and Liliane Crété, *Life in Mexico under Santa Anna, 1822–1855* (Norman: University of Oklahoma Press, 1991), 107.

16. The first quote is in David Pletcher, *The Diplomacy of Annexation: Texas, Oregon, and the Mexican War* (Columbia: University of Missouri Press,

1973), 464; the second and third appear in González Quiroga, "Nuevo León ante la invasión," in Herrera Serna, *México en guerra (1846–1848)*, 443. Residents of Monterrey might have suffered even more damage had General Pedro Ampudia not sent a delegation to Taylor on September 23 to advise him that the cathedral near the main plaza served as an armaments shelter, and that a direct artillery hit on the church would certainly trigger a massive explosion that would take many innocent civilian lives (as well as inflict untold casualties among Taylor's troops). The commissioners informed Taylor that Ampudia would surrender if he could leave Monterrey with his troops and small arms, conditions to which Taylor acquiesced. Richard Bruce Winders, *Crisis in the Southwest: The United States, Mexico, and the Struggle over Texas* (Wilmington, DE: Scholarly Resources, 2002), 106.

17. Nathaniel Cheairs Hughes, Jr., and Timothy D. Johnson, eds., *A Fighter from Way Back: The Mexican War Diary of Lt. Daniel Harvey Hill, 4th Artillery, USA* (Kent, OH: The Kent State University Press, 2002), 28.

18. Johannsen, *To the Halls*, 102; Johnson, *Winfield Scott*, 177–178; and K. Jack Bauer, *The Mexican War 1846–1848* (Lincoln: University of Nebraska Press, 1992 [1974]), 245.

19. Quotes and material in this paragraph come from José María Roa Bárcena, *Recuerdos de la invasión norteamericana (1846–1848)*, 3 vols. (Mexico City: Editorial Porrúa, 1971), 1:294; Kendall, *Dispatches from the Mexican War*, 186; Bauer, *The Mexican War*, 250; and Zeh, *An Immigrant Soldier*, 22.

20. The quotes in this paragraph are taken from Johnson, *Winfield Scott*, 179; and Kendall, *Dispatches from the Mexican War*, 190.

21. Johannsen, *To the Halls*, 89; Hughes and Johnson, *A Fighter from Way Back*, 7; the quotes from Kendall are in *Dispatches from the Mexican War*, 83 and 75; the last citation appears in Johnson, *Winfield Scott*, 193.

22. Miguel Angel González Quiroga, "Nuevo León ocupado: El gobierno de Nuevo León durante la guerra entre México y los Estados Unidos," in Josefina Zoraida Vázquez, coord., *México al tiempo de su guerra con Estados Unidos (1846–1848)* (Mexico City: Secretaría de Relaciones Exteriores, El Colegio de México, y Fondo de Cultura Económica, 1997), 354–355.

23. Charles H. Harris, III, *A Mexican Family Empire: The Latifundio of the Sánchez Navarro Family, 1765–1867* (Austin: University of Texas Press, 1975), 286. Collaborating with the U.S. army as well was the so-called Mexican spy company, also known as the *contraguerrilla poblana*. Comprised of perhaps 200 men and led by Manuel Dominguez, these irregular Mexican troops recruited by General Scott during his stay in Puebla served as scouts, messengers, spies, and guides. Many Mexicans, of course, came to loathe them. Timothy D. Johnson, *A Gallant Little Army: The Mexico City Campaign* (Lawrence: University Press of Kansas, 2007), 130–131; and Antonio García Cubas, *El libro de mis recuerdos*, 7th ed. (Mexico City: Editorial Patria, 1978 [1904]), 564.

24. David W. Walker, *Kinship, Business, and Politics: The Martínez del Río Family in Mexico, 1821–1867* (Austin: University of Texas Press, 1986),

187–193; and Barbara A. Tenembaum, *The Politics of Penury: Debts and Taxes in Mexico, 1821–1856* (Albuquerque: University of New Mexico Press, 1986), 32 and 83.

25. Carlos Rodríguez Venegas, "Las finanzas públicas y la guerra contra Estados Unidos, 1846–1848," in Vázquez, *México al tiempo de su guerra,* 117 and 121.

26. José Antonio Serrano Ortega, "Hacienda y guerra, élites políticas y gobierno nacional. Guanajuato, 1835–1847," in Vázquez, *México al tiempo de su guerra,* 299–301.

27. Jaime Olveda, "Jalisco frente a la invasión norteamericana de 1846–1848," in Vázquez, *México al tiempo de su guerra,*301–302.

28. Olveda, "Jalisco frente a la invasión," in Vázquez, *México al tiempo de su guerra,* 299–301.

29. Michael P. Costeloe, *The Central Republic in Mexico, 1835–1846: Hombres de Bien in the Age of Santa Anna* (New York: Cambridge University Press, 1993), 167.

30. Thompson is quoted in Will Fowler, *Military Political Identity and Reformism in Independent Mexico: An Analysis of the* Memorias de Guerra *(1821–1855)* (London: Institute of Latin American Studies, 1996), 39.

31. Fowler, *Military Political Identity,* 35–38, and 35, n. 131; and William A. DePalo, Jr., *The Mexican National Army, 1822–1852* (College Station: Texas A&M University Press, 1997), 74.

32. DePalo, *The Mexican National Army,* 97.

33. Juan Ortiz Escamilla, "Michoacán: Federalismo e intervención norteamericana," in Vázquez, *México al tiempo de su guerra,* 321; and Antonio López de Santa Anna, *Mi historia militar y política, 1810–1874. Memorias inéditas* (Mexico City: Librería de la vda. de Ch. Bouret, 1905), 70.

34. Pletcher, *The Diplomacy,* 441; and Irving W. Levinson, *Wars within Wars: Mexican Guerillas, Domestic Elites, and the United States of America, 1846–1848* (Fort Worth: Texas Christian University Press, 2006), 35 and 40.

35. Levinson, *Wars within Wars,* 41–48; and appendix A, 123–124.

36. Ralph W. Kirkham, *The Mexican War Journal & Letters of Ralph W. Kirkham,* ed. Robert Ryal Miller (College Station: Texas A&M University Press, 1991), 21.

37. Alcaraz et al., *The Other Side,* 442; and González Quiroga, "Nuevo León ante la invasión," in Herrera Serna, *México en guerra (1846–1848),* 455–456, and 456, n. 102.

38. Pedro Santoni, "A Fear of the People: The Civic Militia of Mexico in 1845," *Hispanic American Historical Review* 68:2 (May 1988), 281–283; and Pedro Santoni, "The Failure of Mobilization: The Civic Militia of Mexico in 1846," *Mexican Studies/Estudios Mexicanos* 12:2 (Summer 1996), 183–184.

39. Lorenzo de Arellano to the Minister of Foreign Relations, Guanajuato, July 15, 1847, Benson Latin American Collection, University of Texas at Austin, Justin Smith Papers G 220, xvii, quoted in Serrano Ortega, "Hacienda y guerra," in Vázquez, *México al tiempo de su guerra,* 260–261.

40. The revolt broke out in response to a decree issued on January 11, 1847, that empowered the government, then headed by *puro* leader and acting chief executive Valentín Gómez Farías, to mortgage or sell ecclesiastical property in order to finance the war against the United States. The national guard units that rebelled against the government came to be known as the *polkos* battalions because they mainly attracted individuals of high-ranking social positions, and the polka had become the most popular dance of elite society in Mexico. Santoni, "The Failure of Mobilization," 191–192.

41. Michael P. Costeloe, "The Mexican Church and the Rebellion of the Polkos," *Hispanic American Historical Review* 46:2 (May 1966), 170–178; Douglas W. Richmond, "A Conservative Prophet Confronts the Northern Menace: Lucas Alamán and US-Mexican Conflict (1822–1848)," *Jahrbuch für Geschichte Lateinamerikas* 43 (2006), 221; *Boletín de la Democracia,* March 2, 5, 6, and 8, 1847; and Salvador Bermúdez de Castro to Primer Secretario de Estado, Mexico City, March 31, 1847, in *Relaciones diplomáticas hispano-mexicanas (1839–1898),* 4 vols. (Mexico City: El Colegio de México, 1949–1968), 4:57.

42. *Legislación mexicana, o colección completa de las disposiciones legislativas expedidas desde la independencia de la república,* eds. Manuel Dublán and José María Lozano, 42 vols. (Mexico City: Imprenta del Comercio, 1876–1904), 5:266–267.

43. *Diario del Gobierno de la República Mexicana,* April 13, 1847.

44. Archivo del Ayuntamiento de la ciudad de México, Actas de Cabildo, Sesiones Secretas, vol. 300, meeting of April 24, 1847; and *El Monitor Republicano,* April 11 and May 10, 1847.

45. *El Monitor Republicano,* May 10, 1847.

46. Prieto, *Memorias,* 257.

47. DePalo, *The Mexican National Army,* 128; Johnson, *Winfield Scott,* 199; and Pletcher, *The Diplomacy,* 512. Yet even at this crucial time some national guardsmen either refused to report for service or deserted. See Minister of War to the Minister of Foreign Relations, Mexico City, August 9, 1847, in *Diario del Gobierno de la República Mexicana,* August 13, 1847.

48. This brief account of Balderas's activities largely comes from my essay, "Lucas Balderas: Popular Leader and Patriot," in *The Human Tradition in Mexico,* ed. Jeffrey M. Pilcher (Wilmington, DE: Scholarly Resources, 2003), 50–51; Balderas's final words appear in María Elena Salas Cuesta, coord., *Molino del Rey: Historia de un monumento* (Mexico City: Consejo Nacional para la Cultura y las Artes, 1997), 226. The assertions about Balderas made by *puro* newspapers are in *Boletín de la Democracia,* March 4 and 9, 1847.

49. Prieto, *Memorias,* 268.

50. García Cubas, *El libro,* 560; and Raymond B. Craib, *Cartographic Mexico: A History of State Fixations and Fugitive Landscapes* (Durham, NC: Duke University Press, 2004), 27.

51. Josefina Zoraida Vázquez, "Breve Diario de Don Mariano Riva Palacio (Agosto de 1847), *Historia Mexicana* 47:2 (October–December 1997), 455. The sense of despair that afflicted Mexico City residents at this time

can also be seen in *A Series of Intercepted Letters Captured by the American Guard at Tacubaya,* August 22, 1847, ed. Robert Hall Smith (Mexico City: "American Star" Print, 1847).

52. José Fernando Ramírez, *Mexico During the War with the United States,* ed. Walter V. Scholes, trans. Elliott B. Scherr (Columbia: University of Missouri Press, 1950), 153 and 156.

53. Alcaraz et al., *The Other Side,* 253.

54. Dennis E. Berge, "A Mexican Dilemma: The Mexico City Ayuntamiento and the Question of Loyalty," *Hispanic American Historical Review* 50:2 (May 1970), 234.

55. Kendall, *Dispatches from the Mexican War,* 373.

56. Luis Fernando Granados, *Sueñan las piedras: Alzamiento ocurrido en la ciudad de México, 14, 15, y 16 de septiembre de 1847* (Mexico City: Ediciones Era, 2003), 100–105; Will Fowler, *Tornel and Santa Anna: The Writer and the Caudillo, Mexico 1793–1853* (Westport, CT: Greenwood, 2000), 247–248; and Alcaraz et al., *The Other Side,* 313.

57. Granados, *Sueñan las piedras,* 32–33, and 40–42; and Johnson, *A Gallant Little Army,* 227 and 237. The quoted phrase is in Hughes and Johnson, *A Fighter from Way Back,* 128.

58. Prieto, *Memorias,* 275; Berge, "A Mexican Dilemma," 234–239; "Impugnación al informe del Exmo. Sr. General D. Antonio López de Santa Anna y constancias en que se apoyan las ampliaciones de la acusación del Sr. Diputado D. Ramón Gamboa," in *Antonio López de Santa Anna: La Guerra de Texas* (Mexico City: Universidad Autónoma Metropolitana, 1983), 309; and Granados, *Sueñan las piedras,* 43, 46, 49, and 61–63. For an insightful analysis of Próspero Pérez's historical significance, see Luis Fernando Granados, "Pequeños patricios, hermanos mayores. Francisco Próspero Pérez como emblema de los *sans-culottes* capitalinos hacia 1846–1847," *Historias* 54:1 (January–April 2003), 25–38.

59. Johnson, *A Gallant Little Army,* 242–243.

60. The first quote is in Ramírez, *Mexico During the War,* 161; the second appears in Johnson, *A Gallant Little Army,* 254.

61. Richmond, "A Conservative Prophet," 222.

62. Over the course of the night the soldiers paid a high price for their actions because they were found dead the next morning. Prieto, *Memorias,* 276.

63. *El Monitor Republicano,* October 19, 1847.

64. Kendall, *Dispatches from the Mexican War,* 421–422.

65. *El Monitor Republicano,* October 21, 1847.

66. Kendall, *Dispatches from the Mexican War,* 421.

67. Roa Bárcena, *Recuerdos de la invasión,* 3:215–216.

68. Berge, "A Mexican Dilemma," 246, 252–255; Moisés González Navarro, *Anatomía del poder en México, 1848–1853* (Mexico City, 1983 [1977]), 20; and Salvador Rueda Smithers, *El Diablo de Semana Santa: El discurso político y el orden social en la ciudad de México en 1850* (Mexico City: Instituto Nacional de Antropología e Historia, 1991), 101–118.

69. Richard Bruce Winders, *Mr. Polk's Army: The American Military Experience in the Mexican War* (College Station: Texas A&M University Press, 1997), 133; Maya Ramos Smith, *El ballet en México en el siglo XIX: De la independencia al segundo imperio (1825–1867)* (Mexico City: Consejo Nacional para la Cultura y las Artes y Alianza Editorial, 1991), 157, and 162–163; Kendall, *Dispatches from the Mexican War,* 409; and *El Monitor Republicano,* October 5 and 16, 1847.

70. *El Monitor Republicano,* November 17, 1847.

71. *El Siglo XIX,* June 3, 7, and 9, 1848, in *La ocupación yanqui de la ciudad de México, 1847–1848,* comp. María Gayón Córdova (Mexico City: Instituto Nacional de Antropología e Historia, 1997), 466–467.

72. Because box tickets to the performances cost one dollar, one U.S. army officer lamented that although the United States had "licked these people [the Mexicans] in battle, they know how to get our money from us[,] and have contrived their ingenuity in every way to invent new methods to extract it." Hughes and Johnson, *A Fighter from Way Back,* 30.

73. Kirkham, *The Mexican War Journal,* 22–23, 26–27, and 32.

74. Francisco Javier Cervantes Bello, "Guerra e iglesia en Puebla, 1780–1863," in Anne Staples, coord., *Historia de la vida cotidiana en México,* tomo IV, *Bienes y vivencias. El siglo XIX* (Mexico City: El Colegio de México y Fondo de Cultura Económica, 2005), 299 and 303.

75. Michael P. Costeloe, "The Junta Patriótica and the Celebration of Independence in Mexico City, 1825–1855," *Mexican Studies/Estudios Mexicanos* 13:1 (Winter 1997), 44; Enrique Plasencia de la Parra, *Independencia y nacionalismo a la luz del discurso conmemorativo (1825–1867)* (Mexico City: Consejo Nacional para la Cultura y las Artes, 1991), 88.

76. Claudio Lomnitz, *Death and the Idea of Mexico* (New York: Zone Books, 2005), 313–314. He quotes *El Monitor Republicano* in 314. Some anonymous Mexico City residents petitioned the archbishop to halt the traditional ringing of church bells during the festivities because the noise might foster even more nervous breakdowns among the city's female population. *Los amigos de la humanidad* (The Friends of Humanity) to the editors of *El Monitor Republicano,* October 15, 1847, in *El Monitor Republicano,* October 17, 1847. I have not found any data that reveals if, or how, the archbishop responded to the request.

77. Hughes and Johnson, *A Fighter from Way Back,* 139.

78. Kendall, *Dispatches from the Mexican War,* 54; and Hughes and Johnson, *A Fighter from Way Back,* 61.

79. Kendall, *Dispatches from the Mexican War,* 393. Winders, *Mr. Polk's Army,* 121 and 123, lists a number of other such establishments

80. *El Monitor Republicano,* October 20, 1847.

81. There is no translation for *jarabe* that would be helpful to readers. For a brief synopsis of its origins and development see John Charles Chasteen, *National Rhythms, African Roots: The Deep History of Latin American Popular Dance* (Albuquerque: University of New Mexico Press, 2004), 139–140.

82. Winders, *Mr. Polk's Army*, 135; the quote is from Johnson, *A Gallant Little Army*, 254.

83. Ramírez, *Mexico During the War*, 161.

84. The most prominent analyses came from José Fernando Ramírez, Mariano Otero, Carlos María Bustamante, and a group of 15 individuals headed by Ramón Alcaraz. A recent analysis of their views on this question appears in Alvaro Matute Aguirre, "Conciencia histórica temprana. Cuatro ejemplos," in Herrera Serna, *México en guerra (1846–1848)*, 41–54.

85. Charles A. Hale, *Mexican Liberalism in the Age of Mora, 1821–1853* (New Haven, CT: Yale University Press, 1968), 11–14; and Carlos María Bustamante, "México en 1848. Principales sucesos políticos y militares," May 3, 4, 13, and 17, 1848, and June 24, 1848. This manuscript can be found at the Bancroft Library of the University of California, Berkeley. Bustamante recorded on a daily basis, in the document above as well as in other works of his, those events that he witnessed or that were mentioned to him.

86. Costeloe, "The Junta Patriótica," 47; Plasencia de la Parra, *Independencia y nacionalismo*, 90–93; Pedro Santoni, "Where Did the Other Heroes Go? Exalting the *Polko* National Guard Battalions in Nineteenth-Century Mexico," *Journal of Latin American Studies* 34:4 (November 2002), 807–844; and Sinkin, *The Mexican Reform*, 28–29.

87. Leticia Reina, "The Sierra Gorda Peasant Rebellion, 1847–1850," in *Riot, Rebellion, and Revolution: Rural Conflict in Mexico*, ed. Friedrich Katz (Princeton: Princeton University Press, 1988), 269, and 276–279; the quote is in Henderson, *A Glorious Defeat*, 174.

88. Foos, *A Short, Offhand, Killing Affair*, 135–136.

89. Patrick J. McNamara, "Felipe García and the Real Heroes of Guelatao," in Pilcher, *The Human Tradition*, 75–89.

90. Enrique Plasencia de la Parra, "Conmemoración de la hazaña épica de los Niños Héroes: Su origen, desarrollo y simbolismos," *Historia Mexicana* 45:2 (October–December 1995), 247–248.

91. Plasencia de la Parra, "Conmemoración de la hazaña épica," 242–243; and Vicente Quirarte, "Tiempo de canallas, héroes y artistas. El imaginario de la guerra entre México y Estados Unidos," in Herrera Serna, *México en guerra (1846–1848)*, 71–74.

92. Plasencia de la Parra, "Conmemoración de la hazaña épica," 273–274; and Thomas Benjamin, *La Revolución: Mexico's Great Revolution as Memory, Myth, and History* (Austin: University of Texas Press, 2000), 155.

93. Mónica Matos-Vega, "El recinto de Chapultepec exhibe un discurso de conceptos y temas," and "Ni tan niños, ni tan héroes," in *La Jornada*, August 11, 2005, http://www.jornada.unam.mx/.

94. Plasencia de la Parra, "Conmemoración de la hazaña épica," 277.

FOUR

Civilians and Civil War in Nineteenth-Century Mexico: Mexico City and the War of the Reform, 1858–1861

Daniel S. Haworth

Violent conflict marked Latin America's uneasy adjustment to in-dependence. In Mexico and Spanish South America, where fierce struggles for self-rule established a precedent for the use of armed force in pursuit of a political objective while disrupting government and the economy, rebellion and civil war proliferated, driven by an interwoven array of precipitating factors that included regional grievances, ethnic tension, and elite antagonism over matters of business, ideology, or personal ambition. Central America achieved independence by peaceful means, yet an attempt at confederation (1824–1838) proved short-lived because the region manifested the same proclivity for political violence. Of the Spanish American re-publics, only Chile, Paraguay, and Costa Rica avoided civil war altogether. Brazil, which separated from Portugal almost without incident in 1822 and remained a monarchy until 1889, also escaped civil war, in part because dependence on slavery made Brazilian elites more circumspect about upsetting the existing social order

This chapter revises and expands upon a series of presentations made to the *Grupo investigador sobre la ciudad de México en tiempo de Guerra* between 1997 and 1998, and originally published as Daniel S. Haworth, "Desde los baluartes conservadores: la ciudad de México y la Guerra de Reforma (1857–1860)," *Relaciones, Estudios de Historia y Sociedad* 84, vol. XXI (otoño 2000): 95–132. Reprinted with permission.

than their Spanish American counterparts. Such apprehensions contributed to stability by confining most intra-elite conflict to government channels, but they did not prevent the emergence in Brazil of the same pressures that led to violence in Spanish America. For example, Rio Grande do Sul, Brazil's southernmost province, tried unsuccessfully to secede in a 10-year struggle known as the War of the Farrapos (1835–1845), while local elites in the northeastern province of Bahía who hoped to replace the monarchy with a federal republic launched the so-called *Sabinada* of 1837–1838.[1]

Mexico attested to the periodic nature of violence in nineteenth-century Latin American politics, as it endured three bouts of civil war between 1810 and 1855. The War for Independence (1810–1821) was the first, inasmuch as Mexican royalist forces formed the backbone of the ostensible Spanish effort to suppress a regionally fragmented anti-imperial insurgency. Spanish rule ended when the royalist army united with its erstwhile rebel foes, whereupon Mexico's original government, a monarchy under Augustín de Iturbide, the royalist officer who had brokered the alliance that secured independence, succumbed in 1823 to a mutiny by disaffected generals. Following Iturbide's fall, elites split into quarreling camps of federalists who advocated regional autonomy and centralists who wanted strong national government. Their enmity sparked a second civil war in 1832 that toppled the centralist administration of General Anastasio Bustamante. Centralists retook the presidency in 1835 and retained the upper hand in Mexican politics until 1854, when a rebellion in southern Mexico against the centralist dictatorship of General Antonio López de Santa Anna grew into yet another civil war, known as the Revolution of Ayutla (1854–1855). Rural Mexicans, the majority of the population, participated in these disturbances or occasionally resorted on their own to armed rebellion. Their motives were as diverse as the communities they inhabited. In many cases they joined a civil war to resist outside influence or oppression, or to assert their vision of national politics. Just as often villagers took advantage of civil war as a pretext to lash out against local rivals. In between its bouts of civil war, moreover, Mexico witnessed dozens of *pronunciamientos*, regionally and/or locally based revolts by dissident elements of the army acting in concert with civilian allies.[2]

For Mexico, as for the other parts of Latin America prone to political violence, the recurrence of civil war belies its physical remoteness from civilian life. The political outcome of war—constitutional reform, policy reversal, the expansion or curtailment of provincial influence, and other changes flowing from the transfer of power—affected civilians more than the process of war. With rare exceptions, combat took place away from population centers. Civil war had the most dramatic impact on civilians caught in the path of an army on the march. Troops on campaign in nineteenth-century Mexico provisioned themselves as they went, requisitioning food, horses, and occasionally money from the settlements through which they passed. This disrupted the economy, but effects were local and transitory. Young men, especially the unmarried and unemployed, risked being drafted either by the government or the rebels. Otherwise the majority of civilians had little direct or sustained physical contact with civil war. However ferocious and deadly a single battle might be, or however unsettled the recurrence of war made politics and the economy, warfare itself remained limited in scope. It never required the mobilization of the entire population.[3] Civilians, in turn, took advantage of whatever opportunities civil war afforded them, while they accommodated or adapted to the limited demands war placed on them.

To test that assertion, this essay explores the context of everyday life in Mexico City during the War of the Reform (1858–1861), a civil war that marked the completion of a gradual shift in the point of division in Mexican politics. The centralist-federalist debate of the 1820s contained within it an ideological disagreement between Liberals and Conservatives, two of the main factions that later emerged and tried to impose their will on national affairs during the first half of the nineteenth century. Liberals and Conservatives disagreed on the relevance to national life of the corporatist social tradition inherited from the Spanish colonial era, which defined society not as an aggregate of individuals, but rather as a collection of distinct interest groups. Corporatism remained extant in early republican Mexico in the legal privileges reserved for the army and the Catholic Church, and the communal landholding tradition of indigenous villages. Liberals desired a federal republic marked by the equality of all citizens in which corporatism neither constrained individual rights nor competed with the state for the individual's allegiance. Conservatives remained committed to a strong central government and contended that Mexico's well-being depended on corporatism; they believed that it had ensured social peace before independence, and that Liberal ideas threatened social dissolution. Between the Liberal and Conservative extremes of the political class stood moderates who sympathized with Liberal aims, but also shared Conservative misgivings about unbridled change.[4]

Middle ground in the Liberal-Conservative dispute began to disappear with Mexico's humiliating loss in its war with the United States (1846–1848). Defeat drove each side to cling to its vision as the only means for the country to recover a sense of national direction. Political polarization intensified after the aforementioned Revolution of Ayutla, when a Liberal administration seized power in the fall of 1855 and adopted a number of measures that set the stage for the War of the Reform. The Liberals proceeded to draft a new national constitution, enacted in February 1857, to which every Mexican was required to swear loyalty. Controversy ensued over provisions within the constitution designed to undermine the corporatist tradition and the interest groups that upheld it—especially the army and the Catholic Church. In response the army mutinied en masse in January 1858 and organized a Conservative government in Mexico City. The Liberal administration fled north under the protection of state governors determined to forestall the formation of a military dictatorship, moving from city to city until eventually settling in the eastern port of Veracruz. By associating their cause with regional autonomy, Liberals cultivated a popular base of support large enough to control the north, south, and east of the republic, while the Conservatives held the center.[5] A string of Conservative victories in 1858 gave way to stalemate in 1859 until the tide of the war at last turned in favor of the Liberals, thanks to the increasing effectiveness of their initially ad hoc military. The capture of Mexico City by Liberal troops late in December 1860 concluded the War of the Reform and brought them temporary victory in their armed struggle with the Conservatives.

MEXICO CITY

In terms of its size and physical layout, Mexico City during the War of the Reform remained much as it had been four decades before when Mexico became independent. The population in the 1850s totaled around 200,000, qualifying Mexico City as the largest city in the country, and among the largest in the Americas. Centuries-old farming communities dotted the surrounding valley, sustained by trade with the city even as they resisted its encroachment.[6] Mexico City itself retained the layout first envisioned by the Spanish in the sixteenth century. Rectangular blocks radiated from its great central square, the *Zócalo*, to form a geometrically ordered urban space that clashed with the hubbub of the streets. People of every station mingled in the public space, but residence patterns conveyed distinctions of class and power much as they had in the colonial era. The poor crowded into the outer blocks. A nascent middle class of professionals, shopkeepers, and prosperous artisans inhabited the interior neighborhoods, while elites resided in imposing homes close to the *Zócalo*, and in the western suburb of Tacubaya, site of the Archbishop's palace.[7]

Neither Liberals nor Conservatives could deny the importance of Mexico City, but for the latter the city was essential. The Conservatives saw the capital as a potent symbol of their legitimacy. Constructed by the Spanish from the rubble of Aztec pyramids, the former capital of the viceroyalty of New Spain embodied both the heritage and the continuity that served as the Conservatives' core ideals. At the city's heart, arranged around the *Zócalo*, massive buildings expressed the power of church and state—to the north, the National Cathedral; to the east, the National Palace; to the south, the offices of the *ayuntamiento*, or city council; and to the west, the offices of powerful merchants and financiers. More importantly, Mexico City represented the Conservatives' claim to rule by virtue of occupying the traditional seat of national power. They needed Mexico City to be the center of the state, a physical counterpoint to the Liberal argument that the center resided in the Constitution of 1857, and not in a fixed geographic locale.

Mexico City also represented a significant military asset, not least of all because the ports, and hence the customs houses, lay in

This lithograph gives an idea of the layout of the key buildings in Mexico City: The cathedral is to the north, the National Palace is to the east, the merchant's archway to the west, and city hall (the *ayuntamiento*) to the south. (Lithograph from *México y sus alrededores,* 3rd ed. Mexico City: Manuel Quesada Brandi, 1965 [1855–56]).

Liberal hands. While Liberals could count on income from international trade, Conservatives had to rely on the population centers of the interior for financial support, Mexico City chief among them. Although reliable economic data for the nineteenth century is notoriously scant, anecdotal evidence suggests a robust flow of trade in and around the capital. According to an 1858 estimate, city residents annually consumed 17,000 cattle, 60,000 pigs, 1,260,000 chickens, 125,000 ducks, 250,000 turkeys, 58 million pounds of corn, 63 million pounds of flour, 18 million gallons of the popular, mildly alcoholic drink *pulque*, 12,000 barrels of brandy, and 20,000 gallons of cooking oil, all produced in the countryside.[8] Besides providing a market for rural products, Mexico City housed a struggling textile industry and a large concentration of artisans; both sectors may have benefited from whatever growth in local demand for their products the war created by disrupting the flow of foreign goods. In addition, the many clergy, lawyers, bureaucrats, journalists, and army officers who called the capital home made for a robust professional class who augmented the city's tax base. In other words, the capital comprised the core of a productive if isolated regional economy vital to sustaining the Conservative cause, as well as a valuable source of manpower for the military. Living in Mexico City amounted to residing in a veritable city-state synonymous with the Conservative project. Conservative rule, in turn, acted as the lens through which the War of the Reform filtered into capital.

Naturally, the Conservatives mounted a stout defense of their most prized possession. The Conservative army proved so effective at carrying the war away from Mexico City that its residents confronted the violence of combat only twice in three years. On October 14, 1858, Liberal commander Manuel Blanco's forces punched into the city through its southeastern quarter. His troops captured a line of positions that brought them within four blocks of the Zócalo before a furious counterattack drove them out. Conservative soldiers carried Blanco's abandoned cannon back to Mexico City as trophies.[9] Six months later, in late March 1859, Liberal forces under Santos Degollado approached from the southwest and pulled up before the Conservatives' hastily constructed earthworks. Degollado's men attempted to breach the Conservative lines on April 2, but fell back to the suburb of Tacubaya after a four-hour struggle. Despite a lull in the fighting, the capital remained under siege for another week. Then, on April 10, Conservative General Leonardo Márquez finally routed Degollado. Cannon fire from the clash could be heard in the city center, where priests had mounted a telescope

atop one of the bell towers of the National Cathedral to watch a
battle unfold that was more spectacle than imminent threat.[10] Thus
protected, Mexico City's residents otherwise lived apart from the
noise, smoke, and death that war inevitably wrought.

Politically, however, the war hovered as an omnipresent reality.
Abrupt changes in leadership spawned by disagreement among
top generals over the conduct of the war played out as public
events scripted to express the legitimacy of the new president. On
January 21, 1858, for example, General Félix Zuloaga, leader of the
mutiny that initiated the war, paraded his troops through the city
to the National Palace. Women waving handkerchiefs in salute
filled the balconies along the route. An enthusiastic throng packed

TOMA del ARZOBISPADO de TACUBAYA por la Division del Gral. MARQUEZ, (el 11 de Abril de 1859.)

This well-worn print shows the battle at Tacubaya, a small town just outside of
Mexico City. The reason for the folds in this picture is that this lithograph was
originally folded into a calendar. The lithograph, by an artist known as Decaen,
appears in the *Calendario reaccionario de 1860*, edited by Vicente Segura. Original
title: "Toma del Arzobispado de Tacubaya por la División del General Márquez
(el 11 de abril de 1859)." The calendar can found at the Biblioteca del Museo
de Antropología (Library of the Mexican National Anthropology Museum) in
Chapultepec Park, Mexico City. (Courtesy of María José Esparza).

the Cathedral to watch the Archbishop consecrate Zuloaga's claim to the presidency, and his association with the Conservative cause, by way of an elaborate mass of thanksgiving. Bullfights and plays marked the occasion, culminating in a colorful display of fireworks in the *Zócalo*.[11] The following day, the Conservative newspaper *El Eco Nacional* hailed Zuloaga's accession as a harbinger of tranquility.[12]

Zuloaga's grasp on the presidency, however, proved brief. That December, with Conservative military fortunes at their zenith, Generals Manuel Robles Pezuela and Miguel María Echeagaray deposed Zuloaga in the belief that he stood in the way of reuniting the country without further bloodshed. Robles Pezuela and Echeagaray assumed that the Liberals would negotiate a truce on Conservative terms rather than face annihilation, but Liberal president Benito Juárez's refusal to bargain forced the politically weakened Robles Pezuela to convene an assembly of notables in Mexico City to "select" a new Conservative chief executive. Instead of ratifying Robles Pezuela's position, the assembly reacted to Juarez's defiance and voted for the doctrinaire commander of the army's northern division, General Miguel Miramón, a dashing figure renowned for his military prowess, who declared his intent to prosecute the war to its conclusion. The degree to which this mattered to the cheering crowds that on January 21, 1859, lined his route to Chapultepec Palace, the presidential residence southeast of the city, remains a matter of conjecture. What can be said is that they welcomed Zuloaga and Miramón with equal zeal. Inasmuch as the average length of a presidential term since 1824 amounted to just under a year, and that in that time there occurred but two peaceful transfers of authority, such events were nothing new. People turned out at the appropriate time, some to signal their sincere support, some to enjoy the show, and others simply to witness the moment. Afterward life returned more or less to normal.

The war might have militarized the Conservative presidency, but it had little effect on municipal government or on the influence of civilians within it. Throughout the conflict generals occupied the key posts of president, governor of the capital district, and chief of police, yet they relied on a civilian *ayuntamiento* to conduct day-to-day administrative affairs. Mexico City's *ayuntamiento* consisted of eight *regidores* (councilmen), assisted by a staff of secretaries and lawyers, who collectively headed the municipal bureaucracy. The *Celadores de Policía*, a select, 26-man mounted police detachment, stood at the *ayuntamiento's* disposition in demonstration of its prestige.[13] City government in the capital, as elsewhere, had mainly been the reserve of the local elite. For the soldier-presidents of the Conservative regime, therefore, the *ayuntamiento* represented a politically and socially critical base of civilian support. Originally an elected body, the *ayuntamiento* at various times since independence had been subject to presidential appointment.[14] This had been the case during the tense early years of Liberal rule prior to the War of the Reform, and it remained so for the war's duration, given the capital's centrality to the Conservative war effort. Even so, relations between the *ayuntamiento* and Zuloaga and Miramón, respectively, indicate that war left the power of Mexico City's civilian oligarchy intact.

Zuloaga was a professional soldier and by all accounts a competent officer. As president, however, his military credentials mattered less than his political inexperience and outsider status in the context of the capital. Zuloaga's only prior political post consisted of serving for a short time in the municipal government of Chihuahua City, in the far north, in the 1840s. Moreover, his military career had kept him away from Mexico City until 1857.[15] Taking up residence there as commander of the Mexico City garrison just months before he led the army in mutiny against the Liberal regime, he had little time to cultivate a stable, influential network of local contacts before coming to power.

Zuloaga retained the *ayuntamiento* originally appointed by the Liberal president he had overthrown, Ignacio Comonfort. The practical need for continuity in city government in the midst of a civil war, not to mention the eminence and evident talents of the *regidores*, may explain Zuloaga's decision. He made one change only, naming Alejandro Arango y Escandón as council president. Arango y Escandón was a prominent public intellectual and Conservative politician who in 1868 would help create the ultraconservative *Sociedad Católica* (the Catholic Society), an organization that coordinated lay religious activity around the country in the absence of a strong national church. He had also been an advocate for the *ayuntamiento's* autonomy. As a *regidor* in 1850, Arango y Escandón had lodged a formal protest with Congress denouncing its decree that the electoral college charged with naming the president and senators would henceforth select the *ayuntamiento* as well.[16] If he was aware of that fact, Zuloaga apparently found it of little or no concern. Arango y Escandón's intellectual achievement, though considerable, paled in comparison to that of *regidor* José Gómez de la Cortina (the Mexican-born son of Spanish nobles who had inherited from his father the title of Conde de la Cortina), a prolific author, linguist, and cofounder of the Mexican Society for Geography and Statistics. Cortina had occupied various high-ranking official posts during the 1830s and 1840s, including a stint as treasury minister and two terms as the governor of the Federal District. He leaned toward conservatism, but his record as an administrator evinced more concern for law and order than for the defense of corporatist tradition per se.[17] The *ayuntamiento's* secretary, Vicente Riva Palacio, was a well-known moderate politician, and a lawyer familiar among the capital's elite circles.[18] Judging from Arango y Escandón, Cortina, and Riva Palacio, at least, the *regidores* who served under Zuloaga represented a diverse body of political opinion, but their shared membership in the local elite set them apart from the *norteño* parvenu Zuloaga.

The social gap between the *regidores* and the president may account for why the *ayuntamiento* displayed a certain disregard for Zuloaga's directives. One of its major responsibilities entailed overseeing the recruitment of troops. Immediately after receiving notice of a conscription drive in February 1858, the *regidores* formed a three-member commission that presented to Zuloaga a formal request for its cessation. Their protest at first glance appears unusual inasmuch as conscription provided an important means of social control. Vagrants, the poor, and the unemployed—the *populacho* in the parlance of the time—were the regular targets of forced military service; state and local governments for many years actually had preferred conscription as a means of providing men for the army while retaining more respectable residents in local national guard units.[19] Zuloaga replied with a stern rebuke. He ordered the *ayuntamiento* to meet in special session to work out the details of the conscription, but the council stonewalled and allowed the matter to languish a full four weeks.[20] A July decree mandating the formation of a civil guard to be composed of property owners took six weeks to implement. The guardsmen-to-be meanwhile began to arm themselves, probably out of concern over the threat posed by Liberal insurgents operating in the nearby mountains, and the fear that the city's poor would take advantage of any disturbance to act out their resentment of the wealthy. Exasperated, Zuloaga dispatched the governor of Mexico City, General Miguel María Azcárrate, to personally convene the *ayuntamiento.* Then and only then did the *regidores* comply with Zuloaga's instructions.[21]

Zuloaga had reason to worry about property owners taking up arms free of government oversight. Earlier that July, even as he issued his instructions to the *ayuntamiento,* he launched a series of ill-advised attempts to wring money from the church and the city's leading families that alienated the elite. Twice Zuloaga pressured the church, whose interests he had pledged to uphold just six months before, to provide the funds needed to cover government expenses.[22] The prelates grudgingly agreed to Zuloaga's first request, but sternly rebuffed the second. Undeterred, he then imposed a forced loan on nine of the richest men in Mexico City, thus dissipating the popularity he had enjoyed at the outset of his tenure.[23]

When viewed against that backdrop, the *regidores'* previous delays resemble acts of intentional resistance motivated by a power struggle between local elites and an alien and unpopular chief executive. This interpretation appears all the more plausible in light of the lack of correspondence between the *ayuntamiento*'s actions and the underlying ideological issues of the war. The presence of a moderate like Vicente Riva Palacio and the fact that every one of his colleagues but Alejandro Arango y Escandón had served under the man whom Zuloaga ousted makes it tempting to view their obstructionism as an act of political revenge, but no evidence indicates that they acted with that end in mind. Furthermore, an *ayuntamiento* president of such Conservative convictions as Arango y Escandón would not knowingly advance the cause of his Liberal adversaries. A desire for political autonomy, as opposed to a strong affiliation with either Conservatives or Liberals, explains the uncooperativeness Zuloaga encountered in his dealings with the *ayuntamiento*. Indeed, relations between the Mexico City *ayuntamiento* and higher authority at the state and national level had long been a contentious affair.[24] By the time Zuloaga was forced from office, civilian elites had seen their mastery of capital challenged but not changed. They had remained in control and managed to impose limits on the executive authority of the general who sought to rule them.

Unlike Zuloaga, General Miramón's personal background seemed to portend a better relationship with the *ayuntamiento*. He was a native of Mexico City who had also married into one of the city's leading families, assuring his place among the capital's upper crust. Yet any affinity these circumstances might have created with an *ayuntamiento* whose members had given Zuloaga so much grief never had a chance to play out, for upon assuming the presidency Miramón replaced those recalcitrant *regidores* with more cooperative appointees; one example was *Regidor* Rafael Roa Bárcena, a prominent writer, intellectual, and Conservative partisan.[25] The exact identity of other *regidores* remains a matter of speculation, but their family names suggest distinct pedigrees. Patricio Murphy may well have been the son of Thomas Murphy, whom Zuloaga had appointed minister to Great Britain.[26] Given Miramón's arch-traditionalist proclivities, it stands to reason that Germán Madrid de Ormachea was related to Juan Bautista Ormachea y Ernáiz, Bishop of Tulancingo. Meanwhile, Sebastián Labastida probably belonged to the extended family of Pelagio Antonio de Labastida y Dávalos, the hard-line Bishop of Puebla and, after 1863, Archbishop of Mexico. Miramón's appointment of these men to the *ayuntamiento* initiated a period of congruence between the presidency and the municipal administration. Vital operations managed by the *ayuntamiento*, such as military conscription or the collection of taxes, functioned smoothly, with no trace of the antagonisms that plagued Zuloaga's time in office.[27] Miramón furthermore left Mexico City for the *ayuntamiento* to administer without his personal supervision, as he was absent from the city for extended periods during much of 1859 and 1860, leading military campaigns in both Veracruz and north of the capital. By that time Mexico City had become more than just the symbolic or material center of the Conservative state. The transition from Zuloaga to Miramón, with the war acting as a catalyst, completed the domination of the Conservative regime by Miramón and his allies among the civilian ruling class of Mexico City.

Just as he often left the civilian *ayuntamiento* in charge of the capital, Miramón made no move to eliminate civilians elsewhere in local government even as he streamlined municipal administration to render it more efficient. He consolidated the number of *cuarteles* (wards) from 32, the number into which the city had been organized prior to his presidency, to eight.[28] An individual *regidor* commanded each *cuartel,* and he in turn counted on the services of an array of lesser officials who combined the functions of law enforcement and municipal administration at the neighborhood level. Every *cuartel* was subdivided into *cuarteles menores,* each with its own inspector who reported to the corresponding *regidor.* An inspector's activities could range from notifying residents of court orders and summons, to gathering conscripts. Each block of a *cuartel* had a subinspector, and every street an *ayudante* (helper).[29] The idea behind these refinements, apparently, was to facilitate Miramon's control of the city via a sympathetic *ayuntamiento.* However, given that inspectors and the officials working under them lived in the neighborhoods they administered, the bounds of kinship, friendship, or *compadrazgo* (ritual kinship) surely tied them to the other residents.[30] Miramón regimented local government, but he did not militarize local authority.

A mid-nineteenth-century lithograph shows one of Mexico City's beautiful buildings, the College of Mines (Colegio de Mineria), with citizens strolling up and
down the street. Living in Mexico City at the time of the War of the Reform was
like living in a protected city-state. (Lithograph from *México y sus alrededores*,
3rd ed. Mexico City: Manuel Quesada Brandi, 1965 [1855–56]).

In light of these findings, it could be said that the structure of municipal government under Miramón functioned as a link between
Mexico City's *barrios* (neighborhoods) and the Conservative regime. The inspector served as an important intermediary between
the city's residents and the *ayuntamiento*. His position allowed him
to communicate local concerns to the *regidor* responsible for his
cuartel. Furthermore, the inspector may have been a client of the
regidor for whom he worked, and he also might have been in a position to dispense limited favors in his neighborhood. In that way the
city government reinforced a direct vertical tie between the population and the state. More research is needed to ascertain exactly how
that social bond between regime and population functioned, and to
what extent it fostered identification with the regime. What is certain, however, is that the structure of municipal government under
Miramón allowed for interaction between the state and the streets,
and facilitated the occasional intrusion of the war into the life of

Mexico City's residents in the form of conscription drives that affected relatively few, or taxation that affected many.

Taxes

War forced both Zuloaga and Miramón to depend on taxes more than other sources of revenue. Previous governments, regardless of their ideological predisposition, used taxation primarily to supplement monies raised through customs receipts and foreign loans because extracting revenue directly from an overwhelmingly rural population scattered across Mexico's mountainous terrain proved difficult and costly. Yet the Conservative regimes had few other alternatives. The Liberals controlled every port and all the towns along the U.S. border, and repelled every Conservative attempt to capture one. This, in turn, made it difficult for the Conservative government to secure loans abroad because they could not barter customs receipts as collateral. Domestic sources of funds were equally limited. Forcing the affluent few to lend the government money carried considerable political liability, as Zuloaga discovered midway through his presidency. Taxes collected from the civilian population of the cities and towns of the interior—especially Mexico City—represented the only reliable means for Conservative leaders to obtain the income they so desperately needed to function and to fight.

A sample of four fund-raising decrees shows how Conservative governments used taxes to target the wealth concentrated in the city. In early February 1858, barely two weeks into his presidency, Zuloaga decreed a 5 percent tax on the value of all goods and real estate. The tax required numerous clarifications as to how exactly it was to be applied and elicited widespread protest and resentment.[31] Undeterred, the following May he imposed a 10 percent tax on the value of all "movable and immovable capital," meaning in effect assets of any kind.[32] General Manuel Robles Pezuela, who presided over the month-long interregnum between Zuloaga and Miramón, declared in January 1859 a more complex tax with defined contribution levels for five categories encompassing assets and economic activity, with payment due within eight working days after January 1 and every four months thereafter. The categories in question were "professions and lucrative exercises," "wages and salaries," "luxury objects," "industrial establishments," and "mercantile earnings."[33] The last example comes from November 1860, when, with Liberal forces closing in on Mexico City, Miramón required every resident to remit monthly cash payments to the government. Contributions were apparently graduated, perhaps according to occupation, the highest level being 2,500 pesos per month, an extraordinary sum at a time when 1,000 pesos afforded one a comfortable life.[34] All of these initiatives represented "extraordinary contributions," as Zuloaga termed his demands, applied in addition to existing municipal taxes. Moreover, the amount of money the government sought to wring from the populace went up over time. War made living in Mexico City an expensive proposition.

Through taxation the war intruded directly into the lives of Mexico City's civilian population. Not only did civilians have to contribute the funds, they also had to administer their collection. Zuloaga ordered that every city block have a resident to act as a commissioner to enforce the submission of payments according to a strict schedule of installments. The other residents were required to provide the commissioner a letter detailing the exact amount they owed, a sum that the commissioner could presumably verify. Additionally, Zuloaga directed governor Miguel Azcárrate to name a qualifying board (*junta calificadora*) to compile and verify the lists of contributions and to punish dishonest commissioners.[35] Likewise, under Robles Pezuela's 1859 plan, local agents (*causantes de contribuciones directas*) collected payments in their neighborhoods, and answered to a citywide qualifying board. The qualifying board in either case probably consisted of wealthy individuals who had to guarantee the potential return of revenue. If so, this system bore a strong resemblance to tax farming, a common feature of Mexican public finance in earlier decades. Allowing the qualifying board to keep a certain percentage of the money they collected would have encouraged its members' cooperation, but ensuring their accountability for the money was another matter. While in all likelihood members of the qualifying board enjoyed political connections with someone in power who trusted them, and such personal relationships may have been sufficient for the government to secure the funds in question, to be sure the government planted a commissioner or agent in each neighborhood for the specific reason that, like the inspector, the tax collector operated in his own community.[36] This made his neighbors less likely to lie to him. The possibility for dissimulation, of course, was hardly eliminated.

Given the absence of hard figures expressing the total amount of revenue these "extraordinary contributions" generated, it is difficult to gauge their success or to discern the level of civilian acquiescence. At first glance, requiring civilian administrators to police one another seems an ineffective means of coercing compliance because of the very real possibility that civilians, upset over repeated government exactions, would collude to evade those requirements. A certain amount of tax evasion was unavoidable, but enough people must have complied to make collecting the money a worthwhile process given that the exigencies of war militated against the repeated investment of resources with no hope of return. Therefore, it stands to reason that most individuals who could do so paid their taxes. If so, then it is equally likely that the elites, professionals, shop owners, and artisans (i.e., those with fixed residences and disposable income) who shouldered the greatest share of the tax burden did so more or less voluntarily, perhaps out of anxiety over the threat of public disorder.

That the propertied classes may have grudgingly paid their taxes because those monies funded the enforcement of social peace in the midst of civil war is not a surprising development. Elite insecurities were reflected in the fear of social upheaval that nagged at Conservative officials in spite of Mexico City remaining largely quiet. Zuloaga issued a draconian conspiracy law in July 1858 that threatened anyone found guilty of plotting against the government with penalties ranging from lengthy imprisonment to execution. The law applied to everyone, including the military, but it also aimed directly at the poor by interpreting loitering, obstreperousness, avoiding the police, and participating in large spontaneous public gatherings as evidence of "conspiracy." Ten months later, General Antonio Corona, Miramón's Minister of War, worried openly over "the neighborhoods' many vagrants and pernicious people."[37] Long-time residents of the capital would have remembered the riots that broke out there during times of political turmoil in 1828, 1838, 1844, 1847, and 1848, or the occupation of the city by peasant rebels from the south in November 1855, whose presence one elite observer likened to the Huns who overran ancient Rome.[38] The Conservative press had long painted the Liberals as demagogues intent on seizing power by inciting the lawless rabble. Taxes helped the government to keep the threat of social upheaval at bay.

Civilian Cooperation with Conservative Governments

Collaboration between civilians and the police lends credence to the notion that civilians cooperated with the Conservative governments. Mexico City during the War of the Reform was, to say the least, heavily policed. In effect a constabulary home guard attached to the army, the police consisted of daytime and nighttime patrols (called the *resguardo diurno* and *resguardo nocturno* respectively). Two hundred men staffed the nighttime patrol. Assuming the daytime patrol consisted of an equal number, Mexico City boasted one police officer for every 500 inhabitants, in addition to troops posted throughout the city around the clock. Nonetheless, law enforcement relied as much on espionage as it did on the public presence of uniformed soldiers or policemen. A network of spies that reported to General Juan B. Lagarde infiltrated the private lives of Mexico City's residents; civilian informants who made up a second, informal tier of surveillance supplemented their efforts.[39]

Civilian informers kept the police supplied with tips such as the one that led to the arrest of Mateo Aguirre in the outlying settlement of San Rafael, northwest of Mexico City, on a charge of "belonging to the ranks of the enemy." Prior to October 1858, when (according to Aguirre) financial hardship forced him to relocate, he had operated a store in Mexico City, on the Plazuela de San Juan Carbonero. Seven months later, one of his former neighbors reported to the police that Aguirre had tried to convince him to "join the revolution," that is, to enlist in the Liberal military, and with that the police mounted a manhunt.[40] In this way civilian networks extended the reach of law enforcement beyond the city proper.

While additional research is needed to determine the mindset of the population, the apparent cooperation between the city's residents and the Conservative regime illustrated by the foregoing discussion of municipal administration raises a tantalizing implication. The Conservative regime derived its legitimacy from the war. Legitimacy, however, required more than a simple claim to rule, and certainly more than countering the Liberals' assertions, because it emanated from the moral economy that characterized the relationship between the ruler and the ruled. Hence, the War of the Reform drove together Mexico City's civilian population and its hybrid government of generals who presided over a preexisting structure of civilian administrators. So important was Mexico City to the Conservative leadership that they could coerce its residents only so much. Conversely, the city's residents undoubtedly benefited from the relative normalcy that prevailed in the midst of war (a normalcy the Conservative regime struggled to preserve). Many, therefore, supported the government. Others merely tolerated it, and those who opposed it laid low.

Civilian perceptions of the war would have shaped their attitude toward the Conservative government. Public opinion, in turn, drew

on accounts of distant events that reached the typical city dweller
long after the fact. Construction of telegraph lines had barely begun
by the outset of the war, leaving information to be carried by post
and word of mouth. Mexico's mountainous terrain and poor roads
slowed the flow of information to the point that a letter posted from
Mexico City took over a week to arrive in Guadalajara, the second
largest city in the country, 300 miles to the northwest.[41] Within the
capital, however, news spread quickly whenever and wherever
people met. For example, vendors, many of them women, kept residents supplied with information as well as goods. Neighborhood
markets thus formed vital links in an expansive network of inter-
personal communication, especially among the poor. The literate
classes could turn to the press for word of current events. Although
periodicals offered more opinion than news, they nonetheless
opened a window into the public mindset through their preserva-
tion of fragments of the collective civilian voice.

Newspapers' Effects on the War of the Reform

Mexico City boasted a thriving press at the outset of the war.
Newspapers flourished on both sides of the political divide. Readers of a Conservative bent could choose between *El Eco Nacional,*
the *Diario de Avisos, La Sociedad,* and *El Heraldo.* Conversely, *El Monitor Republicano* and *El Estandarte* reflected the Liberal point of view.
El Siglo XIX stood out as the voice of moderation in an increasingly polarized political climate. In terms of content, newspapers
combined polemic with a digest of reports carried by other, usually
uncited, periodicals. Meanwhile, the weekly *La Cruz* dedicated itself to religious matters and their connection to politics, the abstract
nature of its discussion contrasting with the pithy presentation of
the secular papers. Given the variety of viewpoints the press represented, newspapers provided a printed medium for public debate.
For example, in September 1857 the Liberal *El Estandarte* prodded
the Conservative *El Eco Nacional* to argue the merits of the constitution. While *El Eco* flatly rejected the challenge, exchanges between
rival papers could be intense, even bitter. The most strident publication of all was *La Sociedad,* whose editor, the noted journalist and
author José María Roa Bárcena, zealously championed the Conservative cause. *La Sociedad* predicted late in December 1857 that the
War of the Reform would be a fight to the death.[42] It subsequently
declared that the Conservative government was the true national
regime, standing, with the support of public opinion, to defend the

cause of justice and the social interests of the people. Then, as a final point in the concluding editorial of a series entitled "Reflections on the governments applied to the Republic," *La Sociedad* accused the Liberals of an unhealthy fascination with the United States. To make its point, the essay played up the differences between Hispanic and Anglo-American cultures, and blamed the ills of the Mexican federal system on its being an alien, North American import.[43]

During the opening months of the war one paper after another closed under pressure from Zuloaga. While Liberal publications all but disappeared, the Conservative press continued to publish, but not always to the government's liking. Such was the case with *La Cruz*. Its editor, the prominent writer Joaquín Pesado, boldly signed all of his political columns. Each one advanced an articulate, intransigent defense of the interests of religion and the Catholic Church. Pesado argued for the absolute liberty of the church from all temporal authority, including the Conservative regime. He went so far as to call for theocracy, and thus indirectly challenged the legitimacy of the military leadership. A subsequent column pronounced insurrection to be a just response to tyranny. Pesado might have been referring to the threat that Liberalism posed to the national interest as he saw it, but he also could have been taking a jab at the increasingly insecure and dictatorial Zuloaga. Until that time Zuloaga had been content with fining opposition newspapers, but Pesado's candor apparently proved too much to bear, and in mid-July 1858 Zuloaga moved to directly censor the press. The surviving Liberal papers ceased publication altogether, as did *La Cruz*, its final edition explaining the journal's demise as a matter of "circumstances beyond our control."[44] For the reading public, Zuloaga's action reduced a once-vibrant press to two printed sources of information: the government's *Diario Oficial*, which published decrees, regulations, and official announcements, and *La Sociedad*, whose doctrinaire stance had assured its survival.

For the remainder of the war *La Sociedad* served as Mexico City's newspaper of record. Its editorial pronouncements aside, the paper regaled its readership with breathless accounts of Conservative battlefield victories. The surrender of Liberal general Manuel Doblado to Luis Gonzaga Osollo at Guanajuato in June 1858 merited a three-page article that not only recounted the action but also listed in detail who and what was captured, and provided a copy of the terms of capitulation. *La Sociedad's* reporting on military developments presented a quasi-mythical view of the war. Nearly every week brought another story of near-invincible troops led by brave commanders, though never any explanation as to why the war dragged on in the face of such military superiority. La Sociedad anointed as heroes the dynamic young generals leading the Conservative offensive in the states north of the capital, Osollo and Miramón. The former's death in June 1858 elicited a front-page eulogy, complete with an ode especially composed by Roa Bárcena, and for weeks afterward readers submitted poems dedicated to the fallen general. Portraits of the martyr, the paper advertised, could be had for four *centavos* (cents) from the Imprenta Litográfica de Decaen.[45]

The extent to which La Sociedad eulogized Osollo paled in comparison to its subsequent deification of Miramón. Indeed, Miramón's rise as a political figure can be tracked through the nature and length of La Sociedad's coverage of his activities. Throughout the spring and summer of 1858, Miramón's conquests—Salamanca in March, Zacatecas and San Luis Potosí in April, his (disputed) victory over Santos Degollado at Atentique, Jalisco in July—were buried on the interior of the paper, confined to small columns. October, however, brought acclaim. The October 4 edition opened with a banner headline proclaiming "General Miramón's Triumph and [Liberal general Santiago] Vidaurri's Defeat," with the first two pages taken up by the announcement of Miramón's victory at Ahualco de Pinos, Zacatecas, on September 29. Later that month an article, entitled "Glory to Valor," described a ceremony held in Miramón's honor at the National Military Academy (*Colegio Militar*). The writer waxed poetic describing the young officers' "youthful aspect admired by the multitude." He went on to laud the "energy and mastery of the military science" that Miramón had displayed in his "short but glorious career."[46] By then Miramón had risen in the pages of La Sociedad from relative obscurity to become the paladin of conservatism. Miramón ascended to the presidency three months later, his media-driven celebrity combining with his military exploits to advance his political prospects.

The popularity of Osollo and Miramón, whom La Sociedad presented as the embodiments of Conservative aspirations, underscores how the press could impact public opinion about the War of the Reform. In years past newspapers reflecting one or another political predisposition had weighed in to sway sentiment on pressing issues like Mexico's tendentious relationship with the United States.[47] Mexico City's reading public, at a time when education, and hence literacy, marked social advancement, held great import for the government because their support of the war effort was crucial. Censorship ensured that media coverage thus fell into either polemic or mythology. At the same time, the press, more so than the spoken word, conveyed a concrete sense of the course of the war. The savvy reader still had to sift the facts from the propaganda.

Miramón's lionization in the pages of *La Sociedad* reveals the intersection of war and public identity. His celebrity derived both from his exploits and from his membership in the army. According to the corporatist logic that suffused Mexican society, and that the Conservatives struggled to preserve, an individual's public identity was a matter of ascription, one mediated not only by action but also by the groups to which the individual belonged. Family, neighborhood, occupation, region, and (in the case of Indians) ethnicity collectively expressed one's quality much as they had in the colonial era. The War of the Reform injected ideology, or more accurately, one's political affiliation, into this mix of criteria. Of course, political affiliation mattered in direct proportion to the individual's involvement in the war. Soldiers and politicians were most subject to categorization as "Liberal" or "Conservative," regardless of the true content of their personal beliefs. This was the case with Miramón, who *La Sociedad* encouraged the public to frame in terms of two overtly political attributes, his membership in the army and his opposition to the Liberals, to which all else was ancillary.

The average civilian in Mexico City could also find his or her identity politicized because the Conservative desire to hold on to the capital created a climate in which the word "Liberal" signified all things treasonous. For this reason Mateo Aguirre, the shopkeeper whom a former neighbor had denounced to the police in May 1859, landed in a Mexico City jail. The ensuing investigation mapped a life on the margins of national politics. In 1853 Aguirre had worked as the inspector of his *cuartel*, a position that linked him then and thereafter with political affairs, though not with Liberalism, since he served the very government the Liberals would supplant two years later. Following the Liberal takeover, according to the police chief, Aguirre had "caused trouble" during local elections. The chief's vague accusation conveys little sense of Aguirre's activities beyond the suggestion that the former inspector remained politically active, or grew more so, after the Liberals came to power. In 1856 Aguirre served in the National Guard, and though he held the rank of captain, he left after serving less than two months to tend to his business, or so he claimed. Nevertheless, his time in the National Guard associated him with the Liberal project inasmuch as the Liberals had organized the guard as a counterbalance to the army. Aguirre's departure from Mexico City for the suburb of San

Antonio in October 1858, just before Liberal forces launched the first of their two attacks on the capital, added to the circumstantial evidence of his guilt. Set against the ideological backdrop of the War of the Reform, Aguirre's past suggested he might be a crypto-Liberal, but the accusation of having bribed his neighbor to join the Liberals could not be corroborated. The lead investigator dismissed the case for lack of evidence.[48]

Men's and Women's Roles during the War

As a man, Mateo Aguirre was susceptible to running afoul of the law on matters of reputation because cultural tradition divided the social space into masculine and feminine spheres. Ingrained notions of masculinity upheld the idea of the man as the public face of the family, concomitantly assigning him a far greater degree of agency in worldly affairs than a woman enjoyed. Politics, the military, the professions, and trades constituted exclusively male pursuits. During the War of the Reform such agency carried a particular risk because jurisprudence, both Liberal and Conservative, held the man, and only the man, responsible for political crimes. Gender thereby factored into Aguirre's troubles, but it may also have been his salvation. Since official suspicion of his political loyalties did not extend to his wife, Dolores Herrera, the court regarded her as a witness and not as a co-conspirator. Her testimony contradicted the accusation of treason anonymously leveled at her husband. Financial extremity, she explained, had compelled her family to leave Mexico City in October 1858. She flatly dismissed the charge against Aguirre. He was, she declared, the victim of lies spread by the enemies "one naturally acquires in the course of serving as a functionary," alluding to Aguirre's tenure as inspector, and to spiteful neighbors who nursed grievances for years thereafter.[49]

Dolores Herrera's role in the investigation of Aguirre offers a fleeting glimpse into the impact of war on the life of a woman. The trial record suggests that the war affected her insofar as it did her husband. Custom and law defined her place in society as subordinate to Aguirre's. She might have contributed financially to the business, making the shop a joint property, but she had no control over it. Neither did she enjoy legal guardianship over their children, if they had any. Though a wide gulf of social rank separated her from Dolores, Concepción Lombardo de Miramón, the wife of General Miramón, likewise felt the touch of war through the demands it placed on her marriage. She found the prominence to which the war catapulted her husband a mixed blessing. Their first days in Chapultepec Palace after Miramón's elevation to the presidency brought her nothing but disruption. The necessities of the army, worries over public affairs, and the constant coming and going of counselors and friends conspired to separate her from her husband as completely as any military maneuver, driving her to lament, "Politics! Politics! What a terrible rival it is for the woman!"[50] Concepción and Dolores thus bore the same burden. Whether through death, imprisonment, or the incessant demands of politics, war threatened to deprive each of her husband, and her principal source of security.[51]

The War of the Reform also touched the life of women in Mexico City through Conservative defense of tradition, a reality that expressed itself in ways at once subtle and contradictory. Though Conservative law made no provision for civil divorce, it did recognize a woman's right to sue for custody of joint property when the husband wrongfully abandoned the marriage. Hence Manuela del Valle, a housewife from the neighborhood of San Agustín in south-central Mexico City whose husband had run away with her sister, appeared before the civil court of her *cuartel*. There she demanded the return of the horse her husband had left at a local boarding house. Because the case turned on the legitimacy of her marriage, and because Manuela lacked her marriage certificate, her neighbors Martín Posadas and Agustín Parra had to vouch for her. It seems she had no recourse to family. Alone and lacking resources, she checked herself into the Convent of San Lorenzo, in the capital's northwest corner.[52]

Convents offered women like Manuela a haven. They had operated in this way since the colonial era, when they developed into complex establishments that enabled women to exercise a degree of self-determination within an otherwise rigidly patriarchal society.[53] As Manuela demonstrated, the residents of a convent were not necessarily nuns. Lay women seeking temporary seclusion from the outside world for whatever reason routinely consigned themselves to convents, and they could stay so long as they respected the rules and did not otherwise disrupt convent life.[54] Behind the walls of the Convent of San Lorenzo, Manuela could regain her composure, removed from her neighborhood and isolated, for the moment, from local rumor. The convent also provided her with room and board in a moment of financial distress, and female consolation to assuage the hurt of betrayal. A devout Catholic, General Miramón's wife likewise turned to a convent in her time of need. Disconsolate at her husband's departure to lead yet another campaign barely two weeks after his inauguration and less than a year into their marriage, she retreated to the Convent of the Incarnation, two blocks north of the *Zócalo,* where her aunt resided as a cloistered nun.[55] For Concepción and Manuela alike, Conservative rule reinforced their subordination but also preserved the convent that each resorted to as an exclusively feminine institution, one that offered emotional and physical refuge to women of all stations.

The convent could also serve as a metaphor for Mexico City under the Conservatives. Their determined effort to defeat the Liberals threw up a figurative wall around the capital, sheltering its residents from the world beyond. That edifice began to crack in the summer of 1860. Guanajuato fell to the Liberals that July, followed by Liberal victories in Jalisco and Veracruz. Each reverse seemingly translated into an increasingly regimented and exacting administration of the city. A November issue of the *Diario oficial del ejército* announced the most sizeable extraordinary contribution to date, and that the public's movements were to be governed by a restrictive passport law in the interests of public safety. The passport decree, consisting of 14 separate articles, made exceptions only for military commanders, and "the Indians and poor people who bring into the city foodstuffs and other articles of first necessity." Though vendors could import such items free of all but municipal taxes, none of the aforementioned goods could leave the city.[56] The population could only wait and wonder at the capital's uncertain fate.

THE UNDERCURRENT OF WAR IN CIVILIAN LIFE

By that time the Liberal noose around Mexico City grew tighter every day. In a last-ditch effort to halt the enemy's advance, Miramón led his weakened army north out of the city into Mexico State, but Liberal forces under Jesús González Ortega routed them two days before Christmas in the Battle of San Miguel Capulapan. "All Mexico City lived in terror," remembered Miramón's wife, frightened by the possibility that the city might be sacked.[57] As it turned out, the Liberals left Mexico City unmolested because they needed the legitimacy it conferred to their claim to rule just as the Conservatives had. Neither did the city's residents invite retribution by resisting the Liberal takeover. González Ortega entered the capital without incident at the head of a 28,000-man army. The *ayuntamiento* met the Liberal commander at the Puente de Santiago, congratulated him, and surrendered the standard of the city in a symbolic act of submission. Mexico City then prepared to welcome the regime cast from the capital three years before by a war that ended where it had begun. Concepción and her beloved husband Miramón meanwhile awaited in Veracruz the ship that would carry them into European exile.

The War of the Reform affected the people of Mexico City in ways more understated than direct. Recurrent taxation displayed the most visible effect of war, as did press censorship, yet only the latter marked an immediate change induced by military imperative. The extraction of revenue, however frequent, never amounted to war-induced government intervention in the economy. Municipal government reflected the local administrative dimension of the Conservative war effort, but nevertheless relied on civilian cooperation. Moreover, with the exception of supplementary taxation, none of the aforementioned developments altered the rhythm of the street, marketplace, or home. The broadest impact of the war on Mexico City derived from the stability engendered by the Conservative war effort. War swirled about the city, but within the city, behind the Conservative defenses, the war formed an undercurrent that only occasionally welled up to disrupt civilian affairs. This was so not only because the Conservative army proved so effective at keeping its Liberal opponent at bay, or because combat remained largely confined to rural areas. The city remained at peace in part because the Conservative regimes depended on the capital for their survival and so worked to preserve an orderly status quo. Civilians in return generally cooperated with these governments, or at least did not outwardly oppose them. For all its destructive fury, the War of the Reform fell far short of demanding the regimentation of everyday of life in Mexico City. There politics, not military action, connected the civilian to civil war.

NOTES

This chapter revises and expands upon a series of presentations made to the *Grupo investigador sobre la ciudad de México en tiempo de guerra* between 1997 and 1998, and published as Daniel S. Haworth, "Desde los baluartes conservadores: la ciudad de México y la Guerra de Reforma (1857–1860)," *Relaciones* 84, vol. XXI (otoño 2000): 95–132. Reprinted with permission.

1. For recent surveys of civil war in nineteenth-century Latin America, see *Rumours of Wars: Civil Conflict in Nineteenth-Century Latin America*, ed. Rebecca Earle (London: Institute for Latin American Studies, University of London, 2000); Fernando López-Alvez, *State Formation and Democracy*

in Latin America, 1810–1900 (Durham, NC: Duke University Press, 2000); and Miguel Angel Centeno, *Blood and Debt: War and the Nation-State in Latin America* (State College: Pennsylvania State University Press, 2002).

2. For a detailed treatment of the federalist-centralist controversy, see Timothy Anna, *Forging Mexico: 1821–1835* (Lincoln: University of Nebraska Press, 1998).

On popular participation in nineteenth-century political violence, see Torcuato S. Di Tella, *National Popular Politics in Early Independent Mexico, 1821–1847* (Albuquerque: University of New Mexico Press, 1996); Florencia Mallon, *Peasant and Nation: The Making of Postcolonial Mexico and Peru,* (Berkeley: University of California Press, 1995); Peter F. Guardino, *Peasants, Politics, and the Formation of Mexico's National State: Guerrero, 1800–1857* (Stanford: Stanford University Press, 1996); and Guy P. C. Thomson and David La France, *Patriotism, Politics, and Popular Liberalism in Nineteenth-Century Mexico. Juan Francisco Lucas and the Puebla Sierra* (Wilmington, DE.: Scholarly Resources, 1999); Nelson Reed, *The Caste War of Yucatán,* rev. ed. (Stanford: Stanford University Press, 2001); and Michael Ducey, *A Nation of Villages: Riot and Rebellion in the Mexican Huastesca, 1750–1850* (Tucson: University of Arizona Press, 2004).

Despite its frequency, scholars of Mexican history have yet to fully study the *pronunciamiento.* The most useful examination of this phenomenon remains Michael P. Costeloe, "The Triangular Revolt in Mexico and the Fall of Anastasio Bustamante, August-October 1841," *Journal of Latin American History* 20:2 (November 1988): 337–360.

3. Miguel Angel Centeno makes this observation for all of Latin America. See Centeno, *Blood and Debt,* 130.

4. On the ideology and evolution of Liberalism in nineteenth-century Mexico, see Charles A. Hale, *Mexican Liberalism in the Age of Mora, 1821–1853* (New Haven, CT: Yale University Press, 1968), as well as his *The Transformation of Liberalism in Late Nineteenth-Century Mexico* (Princeton: Princeton University Press, 1989). See also Jesús Reyes Heroles, *El Liberalismo mexicano,* 3rd ed., 3 vols. (Mexico City: Fondo de Cultura Económica, 1988); Antonio Annino and Raymond Buve, coords., *El Liberalismo en México* (Münster and Hamburg: Asociación de Historiadores Latinoamericanistas Europeos, 1993); and Enrique Montalvo Ortega, coord., *El Águila Bifronte: Poder y Liberalismo en México* (Mexico City: Instituto Nacional de Antropología e Historia, 1995).

The (as yet) definitive study of Mexican conservatism remains Alfonso Noriega, *El pensamiento conservador y el conservadurismo mexicano,* 2 vols. (Mexico City: Universidad Nacional Autónoma de México, Instituto de Investigaciones Jurídicas, 1972); see also Will Fowler and Humberto Morales, coords., *El Conservadurismo Mexicano en el siglo XIX* (Puebla and St. Andrew's: Universidad Autónoma de Puebla/University of St. Andrew's, 1999).

Moderates have received much less attention from historians. For a comprehensive study of moderates during the Reform, see Silvestre Villegas Revueltas, *El liberalismo moderado en México, 1852–1864* (Mexico City: Universidad Nacional Autónoma de México, 1997). On the ideas and activities of moderates prior to the Reform, see Will Fowler, *Mexico in the Age of Proposals, 1821–1853* (Westport, CT: Greenwood, 1998), and María Laura Solares Robles, *Una revolución pacífica: Biografía política de Manuel Gómez Pedraza* (Mexico City: Instituto de Investigaciones Dr. José María Luis Mora, 1996).

5. See Mallon, *Peasant and Nation;* Guardino, *Peasants, Politics;* Thomson and La France, *Patriotism, Politics, and Popular Liberalism.*

6. The frequently antagonistic relationship between Mexico City and the indigenous settlements on its outskirts is covered in Andrés Lira González, *Comunidades indígenas frente a la Ciudad de México: Tenochtitlán y Tlatelolco, sus pueblos y barrios, 1812–1919* (Zamora: El Colegio de Michoacán, 1983).

7. The estimate of Mexico City's population comes from Marcos Arróniz, *Manual del viajero en México* (1858; reprint, Mexico City: Instituto Mora, 1991), 38. Regarding the demography and residence patterns of nineteenth-century Mexico City, see Sonia Pérez Toledo et al., *Población y estructura social de la Ciudad de México, 1790–1842* (Mexico City: Universidad Autónoma Metropolitana, Unidad Iztapalapa, División de Ciencias Sociales y Humanidades, Departamento de Filosofía: Consejo Nacional de Ciencia y Tecnología, 2004).

8. Arróniz, *Manual del viajero*, 38–39.

9. José María Vigil, *La Reforma*, vol. 5 of *México a través de los siglos*, ed. Vicente Riva Palacio (1888; reprint, Mexico City: Editorial Cumbre, 1975) [hereafter cited as *MATS*, 5], 326–328; *La Sociedad*, October 21, 1858. Unless otherwise noted, all newspapers cited were published in Mexico City.

10. Concepción Lombardo de Miramón, *Memorias* (Mexico City: Editorial Porrúa, 1981), 206–208; Vigil, *MATS*, 5:358–361.

11. Regarding the inaugural celebrations celebrating Zuloaga's accession, see Niceto de Zamacois, *Historia de México*, vol. 14 (Mexico City: J. F. Parres y Compañía, 1880), 731, 734; and Lombardo de Miramón, *Memorias*, 102.

12. *El Eco Nacional*, January 23, 1858.

13. On the *Celadores de Policía*, see the following files in Archivo Histórico del Ex-Ayuntamiento de México [hereafter cited as AHAM], Policía, Celadores, vol. 3264: "Estrada, D. Felipe pide se le coloque en una de estas plazas que antes servía," Mexico City, June 1858, file 81; "Zepeda, D. Luis solicita se le coloque en una de estas plazas por haber servido en el Resguardo municipal nocturno," Mexico City, June 1858, file 82; "Paredes, D. Patricio solicita una de las Plazas de Celadores de Policía," Mexico City, January 1859, file 84.

14. For examples of such legislation, see Manuel Dublán and José María Lozano, compilers, *Legislación mexicana o colección completa de las*

disposiciones legislativas expedidas desde la independencia de la república, 34 vols. (Mexico City: Imprenta del Comercio, 1876–1904), 7:632; and 8:295.

15. *Diccionario Porrúa de historia, biografía, y geografía de México*, 6th ed. (Mexico City: Editorial Porrúa, 1995), s.v. "Zuloaga, Félix"; Zamacois, *Historia de México*, 14:35; Ray F. Broussard, "Ignacio Comonfort: His Contributions to the Mexican Reform" (PhD diss., University of Texas at Austin, 1959), 61; Anselmo de la Portilla, *México en 1856 y 1857. Gobierno del General Comonfort* (1858; reprint, Mexico City: Instituto Nacional de Estudios Históricos de la Revolución Mexicana, 1987), 222; Portilla, *Historia de la revolución contra la dictadura del General Santa Anna. 1853–1855* (1856; reprint, Puebla: Editorial José M. Cajica, 1972), 233; Zamacois, *Historia de México*, 14:38.

16. *Diccionario Porrúa*, s.v. "Arango y Escandón, Alejandro"; Ariel Rodríguez Kuri, "Política e institucionalidad: el Ayuntamiento de México y la evolución del conflicto jurisdiccional, 1808–1850," in Regina Hernández Fanyuti, comp., *La Ciudad de México en la primera mitad del siglo XIX* (Mexico City: Instituto de Investigaciones Dr. José María Luis Mora, 1994), 2:87–88.

17. *Diccionario Porrúa*, s.v. "Gómez de la Cortina, José." Cortina's political outlook is described in *Biografía del exmo. sr. d. José M. Justo Gómez de la Cortina, conde de la Cortina, escrita por una comisión de la Sociedad Mexicana de Geografía y Estadística* (Mexico City: Imprenta de Boix, 1860).

18. *Diccionario Porrúa*, s.v. "Riva Palacio, Vicente."

19. José Antonio Serrano Ortega, *El contingente de sangre. Los gobiernos estatales y departamentales y los métodos de reclutamiento del ejército permanente mexicano, 1824–1844* (Mexico City: Instituto Nacional de Antropología e Historia, 1993), 133; and his "Levas, Tribunal de Vagos y Ayuntamiento: la ciudad de México, 1825–1836," in Carlos Illades and Ariel Rodríguez Kuri, comp., *Ciudad de México: instituciones, actores sociales y conflicto, 1774–1931* (Zamora: El Colegio de Michoacán, 1996).

20. Minutes of the Ayuntamiento of Mexico City, February 23, 1858, AHAM, Policía de Seguridad, vol. 3691, file 161.

21. [Miguel María] Azcárrate to Presidente del Ayuntamiento, Mexico City, July 20, 1858, AHAM, Policía de Seguridad, Resguardo Diurno, vol. 3691, file 160, fols. 1r-5r.

22. "Alexis de Gabriac to [French Foreign Minister]," Mexico City, July 2, 1858, in *Versión francesa de México: Informes diplomáticos*, trans. and ed. Lilia Díaz, 4 vols. (Mexico City: El Colegio de México, 1967), 2:27.

23. "Alexis de Gabriac to [French Foreign Minister]," Mexico City, August 1, 1858, in *Versión francesa*, 2:32.

24. See Richard Warren, "Desafío y trastorno en el gobierno municipal: el Ayuntamiento y la dinámica política nacional, 1821–1855," in Illades and Kuri, comp., *Ciudad de México, 1774–1931*.

25. Leonardo Pasquel, *Xalapeños distinguidos* (Mexico City: Editorial Citláltepetl), 591–597.

26. *Diccionário Porrúa*, s.v. "Murphy, Thomas."

27. See, for example, AHAM, Polícia de Seguridad, vol. 3691, file 162–163; *Boletín Oficial* (Mexico City), March, 20, 1859, 1; *Diario Oficial del Ejército*, November 15, 1860, 2.

28. Juan N. del Valle, *El Viajero en México, o sea la capital de la república cerrada en libro* (Mexico City: Castro, 1859), 32.

29. See del Valle, *El Viajero*, 33; regarding the inspector's responsibilities, see "Agustín Landes to [Juez Menor]," Mexico City, September 1, 1859, AHAM, Justicia, Juzgados Menores, vol. 2859, file 4, fol. 16r, and AHAM, Policía de seguridad, vol. 3691, file 161–163.

30. Recent scholarship has shown that government in nineteenth-century Latin America was hardly as top-down and elite dominated as originally supposed. See *Riots in the Cities: Popular Politics and the Urban Poor in Latin America, 1765–1910*, eds. Silvia M. Arrom and Servando Ortoll (Wilmington, DE: Scholarly Resources, 1996), especially Arrom, "Introduction: Rethinking Urban Politics in Latin America before the Populist Era," 1–16.

31. Luis Islas García, *Miramón: El caballero del infortunio* (Mexico City: Ediciones Jus, 1950), 120.

32. *El Eco Nacional*, May 18, 1858.

33. *La Sociedad*, January 5, 1859; see also *Boletín Oficial*, March 20, 1859.

34. *Diario Oficial del Ejército*, November 15, 1860.

35. *El Eco Nacional*, May 18, 1858.

36. *La Sociedad*, January 5, 1859, 3; see also *Boletín Oficial*, March 20, 1859. On tax farming in Mexico prior to the Reform, see Barbara A. Tennenbaum, *The Politics of Penury: Debt and Taxes in Mexico, 1821–1856* (Albuquerque: University of New Mexico Press, 1986).

37. On Zuloaga's anticonspiracy decree, see Vigil, *MATS*, 5:306–307; "[Ministro de la Guerra] to [Ministro de Gobernación]," copy, Mexico City, May [13], 1859, AHAM, Policía de Seguridad, vol. 3691, file 163, fol. 1r.

38. Arrom, "Introduction: Rethinking Urban Politics" in Arrom and Ortoll, eds., *Riots in the Cities*, 4, 8; "M[anuel] Silecio to Manuel Doblado," Mexico City, November, 17, 1855, in Genaro García and Carlos Pereyra, eds., *Documentos inéditos o muy raros para la historia de México* (Mexico City: Editorial Porrúa, 1974), vol. 56: La Revolución de Ayutla según el archivo del General Doblado, 413; see "Soldados del Ejército del Sur," lithograph in García and Pereyra, eds., *Documentos inéditos*, 412.

39. Regarding the night watch, see del Valle, *El Viajero*, 94, 100; evidence of secret police obtained from testimony of policeman Ysidrio Biar, Mexico City, August 3, 1858, Archivo General de la Nación, México/Guerra (hereafter cited as AGNM/G, vol. 105, exp. 1281, 83v.

40. "Contra Don Mateo Aguirre, por pertenecer a las filas del Enemigo," AGNM/G, vol. 32, file 259, fols. 199–220.

41. See Richard Salvucci, *Textiles and Capitalism in Mexico: An Economic History of the Obrajes, 1539–1840* (Princeton: Princeton University Press, 1987), 95, map 3.1.

42. *La Sociedad,* December 27, 1857.

43. *La Sociedad,* January 3 and 6, 1858. Roa Bárcena's argument is misleading, as recent scholarship has shown that federalism was a direct product of the historical development of Mexico. See Anna, *Forging Mexico.*

44. *La Cruz,* July 29, 1858.

45. *La Cruz,* June 25, 1858, 1. For poems, see *La Sociedad,* July 1 and 5, 1858. The advertisement appeared in *La Sociedad,* July 9, 1858.

46. For coverage of Miramón, see *La Sociedad,* March 12, April 21, April 22, July 10, October 4, and October 21, 1858.

47. See Gene M. Brack, *Mexico Views Manifest Destiny: An Essay on the Origins of the Mexican War* (Albuquerque: University of New Mexico Press, 1975).

48. AGNM/G, vol. 32, file 259. Aguirre's military record ensured that a military court would try him. Conservative law observed separate jurisdictions for civilian and military cases, and assigned all current and former soldiers, regular army and national guardsman, to court martial.

49. AGNM/G, vol. 32, file 259, fol. 204 v.

50. Lombardo de Miramón, *Memorias,* 183.

51. On the relative legal status of husbands and wives in nineteenth-century Mexico, see Silvia Marina Arrom, *The Women of Mexico City, 1790–1857* (Stanford: Stanford University Press, 1985). For an examination of patriarchy in nineteenth-century Latin America, see Elizabeth Dore, "One Step Forward, Two Steps Back: Gender and the State in the Long Nineteenth Century," in *Hidden Histories of Gender and the State in Latin America,* eds. Elizabeth Dore and Maxine Molyneaux (Durham, NC: Duke University Press, 2000), 3–32; and *La familia en Iberoamérica, 1550–1980,"* Pablo Rodríguez, coord. (Bogotá: Convenio Andrés Bello, Universidad Externado de Colombia, 2004). The continued use of colonial family law in independent Mexico is discussed in Arrom, *The Women of Mexico City,* 51, and Françoise Carner, "Esteriotipos femeninos en el siglo XIX," in *Presencia y transparencia de la mujer en la historia de México* (Mexico City: El Colegio de México, 1987), 96. See Susan Midgen Socolow, *The Women of Colonial Latin America* (Cambridge: Cambridge University Press, 2000) for a detailed survey of the status of colonial women.

52. "Declaración de testigos que rinde D[oñ]a Manuela del Valle," AHAM, Justicia, Juzgados Diversos, vol. 2963, file 1859.

53. Readers of Spanish will find an exhaustive catalog of life in Mexico's colonial era convents in Josefina Muriel, *Conventos de monjas en la Nueva España,* 2nd ed. (Mexico City: Editorial Jus, 1995); for an English-language survey of convent life in colonial Latin America, see Asunción Lavrin, "Female Religious," in *Cities and Society in Colonial Latin America,* eds. Luisa Schell Hoberman and Susan Midgen Socolow (Albuquerque: University of New Mexico Press, 1986), 165–195.

54. The term "convent" is used here as it is in the original documentation for Manuela's case. In the colonial era, a distinction was observed

between convents, which housed nuns exclusively, and *recogimientos*, which temporarily housed women lacking male protection or family support. The convent and *recogimiento* were similar in most other respects, which would explain their conflation in the court record, if indeed people in the 1850s continued to recognize the distinction between them. A concise comparison of convent and *recogimiento* can be found in Lavrin, "Female Religious," in Hoberman and Socolow, *Cities and Society*, 188–190; regarding the *recogimiento*, see Josefina Muriel, *Los recogimientos de mujeres* (Mexico City: Universidad Nacional Autónoma de México, 1974).

55. Lombardo de Miramón, *Memorias*, 184–185.

56. *Diario Oficial del Ejército*, November 15, 1860.

57. Lombardo de Miramón, *Memorias*, 285.

FIVE

The Brazilian Home Front during the War of the Triple Alliance, 1864–1870

Vitor Izecksohn and Peter M. Beattie

In the 1800s most Brazilians lived far from their national borders in coastal urban centers and plantation zones that insulated them from the depredations of foreign military incursions. Shortly after mid-century, however, the War of the Triple Alliance thrust upon them challenges that they had sidestepped during previous international wars of briefer duration and smaller scale. The length of the conflict (more than five years) as well as the need to mobilize and sustain many more men than any previous campaign on a distant and inhospitable front put the burdens of a modern conflict on the shoulders of the Brazilian imperial state and its citizenry for the first time. The struggle stretched the government's capacity to tax its citizens and to mobilize troops, capabilities crucial to the conduct of modern warfare. This process had profound implications for the civilian sociopolitical and socioeconomic order at home, far from the Paraguayan front.

The English term "front" historically referred to the foremost line or part of an army at war. The term "home front" came into existence during the mobilizations for the twentieth century's great wars to denote "an organized sector of activity," usually those home industrial and bureaucratic activities necessary to support men on a distant battlefield.[1] However contradictory the term, "home front" emphasized the connection between the organization and production of civilians who remained far from the lines of battle and the soldiers who fought to keep the enemy at a distance. Thus, to grasp the impact of the War of the Triple Alliance on Brazil's home front one must relate this experience to the war effort. Even though the conflict mobilized resources and labor on a much smaller scale than World War I and II, the Brazilian state had to attempt the organization of its home front on a scale heretofore unknown. This essay not only explores how the weak institutional capacity of the Brazilian constitutional monarchy shaped its conduct of the war at home and abroad, but also discusses how the war effort affected the lives of Brazilians who stayed behind and their relationship to those who left to fight.

RAISING AN ARMY

For the purposes of the analysis herein, it is sufficient to note that the War of the Triple Alliance derived from tensions between Paraguay and its neighbors that ultimately led Paraguay's president Francisco Solano López to order his army to invade Argentine and Brazilian territory.[2] The governments of Brazil, Argentina, and Uruguay then formed the Triple Alliance to defeat Paraguay, but domestic instability forced Uruguay and Argentina to withdraw most of their troops and left Brazil to bear the brunt of the war.[3] Even without its allies, Brazil dwarfed Paraguay by most standard measures such as population, trade volume, wealth, and productive capacity. This superiority led Brazilians to believe condescendingly that the war would be quickly won, but the Paraguayans fought a tenacious defensive campaign that precluded a speedy victory.[4]

To fight the war the Brazilian monarchy called up some 140,000 men to the Paraguayan front. This army, whose makeup reflected Brazil's history of African and Indian slavery and race mixture as men of all races and many former slaves served in its ranks, represented a rather small fraction (approximately 1.6 percent) of the country's estimated 9.1 million inhabitants in 1865. According to Brazil's 1872 census, only some 4.2 million of its population of 9.9 million (including slaves) were males of military age (15 to 39). If one takes this lower number, 140,000 mobilized still signifies only about 3.3 percent of Brazil's men and adolescents available for military service.[5] Nonetheless, this relatively minute mobilization required both a collective and bureaucratic effort that created serious and unanticipated strains for Brazil's social, institutional, and political fabric.

Much of the strain caused by wartime mobilization related to the centrality of slavery to the socioeconomic and political fabric of Brazil, the last nation to abolish slavery in the western hemisphere in 1888. Slavery's longevity derived in large part from Brazil's relative political stability in the nineteenth century, which contrasted starkly with the civil wars that followed independence in most Spanish American nations as well as the bloodiest breakdown of political authority in the western hemisphere, the U.S. Civil War (1861–1865). These conflicts weakened slavery or resulted in its outright abolition in much of the Americas. On the other hand, for Brazil, which had existed as a constitutional monarchy ever since its citizens won independence from Portugal in 1822, the reign of Pedro II (1840–1888) ushered in a period of peace and stability that helped sustain Brazilian slavery (and its legitimacy) through the late 1880s. Nonetheless, Brazil's slave population began to gradually drop during the 1850s as the state enforced laws that banned the international slave trade. According to the 1872 census, slaves (approximately 1.5 million) constituted some 15 percent of the national population; this represented a decline from the previous generation, when almost one-third of the country's inhabitants lived in bondage. The diminishing number of slaves, coupled with the increasing demand for troops required by the War of the Triple Alliance, diminished the status of Brazil's free poor civilians, changed the meaning of the war, and altered military service requirements for Brazilians at home.

At the war's outset, however, these potential consequences did not figure prominently in the minds of Brazilian citizens. When war broke out what concerned most Brazilians, rich and poor, was a sense of outrage that their national territory had been violated, and that Brazilian citizens had suffered well-publicized depredations at the hands of Paraguayan soldiers. The governor of Bahia articulated the patriotic mood and likened the Paraguayan campaign to a crusade against barbarity: "I hope you will enlist for this war of law against violence; of justice against arbitrariness, of civilization against barbarism, and of freedom against despotism."[6] As a result, many young men put aside their contempt for enlisted military service and volunteered in fits of nationalistic fervor to defend the honor of their homeland.

In spite of declarations like the one above, the number of Brazilians who enrolled in the army proved insufficient for the size of the task. This was partly due to the attitude widely held among Brazilians that military service as an enlisted man was unpalatable. Unlike the United States, where most men associated service in the armed forces with racial privilege and the duties of republican citizenship that emphasized voluntary enlistment in peace and wartime, military recruitment in mid-nineteenth-century Brazil relied heavily on coercion. Authorities practiced summary punishment (i.e., without trial) of males of all races who they considered troublemakers, vagrants, and nonhomicidal criminals. Government officers also used military impressment to make an example of men who offended public morality by abandoning their wives or seducing young women with marriage promises that they failed to honor, as Brazilian (and formerly Portuguese) law had long protected married men from impressment if they upheld their responsibility to provide for and to protect the honor of their wives and dependents. In addition, local political bosses penalized disobedient clients by sending them to serve in the army. In 1867, for example, a National Guard officer in Rio Bonito justified just such a decision with the following explanation: "His behavior as a guardsman and a citizen is abominable."[7] What's more, the brutal methods employed to capture military recruits resembled those used to capture runaway slaves and criminals. Even the living arrangements of soldiers approximated stereotypes of slave life. On large plantations, most slaves lived like soldiers in sexually segregated barracks-like housing, and as a result most free Brazilians typecast slaves and soldiers as immoral and uncouth because they were not "of family."[8] These unfavorable stereotypes plus the subordination demanded of common soldiers smacked of the servility expected of slaves, and insured that most Brazilians in the mid-nineteenth century loathed enlisted military service.

To address the shortfall in manpower, the imperial government created the Corps of Volunteers of the Fatherland in January 1865. Those young men who spontaneously presented themselves as volunteers henceforth would be entitled to enlistment bounties, and as discharged veterans they were to receive pensions, land grants, and preferences for government jobs. Parliament intended the measure to stimulate the willing enrollment of great numbers of troops in a short period, and government records list some 37,838 men as Volunteers of the Fatherland. While many of these men presented themselves for service to take advantage of the new benefits, authorities dragooned numerous others but officially designated them as Volunteers of the Fatherland in any case.[9]

Despite the attraction of new benefits and continuing impressment, the number of Brazilians serving as Volunteers of the Fatherland did not provide the necessary manpower to sustain the campaign against Paraguay. As a result, by 1866 the government had little choice but to call up National Guardsmen and members of its provincial police forces for frontline duty. Created in 1831, the National Guard was an auxiliary militia responsible for keeping peace at the local level. It also cooperated with the imperial army when major insurrections broke out, and helped local police to support the criminal justice system and guard against slave rebellions. Common free laborers tended to view National Guard officers as capable patrons whose authority bolstered their ability to protect clients from impersonal imperial authority. An 1850 decree issued by Parliament threatened this state of affairs because it allowed the government to call up National Guardsmen for regular military service in times of war. The monarchy did not implement the law on a large scale prior to the War of the Triple Alliance, but in 1866, when wartime manpower needs became preeminent, it used the 1850 legal precedent to justify calling up guardsmen.[10]

The creation of the Volunteers of the Fatherland and the call-up of National Guardsmen also created new forms of stratification that defied old social hierarchies within the army and larger Brazilian society. Local political bosses had sought out National Guard commissions to name their clients to guard posts, a status that exempted them from peacetime recruitment in the regular army. In return for this and other types of protection, bosses expected the submission and loyal support of clients at election time when conflicts between rival factions often flared. As a result, those poor free men who possessed influential patrons that could defend them from impressment belonged to the "protected" (*protegido*) poor, while those who could not formed part of the "unprotected" (*desprotegido*) poor, whose respectability was questionable, if not notorious. However, because the Volunteers of the Fatherland differentiated regular army troops from the new "volunteers," it called attention to the government's efforts to accommodate the status-conscious sensibilities of members of the protected poor who they hoped to attract to the ranks. The new practice of calling up National Guardsmen to serve at the Paraguayan front under the command of strangers came to be seen as a challenge to the norms, status, and habits of respectable free poor men who looked to their local patrons for protection and leadership. In an attempt to soften the blow the government issued legislation in August and October 1865 that granted guardsmen designated for regular wartime army service the same benefits promised to the Volunteers of the Fatherland, but most guardsmen considered the grant a poor consolation. Evidence indicates that authorities had to capture many guardsmen called up for wartime service at the front.[11]

Wartime mobilization also diminished the ability of Brazil's free poor to protect themselves and family members from military impressment, as illustrated in the 1866 cartoon from the northeastern province of Pernambuco reproduced below.[12] The caricature shows a "white" *matuto* or country bumpkin requesting the well-dressed, urbane Dr. Recife to help him to have his liberty restored. When Dr. Recife asks who apprehended him, the *matuto* replies that the local police authority "recruited" him as a "volunteer" because he did not vote for the right political party. The fact that the *matuto's* hands are bound and the police delegate has his hand on his sword highlights the authorities' common abuse of the term "volunteer" when designating recruits.[13]

The cartoonist's inclusion of the *matuto's* wife and children, who accompany him in his misfortune, also illustrates how abusive wartime recruitment threatened the honor of respectable poor heads of household. While many wives and children followed husbands and fathers to the front, recruitment also separated many wives

A *matuto*, or bumpkin, is forced to volunteer in this 1866 cartoon. (From *O Recife Illustrado*, Recife, December 16, 1866).

and consensual lovers (*amazias*) from their "natural" male protectors. Even though many single Brazilian women headed households and raised their children by means of licit employment, authorities commonly voiced the fear that poor women who had been separated from their husbands would turn to prostitution to support themselves, or at least that they would be more vulnerable to aggressive male sexual abuse. Male household heads thus provided protection in two basic ways: first, they shielded their wives and dependents from the sexual advances of other males; second, through the dint of their labor they provided housing and sustenance for their household.

The imperial regime's decision to include large numbers of slaves as soldiers for the war further clouded attempts to respect traditional lines of social stratification. The low status of soldiering in Brazil, and its mostly nonwhite citizenry, led government officials to abandon attempts to segregate troops on the basis of race by the mid-1800s, but legally slaves could not be recruited for military service because they were the property of citizens. In 1866, however, Parliament issued a legislation that gave the government permission to purchase slaves who would be manumitted if they served in the military at the Paraguayan front. The decree also encouraged slave-owning patriots to donate slaves to the war effort, or to present slaves as substitutes for themselves, relatives, or friends recruited for the war. As the war dragged on, the government even tapped homicide convicts on the penal colony of Fernando de Noronha Island for service at the front. Again, authorities made little effort to segregate these men, considered to spring from the most dishonorable strata of society, from those troops of respectable status in the ranks. Indeed, the high command at the Brazilian front eventually disbanded all black volunteer units raised in the provinces of Bahia and Pernambuco, and integrated them into multiracial units.[14]

Wartime mobilization also posed a challenge to hierarchies of age and gender. Many children became army enlisted men when the government reassigned apprentices from arsenal schools to the frontlines, where the boys served as adjutants, drummer boys, and soldiers. Some infants even followed their parents to the battlefields. Alfredo d'Escragnolle Taunay, a Brazilian officer at the front, noted that many mothers who accompanied the troops carried babies (*crianças de colo*) in their arms. In these cases, whole families marched with soldiers to the front and as a result some women engaged in fighting.[15] The Count D'Eu, the Emperor Pedro II's Austrian son-in-law and commander of the Brazilian army during the final phase of the war, observed "the interminable rear guard procession of women, carts, and animals loaded with the most extraordinary baggage."[16] While some soldiers and a few officers traveled to the front with their spouses, other lonely soldiers and officers had campaign wives (*esposas de campanha*), in other words, women who they lived with as a spouse during their time at the front. For most soldiers, however, the war was not a family affair but rather a trying experience that separated them from kith and kin for years.

The government's attempt to create a more respectable class of soldiers through the creation of the Volunteers of the Fatherland Corps did not succeed. Eventually, recruitment policies opened the ranks of the imperial military to individuals whose low status would have normally excluded them from the regular peacetime army. As the 1866 *matuto* cartoon from Pernambuco illustrated, many "volunteers" had been pressed into service against their will in a fashion that violated traditional ideas of the propriety and rights of free men. The danger of the front, traditional associations of enlisted military service with low status and criminality, and the integration of men from such different backgrounds in the enlisted ranks all contributed to make many Brazilians loath to cooperate with mobilization efforts. Such efforts, in turn, had other significant ramifications for Brazilians distant from the front.

MOBILIZATION AND THE HOME FRONT

Mobilization for the War of the Triple Alliance not only impacted Brazilians who stayed behind, but the government as well. The monarchy found the war a costly endeavor. The Ministry of War's expenditures doubled between 1863 and 1870, forcing the national debt to grow four times the amount in relation to 1863 and 1864. The War Ministry's budget mushroomed from 21.9 percent of public spending in 1864 to 49.5 percent in 1865, and this percentage never dropped below 41 percent during the years of the conflict. Wartime military spending cost Brazilians the rough equivalent of 11 years of tax revenues based on prewar budgets.[17] To defray the costs of the war, Brazilian policy makers did not squeeze their citizens by raising taxes—a move likely dictated by the unpopular methods of recruitment discussed later in this section. Instead, and unlike their landlocked Paraguayan adversaries, the Brazilian government borrowed funds from European (mostly English) lenders, and it also prescribed a moderate tariff hike on imports. The former measure, however, led to debt, higher taxes, and economic stagnation following the war, while the latter raised the costs of many basic and luxury imported goods that adversely affected consumers of all classes.[18]

Meanwhile, most Brazilians distant from the front carried on with their lives as best they could. While scarcity was not the norm in coastal areas where the ability to import goods allowed residents to overcome whatever shortfalls recruitment or other factors caused in local production, several inland regions did experience shortages in the supply of food and other products as a result of the war. The situation was worse in the western interior province of Mato Grosso, where the Paraguayan invasion disrupted many economic activities, especially cattle-raising. Natural calamities also adversely affected production. For example, exceptional rainfalls in the neighboring province of Goiás lessened the production of manioc flour (the main starch in the Brazilian diet of the era), forcing the government to buy and transport rice, all of which increased the costs of normal patterns of consumption.

The misfortunes of those civilians who experienced periodic shortages of typical items of consumption did not compare, however, to the situation of Brazilian soldiers on the frontlines, where the lack of adequate nutrition, medical treatment, clothing, footwear, and portable housing made their lives miserable. The ordeal of the expeditionary forces in Mato Grosso typified what Brazilian soldiers had to endure. Describing their terrible conditions in February 1867, its commander Carlos de Moraes Camisão reported:

The question of alimentation has been the most significant obstacle to troop movements at the front because it has not been possible to herd a sufficient number of cattle to support military operations. The food supply serves only for the troops' daily consumption because there are not enough cattle in the area and those that exist are widely scattered. Herding stray cattle is slow and difficult because we lack adequate horses and therefore, I have been obliged to take possession of the few horses remaining in the First Calvary Regiment whose troops currently have no mounts.[19]

A moving army on a distant, sparsely inhabited front required ample mobile food supplies like cattle to remain militarily effective, and Paraguayan raiders plundered these resources whenever they could to hinder their enemies' movements.

The war years may have proved difficult for many who stayed behind as well as for the troops, but a privileged few—namely those with connections and capital—prospered because of government contracts to supply goods, services, and slaves that the armed services required. A small portion of these expenditures benefited home front laborers employed by government contractors. Army arsenal tailors, for example, parceled out much of the process of uniform-making to poor female seamstresses, a practice that army reports to the Parliament often likened to a productive form of public charity.[20] In addition, the coerced labor of slaves and criminals who remained free from the clutches of recruitment agents contributed to the war effort. The company of convict cobblers on the penal colony island of Fernando de Noronha churned out new boots for the troops, and army-owned slaves at the army's ironworks in Ipanema, São Paulo, worked alongside free workers and soldiers to produce musket and cannon balls.

The War of the Triple Alliance also benefited some incipient industries—textiles, for example, had gained toeholds in Rio de Janeiro and Bahia in the 1850s and 1860s—as the imperial government prescribed the aforementioned small hike in tariff rates on imports that protected them to some extent from foreign competition. Still, Brazilians remained heavily dependant on imported cloth and apparel for basic products such as soldiers' uniforms, not to mention modern arms, and Brazilian contractors complained bitterly that the government imported shoddy goods from abroad rather than tender more contracts to native entrepreneurs. Moreover, the war's overall stimulus to industrialize Brazil's economy and strengthen the state's extractive power proved far more modest than that which the U.S. Civil War gave to already developed Union industries.[21]

Home front production may have brought a new dynamism and organizational apparatus to Brazil's productive capacities, but military recruitment often proved a disruptive force. Males of military age would often flee if police or National Guard units approached local communities out of fear that they would be dragooned for embarkation to the front. Newspaper cartoons showed Brazil's urban centers abandoned and full of wild animals, while men fleeing military service camped out in the wilderness to hide from recruitment agents. The phrase "club and rope recruit" became part of the popular vocabulary on the home front, and it described the crude methods gangs of recruiters used to subdue and secure future soldiers. Armed and aggressive, impressment gangs had little incentive to hold back because they were paid only when they presented new recruits to army depositories. These impressment sweeps sometimes led to violent conflicts between recruiters and their prey, as when those dragooned for imperial military service resisted their captors, or when groups attacked press gangs to free captured relatives and friends.

As the war dragged on, many sectors of Brazilian society reacted against the increasing demands for military manpower. Planters and manufacturers sought to deter recruitment near their farms and businesses because it affected the provision of free labor at a time when the slave population was aging and dwindling. Local leaders complained that the removal of local militia, police, and military forces to fight at the front left them more vulnerable to slave rebellion and criminal activity. The combined reactions of local elites and respectable poor families created great tensions between the central government and provincial authorities that commonly came to a head in disputes over the military exemption status of men caught up in coercive recruitment sweeps.[22]

Short of desertion, the most common way to escape the military once government agents apprehended a recruit involved proving one's legal exemption. Parliament recognized some wartime exemptions to protect men with work skills crucial to the economy, such as railway workers, for example. Desertion, however, became increasingly common as the population's dissatisfaction with the war grew. By 1867, as the war entered its third year, a National Guard commander in the province of Rio Grande do Sul warned about the rising tide of public cynicism when he wrote that "the people have arrived at a distressing state of demoralization because parents themselves are now advising their sons to desert [the army]."[23] Desertion also escalated as wartime manpower demands began to undermine the ability of National Guard commanders to protect clients from recruitment. Indeed, most deserters came from National Guardsmen called up for service at the front and those individuals pressed into service against their will. Approximately 30 percent of National Guardsmen who initially reported for wartime duty in Paraguay deserted before the army could embark them to the front. Many more guardsmen simply failed to report for duty. An 1865 report presented by the governor of the northeastern province of Maranhão's governor illustrates the timing of desertion. From a total of 910 Maranhense guardsmen designated to transfer to the army, only 546 (60 percent) embarked for the front.[24]

Feigned illness and self-inflicted mutilation further hampered the imperial state's recruitment capabilities, as the following case illustrates. In 1869 the governor of the northeastern province of Ceará reported to the War Ministry that four army recruits had "made themselves useless for military service by cutting their Achilles tendons." One can only imagine the dread that drove these men to such desperate and painful extremes. Because the army's penal code considered self-mutilation a crime, the War Ministry recommended that the recruits submit to a court martial in Ceará. Available documentation does not reveal the crippled troops' ultimate fate, but the War Ministry's decision to prosecute them was likely intended to discourage others who might want to follow their harrowing example.[25]

Episodes like the one recounted above did not win public sympathy for the government's crude efforts to prosecute the campaign, and regional disparities in troop mobilization exacerbated such sentiments as the war progressed. While citizens in northeastern provinces resented sending a disproportionate number of their young men to fight a campaign hundreds of miles from their homes, those from the southernmost parts of Brazil felt even more overwhelmed. The sense of distress was particularly acute in Rio Grande do Sul, which had been invaded by Paraguayan troops and whose sons bore the bulk of wartime sacrifices. The anger of Rio Grandeses focused especially on Brazil's most populous province, Minas Gerais, an interior region rich in mines and fertile farmlands. Minas's mountainous topography and the considerable political influence it wielded within Parliament enabled its authorities to contribute a disproportionately low number of troops for the war. According to an 1872 War Ministry report, Minas Gerais had only contributed 4,070 recruits for the war despite having more than 20 percent of the nation's inhabitants, while Rio Grande do Sul, with less than 5 percent of the population, had made available 4,483 men.[26] Such disparity did not go unnoticed. An 1867 Rio Grande do Sul cartoon compared everyday life in the two provinces. In Minas Gerais the artist depicted families dancing and enjoying the pleasures of a happy, peaceful life. By contrast, the cartoonist showed women in Rio Grande do Sul praying and mourning their dead loved ones who had fallen in battle.[27]

All these local and provincial conflicts had their counterpart at the national level between the two dominant political parties. The commander of Brazilian forces in Paraguay, the Marquis de Caxias, was also a senator and a member of the Conservative Party. Caxias complained that members of the incumbent Liberal

An 1867 Rio Grande do Sul cartoon compared everyday life in two provinces: In Minas Gerais, families dance and enjoy pleasures of a happy, peaceful life. In Rio Grande do Sul they pray and mourn their loved ones who have died in fighting. (*A Sentinella do Sul,* Porto Alegre, July 7, 1867).

Parliament used their political clout irresponsibly to intrigue with his officers, all of which undermined his authority at the front. Caxias warned the emperor that he would resign his command unless he rectified the situation. Fearful that Caxias' exit could undermine the unpopular war effort, the emperor used his constitutional powers to nominate a new Conservative cabinet and call for new elections.

As in the past, the result of the emperor's decision brought the opposition Conservative party to power, but it also fueled new conflicts across Brazil. Liberals accused the new Conservative cabinet of using electoral fraud to win the elections; one of their chief complaints was that Conservative authorities used threats of military recruitment to intimidate voters. Since there was no secret vote in Brazil at this time, local Conservative bosses could easily monitor votes and punish those who supported Liberal candidates. Indeed, the turmoil of this political transition amid a war led some to take advantage of the situation to settle old scores. As one Liberal senator fumed: "The legal authority disappeared and in its place ruled one entity known as the 'recruiter' (*recrutador*) . . . all those who claimed to be of the Conservative Party made themselves into recruiters . . . if they had vengeance to take, they asked for a squad saying that they planned to arrest John Doe, then proceeded to the house of their enemy and arrested him; [from this resulted] a conflict and a death."[28]

As a result of the 1868 elections and the recruitment abuses that accompanied them, relations between members of the Liberal and Conservative parties became increasingly rancorous. While Liberals had also used impressment to secure electoral victories in the past, the relative dominance of Conservative Parliaments during the Brazilian Empire (1822–1889) meant that supporters of the Liberal Party had more often been the victims of this practice. Some members of the Liberal Party could not be mollified by the new, more radical platform adopted by their leadership, which called for, among other things, the abolition of both military impressment and slavery. A splinter group of embittered Liberals formed a new organization—the Republican Party—which also adopted a critical stance against military recruitment. More significantly, this party represented a departure in Brazilian politics because it questioned the legitimacy of the constitutional monarchy and sought to use the ballot box to replace it with a republican system of governance. In short, wartime military impressment contributed to deepening political divisions that shaped the last two decades of constitutional monarchy and foreshadowed the promulgation of a republic in 1889.

WOMEN AND THE WAR

Military mobilization may have fomented conflict at several levels for Brazilians from all walks of life, but the enlistment of men for the War of the Triple Alliance provided new possibilities for Brazilian women of almost all classes to participate in public life. Most privileged women did not have to worry that their husbands or sons would go off to war,[29] but many of them did offer goods, services, money, and moral support to the war effort. Some wealthy females sponsored bazaars whose proceeds assisted the soldiers, while others produced bandages destined for the wounds of injured troops, or sewed flags to be sent to the front or displayed at patriotic celebrations. Journalists extolled these gender-appropriate patriotic roles as *"piedade feminil"* (feminine piety) which linked their actions to the works of church charity that stereotypically characterized the highest ideal of feminine public action in times of peace.[30] This did not entail a radical departure from assumptions about gender-appropriate behavior, but it likely afforded a breath of fresh air to many elite women whose roles were often limited to the domestic and religious spheres.

The experiences of poor, mostly illiterate women during the war are more difficult to analyze in a systematic fashion. Nonetheless, evidence from the home front indicates that many could not afford to follow traditional gender roles as they sought to provide for themselves and their families (especially if their husbands or older sons were off to war). The absence of many men in urban centers due to wartime mobilization and fears of impressment sweeps required poor women to carry out jobs that men ordinarily performed. The next caricature shows a National Guardsman apprehending a woman who has been driving a wood cart. She protests his actions, declaring, "Can't you see that I am a woman?" The guardsman insists that women do not drive wood carts, and informs her that a health inspection at the recruit depository will prove her exemption from military service. The cartoon highlights the gender subversion and danger that wartime mobilization could bring to the home front. Both the guardsman's manhandling and the ensuing inspection implied an examination of her private parts. This kind of treatment threatened this working woman's honor. In addition, the cartoon plays on the sexual danger that such an examination would entail for all respectable poor women who performed traditionally masculine work, and it more subtly suggested that some men resorted to the ruse of cross dressing to avoid military impressment.[31] Both implications hint at the ways that the war effort subverted gender norms and opened new employment fronts for free poor women who remained at home during the war. The new roles required that some gender stereotypes be adjusted, at least temporarily, and they exposed some working poor women to disparaging treatment and rhetoric.

The emerging anxieties about gender subversion on the home front led some male journalists to reaffirm that those Brazilian women who took on more public roles should do so in a proper fashion. The 1865 cartoon that appears on page 139, which contrasted the gender appropriateness of Brazilian women's patriotic volunteerism to the improper actions of the Paraguayan enemy, clearly illustrates this development. The artist has depicted well-dressed Brazilian women, including nuns, the epitome of feminine

In this cartoon, a working woman is harassed for both having a cart—because only men should have them—and for not being in the army, because she might be a man in disguise. (*O Cabrião*, São Paulo, December 2, 1866).

chastity and piety, signing up as Volunteers of the Fatherland with the symbol of Brazil, the Tupi Indian warrior, registering them in orderly fashion. The caption notes that "Brazil recruits warrioresses that will serve on the battlefield as camp followers, inspire courage, reward acts of bravery, encourage the wounded, work in infirmaries, prepare cartridges, laugh at bullets and scoff at cannon blasts." By contrast the caricaturist shows Paraguay's Solano López "recruiting children, old men, and women as instruments of war without caring that they will be lambs at the slaughter." The cartoon suggests that the difference between liberty and oppression lay in Brazil's ability to enforce suitable age and gender roles in war while allowing women to spontaneously express their patriotism as volunteers. Solano López, however, disrespected proper age and gender roles by forcing bedraggled women, children, and old men to serve in the war as regular soldiers.

The works of Alfredo d'Escragnolle Taunay shed further light on the social tensions and pain that military recruitment could wreak on the lives of young families in formation. In 1871 Taunay authored Brazil's most famous firsthand historical account of the War of the Triple Alliance—*A retirada da Laguna*—and several years later he wrote a lesser-known short story, "*Juca o tropeiro*" (Juca, the Muleteer), that treats the lives of the common folk who lived in Minas Gerais, the province that gained national renown for its disproportionately small troop contribution to the war effort. A stock Brazilian

This cartoon states that "Brazil recruits warrioresses that will serve on the battlefield as camp followers, inspire courage, reward acts of bravery, encourage the wounded, work in infirmaries, prepare cartridges, laugh at bullets and scoff at cannon blasts. . . ." ("Liberty and Oppression." 1865).

literary figure of the era, Juca was a *sertanejo* (backwoodsman), a carefree youth who took great pride in his knowledge of the frontier. Juca loved the traveling life of the muleteer, and Taunay described him as a "great companion, happy and popular" with his peers because of his bravery, affability, trustworthiness, and religiosity.

When not traveling to the distant frontier provinces of Mato Grosso and Goiás, Juca lived in Uberaba, a town in Minas Gerais that Taunay characterized as distant in both cultural and geographic terms from Brazil's civilized urban centers. His fiancé Babita also resided in Uberaba, but their marriage plans were put on hold when Juca was called up for military service in the war against Paraguay. Although Juca's membership in the local National Guard unit made him part of Uberaba's "protected poor," he reported for duty in the regular army. Juca reluctantly took an oath on the Bible and to the Brazilian flag required by law of all army recruits, but unlike so many of his compatriots he took seriously the promise to fulfill his patriotic service. Even when almost all those recruited with him deserted and slipped away into the sheltering frontier wilderness before marching to the distant Paraguayan front, Juca stayed with his regiment because he had given his word and would not break it.

Juca's military service kept him away from Uberaba for five years, during which he never heard a word from his beloved Babita. Upon returning home, however, Juca found out that Babita had married a friend of his because comrades who had returned from the war had informed her that Juca had been killed. At this point in the story Taunay informs his audience that in Uberaba "the soulless men who had trifled with Juca's honor trembled with fear" when they learned he had returned. He thus leads readers to expect a stereotypical act of blood vengeance by the veteran Juca to restore his besmirched honor that could require the murder of his friend and even his beloved Babita. The author, however, does not resort to this predictable literary drama; instead he has Juca judiciously come to the conclusion that there was not an intentional plot to betray him, so he forgives both his friend and his former fiancé. Nevertheless, Taunay made it clear that the experience of war abroad and lost love at home deeply affected Juca. He was never again the happy genial person he had once been because the sacrifices and disruptions of the war had hardened him considerably.

Taunay's short story recognizes the many personal sacrifices common Brazilian men and women stoically endured during the war, both at home and abroad. The tale also suggests a desire for a postwar reconciliation between resentful soldiers who returned from the front and those at home who had shirked their service or abused their authority to press men into duty. Taunay's decision to set his story in Minas Gerais was probably not accidental. Not only does the story reflect the deep social divisions wartime mobilization exacerbated at home, but it also suggests the need for a larger postwar reconciliation between the inhabitants of provinces like Rio Grande do Sul, where so many families sacrificed sons in the war, with those of Minas Gerais, who lost relatively few in the defense of Brazil's national honor.[32] Unfortunately the type of reconciliation that Taunay's story portends would not be easily achieved, as memories of the war thwarted efforts to reconcile disaffected political factions and reform military recruitment in the decades that followed.

CONCLUSION

As detailed in the preceding pages, mobilization for the War of the Triple Alliance had significant economic, political, and social repercussions for Brazilian civilians who stayed behind. Taken as a whole, these ramifications created a credibility deficit for the imperial state in the postbellum period clearly illustrated in the next cartoon, entitled "Attention, All Brazilians Above 19 Years Old." In 1874 Parliament passed a recruitment law that sought to implement a modern conscription system to replace the abuses of impressment. A draft lottery would ideally level Brazilians in terms of shouldering the burden of enlisted military service, but the mistrust engendered by the war with Paraguay proved too powerful a barrier to recruitment reform. The caricature shows the leader of the Emperor's Council of State in 1874, the Marquis of Caxias, who had led Brazil to victory in the War of the Triple Alliance, attempting to console the dejected Tupi Warrior who symbolized Brazil. In what approximates a crucifixion scene, he holds the Indian under a post commonly used to measure the height of recruits by the army. In his hand the Tupi warrior holds a parchment that reads "Brazil prepares itself for peace." To the side the artist portrays a dark vision of the recruitment lottery process and foregrounds the very instrument of the conscription lottery, a cylinder that randomly mixed different colored balls to determine who would be drafted. In the first scene in the left corner a young man has drawn a black ball in the lottery that designates his selection for military service. The cartoon then traces his military career: training, inspection, "baptism of blood" in battle, and ultimate dismemberment that at a young age incapacitates him for work. He, like many Brazilian disabled veterans of the War of the Triple Alliance, has ended up as a beggar instead of as a producer for the nation.

The cartoon expressed the cynicism about the draft that pervaded much of Brazilian society in the postwar period. The mistrust engendered by the War of the Triple Alliance remained a staunch barrier to military recruitment reform for the next four decades. For the "protected poor," the conscription lottery was akin to drawing lots to see whose son should serve a dangerous jail term. Moreover, the leveling implied by the draft lottery was

"Attention, All Brazilians Above 19 Years Old." This caricature depicts popular suspicions about the draft for military service instituted by the government in 1874. Such misgivings were a direct byproduct of recruitment during the War of the Triple Alliance.

anathema to the status-conscious orientation of most Brazilians, poor and rich alike. Ultimately, it took the events of World War I to overcome the reluctance of Brazilians to cooperate with a system of military conscription. The savagery and carnage engendered by that conflict in the heart of civilized Europe shook the confidence of Brazil's elites in the ability of diplomacy and geography to defend their national sovereignty. Most privileged Brazilians concluded that conscription was essential to secure their nation in an age of unabashed imperialism. At the same time, the government and its allies worked for years after the war with Paraguay to improve the conditions and terms of enlisted military service and to improve the public image of soldiering. In so doing, the Brazilian state finally overcame the unpleasant memories and legacies of coercive recruitment on the home front that remained as a legacy from the War of the Triple Alliance.

NOTES

1. See *The Oxford English Dictionary*'s Web site: http://dictionary.oed. com/cgi/entry/50090253/50090253se10?single=1&query_type=word&qu eryword=Home+Front&first=1&max_to_show=10&hilite=50090253se10.

2. For recent debate on the war's causes and course see Francisco Doratioto, *Maldita Guerra. Nova História da Guerra do Paraguai* (São Paulo: Cia. das Letras, 2002) and Thomas L. Whigham, *The Paraguayan War, Volume 1, Causes and Early Conflict* (Lincoln: University of Nebraska Press, 2002).

3. Ariel de la Fuente, *Children of Facundo: Caudillo and Gaucho Insurgency during the Argentine State-Formation Process (La Rioja, 1853–1870)* (Durham, NC: Duke University Press, 2000).

4. Diego Abente, "The War of the Triple Alliance: Three Explanatory Models," *Latin American Research Review* 22:2 (June 1987), 47–69.

5. Instituto Brasileiro de Geografia e Estatísticas (IBGE), *Estatísticas históricas do Brasil*, 2nd ed. (Rio de Janeiro: IBGE, 1990), 32–33.

6. Proclamação do Presidente da Bahia Luiz Antonio de Barboza Almeida, Arquivo Nacional do Rio de Janeiro, Série Guerra (code IG) IG-1–125, Salvador, January 7, 1865.

7. Superior Commander of the National Guard of Rio Bonito to the Vice President of Rio de Janeiro, Rio Bonito, Sept. 10, 1867, Arquivo Público do Rio de Janeiro, Documentos da Presidêda Província, 1862–1867, Collection 215–216, Guarda Nacional—Box 176.

8. Recent research, however, has shown that many more Brazilian slaves had church-sanctioned marriages and maintained a family life within bondage than previously thought. See Robert Slenes, *Na senzala uma flor: Esperanças e recordações na formação da família escrava. Brasil sudeste, século XIX* (Rio de Janeiro: Nova Fronteira, 1999).

9. The official number of Volunteers of the Fatherland is inflated. As the 1866 cartoon from Pernambuco later analyzed in this section and ample other evidence indicates, authorities often abused the term "volunteer" to cover up coercive recruitment. The government's data on wartime recruitment can be found in *Relatório da Repartição dos Negócios do Ministério da Guerra apresentado ao Parlamento* (Rio de Janeiro: Imprensa Nacional, 1872), annexos. For evidence of pressed soldiers who received the designation of "volunteers," see Peter M. Beattie, *The Tribute of Blood: Army, Honor, Race, and Nation, 1864–1945* (Durham, NC: Duke University Press, 2001), chapters 2 and 3.

10. On the Brazilian National Guard, see Fernando Uricoechea, *O Minotauro Imperial. A Burocratização do Estado Parimonial Brasileiro no Século XIX* (Rio de Janeiro: Difel, 1978).

11. The laws that equalized the advantages of National Guards to those of the Volunteers of the Fatherland appear in *Collecção das Decisões do Governo do Império do Brasil de 1865* (Rio de Janeiro, Typographia

nacional. Rua da Guarda Velha, 1865), tomo XXVIII, 580–581. For examples of the arrests of national guardsmen, see Beattie, *The Tribute of Blood*, 45–47.

12. Beattie, *The Tribute of Blood*, provides an overview of army recruitment from 1865 to 1945. For the Brazilian navy, see Álvaro Pereira do Nascimento, *A ressaca da marujada. Recrutamento e disciplina na Armada Imperial* (Rio de Janeiro: Arquivo Nacional, 2001).

13. *O Recife Illustrado*, Recife, December 16, 1866.

14. Hendrik Kraay, "Patriotic Mobilization in Brazil: The Zuavos and other Black Companies," in *I Die with My Country: Perspectives on the Paraguayan War, 1864–1870*, eds. Hendrik Kraay and Thomas L. Whigham (Lincoln: University of Nebraska Press, 2005), 61–80.

15. See Alfredo Escragnolle Taunay, *A retirada da Laguna*, trans. Ramiz Galvão, from the 3rd French ed., 5th Portuguese ed. (São Paulo: Typ. Ideal, 1919 [1871]).

16. Conde D'Eu to Consilheiro José Antonio Saraiva, May 20, 1869, Arquivo do Museu do Imperial, Pack 145, Document 7065.

17. Liberato de Castro Carreira, *História Financeira e Orçamentária do Império do Brasil desde a sua fundação, precedida de alguns apontamentos acerca de sua independência* (Rio de Janeiro: Imprensa Nacional, 1980), 402–462.

18. Richard Graham, "1850–1870," in *Brazil: Empire and Republic 1822–1930*, ed. Leslie Bethell (New York: Cambridge University Press, 1989), 133; Miguel Angel Centeno, *Blood and Debt: War and the Nation State in Latin America* (University Park: Pennsylvania State University Press, 2002), *passim*.

19. Camisão to Minister of War, Nioac, Mato Grosso, February 23, 1867, Arquivo Nacional, box IG-1–241, 23.

20. Graham, "1850–1870," 133.

21. Centeno, *Blood and Debt*, 116–126.

22. Fábio Faria Mendes, "Encargos, privilégios e direitos: o recrutamento militar no Brasil nos séculos XVIII e XIX," in *Nova História Militar Brasileira*, comps. Celso Castro, Vitor Izecksohn, and Hendrik Kraay (Rio de Janeiro: FGV/Bom Texto, 2004), 111–138.

23. Victorino José C. Montim to Francisco Inácio Marcondes Homem de Melo, Itaquá, Paraguay, April 13, 1867, Letter 49, in *Correspondência Oficial Sobre a Organização do Terceiro Corpo do Exército da Guerra do Paraguai*, Biblioteca Nacional, Seção de Manuscritos (4, 3, 21).

24. Lt. Colonel José Caetano Vaz Júnior to Counsilor José Antonio Saraiva, August 14, 1865. Arquivo Nacional, Sessão Estadual e Provincial, box IG-1–530, 76, quoted in Vitor Izecksohn, "Resistência ao recrutamento para o Exército durante as guerras Civil e do Paraguai: Brasil e Estados Unidos na década de 1860," in *Estudos Históricos* 27:1 (2001), 85.

25. Tenente Coronel Francisco Egidio Mora, Chefe de Seção da Repartição do Ajudante General to the Office of the Governor of Ceará, January 25, 1869, Arquivo Nacional de Rio de Janeiro, box IG-1–40, no page numbers.

26. *Relatório da Repatição dos Negócios do Ministério da Guerra apresentado ao Parlamento* (Rio de Janeiro: Typ. Universal de Laemmert, 1872), anexos.

27. *A Sentinella do Sul,* Porto Alegre, July 7, 1867. For a fuller analysis of this cartoon in the context of the war, see Vitor Izecksohn, *O Cerne da discórdia. A Guerra do Paraguai e o núcleo profissional do exército* (Rio de Janeiro: E-Papers, 2002), 183.

28. *Annaes do Senado Brasileiro* (Rio de Janeiro: Typ. Nacional, 1870), vol. 1–2 of 6 vols., June 28, 1869, 329.

29. A number of elite males volunteered and served at the front as officers, but most wealthy men stayed home and busied themselves with farms, businesses, or politics. More prosperous families could always pay for a pecuniary exemption for their loved ones to exempt them from service.

30. Wiebke Ipsen, "Delicate Citizenship—Gender and Nation Building in Brazil, 1865–1891" (PhD diss., University of California at Irvine, 2005), chapter 2.

31. *O Cabrião,* São Paulo, December 2, 1866.

32. Visconde de Taunay, *Visconde de Taunay: Páginas escolhidas* [Selection and presentation by Alberto de Oliveira and Jorge Jobim] (Rio de Janeiro, Carnier, 1922), 257; Peter M. Beattie, "National Identity and the Brazilian Folk: The Image of the *Sertanejo* in Taunay's *A retirada,* 1871," *Review of Latin American Studies* 4:1 (1991), 7–43.

SIX

Civilians and the War of the Pacific, 1879–1884

Bruce W. Farcau

Most Americans would assume that the War of the Pacific refers to the struggle against the Japanese in the Second World War. In Latin America, however, the term relates to the conflict that set Chile against Peru and Bolivia during the last quarter of the nineteenth century (1879–1884). This conflict was not fought nearly on the scale of the Pacific theater of the Second World War and did not result in the same toll in civilian lives caused by the Japanese massacres of millions in China, or the United States' strategic bombing campaign against Japan in which tens of thousands perished in a single night. Nonetheless, the inhabitants of all three countries involved in the earlier War of the Pacific paid a much heavier price for the conflict than the casualty count of the battles themselves, numbering *only* in the thousands, would imply.

Although the war's impact on the civilian population might appear to have been minimal, given that no major cities were devastated nor farmland or industrial areas laid to waste, the conflict profoundly affected victors as well as vanquished. Bolivia's early and ignominious exit from active campaigning deprived its citizens of faith in any government for years to come and ensured endemic political instability. The refusal of its ally, Peru, to surrender resulted in a virtual Chilean conquest of the country, which led to civil war between irreconcilable Peruvian nationalists and the

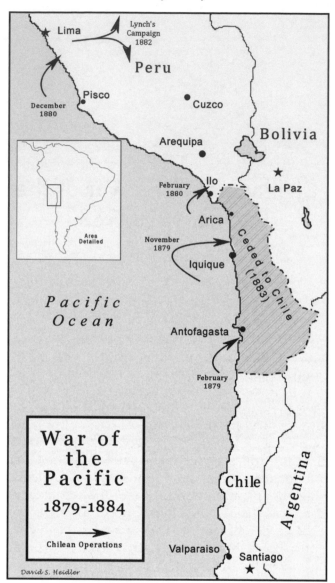

War of the Pacific. (Map courtesy of David S. Heidler).

collaborationist regime sponsored by Chile. Occupying Chilean forces instituted severe measures against civilians in an effort to end the conflict, but such actions vastly increased the suffering of Peruvian civilians anxious to be left alone. Finally, even victorious Chile paid for its hubris over time. The conflict not only brought economic disruption to the entire populace, but also increased the burdens of military service on the lower classes for the drawn-out guerrilla war in Peru. The government had to forcefully conscript the poor for that struggle once Chilean elites lost their enthusiasm for the war and began to use their power and influence to avoid enlistment.

ROOTS OF THE CONFLICT

The War of the Pacific has sometimes been called the "Ten Cents War" in reference to a modest municipal tax the local Bolivian administration in the tiny port of Antofagasta attempted to impose on businesses, mostly Chilean, that indulged in the extraction and exportation of nitrates from the coastal strip separating Chile from Peru. Nitrates had become a particularly valuable commodity in the late nineteenth century for the production of both fertilizers and munitions, and fortuitous circumstances had assured their presence in the virtually uninhabited and uninhabitable Atacama Desert (located in what is now northern Chile): an abundance of marine life in the waters of the Pacific Ocean just off the coast, which had attracted millions of nesting sea birds, coincided with the supreme dryness of the area (caused by the Andes Mountains pressing hard up against the coast and preventing rain from falling, literally for decades at a time). As a result, the birds' nitrate-rich droppings had accumulated over the centuries to a depth of tens of meters, allowing easy extraction. This twist of fate, which might have provided work and wealth for anyone with the initiative to take advantage of it, instead became the war's proximate cause for reasons all too common in the former Spanish colonial world.

As often happened in colonial regions, not just in Latin America but in Africa and Asia as well, the boundaries that separated administrative units had been drawn rather arbitrarily because any dispute in jurisdiction could always be referred to higher authorities in the mother country. When those colonial provinces achieved independence and became sovereign nations, the former boundaries became part of the "national patrimony," unalterable without grievous damage to national prestige. Higher authorities to whom to refer disputes over territory no longer existed. Disagreements that now arose in the interpretation of vaguely worded colonial divisions of land could only be resolved through recourse to arms.

In postcolonial South America, the portion of the Spanish empire that became Bolivia consisted of a vast territory, originally twice the size of California. Its relatively small population concentrated in the high plateau and valleys in the center of the country, leaving vast stretches of land along the fringes virtually uninhabited. Furthermore, Bolivia's predominantly Indian population was exceptionally sedentary, unwilling to move from ancestral lands despite overcrowding and infertile soils there, to the agriculturally rich eastern lowlands or the uninviting coastal desert with its vast mineral potential and access to the sea. Bolivian business interests likewise stayed close to home in the highlands, investing in the nation's traditional fortes, first silver mining and then tin when silver ran out. These factors facilitated the intrusion of Chilean capital and surplus labor into the Atacama Desert, and so Chileans largely discovered, developed, and exploited the nitrates and port facilities that served as Bolivia's only outlet to the world. The stage was set for the dynamic and increasingly powerful Chilean state to "rectify" the errors of the original division of the Spanish empire.

Chilean statesmen and their Peruvian counterparts had both long looked at Bolivia as the possible key to dominance of the western part of the continent. Chile and Peru appeared roughly evenly balanced in terms of population, economic assets, and military power, but if either managed to add Bolivia's resources the scales would likely tip in their favor, as Bolivian territory conveniently flanked the two coastal nations. Although both countries had vied for influence in Bolivia, Peru might not necessarily have been drawn into a conflict with Chile. However, an 1873 "secret" alliance between Peru and Bolivia that nonetheless became widely known in all three countries obliged the former to support the latter in the event of war.

At this juncture Peru had little to gain from a war with Chile. Moreover, Peru was also indebted to Chile for support during a brief Spanish attempt to reassert their colonial dominance in the previous decade. Nonetheless, Peruvian authorities decided that their credibility as an ally would disappear should they stand and watch Chile defeat Bolivia. In that case, furthermore, Chilean dominance of the highland nation would permanently insure Peru's inferiority. The Bolivian government's decision in December 1878 to impose the previously mentioned municipal tax in Antofagasta prompted an exchange of angry ultimatums with Chile that paved the way for a much larger conflict. Bolivian president Hilarión Daza, like many dictators, felt too insecure in his position to offer any kind of compromise, and the Chileans, hungry for actual control of not only disputed border areas but also the nitrate-rich guano deposits in the southern portion of Peru, were hardly amenable to anything less. War broke out in February 1879.

BOLIVIA

The conflict did not start auspiciously for Bolivia. It possessed a modest professional army of slightly more than 2,000 men that, as was true of many Latin American armies, were not deployed along the borders facing potential aggressors. The government instead had conveniently stationed the army's most potent units near to the capital so they could be on hand to participate in Bolivia's frequent coups d'etat. Consequently, only a handful of isolated troops (and no navy whatsoever) confronted the Chilean fleet when it occupied the port of Antofagasta in February 1879, and these troops quickly escaped inland to raise the alarm.

Bolivia first offered serious resistance at the town of Calama, a small way station on the trade route from the Bolivian highlands to the cities across the desert and down to the coast. The brief, heroic, doomed resistance against overwhelming force by the handful of defenders comprising scattered troops from small outposts and a militia of local residents later found its way into Bolivian history and mythology, but the battle, unlike the vaguely similar situation of the Alamo in U.S. history, only served to undermine the faith of Bolivian citizens in the capacity and honor of its own armed forces. While the tiny garrison included no less than 5 colonels, 2 lieutenant colonels, 6 majors, 2 captains, and 25 lieutenants of the regular army, the defense was actually organized by Ladislas Cabrera Vargas, the civilian lawyer-prefect whose only claim to authority was that he was brother-in-law to Bolivia's minister of foreign relations, and Eduardo Abaroa, a petty bureaucrat whose profane refusal to a Chilean offer to surrender just before his death became legendary. His impolite, *"Que se rinde su abuela, carajo!"* ("Let your grandmother surrender, damn it!" with *carajo* being somewhat stronger than the English version and the reference to surrender implying the old lady surrendering herself) has given Bolivian schoolchildren a pretext for swearing ever since—it was good enough for a national hero, after all.[1] The fact that civilians stepped forward to perform the role of a professional army that had squandered substantial portions of Bolivia's resources since independence, to say nothing of its habit of using armed might to seize and abuse political power, was not lost on the Bolivian people, even as they celebrated the glorious sacrifice.

After this and other initial skirmishes and the rapid Chilean occupation of the entire Bolivian littoral, the war began in earnest. Bolivia undertook the conflict with two armies. The first, the permanent and professional one, was centered on three regiments, each known by the color of its jackets, red, yellow, or green, for the colors of the Bolivian flag. The most significant of these were the *Colorados* (redcoats), who numbered approximately 1,000 men and were organized as the personal praetorian guard of President Daza. A former commander of the *Colorados,* Daza had used them to install Tomás Frías in the presidency in 1874; two years later he repeated the same trick to install himself as head of state, keeping command of the regiment as well. Although Daza treated all professional soldiers well, he lavished special attention and largess on the *Colorados.* He set the pay for a private soldier at approximately that of a captain in any other regiment, provided the best uniforms, quarters, and mess, and took the precaution of reserving for them the entire Bolivian army's supply of modern Remington repeating rifles and even their own small artillery section; the rest of the army had to make do with inferior Martini-Henrys or even cap-and-ball muskets of U.S. Civil War vintage. The *Colorados* might have enjoyed more firepower than the rest of the army combined, ensuring their ability to protect Daza's regime and their willingness to do so against all comers, but they still lacked the military capability of Chile's forces.[2]

The other army that marched down from the Bolivian highlands was a popular one, not mobilized by the Daza government so much as by the people themselves in spite of the regime's preference for keeping monopolistic control over all armed force. Bolivia had not been involved in the war long enough to make conscription a serious issue, as the patriotic fervor to defend the nation made a draft unnecessary. The streets of every city were clogged with demonstrations led by brass bands, subscriptions for the war effort were routinely over-fulfilled, and towns and cities competed with each other to raise more and larger regiments of volunteers. The sons of the very "best" families of La Paz, Bolivia's capital, formed the *Murillo* cavalry squadron of 300 men, dressed in elaborately tailored uniforms and equipped with state-of-the-art gear. Not to be outdone, the city's skilled worker guilds raised three infantry regiments of their own, and Bolivia's other major urban centers followed suit, more than tripling the size of the peacetime army. Despite the existence of a large pool of underemployed senior officers in the Bolivian army, the volunteer units all chose to elect their own officers, and Daza found it politically expedient to let them have their way. Nonetheless, the emergence of these units made him uneasy about his own security, so he largely excluded citizen soldiers from his inner councils as he led the army to war.

The combined army under Daza's command completed the approach march down to the coast to join up with their Peruvian allies at Arica without incident. Because a series of running fights at sea in the early weeks of the war had virtually destroyed the Peruvian navy, to challenge the Chilean invaders and hopefully drive them back the allies would have to move by land and undertake a difficult crossing of some 45 miles of open desert, their seaward flank always open to a possible Chilean amphibious descent to their rear. The Peruvians accomplished the task with little effort in two or three days, marching at night to avoid the heat, and with officers taking care to ensure that their men carried only the essentials, including as much water as possible, since it was still possible to run occasional small transports down along the coast, evading the Chilean navy, and bring in supplies.

Daza, however, chose to ignore the advice of his allies. He claimed extensive experience in the movement of troops, but his actual military background largely consisted of marching from barracks to presidential palace to defend or overthrow a government, his combat record to brief skirmishes around the House of Delegates or occasionally firing into unruly crowds of unarmed civilians. Thus, the Bolivians marched by day because Daza took pride in the belief that his countrymen were used to hardships. Moreover, and in the manner of green troops, soldiers loaded themselves up with useless baggage, and their equally inexperienced officers followed their commander's example and brought along furniture, china, dress uniforms, and luxury provisions. Discarded packs and weapons, and eventually the bodies of dehydrated men and animals, littered the advance route as the march dragged on for more than five days in unbearable heat.

But neither the poor management of the march nor the wastage suffered en route produced the greatest disaster for Bolivian fortunes; responsibility for that catastrophe fell on the president's shoulders. The Bolivian army arrived at the town of Camarones after their harrowing march with plenty of water and forage, but President Daza suddenly realized that he now found himself in the midst of a real war. Somewhere to his front, and no one knew exactly where, were two armies, the invading Chileans under General Erasmo Escala, and the allied forces under Peruvian General Juan Buendía. Neither had chosen to wait for Daza to bring up the bulk of his army. It now occurred to Daza that, if he continued to advance, his troops would eventually come under hostile fire, perhaps alone if he failed to find Buendía to join forces first. Now, that might not seem surprising, this being a war and all, but Daza knew perfectly well that his grip on power rested solely on the loyalty of his beloved *Colorados*, and because that loyalty depended on their lavish pay and pampering, it might not survive being led into a hell of bullets and shrapnel. The concept of defending the nation, despite a torrent of patriotic speeches Daza had unleashed since the start of the conflict, at this point seemed of secondary importance. He decided to go home.

Daza cloaked the betrayal of both his allies and of several thousand Bolivian troops already serving with Buendía's army with an implausible new plan. He would now lead his army back to Bolivia to link up with fresh forces being raised there, and then launch a new invasion to the south, far to the Chilean rear, aimed at recapturing the port of Antofagasta.[3] The maneuver, which would have taken weeks to execute, might have been a viable strategy had it not involved marching back and forth over the spine of the Andes and crossing and recrossing waterless desert regions. Daza's plan also seemed a bit late to think of after bringing his own army to within striking distance of the enemy and with a Peruvian force handy that would have given the allies combined combat power easily superior to the Chileans. It is unlikely that anyone took the ploy seriously, but Peruvian president Mario Ignacio Prado sent a gracious note to Daza acknowledging the "impossibility" of his further advance and advising that his council of war had issued orders for Buendía to attack the Chileans without delay. Prado perhaps hoped to shame Daza into discarding his plan and joining the fight, but most likely he feared that openly opposing Daza's move might prompt the prickly dictator to withdraw not only his own army but also those Bolivian troops already with Buendía, a move that would leave the Peruvians badly outnumbered. Prado may also have thought it possible that his politeness might persuade Daza's officers to talk him out of the withdrawal so long as he had not been openly alienated or humiliated.[4]

The attempt to keep Daza and his troops in the field failed, so the Bolivian army duly countermarched. They suffered through the desert only to be greeted with jeers and a barrage of dung and garbage by the citizens of Arica as they shuffled through the streets. Meanwhile, the Chileans went on to defeat the forces under Buendía in November 1879 at the battle of Dolores. Buendía had postponed his attack as he waited for Daza. The delay had allowed the Chileans to bring up reinforcements, but they were still slightly outnumbered by the 7,000 allied troops. Had Daza's troops been present, increasing the size of the attacking force by more than 50 percent, the outcome might well have been different.

This turn of events shamed and disgusted Daza's troops, particularly the volunteers, and they took matters into their own hands. Just over a month later, a cabal of junior officers organized a coup d'etat with the connivance of the irate Peruvians, who obviously would be glad to be rid of Daza but who also did not want to foment a Bolivian civil war on their own territory in the midst of an invasion. Peruvian Vice Admiral Lizardo Montero invited Daza, who had moved on to Tacna, to travel by train back to Arica to discuss Daza's new strategy. The Bolivian president accepted, necessarily leaving his precious *Colorados* behind. The conspirators then ordered the *Colorados* to stack arms and proceed to the river to bathe and also to launder their uniforms. When the clean and refreshed praetorians returned to camp they found several volunteer regiments formed up, under arms, between them and their weapons. The *Colorados* sensibly accepted the situation, some actually cheering, and the deed was done. Daza at first demanded that Peruvian troops help him regain power, which they refused. Then, after learning that a coalition of government leaders and opposition politicians had declared for the insurrection, he gave up and escaped to Europe.[5]

Daza's departure freed the Bolivians to sign up for the war out of a sense of patriotism rather than on the whim of their mercurial president, but joining out of patriotism was out of the question because the war had not gone well and much of the initial enthusiasm had worn off. In an attempt to refurbish popular morale, the new Bolivian and Peruvian governments, following the abrupt departure of both Daza and President Prado, reaffirmed the two countries' commitment to their alliance and solemnly promised not to consider any sort of negotiated settlement, either separately or jointly, as long as a single Chilean soldier stood on the soil of either nation. But these were largely empty words because neither Peru nor Bolivia made a serious effort to mobilize the resources necessary to carry on a prolonged conflict. The ragged, demoralized allied army had managed to inflict a stinging reverse on the otherwise victorious Chileans at Tarapacá, but the overall strategic picture remained extremely bleak by the end of 1879. The Chileans had demonstrated an ability to use their naval superiority to leapfrog to any point on the Peruvian coast, making any coherent defense by the allies virtually impossible.

The Bolivian army and their Peruvian allies made a final stand at the Battle of Tacna in May 1880, but they suffered a decisive defeat.

At this point the Bolivian commander, Narciso Campero, who co-incidentally had been elected president of the republic, and his Peruvian counterpart Lizardo Montero, agreed that further resistance was useless and returned to their respective capitals. The battered, weary Bolivian survivors, who had marched hundreds of miles and fought several bloody engagements, faced a grueling march across deserts and icy mountain passes reaching to 10,000 feet; many wounded soldiers dropped out of the column along the way to die. Bolivian troops also had to endure the humiliation of marching through the Peruvian city of Tacna, where residents considered the Bolivians responsible for the defeat and pelted them with garbage. Then, upon reaching the Bolivian border, the soldiers endured a final disgrace when a strong cavalry forcibly disarmed them for fear that the armed rabble would turn to brigandage. Their return to La Paz stood in stark contrast to their joyous, spirited departure months before.

By mid-1880, thus, Bolivia was effectively out of the war. The fighting continued in Peru, but no Bolivian statesman considered honoring President Campero's word and standing by the Peruvians as they had stood by Bolivia in compliance with the 1873 "secret" alliance. Having abandoned an ally that entered a war largely to comply with treaty commitments rather than specific national interests, Bolivia could not expect Peru to protect its well-being when peace talks began. One serious problem in those discussions arose because Chile had seized large tracts of Peruvian territory in addition to the Bolivian littoral. Thus, while Chile would have gladly allowed Bolivia a corridor to the sea along the new Chilean-Peruvian border that would have also served as a buffer between Chile and the possibly vengeful Peruvians, the Peruvians were quick to point out that this land would necessarily have consisted of *Peruvian* territory. If the Chileans wanted to divest themselves of that corridor, they should return it to the original owners and not to the traitorous Bolivians.

Instead of delivering salvation, diplomacy doomed Bolivia to a future as a landlocked nation with all the handicaps this implied for their economic development. While the final terms of the peace accord guaranteed Bolivia unrestricted right of importation through both Chilean and Peruvian ports, that assurance was not always honored. During the Chaco War of the 1930s, for example, a conflict largely fought as a result of Bolivia's frantic yearning to find another access to the sea, Chile and Peru briefly blocked arms shipments to Bolivia across their territory. Furthermore, the railroad that the Chileans later constructed between the port of Arica and La Paz, supposedly in "payment" for the Bolivian territory seized, inextricably subordinated the Bolivian economy to Chile's. Bolivian schoolchildren still link arms and march forward and backward singing:

> Ferrocarril, carril, carril
> Arica-La Paz, La Paz, La Paz
> Un paso para atrás, atrás, atrás!
> (Railroad, railroad
> Arica-La Paz, La Paz, La Paz
> A step back, back, back)

CHILE

Chile came out of the War of the Pacific with significant advantages over the other belligerents. Because none of the fighting took place on Chilean soil, the conflict did not directly affect Chilean civilians. In addition, the fact that Chile emerged victorious from the war helped assuage any suffering the Chilean people might have felt due to the inevitable butcher's bill. In the end, however, the Chilean population did not emerge unscathed.

Chileans initially supported the war because the government ostensibly undertook it on behalf of the *rotos*, the landless workers who had sought employment in Bolivian and Peruvian territory due to the downturn in the Chilean economy in the second half of the nineteenth century. With the consolidation and mechanization of Chilean agriculture, thousands of surplus laborers had gone to work in the nitrate facilities of the Atacama Desert and along the Peruvian coast in enterprises largely funded by Chilean capital.[6] The corruption and inefficiency of the Peruvian and Bolivian governments, and their perceived rapaciousness, seemingly threatened the livelihoods of these men and the investments of Chilean concerns. The xenophobia that accompanied the rising tensions between the belligerents prior to the outbreak of hostilities drove thousands of *rotos* from their jobs, adding fuel to the fire. For example, Chilean nationals comprised as much as a third of the personnel of the Peruvian navy, all of whom were expelled when war broke out. These men, along with the *rotos*, proved to be eager recruits for the Chilean military in the early days of the conflict.[7]

Not surprisingly, the initial victories by the Chilean navy and army further encouraged popular enthusiasm for the war because casualties were not so extensive as to dampen the nationalist spirit.

Furthermore, the fact that Chilean forces had consistently emerged triumphant, conquering vast stretches of valuable land and achieving all of the nation's prewar goals and then some, served to ameliorate the blow on the Chilean populace. There was also a certain sense, toward the end of the nineteenth century, that a people needed an occasional blooding to enhance their warrior nature and to purify the race. Chilean president Aníbal Pinto had stated as much during the April 1, 1879, cabinet meeting to decide whether or not to go to war with Bolivia and Peru: "War and victory are the only means by which we can obtain effective dominion. On occasion, a people need to go to war to irrigate with blood the tree of life of the country."[8]

Technically, Chile did not resort to conscription because all able-bodied men between the ages of 18 and 45 were supposed to belong to the National Guard and attend regular drills. Because this requirement for service was honored more during times of peace prior to the outbreak of the War of the Pacific, the army began the conflict short-handed in comparison to its paper strength,[9] but displaced *rotos* from Bolivian and Peruvian territory, eager not only to avenge themselves on their former masters but also to earn even the modest stipend paid by the army, swelled up the ranks of the armed services in the early days of the conflict. Likewise, as in Bolivia, the sons of the upper classes flocked to the banners, eager for adventure and possibly with an eye toward establishing a war record that would prove useful if one were considering a political career later on. As the war dragged on, however, the propertied classes' enthusiasm for military service wore off, forcing the government to turn to mass conscription. A new problem then surfaced: the lack of sufficient funds to make good even the modest salaries promised the troops. The shortage of money reduced to penury the families of common soldiers and further exacerbated the reluctance of men to join the ranks. Moreover, corruption in the system—such as the wealthy bribing government officials, obtaining false medical waivers, or paying for substitutes—severely restricted the available pool of manpower. Chilean officials had to send out press gangs to sweep the countryside, and the inevitable brutalities and abuses they committed in their efforts to raise troops further alienated the lower classes from the government.

Despite the growing disaffection, the Chilean government managed to adequately fill the ranks of the army, and the ease of its early battlefield successes led officials to pursue broader goals that reduced the likelihood for a negotiated settlement. Had Chile been satisfied with the quick seizure of the Bolivian littoral, the allies could have done little to take it back, especially once Chile gained control of the sea. However, the Chilean high command's desire to strike at and destroy enemy land forces led to the invasion of Peruvian territory, which also fell to them with relative ease. This turn of events made it less probable that any regime in Lima, Peru's capital, would accede to a peace that recognized the loss of the rich guano deposits along the southern Peruvian coast, a piece of real estate that Chileans now felt was theirs by right of conquest. With Peru unwilling to accept a settlement on these terms, Chileans had little choice but to drive on and attempt to dictate a peace treaty in Lima itself. Chile's navy first blockaded Lima's port of Callao and then its army drove through the fortified defenses on the approaches to Lima. The Chileans then marched into the city as conquerors.

The war, however, did not end with the fall of Lima, and the nature of the conflict and the fighting underwent a dramatic transformation. Rather than a classic clash of armies between uniformed troops who followed their flags into battles that produced clear victors and losers, the war became a counterinsurgency operation—with no clear front lines or tangible measure of victory—characterized by the brutal *ratissage* of guerrilla warfare: ambushes, search-and-destroy sweeps, and the systematic destruction of civilian infrastructure that might sustain the elusive guerrillas. Entire Chilean garrisons were wiped out to the last man, with the bodies of the dead allegedly mutilated by Peruvian guerrillas,[10] and Peruvians repeatedly used what today might be called "improvised explosive devices." These consisted of small naval craft, conveniently loaded with fresh fruits and vegetables, left for the Chilean blockaders to find. The launches would also be packed with explosives; one such contrivance destroyed the frigate *Loa* along with over 100 of her crew.

This development, of course, led to a certain brutalization of the occupying force and to a further decline in Chilean public morale, with large numbers of conscripts from the lower classes being sent to fight in a seemingly endless war with no identifiable goal in sight. The conflict's changing nature also brought about an increasing chorus of criticism, not of the war itself, which was generally considered by consensus in Chile to have been justified as a matter of national honor, but rather against the leaders responsible for its conduct. Public-spirited Chileans questioned why the telling battlefield victories had not translated into political victory and a quick and prosperous peace.[11]

Other issues raised questions in Chile as to the wisdom of the war. The conflict cost Chile some $2.5 million pounds sterling per year (over $12 U.S. million at the time), a sum that largely swallowed up the money being made from nitrate sales in the conquered territories and the "taxes" imposed by Chilean forces on the towns they raided far up the Peruvian coast. Some wondered whether Chilean elites were profiting from the venture that was being paid for in the blood of the poor, thus driving a further wedge between the upper and lower classes.[12] This attitude served to undermine popular faith in the ruling class, a lack of confidence that endured long after the end of the war and became exemplified in the increasingly strident tone of political debate and the rise of more and more radical political parties.

In addition, the very nature of the windfall resulting from the capture of the nitrate lands of Bolivia and Peru significantly distorted the Chilean economy.[13] With the irresistible prospect of easy fortunes to be made in the extraction of nitrates, be they from the deposits in the Atacama Desert or from Peruvian guano, at a time when the demand for nitrates for the manufacture of both fertilizers and explosives seemed inexhaustible, Chilean investment capital naturally flowed into the nitrate industry to the exclusion of virtually all others. The nitrate market, however, subsequently collapsed in the early twentieth century due to Franz Haber's creation of a method for synthesizing ammonia. The downfall depressed the Chilean economy for decades, not unlike the boom and bust often seen with the oil-based economies of the Persian Gulf, the difference being that there was no underlying dependence of the world's industrial base on nitrates as there has been on oil.[14]

PERU

The Peruvian people had no real interest or even any real prospect of benefiting from the War of the Pacific, yet of the three belligerents they paid the greatest price for the conflict. Not only did Peru lose thousands of men in combat and a substantial chunk of valuable territory to Chile, but the war also degenerated into a foreign occupation and a guerrilla resistance with a virtual civil war overshadowing the entire affair. Therefore, the disruption of the Peruvian economy and the emergence of societal conflicts between its large Indian population and the white elite far outstripped anything that occurred to either of the two other belligerents.

When war broke out Peru found itself in no condition to challenge Chile, the region's predominant power. After a series of profligate administrations, by the mid 1870s *all* of the income from guano sales abroad, some 2.5 million pounds sterling per year, was committed to debt service. The government could still count on the income from nitrate sales in the Tarapacá region to help cover government expenditures, but these earnings would be lost to Chile once the campaign started.[15] As a budgetary measure shortly prior to the outbreak of the war, the government cut the size of the army by three quarters to 2,500 men, a reduction that prompted the secret alliance with Bolivia (to which it hoped to add Argentina at a later date) as a source of protection against Chile. In addition, a series of coups and attempted coups just prior to the war had left Peru in a virtual state of bankruptcy and with a violently divided political community.

With President Prado's decision to honor his commitment to Bolivia following the Chilean invasion of Bolivian territory, Peru found it immediately necessary to resort to conscription. There had been a brief flurry of patriotic enlistment as is not uncommon early on in a war, but nothing like that seen in either of the other two belligerent nations because Peruvian territory had not yet been violated. Furthermore, the dismal state of Peruvian finances precluded offering bounties for new recruits or an increase to the miserly pay of the common soldiers. Thus, there was little incentive for any but the totally destitute to volunteer for the hazardous life of a soldier, and those heads of households who were conscripted could not provide even basic necessities for their families left at home. As a result, a marginally popular war became reviled almost from the outset.

This poor start might not have been insurmountable had the initial campaigning gone better. However, the early annihilation of its fleet virtually cut Peru off from sources of imported goods, both for the war effort and for private consumption, to say nothing of the markets for Peruvian exports, thus crippling the country's already staggering economy. The quick Chilean conquest of the guano and nitrate producing territories, therefore, actually had limited immediate additional impact in itself, since Peru would have had no way to transport the goods to European or American buyers in any event. The naval blockade could have theoretically been broken or lifted at any moment, but even in that event the occupation of the nitrate production regions meant that no goods would be available for export. Peruvian morale would also naturally have been hurt by the certain knowledge that the Chileans would not be likely to release the valuable territory willingly.

Still, Peruvian forces, even if ultimately unsuccessful, fought courageously. Despite facing tremendous odds against the Chilean fleet, either of whose two newest ironclads outgunned all the Peruvian vessels put together, the navy provided grist for the war hero mill. Peruvian admiral Manuel Grau outmaneuvered the superior Chilean forces and caught a portion of the Chilean fleet unsupported, and thus was able to deliver a morale-lifting victory off the coast of Iquique on May 21; the triumph, however, was tempered by the accidental sinking of the Peruvian *Independencia,* dashing any hope of matching the Chilean fleet and forcing Grau to conduct what amounted to a form of naval guerrilla warfare for weeks until his own death on October 8, 1879. Even the allied armies gave a fair account of themselves, bloodying the invaders repeatedly even as they retreated deeper into Peruvian territory.

Suddenly, however, President Prado dealt his nation's morale a blow similar to the one Daza inflicted on Bolivia. Late in November 1879, just before the minor Allied victory at the Battle of Tarapacá, Prado unexpectedly turned over command of the army to his deputy, Vice Admiral Montero. He returned to Lima to better organize the war effort—hardly an unreasonable action in itself—but found city streets teeming with violent protests against the incompetent handling of the war. In the popular view the combined allied armies theoretically should have easily outnumbered the Chileans, who also operated at the end of a long supply line, and only the government's poor coordination of the troops, along with Daza's treachery, had allowed the Chileans to emerge victorious. Within two weeks of his return Prado had dissolved the government and turned to Nicolás Piérola (a former coup plotter against the regime then in exile) to form a new one. On December 18, however, before Piérola could take up this task, Prado suddenly gathered up his belongings, along with some 6 million pesos in gold from the treasury, and took ship from Callao for Panama. The alleged purpose of the trip was to oversee the purchase of arms in Europe, but neither he nor the money were seen in Lima again.[16]

Prado's abrupt departure provoked a political crisis. The vice president, General Luis de la Puerta, nominally assumed control of the government but Piérola, upon his return to Peru, saw no reason to share power and attempted a coup that proved unsuccessful. Piérola regrouped his forces at Callao and was preparing a second drive on the capital when a delegation of bishops and senior military officers convinced de la Puerta to step down peacefully. Piérola assumed the presidency on December 23, and then quickly drafted a new constitution that disbanded the legislature and reserved all power to himself. He also declared a call-up of all men between the ages of 18 and 45 for the army, although in practice the country lacked the means to provide weapons or uniforms for even a fraction of those conscripted.

Piérola's political and military measures, however, failed to reverse the course of the war, and the situation worsened with the June 1880 fall of the port of Arica to the Chileans, which freed the Chilean fleet to come north and blockade the harbor of Callao. With no means to challenge the Chileans at sea, the Peruvians resorted to unconventional tactics, such as the previously mentioned "improvised explosive devices." Such ploys prompted a howl of rage in Chile, and the government authorized a series of punitive raids north along the Peruvian coast, both to destroy Peru's one remaining source of foreign exchange, the large sugar plantations there, and to raise the level of pain to force Peruvians to lay down their arms.[17]

Piérola's response to those expeditions, however, left the civilian population without protection, facing inevitable destruction at the hands of either friend or foe. In those raids Chilean troops demanded large "reparations" from the local landowners under threat of the destruction of their buildings, crops, and livestock. But instead of launching a military operation to drive the raiders into the sea because he preferred to keep his forces concentrated around Lima, Piérola decreed that any Peruvian found to have paid extortion money to the Chileans would be tried and executed as a traitor.[18] Most of these unfortunate landowners chose loss of property to loss of life and refused the Chilean demands. Apart from seizing any cash and other items of value, and destroying rail lines, crops, and buildings, Chilean soldiers also "freed" hundreds of Chinese laborers. These Chinese immigrants had labored in conditions that bordered on slavery, and now often turned on their former employers with homicidal rage. One suspects that the Chileans would not have felt this same emancipatory urge had landowners chosen to pay their "contributions."

Scholars are divided on whether the raids served their purpose and intimidated the Peruvian government to open talks or whether Peru entered into negotiations because the prospects for a military victory grew increasingly hopeless. In any case, peace talks were

conducted fitfully throughout the middle of 1880 but without result. Chileans demanded not only the cession of the nitrate lands
that belonged to both Peru and Bolivia, but also reparations of
some 20 million gold pesos and a public abrogation of the "secret"
Peru-Bolivia treaty, with the provision that Chile would hold Arica,
Tacna, and Moquegua as collateral until the full terms were met.[19]
The allies, for their part, insisted on a Chilean withdrawal *prior* to
formal negotiations and that the entire dispute should be submitted to international arbitration. Despite the encouragement of the
U.S. envoy to Peru, the talks came to nothing.

When negotiations collapsed Chile decided to press forward
with the military campaign and take Lima. The move would likely
force Peru to capitulate, although the similar Prussian experience
in France just a decade before might have led one to believe that
surrender might not follow after all. In any event, Chile's determination raised Peruvian enthusiasm for the war; the conflict now
entailed defending the homeland, and the population responded
with more vigor. Besides filling out the ranks of the line regiments
that had survived the debacle in the south, a reserve army was
raised around the capital with divisions formed of members of various professions: one each of employees of the ministry of justice,
of public school teachers, of economists, of construction workers,
of government-owned industries, of artisans, of journalists, of re-
tail merchants, of railroad workers, and, not to be outdone, one of
decorators and hairdressers. The government also brought in some
3,000 Indians from the remote Jauja Valley armed with deadly poisoned arrows and blowgun darts.[20]

Despite the promising mobilization, Peruvian forces remained
largely inert as the Chileans approached Lima at their leisure.
Meanwhile, massive fortifications were dug all around the capital, expending huge sums and tens of thousands of man-hours on
works that ultimately had no influence on the upcoming battle.
When the Chileans finally struck in January 1881, the lines protecting the city crumbled despite isolated scenes of bravery, notably by
troops under General Andrés Avelino Cáceres, and defenders fell
back to the suburb of Miraflores. Perhaps frustrated by the continuing Peruvian resistance, during the final advance on Lima Chilean
troops apparently ran rampant through the neighboring suburb
Chorrillos, massacring escaping Peruvian troops and civilians alike
and burning the town, possibly aided by several thousand "freed"
Chinese laborers. Chilean officers did little to halt the killing until
the violence had run its course.[21]

A brief truce followed during which diplomats of various neutral countries resident in Lima attempted to negotiate the city's orderly surrender. The talks apparently got under way without anyone informing the Peruvian defenders, and fighting broke out anew as they were held, probably without premeditation by either side. The Chileans pressed home their attack against the demoralized Peruvian army, which briefly resisted but then literally disintegrated in the face of overwhelming Chilean firepower. While Cáceres frantically tried to organize a counterattack, Piérola, who may have suffered a nervous breakdown, ordered the bulk of the Peruvian troops to discard their uniforms and return to their homes. Most of the exhausted defenders were only too happy to obey.[22]

Piérola's decision might have been understandable had he planned to end the war, but the president apparently could not bring himself to surrender. On the night of January 15 he escaped on horseback to the town of Canta with a small band of aides; he did not bother to destroy any sensitive state documents or to bring along funds from the national treasury. While Piérola did announce that Peru's capital would be wherever he was found and that the war would go on, he failed to ensure any sort of order in Lima. City streets quickly filled with hordes of ragged, undisciplined troops, many still with their weapons, and terrified civilians, the wealthiest of whom desperately tried to purchase vehicles or horses to get out of town. Looting and burning began that evening and continued throughout the next day, both in Lima and the port of Callao. In the end, Lima's mayor had to call on the foreign envoys to set up an "urban guard" of their own nationals, mainly sailors and marines from ships in the harbor, to reestablish order. They finally did so on January 17, killing over 200 looters in Lima and 150 in Callao in the process.[23] A limited number of Chilean troops entered the capital under strict discipline the next day.

Piérola's declarations notwithstanding, the Chileans had cause to believe that the war was over because the enemy capital had fallen and virtually all of the organized units of the regular army had been destroyed or captured. In the weeks that followed, however, General Cáceres, who had been badly wounded in the fighting, recovered from his injuries and prepared to wage a guerrilla war that would make the occupation of Peru too costly for the Chileans. In a situation not all that different from that of insurgent forces in Vietnam in the twentieth century or present-day Iraq, Cáceres believed that every day he could force the Chileans to keep thousands of men mobilized far from home, and every casualty he could inflict, would encourage opposition politicians in Chile to pressure their government into accepting some sort of settlement with Peru that would be better than the punitive terms already on offer.

Cáceres met his match in General Patricio Lynch, who had commanded some of the more destructive Chilean raids into northern Peru and who in May 1881 assumed command of Chile's expeditionary forces. In his new post Lynch put into practice similar tactics as in the past. He demanded that Lima's citizens pay a "war tax" under the threat of imprisoning their family members and/ or destroying their property. Piérola, from the safety of the mountains, continued to insist on his policy that anyone paying the "tax" would be treated as a traitor.[24] Consequently, peasants not only suffered because they had to pay double taxes, which the Chileans in particular collected with total disregard to leaving the people enough to survive on, but also because they remained under the threat of dreadful punishment from both sides for either failing to pay the one or for collaborating with the other.

Given that Piérola did not appear willing to negotiate a proper surrender, the Chileans decided to create a Peruvian government that would. They did not allow the new regime, under President Francisco García Calderón, to establish itself in Lima, but rather ordered it to reside in the town of Magdalena. Chilean authorities even allowed the collaborationist government to raise and arm a few hundred soldiers, more for the protection of its officials than anything else, as Peruvian nationalists had identified the collaborationists as traitors and placed them under threat of death. In his defense, let it be noted that García Calderón sincerely believed that continued resistance was futile and would only result in more death and destruction for Peruvian civilians, and that the highest priority was to get the Chilean troops out of the country as quickly and painlessly as possible.

Meanwhile, columns of Chilean troops roamed the rich farm country farther inland in search of Cáceres and his forces. Cáceres had no trouble avoiding the plodding infantry, but civilians did not have such luck. Chilean soldiers were in a foul mood due to the brutal cold of the Andes, the largely fruitless campaign in search of Peruvian nationalists, and the lack of quartermaster support that had forced them to live off the land. The expeditions thus seized food and goods, and extorted money from the wealthier inhabitants. Such actions soon drove the desperate civilian population into a rage, but the Chileans relied on rapid-fire rifles and artillery to easily repel, with considerable slaughter, the attacks of unarmed farmers. Although the army court-martialed the commander of at least one of these columns for his brutality and for taking a "commission" of all the goods and money seized, the trial failed to improve relations between the occupying army and the natives.[25]

What's more, the brutality of Chilean troops in their quest for food, draft animals, and money facilitated Cáceres's recruitment efforts. The army of resistance under his command grew steadily, swelled by stragglers from the old Peruvian army and deserters from García Calderón's troops. Thousands of highland Indians, previously exempt from the draft, also flocked to his banners to help drive out the foreign invader. In addition, Peruvian claims that Chilean troops insisted on being supplied with a number of "virgins" in each town where they bivouacked naturally incensed the local inhabitants and fostered continued resistance.[26] While the specification of "virgins" smacks decidedly of Peruvian propaganda, such stories were likely given wide credence by the Peruvian people whether they were precisely true or not.[27]

In an effort to break the stalemate, General Lynch launched a new counter-guerrilla campaign early in 1882 to eliminate Cáceres and his troops once and for all. Flying columns again penetrated the hinterland, sweeping through farmland and extorting whatever supplies they required, dealing harshly with any resistance from the locals. However, the marching was hard; the troops suffered from cold, altitude sickness, and typhoid, losing more men to disease than to enemy fire. Cáceres, for his part, could only wait for Chilean foraging parties to seize a stock of goods on one of their operations and then attack the Chileans, stealing what they had already stolen. This was the only way Cáceres could avoid alienating the local inhabitants whose goodwill was vital to his survival, but Chilean depredations meant there was little surplus for even the most willing farmers to spare him. Cáceres's forces survived the campaign, but that April, Peruvian General Miguel Iglesias suddenly emerged in northern Peru, claimed to be the true head of state, and called for peace with Chile on any terms. This was just the message that Chilean officials wanted to hear, and they recognized Iglesias as the head of the legal Peruvian government. With this encouragement, they ordered Lynch to launch a final campaign and eliminate armed resistance once and for all. This he finally accomplished in July, trapping and crushing Cáceres's remaining ragtag army, dispirited after suffering repeated defeats in the war and being forced to live off the land for months.

Cáceres's demise meant that Chileans could freely negotiate with the Iglesias government, and the peace agreement was signed on October 20, 1883. No accurate record was kept of the Peruvian civilians killed by the occupation forces or even of the Peruvian soldiers who died in combat or from disease during the four years of war. Given the essential lack of interest in such statistics on the part of the Chileans and the total chaos on the Peruvian side, with no coherent government structure in existence during this period, this lack of recordkeeping is hardly surprising. Nonetheless, the total number of the dead must have been in the tens of thousands, not counting those who may have died from malnutrition or disease brought on by the depredations of the contending armies in the Peruvian highlands.

"El Repase," a painting by Ramón Muñiz, symbolizes the sacrifices that courageous Peruvian women were willing to make in the War of the Pacific. (Courtesy of *Museo del Ejército Real Felipe,* located in Callao, Peru. Photo by Captain José Perales Wong. Courtesy of Colonel Manuel Ríos Lavagna, the Director of Museums for the Peruvian Army).

CONCLUSION

Compared to some Latin American conflicts such as the 1910 Mexican Revolution or the ongoing guerrilla war in Colombia, civilian suffering in the War of the Pacific was relatively modest. Most of the fighting took place in virtually uninhabited regions and might have been limited to that had the belligerents come to an early settlement after the initial Chilean victories. As Bolivia quickly dropped out of the war, the physical cost of the war was limited. However, the Bolivian nation lost its only outlet to the sea, and the disastrous and disgraceful performance of its leaders left the Bolivian public with a justifiably abysmal view of the quality of their own political class. Since none of the fighting took place in Chile, its population only suffered having to support a long and bloody war at a distance, with consequent indirect disruption of their economy. Peru endured considerable hardship, not just the disgrace of military defeat and economic loss, but also years of heavy-handed foreign occupation.

The war, however, has had severe long-term costs for the three participating countries. The most enduring cost has been the animosity between the governments and peoples that was born of the conflict and which the years have done little to erase. While relations between Chile and its northern neighbors had never been particularly warm since the achievement of independence from Spain in the 1820s, the seizure of the entire Bolivian coast as well as the southern portion of Peru as spoils of war created a permanent atmosphere of mutual distrust that has never completely dissipated. Chile may have had an arguably valid claim to some kind of border adjustment with Bolivia initially, but the wartime territorial acquisitions could hardly be categorized as anything other than blatant depredation. Perhaps the May 2006 meeting between current Chilean president Michelle Bachelet and her Bolivian counterpart Evo Morales in which they discussed the possibility of renewing diplomatic relations (which broke down in 1978) will be a first step toward dissipating the ill feelings that have endured for more than a century.[28]

NOTES

1. Andrés Lizardo Taborga, *Apuntes de la Campaña de 50 Días de las Fuerzas Bolivianas en Calama, con Motivo de la Invasión Chilena* (Sucre: Tipografía de la Libertad, 1879), 6.

2. Roberto Querejazu Calvo, *Guano, Salitre, Sangre: Historia de la Guerra del Pacífico* (La Paz: Editorial Los Amigos del Libro, 1979), 263.

3. Querejazu Calvo, *Guano, Salitre, Sangre*, 423.

4. Edgar Oblitas Fernández, *Historia Secreta de la Guerra del Pacífico* (Sucre: Editorial Tupac Katari, 1978), 225.

5. Diego Barros Arana, *Historia de la Guerra del Pacífico, 1879–1881* (Santiago: Editorial Andrés Bello, 1979), 175.

6. Simon Collier and William F. Sater, *A History of Chile 1808–1994* (New York: Cambridge University Press, 1997), 125.

7. Andrés Avelino Cáceres, *La Guerra del '79: Sus Campañas* (Lima: Editorial Milla Batrea, 1973), 13.

8. Querejazu Calvo, *Guano, Salitre, Sangre*, 344.

9. Willam F. Sater, *Chile and the War of the Pacific* (Lincoln: University of Nebraska Press, 1986), 76.

10. Cáceres, *La Guerra del '79*, 179.

11. Sater, *Chile and the War*, 54.

12. *The Chilean Times* (Valparaíso), September 2, 1882.

13. Sater, *Chile and the War*, 192.

14. William Jefferson Dennis, *Tacna and Arica: An Account of the Chile-Peru Boundary Dispute and the United States Arbitrations* (New York: Archon Books, 1967), 195.

15. Pedro Dávalos y Lisson, *La Primera Centenia: Causas Geográficas, Políticas, y Económicas que Han Detenido el Progreso Moral y Material del Perú en el Primer Siglo de su Vida Independiente*, 4 vols. (Lima: s.n., 1926), 4:369.

16. Fernández Oblitas, *Historia Secreta*, 286.

17. Martín Congrains, *La Expedición Lynch* (Lima: Editorial Ecoma, 1973), 58.

18. Congrains, *La Expedición Lynch*, 59.

19. Valentín Abecia Baldivieso, *Las Relaciones Internacionales en la Historia de Bolivia*, 3 vols. (La Paz: Editorial Los Amigos del Libro, 1979), 2:135.

20. Querejazu Calvo, *Guano, Salitre, Sangre*, 619.

21. Mariano Felipe Paz Soldán, *Narración Histórica de la Guerra de Chile contra el Perú y Bolivia*, 3 vols. (Buenos Aires: Imprenta de Mayo, 1884), 2:72.

22. Cáceres, *La Guerra del '79*, 79.

23. Gonzalo Bulnes, *Guerra del Pacífico*, 2 vols. (Santiago: Editorial del Pacífico, 1955), 2:302.

24. Querejazu Calvo, *Guano, Salitre, Sangre*, 635.

25. Bulnes, *Guerra*, 2:21.

26. Florencia E. Mallon, *Peasant and Nation: The Making of Post-Colonial Mexico and Peru* (Berkeley: University of California Press, 1994), 192.

27. Chilean sources imply that the recourse to Indian fighters was a kind of unsportsmanlike servile insurrection, and that the war should have been restricted to the European and mixed-blood (*mestizo*) races. Bulnes, *Guerra*, 2:89. Of course, Chileans had a rather different ethnic take on warfare given that the bulk of their population consisted of Europeans and

mestizos, with the surviving Araucan Indians being largely restricted to the wilds of the southern frontier and looked upon as barbarians. In Peru, on the other hand, the indigenous population, then as now, comprised a substantial majority and could hardly be excluded from participation in all aspects of national life.

28. *El Mercurio* (Santiago), May 13, 2006.

SEVEN

"¡No Vamos a la Revolución!" Civilians as *Revolucionarios* and *Revolucionados* in the 1910 Mexican Revolution

John Lear

"*¡Vámonos con Pancho Villa! ¡Vamos a la bola! ¡Vamos a la Revolución!*" Such phrases, sanctified in *corridos,* novels and films, have come to characterize the widespread armed participation of Mexicans in the first major social uprising in the Americas in the twentieth century. And yet, for all of its massive participation and related social transformation, only a small fraction of the 15 million people living in Mexico in 1910 joined any of the armed factions of the Revolution. Though most citizens lived the revolution as noncombatants, it is the experience of armed combatants that looms large in modern memory. Few scholars have directly researched the daily lives of civilians during the military decade of the Revolution (1910–1920), as historical monographs and oral histories of the period tend to favor the experience of combatants.[1] Even so, the civilian experience is inevitably a piece, albeit indirect, of the extensive historiography of the Revolution. This essay suggests a variety of patterns that illuminate the experience of the majority of Mexicans, those who did not take up arms. For many such individuals, direct support or overt rejection of the armed Revolution could be a crucial alternative form of political participation; for others, daily encounters with armed factions and the devastating material conditions brought on by a decade of fighting proved as transformative as the ideas, conditions, and events that brought on the armed Revolution.

The different phases and factions of the Revolution, which began when a crisis over political succession in 1910 exploded into an armed revolt that continued through much of the decade, extended throughout the country and across social classes. In 1910 a wealthy liberal reformer from the north, Francisco Madero, ran unsuccessfully in fixed elections against aging strongman Porfirio Díaz, who had presided for 34 years over rapid but unequal growth, fueled largely by agricultural and mineral exports and Euro-American investment. Supported mainly by country people, Madero then led an armed rebellion that triumphed in a few brief months of fighting in the spring of 1911. As president, however, Madero could not contain for long either the factions of the Porfirian elite and foreigners that opposed change, or those groups, largely peasants and rural workers, that pushed for far deeper reforms than those advocated by the new president and middle-class politicians. As a result, in February 1913 conservative sectors led by Porfirian General Victoriano Huerta overthrew his presidency. The subsequent assassination of Madero and Huerta's attempts to consolidate a militarized regime spurred another round of popular rebellion through much of the country. Over the next 18 months, guerrilla and more formal armies throughout the country rallied to defeat Huerta and eliminate the remaining elements of the Porfirian army.

Within months of Huerta's fall in mid-1914, the revolutionary forces that defeated him divided into two factions: the northern-based "Constitutionalist" forces headed by Venustiano Carranza and his key general, Alvaro Obregón; and the "Convention" forces based on the peasant armies of Emiliano Zapata in the southern state of Morelos and the more diverse northern rural constituency led by Francisco Villa. By 1916 Constitutionalist forces emerged triumphant from this civil war and began the process of incorporating many of the social aspirations of the revolution into what became the Constitution of 1917, even as remnants of the Convention armies and other dissident forces remained at large. Elected president in 1917, Carranza provoked the United States, ignored reform pressures from popular sectors, marginalized domestic rivals, and tried to impose his successor. These developments prompted Carranza's ouster and assassination in 1920 in a coup led by his former ally Obregón, who was able to negotiate with popular sectors, armed dissidents, and the United States. This change closed the military phase of the Revolution and began the slow process of "institutionalizing the Revolution" over the next two decades.

Scholars have long proposed differing interpretations of the Revolution that in turn influence their views of the civilian experience. The orthodox, populist view that emerged in the 1930s portrayed the revolution as a peasant and nationalist revolution in which the peasant masses rebelled against the injustices of the old regime, and gave rise to a revolutionary government dedicated to social justice and a national development of Mexican resources.[2] In the 1960s, in the context of the more radical Cuban revolution and after the Mexican army massacred student protesters in Mexico City in 1968, the orthodox view came under attack, as revisionist historians emphasized continuities between the Porfirian and the postrevolutionary periods, in particular, unequal capitalist development, economic dependence on the United States, and state manipulation of the masses from above. Since the mid-1980s, historians have salvaged elements of the populist view of the revolution. In particular, Alan Knight and John Mason Hart have helped reestablish the central role of the mobilization of peasants in narratives of the revolution, while acknowledging the interplay between mobilizations from below and the manipulation and intermittent repression of the lower classes from above.[3]

While historians argue over the significance and outcomes of the Revolution, there is little disagreement over the extensive scale of participation in the armed struggle. The type and extent of armed mobilization varied over space and time, but estimated figures for two key moments are indicative of the scale. By the spring of 1914 General Huerta had expanded federal troops to 250,000, while the four revolutionary armies that defeated him assembled some 115,000 troops between them. The size of the federal troops and their eventual defeat was largely due to massive forced recruitment (discussed below). After Huerta's fall, mobilization and violence (if not total numbers) peaked during the civil war of the first half of 1915, with some 160,000 soldiers fighting on behalf of either the Constitutionalist or Convention forces.[4] Even after the virtual triumph of the Constitutionalists in 1915, the ranks of its army continued to grow, reaching 200,000 in 1916.[5] The size of standing armies was perhaps doubled at any given moment by participation of *soldaderas*—the women who accompanied both federal and revolutionary armies and served as soldiers, cooks, mistresses, and nurses.[6] Over a 10-year period of cycles of recruitment, the total number of soldiers and cohorts participating in the different factions may have doubled these peak figures, thus approaching 1.5 million, or 10 percent of the 1910 population. Estimates of mortality figures for the decade of the Revolution range broadly in numbers and causes, but do suggest the scale of participation and devastation in the Revolution. For example, Robert McCaa estimates "excess deaths" from the Revolution, including both military casualties and disease, to number 1.5 million, with over 350,000 more male than female deaths. The size of troops and the high number of casualties related to the Revolution suggest a war of great mobilization and costs. Indeed, McCaa ranks the Mexican Revolution 9th among 26 major wars of the nineteenth and twentieth centuries in terms of human costs, and Mexico's most traumatic event since the conquest and pandemics of the sixteenth century.[7]

And yet, the vast majority of the 15 million people living in Mexico in 1910 neither directly joined troops nor died as a result of widespread fighting and disease, which begs a return to the understudied topic of the civilian experience of the revolution. The orthodox, populist view of the Revolution assumes a fairly direct overlap between the armed masses and the general civilian population from which they arise. By contrast, for the revisionist historians of the 1960s and 1970s, the explicit argument that the Revolution was a trick by a reformist middle class on the peasants who fought its battles leads to an implicit suggestion that the Revolution—generals and soldiers, winners and losers—was imposed on an unwilling and long-suffering civilian population.[8] But a postrevisionist synthesis of the civilian experience might echo the dialectic of manipulation and resistance suggested by recent historians of the Revolution, acknowledging the intimate ties and coincidence of goals between some armed revolutionaries and civilian populations on the one hand, while acknowledging the frequent tensions or outright antipathy between them, as well as the enormous civilian suffering, on the other. Over time and place, civilians wavered between politics and armed insurrection, between support for different factions and a virtual or eventual rejection, between pursuing goals rooted in the rhetoric of the Revolution and simply struggling to survive.

Certainly at several moments in the Revolution, civilians played the key role in national events. Madero's first campaign was an electoral one, and it was dissident elites and the urban middle and working classes that rallied to the possibilities of electoral politics. Even the fall of President Díaz was not simply the result of military force, but also reflected the lack of widespread civilian support at the moment of his fall. Indirectly, the withdrawal of civilian support from Díaz "made the actions of the revolutionaries viable."[9] Similarly, during the 15 months of Madero's presidency, civilian

This broadside, created in 1915 by one of Mexico City's leading publishers, Antonio Vanegas Arroyo, shows a woman with a shawl around her shoulders and hands on her hips, and contains the words to the ballad of *la cucaracha* (cockroach). During the Mexican Revolution the term became synonymous with "camp follower," and denoted those women who followed their male partners into battle. The song details the difficulties of camp life—the lack of starch, soap, or money. (Courtesy Library of Congress).

politicians wielded considerable power, and urban civil society grew much stronger.[10] But ultimately, and certainly during the civil war of 1914–1915, the military minority decided Mexico's fate. The key civilian decision, individual and collective, was whether to take up arms (and stop being civilian), since arms became the most effective path to change.[11] For conservative critic of the Revolution Jorge Vera Estañol, this meant that "the armed citizen was the only true citizen of the republic; all others were denied citizenship rights."[12] But the role of noncombatants in the Revolution, albeit secondary to that of "armed citizens," hardly diminishes their importance, which is rooted in their numbers, their agency, and their sufferings.

This essay considers a variety of ways that civilians participated in and experienced the Revolution, ways that include actively supporting or opposing revolutionary factions, seizing the opportunity for parallel and nonviolent organization, actively fleeing, simply surviving, and of course, losing their lives to the violence, disease, and hunger. The article pays attention to divisions of class and gender, country and city, but it is organized around three somewhat broad and overlapping categories. First the essay examines civilians as *"revolucionarios"* who often shared common origins and goals with particular rebel factions, or in the case of urban areas, used the opportunities of the revolution to organize and assert themselves without necessarily taking up arms. Secondly, the piece considers civilians as *"revolucionados,"* a term used by Luis González to describe those who were swept up by the military forces and material deprivation of the Revolution without necessarily identifying with the Revolution as anything but a challenge to their survival. The article finally addresses what might be called civilians *"revolución adiós,"* that is, the many civilians who fled their rural homes and perhaps the Revolution to migrate to cities and to the United States, some of them leaving permanently. Of course, the three categories are hardly exclusive, and many civilians moved back and forth between being *revolucionarios* and *revolucionados,* or ended their experience of the Revolution with an *adiós.*

CIVILIANS AS *REVOLUCIONARIOS*

The Countryside

In an isolated Morelos village in 1915, an old woman answered a city slicker's query about Zapata: "What do you want us to say? . . . us poor mountain Indians who go along hanging on tight to the tail of our jefe Zapata's horse."[13] The rustic metaphor suggests the intimate relation between civilians and revolutionaries in many rural areas. The Revolution was above all a rural phenomenon, fought primarily by peasants and rural workers and fueled by the increasingly unequal structure of landholdings, deteriorating

rural wages, and incursions of central power. Alan Knight identifies two prototypes for peasant participation in the Revolution, the
agrarian revolt and the *serrano* (mountaineer) revolt, each based in a
particular kind of rural community in which armed combatants and
civilians were tightly bound.[14] The rural village was at the heart of
each pattern of mobilization, and it is inevitably there that one must
first look to generalize about civilian experiences in the countryside.

Agrarian revolt was rooted in the ancient and accelerating conflict
between the free village, or *pueblo,* and outsiders (hacienda owners,
mid-sized farmers, and local political bosses) over land, forest, and
water, as well as local autonomy. Thus the free village—with its
deep roots in location and land, its corporate structure and relatively
equal internal social relations, and its tradition of revolt and ongoing conflicts over land—became the basic unit for agrarian revolt.
This pattern proved more powerful and enduring in Zapata's home
state of Morelos, south of Mexico City. The very strength of the Zapatista movement in some ways makes it and the related civilian
experience atypical. The existence of lesser Zapatismos throughout
Mexico, however, makes this most-studied of regions a good place
to begin generalizing about the rural experience of civilians, as well
as to consider variations on that experience.[15]

John Womack identifies Zapata's "Liberating Army of the South
and Center" as "an armed league of the state's municipalities " in
which being "people" counted more than being "army." The centrality of the struggle to recover land lost in the recent expansion of
Morelos' great sugar estates, a struggle sanctified in Zapata's 1911
Plan of Ayala, gave purpose to these agrarian rebels and to the *pueblos* that supported them. Many women served alongside the men
as *soldaderas,* private quartermistresses and occasional soldiers, and
villagers "looked more to their village chiefs than to their revolutionary army officers," who were indeed often the same. Even so, the
line between civilian villagers and Zapata's guerrilla army shifted
throughout the 10-year conflict. During the fight against Huerta, a
degree of centralization and professionalization of the guerrillas occurred, though far less than among the Constitutionalist armies of
the north. Even so, during the periods of peace, such as the one that
followed the fall of Huerta in mid-1914, momentum and individuals shifted again toward civilian life as "villagers refounded local
society in civil terms."[16]

While many villagers moved according to the season or cycle
of fighting between military and civilian roles, others more consistently inhabited their civilian, or *pacífico,* status. Though women

fought and served as *soldaderas*, many remained in their villages, along with children, older men, and even men of fighting age. Indeed, whether villagers were peaceable reformers, passive admirers, or even antagonistic to the Zapatistas, their presence insured the continued functioning of the villages as civil and productive entities, which was both the central purpose of the revolutionary armies and essential to their everyday survival. Armed Zapatistas moved in and out of villages, whether returning home to harvest, to obtain resources, or to seek refuge from or information about invading armies.[17] Thus villagers not only hung on to the symbolic tail of Zapata's horse, they also hid, fed, and informed the horse and rider.

The intimate ties between villagers and armed Zapatistas in turn led the successive invading armies sent from Mexico City to target supportive villages rather than invisible guerrillas. General Juvencio Robles, sent by President Madero to lead the federal army against the newly insurgent Zapatistas, declared in 1912 that, "All Morelos, as I understand it, is Zapatista, and there's not a single inhabitant who doesn't believe in the false doctrines of the bandit Emiliano Zapata."[18] And so Robles began a policy of "resettlement" inspired by Spanish and British techniques developed in the late nineteenth century against independence movements in Cuba and in Africa. The federal army removed residents from Zapatista villages to concentration camps before burning their houses to the ground. Anyone found remaining in evacuated areas was assumed to be a Zapatista, and shot. By the summer of 1913, Robles had drafted thousands of villagers into the federal army and sent them to fight rebels in northern Mexico.[19] While separating the guerrillas from their civilian base, the policy also convinced many wavering *pacíficos* to join the armed Zapatistas. When Robles emptied and burned the village of Nexpa, for example, he found only 136 people left, and all but 5 were women and children. With each successive revival of Zapatista fortunes, civilians would return to rebuild their towns. Almost as often, the next wave of invading troops, sent by Huerta in 1913 or Carranza from late 1915 on, would resume policies of resettling, deporting, or conscripting villagers, and eradicating their villages.[20]

As Samuel Brunk has shown, the intimate relation between Zapatista guerrillas and villages was rife with tensions, even in the best of times. Bandits often assumed the banner of Zapatismo and some groups within the loosely federated Zapatistas did loot, rape, or exact revenge on rival towns and villages. Zapata tried to balance civilian and military needs, and whenever possible diverted his men's looting and forced loans to the rich or prosperous, in particular hacienda owners or urban merchants, rather than to friendly villages.[21] Villagers sometimes asked rebel chiefs to keep their distance, so as not to attract the wrath of the federal army. Even during the "utopia" of Zapatista control in Morelos from late 1914 to early 1915, when Zapatistas began carrying out extensive agrarian reforms, local military chiefs sometimes abused municipal authorities or were reluctant to give up nationalized property claimed by villages.[22]

If tension characterized Zapatista relations with villages in the best of times, in the worst of times they deteriorated rapidly. By the fall of 1915, Obregón's armies in the north had routed Villa's forces, which allowed the triumphant Constitutionalists to send yet another invading force to Morelos. Zapatista soldiers steadily lost control over much of the state and found themselves increasingly on the run, reduced once again to a guerrilla force. Like Generals Huerta and Robles before them, the invading Constitutionalists considered the villagers themselves to be outlaws, and unleashed similar scorched-earth policies against them, executing women and children, sending nearly 1,300 prisoners to Mexico City in the spring of 1916, and forcing thousands of *pacíficos* to seek refuge in towns or in neighboring states.[23] The depredations of invading armies had pushed many peasants to support or join the Zapatistas in the first years of the revolution; but from late 1915, after years of fighting, and as Zapatista territory, unity, and victories steadily and irrevocably declined, intimate relations between guerrilla and village often broke down. In spite of Zapata's attempts to control his men, soldiers increasingly abused and coerced hard-strapped civilians. Villagers in Huaquechula and Tlapanalá dismissed the gains of Zapata's agrarian reform and insisted that "the ambition that they have at the moment is just to obtain a guarantee that they'll live." Some villages refused to feed Zapatista soldiers, and in some cases even fired on Zapatista troops. One witness remembered that after 1915, village loyalties to Zapata declined, as "the government would come and burn the *pueblos,* the Zapatistas would come and assault [us], so that when Zapata died the people desired peace more than anything, even if the Plan of Ayala was not fulfilled."[24]

Not only did the cohesion of Zapatismo with civilians fluctuate over time, it also varied over space. Villages in eastern Morelos that had managed to preserve much of their land against haciendas in the Porfirian period were slow to support and quick to diverge from Zapatismo. Resident hacienda peons—who lacked roots in the villages and clung to the security of their hacienda employment—often joined up only when the destruction of the hacienda eliminated their jobs and forced them and their patrons to abandon the haciendas. Similarly, the wealthy and the sparse middle class of Cuernavaca and other provincial towns, subject to forced loans by the Zapatistas and fearful of the dark peasant masses, were more likely to favor, depending on the moment, continued Porfirian rule, Madero-style reform, or control of Morelos by just about any other outside revolutionary faction.[25]

The divergence from the model of pueblo support for rebellion within Morelos sheds light on the broader patterns of mobilization and civilian response elsewhere. Certainly where "lesser Zapatismos" prevailed, civilian support for rebels varied even more over time and space. In much of northern Mexico, for example, the model for revolt more closely resembled what Alan Knight calls a *serrano* revolt. If free peasants were at the heart of agrarian revolt in the south, the *serrano* revolt, embodied in the early movements led by Pancho Villa, contained a mixture of urban and rural workers, ex-military colonists, and peons. *Serrano* rebels were less rooted to the land and more mobile than the free peasants of the south, and village cohesion extended vertically across different social classes and to urban areas. As a result, the central conflict around which revolt occurred was less over land than over the impositions of local monopolies, local political bosses, and the centralizing authority of state and national governments. With land reform a secondary concern, *serrano* movements were less rooted in particular villages and had less clear ideologies and goals. Following the defeat of local bosses and the destruction of the Porfirian state in the early years of the Revolution, *serrano* rebels moved away from their communities of origin and found themselves easily absorbed into the more corporate structures, soldiers' wages, and personal loyalties of the Constitutionalist troops.[26]

As a result, ties between local communities and rebels frequently were more precarious than in Morelos, and more quickly deteriorated into the impositions of invading armies. Friedrich Katz notes that by the time Villa gained control of the state of Chihuahua in the spring of 1914, fighting "had largely destroyed the revolutionary civilian infrastructure, so that the only 'revolutionary organization' at Villa's disposal was his army." Municipal councils came under the supervision of men with popular origins, but they were often outsiders and ultimately military authorities. These leaders often abused local communities, which frequently and unsuccessfully demanded local elections. In addition, Villa confiscated the large haciendas of his state, at least those owned by Mexicans, but he postponed distribution of land until an eventual, hoped-for victory, so that his soldiers would not stop fighting. Instead, he used revenues from confiscated estates to run his army, distributing a portion in the form of cheap food to the large nonpeasant population in Chihuahua's towns and mining communities. With wages and food for his army assured, Villa depended less on the good will of civilian communities for survival, at least as long as the bounty from confiscated properties lasted. In spite of Villa's enormous popularity in the state and the loyalty of his men, the militarization of municipal control and the limits on agrarian reform ultimately distanced this popular revolution from its community roots.[27]

After Obregón's rout of Villa's army in the decisive battles of Celaya and León in mid-1915, Villa's popularity in Chihuahua plummeted, as did economic production and the value of Villista currency. His army began to disintegrate as many soldiers deserted or became more interested in pillaging and killing than in fighting the Constitutionalists. Villa further alienated many free

Mexican *insurrectos* (rebels) with homemade cannon in Ciudad Juárez, c. 1911. (Courtesy Library of Congress).

peasants and tenants by taking food for his troops. He managed to regain a degree of public legitimacy thanks to his 1916 attack on Columbus, New Mexico, and the subsequent pursuit by U.S. troops led by General John Pershing, as well as by his decision to finally divide up haciendas among peons and tenants in the territory he managed to retake. But his resurgence in popularity and control of territory in late 1916 would be partial and short-lived. As Pershing withdrew from Mexico, Villa's confiscations alienated the middle class and foreigners whom he had previously protected, and his forced recruitments alienated the lower classes. In the sustained fighting that continued in Chihuahua between 1917 and 1920, the people of Chihuahua found themselves trapped between the abuses and confiscations of the armies of Villa and of Carranza. At the request of then-president Carranza, many communities organized *"Defensas Sociales,"* local militias to defend against Villista incursions, though these militias were almost as likely to resist troops sent by Carranza. By the end of the decade, neither the federal forces nor Villa's guerrilla forces enjoyed the support of the hard-pressed Chihuahua population who had been at the heart of the region's *serrano* revolts.[28] Thus, among both Villista and Zapatista villages, civilian *revolucionarios* could over time become *revolucionados.*

Women and children flee the battlefield at Ojinaga, Chihuahua (located near the border with Texas) during Venustiano Carranza's struggle against the Huerta government, c. April 1914. (Courtesy Library of Congress).

The Cities

The vision of counter-revolutionary cities was formalized by historian Frank Tannenbaum, who wrote in 1933 that "the cities have been reactionary and the country radical," and declared that "the City of Mexico has been and is at present the great enemy of the Mexican Revolution."[29] This vision of reactionary cities was rooted in the experience of the northern, middle-class leaders who ultimately came to dominate the revolution. For example, General Obregón, soon after taking Mexico City for the first time in August 1914, made a speech at the site of Madero's grave in which he denounced the men of Mexico City for sitting out the revolution. To add insult to injury, he singled out of the crowd the northern schoolteacher María Arias Bernal, who had accompanied the Constitutionalist troops in the fight against Huerta, and declared, "Men who can carry a gun and did not, for fear of leaving their homes, have no excuse. I abandoned my children, and as I know how to admire valor, I cede my pistol to the señorita Arias, who is the only one worthy of carrying it." Obregón's intention was to question the masculinity of the men of Mexico City for failing to fight in the revolution, rather than to urge women to transgress gender boundaries by becoming *soldaderas*.

Certainly the urban experience of the Revolution differed from the rural one. None of Mexico's major cities experienced any kind of armed uprising that approached the enduring cohesion and focus of the agrarian revolt or the initial explosiveness of the *serrano* rebellions, both of which were organized around a clear identification with a particular community and a set of specific gripes or goals. Nor did any of the principal leaders of the Revolution come from major urban areas, though some secondary leaders did, and virtually all of them incorporated "city boys," civilian professionals and intellectuals, as key advisers and secretaries. Although aggregate data is limited, it is reasonable to assume that only a small percentage of nonconscripted soldiers in the revolutionary factions came from urban areas (many of them participants in the union-sponsored "Red Battalions" discussed below). Some sectors of urban society, particularly wealthy Mexicans and foreigners, and the Catholic Church, were decidedly hostile to all revolutionary factions. Moreover, much of the urban population, at least in Mexico City and Guadalajara, probably felt little automatic sympathy for invading troops. In short, the Revolution was primarily a rural phenomenon.

Despite the rural dynamic, the Revolution unleashed unprecedented cycles of urban mobilization that cannot be generalized as
reactionary, either in a political or purely reactive sense. As suggested earlier, the Revolution began as a civilian movement around
the 1910 election campaign of Madero, and citizens of the middle
and working classes in the country's main cities—Monterrey, Mexico City, Puebla—rallied to the promise of "a real vote, and no boss
rule."[30] When Madero's aborted presidential campaign turned to
armed rebellion, his source of support came from the countryside,
while the cities remained largely quiet. But for much of the first year
after the fall of Díaz, urban politics formed the heart of Madero's
Revolution, including his second, victorious campaign for the presidency, as well as congressional and municipal elections. Stimulated
by free elections and a free press, urban civil society flourished
around elections, demonstrations, and the lobbying that ensued
around a variety of issues. Ultimately, however, the possibilities of
political participation for workers explicit in 1910 proved limited
and frustrating during Madero's brief presidency (November 1911
to February 1913). Real power was increasingly exerted through
arms, whether those of dissatisfied rebels like Pascual Orozco in
the north and Zapata in the south, or those of the disgruntled Porfirian army. Huerta's coup and presidency (February 1913 to August 1914) effectively shut down the legislature, limited the press,
and accelerated a process of militarization of society that continued
well beyond the inauguration of the 1917 Constitution.

In spite of this militarization, city dwellers were not passive subjects and pursued forms of mobilization short of taking up arms.
As political avenues closed, urban workers moved to strengthen
their own organizations in the workplace and their own communities. Although strikes occurred and workers formed organizations with increasing frequency at the turn of the century, these
initiatives clearly accelerated after the fall of Díaz and continued
even under the heavy-handed rule of Huerta. Aided in part by the
anarchist-inspired *Casa del Obrero Mundial,* a working-class cultural
organization founded in Mexico City in 1912, a variety of skilled
and unskilled, male and female workers organized mutual aid societies, unions, and federations in the capital. In related initiatives,
working people organized in Puebla, Veracruz, Orizaba, and various mining and oil towns.

In spite of occasional bouts of repression, such as the imposition
of martial law against a wave of strikes throughout the country in
mid-1916, the general pattern by the fall of Huerta was for military

leaders of all revolutionary factions to encourage the organizational efforts of workers and tolerate strikes or even intervene on behalf of workers, particularly when strikes involved foreign companies and occurred in strategic industries.[31] Indeed, when at the end of 1914 the triumphant Constitutional forces split, the *Casa* reported a membership of 52,000 in Mexico City alone. By mid-1916, they claimed a membership of 90,000, almost a third of the city's labor force, making it the largest and most unified labor organization in the nation up to that date.[32] With support from revolutionary generals, and energized by the dire material conditions of 1914–1916, strikes increased dramatically in frequency, culminating with the general strike of July-August 1916 in Mexico City. The material hardships of the Revolution motivated urban workers to organize and strike in an effort to prevent living standards from falling too far, but they also continued to push for long-standing demands such as recognition of unions and control over arbitrary treatment and firings, and to defend the public participation they had achieved since 1910.

At various moments, urban mobilization extended beyond the organized working class, particularly when related to politics or consumption issues. For example, on May 24, 1911, a massive and largely spontaneous protest against Díaz of some 15,000 poor citizens in the central plaza of Mexico City hastened his resignation the next day.[33] The April 21, 1914 landing of U.S. troops in Veracruz, a move by President Woodrow Wilson to undermine Huerta's regime, created an intense anti-Americanism in Guadalajara, Veracruz, and Mexico City, where anti-American riots briefly filled the streets, and groups of students and workers offered to form battalions to battle the "gringo pigs."[34] Unions and tenant unions also took on problems that extended beyond work to consumption issues of food, rent, and provision of basic services. These concerns were a relatively natural link, given mutualist and anarchist traditions, the increasing concentration of production and commerce in the capital, and drastic changes in the city's material conditions. For example, the *Casa del Obrero* presented a petition to Constitutionalist military authorities in October 1914 that went beyond its ambitious labor proposals to demand a mix of regulations to force prices of basic goods down to their 1912 levels, to drop rents by a third, to triple the tax on empty rooms, and to enforce housing sanitation regulations, with workers acting as inspectors and construction teams to implement improvements.[35]

The link to issues of consumption had important consequences for the mobilization of women, within or outside of unions. Women provided the initiative and primary participation for a series of mobilizations that ranged from taking over food shops in order to administer a just exchange, to occupying government buildings and pressing demands for food and services. Throughout much of July 1915, women in Mexico City led widespread food riots and confiscations, even taking over the parliament formed by Villista and Zapatista delegates to demand a resolution to the problem of hunger in the city. The difficult material conditions in cities stimulated the extent of mobilization around consumer issues, but as with workers, these male and female civilians invoked the rhetoric and promises of the different revolutionary factions to justify their demands for social justice. After the suppression of a food riot in Mexico City, a neighborhood group sent a petition to the Convention congress asking whether "the grandiose revolution, brought about in favor of the humble people, has triumphed, or are we still in the times of tyranny, when the unprotected were assassinated with impunity?"[36]

The reality of often direct collaboration between civilians and occupying revolutionary forces over issues of work and consumption also raised the possibility of armed collaboration, if not insurrection. Many city folk were of course conscripted into the federal army during Huerta's rule. A trickle of sympathizers joined one revolutionary faction or another out of ideological sympathy or ambition, and many more joined as an immediate solution to the hunger and unemployment that affected numerous areas, as discussed in the next section. Perhaps the most noteworthy example of collective, armed participation in the Revolution by city dwellers, both in numbers and symbolic significance, was that organized by the *Casa del Obrero Mundial*. In February 1915, a portion of the *Casa* leadership and component unions abandoned their stance of political neutrality by signing a "Pact" to take up arms in Carranza's Constitutionalist forces in their battle against Villa and Zapata. In March some 5,000 to 7,000 soldiers in five "Red Battalions" abandoned Mexico City and followed General Obregón to Veracruz, and their numbers possibly doubled with the addition of workers from other urban areas. Thus the principal collective participation of workers in the armed movements of the revolution took the form of an alliance, or "pact," rather than an insurrection. Various factors and explanations for the alliance bear mentioning: the dire shortages and unemployment in the city that made the guaranteed pay and corporate structure of the "Red Battalions" attractive; the personalist-style intervention of General Obregón and his middle-class intellectual allies; the failure of the Convention forces to appeal to or court urban workers, or to resolve urban shortages; internal conflicts within the *Casa;* and the promise of Constitutionalist support for the expanded organization of unions.[37] In spite of the symbolic significance of the pact at the time and after the Revolution, the "Red Battalions" remained a distinct minority of the capital's working class and of the Constitutionalist forces, and the alliance proved brief and ill fated. At best, then, the Revolution provided city dwellers with an opportunity to assert themselves in politics, in the workplace, and in their communities; in spite of militarization, civil society continued to engage revolutionary authorities. At worst, the Revolution was a struggle for urban civilians to survive the invasions and impositions of multiple armies and the material consequences of nationwide fighting. For some, the Revolution meant both.

CIVILIANS AS *"REVOLUCIONADOS"*

Esther Torres struggled through the toughest years of the Revolution working, between prolonged periods of unemployment, as a seamstress at a variety of sweatshops in Mexico City. Remembering her search for work and food years later, she explained, "We were in the time of the revolution, miss, and in the time of the revolution, one wants to just live, nothing more, right?"[38] Torres's comment might suggest what Luis González has characterized as *"revolucionados,"* those individuals who were swept up by the military forces and material deprivation of the Revolution without necessarily identifying with the Revolution itself. Indeed, most citizens had little global sense of the Revolution while it happened, tended to see multiple Revolutions (that of Madero, Villa, Zapata, etc.), and over time carried the most painful and vivid memories of the years 1913–1917. According to González, the civilians' perspective was characterized not by the heroic feats of soldiers, but rather by years of "atrocious crimes, robberies, kidnappings, hanging bodies, raped women" and the desecration of religious images.[39]

If civilian *revolucionarios* saw in the Revolution the possibility of liberation, civilian *revolucionados* saw the Revolution as distant or barbaric in inspiration and often tragic in its immediate results. This section considers those in rural and urban areas who were either largely passed over by the Revolution, directly experienced the armed revolutionaries as coercive and violent, or suffered from the broader material conditions created at some level by the Revolution. And while these two categories assume distinct groups, *revolucionarios* could indeed become *revolucionados,* as was so for some beleaguered Zapatista and Villista *pueblos,* and *revolucionados* might in turn become *revolucionarios.*

If Morelos and Chihuahua represent two central but not opposite poles of the intimate relations between armed rebellion and sympathetic civilian populations, other patterns previously hinted at are worth developing here. In the southern state of Oaxaca, traditional communities retained much of their land and a considerable degree of agrarian equality, while haciendas were limited in size and number. As a result, revolutionary activity came slowly to the state and was often led by middle-class urban dissidents and *rancheros* seeking more regional autonomy, with limited peasant participation and only isolated agrarian conflicts. Similarly, rural land in the northern state of Nuevo León was fairly evenly divided, which helps explain why it played a limited role in the armed Revolution.[40] As suggested regarding Morelos, hacienda peons and tenants throughout Mexico rarely initiated revolt and were as likely take up arms on behalf of their *patrón.* In southern states like Veracruz, Yucatán, and Chiapas, planter control was so oppressive that it resembled slavery, and peons rarely broke with the protection and social control of the hacienda without the imposition of outside forces, be they rebels from nearby free villages or the invading armies from the north. On the henequen plantations of the Yucatán, serf-like peons clearly benefited from the interventions of Constitutionalist authorities, who eliminated the worst abuses of landowners and encouraged rural workers to organize, though not to take up arms.[41]

In many towns marked by social inequalities, like Michoacán's San José de Gracia, social solidarities between rich and poor prevailed over conflict. There the Revolution came late and from the outside. Madero's electoral and military campaigns brought newspapers, the town's first election, and ripples of gossip from the capital. Otherwise, as Luis González tells us about his childhood town, the most notable event of the Madero years was "Elías Martínez's attempt to become a bird." Only after Madero's fall did the Revolution become tangible, first when Carrancistas demanded forced loans and then as Huertistas called for men to fight against the gringos who had invaded Veracruz. Residents of San José, however, "were disinclined neophytes in patriotism, and they had not yet come to identify with the state." They were more likely to follow the village priest than the revolutionaries, and made little distinction between the various invading armies who came to extract loans, loot the town, and carry off women. Only in the 1920s would citizens of San José take up arms collectively, led by the town priest in the Cristero rebellion against the anticlerical impositions of the postrevolutionary state. Just as there were "Zapatismos" and *serrano* revolts throughout Mexico, many rural communities like San José de Gracia simply endured the revolution rather than generating rebels and civilian networks of support.[42]

Regardless of the response of civilians to the revolutionary factions, war and its consequent material devastation and disease profoundly shaped the daily experiences of civilians during the revolutionary decade. Many major battles of the Revolution, such as that associated with the city of León in 1915, took place in the countryside at a distance from large civilian populations. Mexico City and Guadalajara never experienced large battles; instead, minor skirmishes occurred on the peripheries as the different factions occupied or abandoned these major cities that held more symbolic than strategic value. Still, many provincial towns (Cuautla in 1911, Torreón in 1913, Zacatecas in 1914, and Celaya in 1915) lived through major military engagements that took thousands of civilian lives and destroyed buildings and infrastructure.

If these and other battles affected targeted urban centers, the indirect disruptions associated with fighting affected the entire population. Huerta began a process of militarizing already weak civilian authority in cities and towns that would continue, in different form, under Constitutionalist occupations. One of the most devastating aspects of Huerta's rule was *la leva*, the massive conscription of poor civilians into the army, a tradition well-entrenched in the nineteenth century, but raised to unprecedented levels as Huerta expanded the federal army in response to the Constitutionalist rebellion. In the countryside, soldiers rounded up Indians and peasants, often 15 years old or less, by the trainload. In the cities, working people were picked up at factories, hospitals, cinemas, and theaters, labeled as "vagrants," and shipped off to fight in the federal army. Few policies created more resentment against Huerta and more sympathy for the revolutionary factions that opposed him than this conscription. Moreover, conscripts proved dispirited fighters, quick to defect and even to join rebels.[43] By contrast, the revolutionary armies rarely resorted to forced recruitment, or did so on a much smaller scale than that of Huerta, as for example Villa after 1916.

When Revolutionary armies occupied cities and towns, tremendous disruptions occurred. These armies often imposed martial law to neutralize hostile civilian authorities and to limit the sacking of stores and houses. Constitutionalist forces often turned the traditional order on its head. In Mexico City and Guadalajara, officers and troops occupied the houses of the wealthy, desecrated church buildings by turning them into barracks or giving them to workers' organizations, and forced wealthy residents, merchants, and church officials to provide "loans" and engage in public displays of humiliation, such as sweeping the streets.[44] Such largely symbolic actions created fear among urban elites and antipathy among devout Catholics of all social classes. Mixed sympathy resulted among the urban poor and working people, especially when federal army domination was combined with army embrace of labor unions and periodic distribution of food and currency. Similarly, in Chihuahua in 1914, Villa squeezed the wealthy for contributions and brought in cattle from confiscated haciendas to assure a cheap and plentiful supply of meat.[45]

But the redistribution of wealth in cities was often more symbolic and temporary than real, and the invading armies, particularly the Constitutionalists, often engaged in random and systematic looting. For example, before abandoning Mexico City in March 1915 to the Zapatistas, Constitutionalists stripped two of the main hospitals of all medicines, instruments, and sheets. The Englishwoman Rosa King recalled finding in Mexico City a year later the bathtubs from her Cuernavaca hotel, after they had been confiscated and sold by Constitutionalist soldiers. While Convention forces seem to have been less systematic in their theft, Zapatista and Villista soldiers were known for random sacking in towns and cities. In the countryside, revolutionaries who plundered towns and carried off horses and women were often indistinguishable from bandits.[46]

Popular wisdom reflected veiled hostilities. Broadsheets and songs particularly lampooned the Carrancistas, often referred to as *"Con-sus-uñas-listas"* ("With nails ready to dig in"), for their propensity to grab everything of value before evacuating a town. The attitude of many urban civilians toward all military factions was perhaps expressed by a version of the Villista anthem *"Adelita,"* popular in Mexico City in 1915:

If Carranza gets married with Zapata
Pancho Villa with Alvaro Obregón
Adelita and I will get married
And so ends the Revolution.[47]

But for many civilians, the greatest challenges of the Revolution came not from direct contact with armed factions, but rather from the dire conditions that years of fighting brought to both town and countryside. Fighting disrupted transportation, cut off supplies, and sporadically closed down mines and factories, thus raising unemployment. Workers had a vested interest in continued industrial production, and their greatest participation in the Revolution coincided with the period of greatest economic disruption and unemployment. In mining areas like Chihuahua, workers shared an interest in the continued operations of foreign-owned mines, and violence against the property of the mining companies, or recruitment into the ranks of the revolutionaries, was most likely to occur when the mines were closed down.[48]

Agricultural production plummeted between 1915 and 1917, devastated by drought and fighting, and remained low as hostilities subsided. A 1915 report commissioned by Carranza reported that the amount of corn and wheat production reaching markets was less than 10 percent of the levels of 1910, a situation worsened by damage to the railroad system, the continued diversion of much railroad equipment to military use, and the banditry that plagued roads.[49] The situation was further worsened because virtually every revolutionary faction financed war and government by printing its own currency, unsupported by any bank or gold guarantee. By August 1915, the paper peso had dropped from its 1910 value of 50 U.S. cents to 7 U.S. cents, and the decline would continue over the next year.[50] The repeated printing of unbacked new currencies was an invitation to speculate, something soldier and shop owner alike were ready to do. Food prices in Mexico City rose 15-fold between July 1914 and July 1915. Inflation had its redistributive aspects, as the wealthy were forced to sell their jewels for a pittance, but ultimately the poor suffered most.[51]

In rural areas, civilians could protect themselves somewhat from inflation and the disruption of production and transportation by relying on traditional subsistence crops. In 1915 the state of Morelos found itself in the midst of the most extensive agrarian reform during the Revolution, and so enjoyed abundant foodstuffs. Residents of San José de Gracia, Michoacán, began once again to consume products they had once shipped to cities.[52] By contrast, urban areas suffered much more from hunger. In the spring and summer of 1915, while Morelos enjoyed its agricultural bounty, a short distance away the metropolitan press was full of stories of desperate women selling their bodies, of despairing mothers who attempted suicide because they could not feed their children, of soaring death rates related to food problems, of those who chopped down trees in the Alameda and Chupultepec parks for fuel, and of furious fights over garbage.[53] Hunger, inflation, and unemployment in Mexico City made the population desperate, and contributed to what critics of the "Red Battalions" referred to at the time as "conscription by hunger." Even in rural areas of northern Mexico, many Carrancista recruits joined the ranks in 1916 as an alternative to starvation.[54]

Hunger, in turn, greatly weakened the population and made them particularly vulnerable to disease. Typhus cases peaked throughout the country between 1915 and 1917, hitting urban areas and the cities of Mexico, Durango, and Zacatecas particularly hard. Reported disease-related deaths in Mexico City, exacerbated by hunger, reached almost 25,000 for 1915, or 5 percent of the population, and remained almost as high for 1916.[55] By 1918, with Carranza formally elected president and much of the country at peace, the Spanish flu pandemic hit Mexico hard in both rural and urban areas. Mexico City lost 23,000 to the flu, and Morelos lost a quarter of its population in 1918 to mostly disease-related deaths and emigration. By the time of the 1921 census, the combination of fighting, migration, and disease had reduced the population of Morelos by over 40 percent from what it had been in 1910. Nationally, mortality estimates for the Spanish flu run as high as 450,000 deaths. By contrast, flu deaths reached 550,000 in the United States, whose population was more than six times that of Mexico. Overall, disease took a toll certainly made far worse by the material depredations of the Revolution, a toll that may have equaled the deaths directly related to fighting.[56]

Of course *revolucionados* were not simply passive victims of looting, unemployment, hunger, and disease. As suggested in the previous section, one response to the material deprivations of the Revolution was to organize, and indeed hunger and unemployment first brought Esther Torres ("one wants to just live, nothing more, right?") to the *Casa del Obrero Mundial*, where she received work distributing food in outlets organized by the *Casa* and municipal authorities, and eventually organized a seamstress union and played a key role in the general strike of 1916.[57] Those forced by the *leva* or by necessity to take up arms were inevitably transformed by mobility and experience.

¡Revolución Adios!

Yet another active response of *revolucionados* was to flee. Pablo Mares sold everything in his store and shut it down after soldiers harassed him in his home town in Jalisco. Even so, the Villistas soon pressed him into service. "But I didn't like that," he remembered, "because I never liked to go about fighting, especially about things that don't make any difference to one." When his regiment got to the city of Torreón, he made for the Texas border and got a job working on the railroad. Concha Gutiérrez del Río taught school in a small town in Chihuahua until "with the revolution they ceased paying us," and she and her husband left to find work in the United States. Pedro Chausse joined up with Carranza after his high school was closed because of the Revolution. "When the campaign was over and I was not able to find employment, I went to join my brother who was already working in the United States."[58] A common response of many civilians to the violence and hardship of the Revolution was to leave their homes, not only to join one military faction or another, but also to escape to less violent regions or cities, or to the greater safety and employment possibilities in the United States.

In the early years of the Revolution, wealthy foreigners and Mexicans became ready targets of taxation, violence, and confiscation, and so they were often the first to leave their homes. The U.S. reporter Herman Whitaker wrote from the city of Chihuahua in 1914 that "since the revolution began the foreign population has dwindled from about 800 in the city and 4,000 in the surrounding districts to some eighty people." Many were skilled American mine workers who feared violence or suffered the suspension of operations.[59] As Huerta's regime faltered in the face of revolutionary forces, many wealthy citizens—landed elites, urban landlords, professionals, and "respectable" families—chose to flee their haciendas and urban homes rather than face or resist revolutionary troops.

Internal migration was an obvious option. When the cities of Durango, Chihuahua, and Guadalajara fell to Constitutionalist forces in 1914, a wave of wealthy and middle-class refugees fled south, and cities of the central region, where much of the heaviest fighting occurred, lost population during the course of the entire decade of fighting. By the end of the summer, over 15,000 refugees, many of them well-to-do, had crowded into Veracruz, then under United States occupation. Migration into Veracruz continued over the next two years, as the port served as Carranza's headquarters and escaped the worst fighting of the civil war.[60] Rich and poor alike continued to crowd into Mexico City. In spite of the toll of hunger and disease, the capital expanded almost by 30 percent over the decade, to 615,000 in 1921, during a period when the country as a whole lost population. Females outnumbered males two to one in this additional population, and sex imbalances in the city were greatest between the ages of 15 and 24.[61]

Perhaps just as obvious, particularly for northerners, was the possibility of heading "*al norte*" to seek refuge and work. Border crossings were fairly casual, making it easy for migrants to cross, but difficult for historians to measure the hundreds of thousands who traversed the border as legal immigrants, temporary workers, refugees, and illegal aliens. Official U.S. figures for the first two categories put the total legal migration across the border into the United States for the decade at 890,000, a figure that undoubtedly underestimates the actual movement. Some scholars estimate a total close to 1.5 million.[62]

While historians generally agree on the massive and unprecedented scale of migration to the United States, there is less conformity on the degree to which migrants were fleeing the Revolution to embrace opportunities there. In spite of incompleteness and the bias towards legal immigration, the data suggest a variety of interesting patterns. Migration to the United States increased from the very beginning of the Revolution, but jumped by 50 percent in 1913 after Huerta overthrew President Madero and fighting spread throughout the country. But the rise in migration does not directly correspond with a rise in violence. In the worst years of fighting, 1914 and 1915, the number of legal immigrants actually dropped by 20 percent over 1913, to roughly 65,000, most probably because revolutionary factions controlled the major railroads, making it difficult for many in central Mexico to reach the border. By contrast, immigration jumped dramatically in 1916 to approximately 100,000, and dropped below that figure only once in the next five years. Emigrants continued to be mostly peasants and rural workers, but the percentage of wealthy hacienda owners, professionals, and skilled workers increased during the Revolution. So too did the percentage of women and families, rather than single men.[63]

The rise in emigration to the United States from 1916, after the worst fighting of the Revolution had subsided, suggests that people left Mexico as much because of the economic and social devastation there as because of the fighting. Hunger, unemployment, and inflation devastated Mexico from the second half of 1915. Some troops were demobilized after the devastating defeats of Villa in the fall of 1915, and the former soldiers found limited opportunities for employment. Migrants may also have come as much for the opportunities in the United States as for the lack of them in Mexico. By contrast to Mexico's, the U.S. economy was booming, particularly in

California and Texas, and employment opportunities for Mexicans increased once the United States entered World War I, as much of the U.S. male population left to fight in Europe, and war and the 1917 Immigration Act cut off competing immigration from Europe. Authors of one quantitative analysis of migration patterns during the decade of the Revolution see the rise of Mexican migration during the decade of the Revolution to be largely part of a broader pattern, spurred by economic expansion in the United States, which began before 1910 and continued after 1920. In their estimate, the Revolution itself produced one-fourth more migrants than there might have otherwise been.[64]

As always, migrants were a highly transient population, and many returned to Mexico during the course of the decade. For example, the U.S. census for 1920 shows the Mexican population resident in the United States increasing by 265,000 when compared with 1910, a modest portion of the 890,000 who had formally migrated during the previous 10 years.[65] At any rate, motives for migration were mixed and multiple. Fleeing was not only a way to deal with the violence, confiscations, and material devastation of the Revolution; it was also a means—as it would continue to be into the twenty-first century—to seek opportunities available in the United States.

CONCLUSION

Although civilians were subordinate to the armed soldiers of the Mexican Revolution, and have long been treated as such by revolutionary leaders, by their troops, and by scholars, they nonetheless played important roles in shaping the Revolution. The civilian populations of rural villages provided a crucial base of support for revolutionary factions, both for those organized around the demand for agrarian reform and for those determined to regain village autonomy. The shift from *pacífico* to armed revolutionary was frequent and the dependency between them was to some extent natural, given the importance of rural villages as a basis for rebellion. But even the most coherent and focused revolutionary movements, such as that led by Zapata, were prone to tensions with local populations, and civilian *revolucionarios* could also come to feel that they were *revolucionados*. In urban areas, the armed revolution brought opportunities for civilian organization and mobilization, though the overlap of rural and urban goals was limited, and urban civilians were less likely to cross directly over to armed rebellion. Finally, many civilians experienced the armed Revolution and its attendant unemployment, hunger, and disease not as liberation, but as an affront to their way of life or a challenge to their very survival. The response of many, from hacienda owners to the poorest peasants, was often to flee to greater safety and opportunities.

After 1920—with the return of a relative peace, a measure of civilian government (albeit dominated until 1946 by former generals), and an official promise of social justice—taking up arms remained a strategy for new and former rebels, but one that was increasingly desperate and never again successful. Postrevolutionary Mexico experienced a level of stability unusual for Latin America, though it was not completely devoid of the guerrillas and "dirty wars" that devastated so much of Latin America in the 1960s and 1970s. Its modern history could instead be characterized by the often tense interaction between a civilian state that clung to power and claimed legitimacy as the embodiment of the Revolution's struggle for social justice, and its unarmed citizens (including workers, campesinos, the urban poor, and a growing middle class) who demanded greater democracy and the fulfillment of promises of social justice. Even the famous neo-Zapatista rebellion in 1994 shifted quickly, after 12 days of fighting, to protracted negotiations and political maneuvering. As a result of this interaction, rooted more in social mobilization and negotiation than in armed confrontation, civilians retained the central role in local and national affairs, and became once again subjects worthy of the attention of historians.

NOTES

1. See the comments of Luis González on this neglect in "La Revolución Mexicana desde el punto de vista de los revolucionados," in *Historias* 8–9 (Enero–Junio 1985), 5–13. Exceptions are his own book, *San José de Gracia: Mexican Village in Transition* (Austin: University of Texas Press, 1974), and Rafael Torres Sánchez, *Revolución y vida cotidiana: Guadalajara, 1914–1934* (Mexico City: Universidad Autónoma de Sinaloa, 2001).

2. Frank Tannenbaum, *Peace by Revolution, Mexico after 1910* (New York: Columbia University Press, 1966).

3. For a succinct overview of interpretations of the Revolution, see Alan Knight, "Mexican Revolution: Interpretations," in *Encyclopedia of Mexico: History, Society & Culture,* ed. Michael S. Werner (Chicago: Fitzroy Dearborn Publishers, 1997), 869–873. The most important overviews of the Mexican Revolution remain Alan Knight's *The Mexican Revolution,* 2 vols. (Cambridge: Cambridge University Press, 1986) and John M. Hart's *Revolutionary Mexico: The Coming and Process of the Mexican Revolution* (Berkeley: University of California Press, 1987).

4. Figures on troops are from John Womack, "The Mexican Revolution, 1910–1920," in *Mexico since Independence*, ed. Leslie Bethell (Cambridge: Cambridge University Press, 1991), 148, 154–156, 162–163. Edwin Lieuwen puts federal troops under Huerta in August 1914 at a much lower level, somewhere between 40,000 and 68,000. He puts Constitutionalist forces at 150,000 at the time of the Aguascalientes Convention in the fall of 1914. *Mexican Militarism: The Political Rise and Fall of the Revolutionary Army, 1910–1940* (Albuquerque: University of New Mexico, 1968), 19, 27.

5. Lieuwen, *Mexican Militarism*, 45.

6. Knight, *The Mexican Revolution*, 2:143.

7. Robert McCaa, "Missing Millions: The Human Cost of the Mexican Revolution, 1910–1930," published online by The Population Center, 2001, http://www.hist.umn.edu/%7Ermccaa/missmill/index.htm.

8. González, "La Revolución Mexicana desde el punto de vista de los revolucionados," 3–13.

9. John Hart, "Mexican Revolution: Causes," in Werner, *Encyclopedia of Mexico*, 848.

10. John Lear, *Workers, Neighbors, and Citizens: The Revolution in Mexico City* (Lincoln: University of Nebraska Press, 2001), chapters 4 and 5.

11. Knight, *The Mexican Revolution*, 1:273.

12. Vera Estañol is cited in Lieuwen, *Mexican Militarism*, 29.

13. John Womack, *Zapata and the Mexican Revolution* (New York: Knopf, 1969), 228.

14. Knight, *The Mexican Revolution*, 1:78–126.

15. Knight, *The Mexican Revolution*, 1:105.

16. Womack, *Zapata*, 225.

17. Womack, *Zapata*, 131–132; Samuel Brunk, *Emiliano Zapata! Revolution & Betrayal in Mexico* (Albuquerque: University of New Mexico Press, 1995), 72.

18. Womack, *Zapata*, 138.

19. Brunk, *Emiliano Zapata!*, 89.

20. Womack, *Zapata*, 138–139, 165, 169.

21. Brunk, *Emiliano Zapata!*, 44, 73–75.

22. Womack, *Zapata*, 152, 227.

23. Womack, *Zapata*, 254.

24. Brunk, *Emiliano Zapata!*, 199, 211; Samuel Brunk, "The Sad Situation of Civilians and Soldiers: The Banditry of Zapatismo in the Mexican Revolution," *American Historical Review* 101:2 (April 1996), 341.

25. Brunk, *Emiliano Zapata!*, 72–74.

26. Knight, *The Mexican Revolution*, 1:115–127; Friedrich Katz, *The Life and Times of Pancho Villa* (Stanford: Stanford University Press, 1998), 389–390.

27. Katz, *Life and Times*, 401–403.

28. Katz, *Life and Times*, 514, 585–586, 596–597.

29. Francisco Ramírez Plancarte, *La Ciudad de México durante la Revolución Constitucionalista* (Mexico City: Ediciones Botas, 1941), 65–66; Tannenbaum, *Peace by Revolution*, 122–123.

30. Lear, *Workers, Neighbors, and Citizens*, 123–191; Rodney Anderson, "Mexican Workers and the Politics of Revolution, 1906–1911," *Hispanic American Historical Review* 54:1 (February 1974), 94–113.

31. Lear, *Workers, Neighbors, and Citizens*, 192–241.

32. Membership reported in *Mexican Herald*, February 12, 1915; Luis Araiza, *Historia del movimiento obrero mexicano* (Mexico City: Ediciones de la Casa Mundial, 1966), 3:112.

33. Lear, *Workers, Neighbors, and Citizens*, 138–141; Ariel Rodríguez Kuri, *La Experiencia Olvidada: El Ayuntamiento de México: Política y Gobierno, 1876–1912* (Mexico City: UAM/Colegio de México, 1996), 226–227.

34. Knight, *The Mexican Revolution*, 2:67, 158; Javier Garciadiego, *Rudos contra Científicos. La Universidad Nacional durante la Revolución Mexicana* (Mexico City: El Colegio de México, 1996), 228–232; Ramírez Plancarte, *La Ciudad de México*, 49–50.

35. "Peticiones de la Casa del Obrero Mundial," in *El Demócrata*, October 3, 1914; see also the *Casa*-organized march of the unemployed, "Al Pueblo Obrero," in *El Pueblo*, October 3, 1914.

36. On food riots and confiscations, see Lear, *Workers, Neighbors, and Citizens*, 299–315.

37. Lear, *Workers, Neighbors, and Citizens*, 269–291.

38. "Entrevista con la Señora Esther Torres, viuda de Morales, realizado por María Isabel Souza y Carmen Nava los días 12 y 25 de febrero de 1975 en la Ciudad de México," PHO/I/145, 22–23, in Archivo de la Palabra, Instituto de Investigaciones Dr. José María Luis Mora.

39. González, "La Revolución Mexicana," 11–12.

40. Knight, *The Mexican Revolution*, 1:99.

41. Gilbert Joseph, *Revolution from Without: Yucatán, Mexico and the United States, 1880–1924* (Cambridge: Cambridge University Press, 1982).

42. González, *San José de Gracia*, 121–127, 153–160.

43. Knight, *The Mexican Revolution*, 2:78–79.

44. Rafael Torres Sánchez, *Revolución y vida cotidiana*, 137; Lear, *Workers, Neighbors, and Citizens*, 272–273.

45. Katz, *Life and Times*, 421.

46. Ramírez Plancarte, *La Ciudad*, 526; Cardoso de Oliveira to Secretary of State, March 6, 1915, *Records of the Department of State relating to internal affairs of Mexico, 1910–1929 [microform]*, Washington, D.C.: National Archives and Records Service, General Services Administration, 1959, 812.00/14515; Rosa King, *Tempest over Mexico* (Boston: Little, Brown, 1935), 302.

47. Ramírez Plancarte, *La Ciudad*, 338.

48. William French, *A Peaceful and Working People: Manners, Morals, and Class Formation in Northern Mexico* (Albuquerque: University of New Mexico Press, 1996), 141–241.

49. Study by Eduardo Fuentes, in Archivo Histórico del Centro de Estudios de Historia de México, Mexico City (Condumex archive), Fondo XXI, L 5861 carpeta 53, p. 22; for a more moderate estimate of production losses, see Womack, "The Mexican Revolution," 133.

50. Edwin W. Kemmerer, *Inflation and Revolution: Mexico's Experience of 1912–1917* (Princeton: Princeton University Press, 1940), 45–46.

51. Knight, *The Mexican Revolution*, 2:410–413. See also Ariel Rodríguez Kuri, "Desabasto, hambre y respuesta política, 1915" in *Instituciones y ciudad: Ocho estudios históricos sobre la ciudad de México*, eds. Carlos Illades and Ariel Rodríguez Kuri (Jalapa, Mexico: Unidad Obrera y Socialista, 2000), 133–161.

52. Womack, *Zapata*, 241; and González, *San José*, 124.

53. *Mexican Herald*, February 18 and 21, 1915; Ramírez Plancarte, *La Ciudad*, chapters 14 and 15; Knight, *The Mexican Revolution*, 2:317, 425.

54. Ramírez Plancarte, *La Ciudad*, 367; Katz, *Life and Times*, 595.

55. Knight, *The Mexican Revolution*, 2:420; deaths in Mexico City are from McCaa, "Missing Millions," 8, 13.

56. Knight, *The Mexican Revolution*, 2:422; Womack, *Zapata*, 311; McCaa, "Missing Millions," 8.

57. "Entrevista con la Señora Esther Torres," 58.

58. Manuel Gamio, *The Mexican Immigrant* (Chicago: University of Chicago Press, 1931), 2, 165, 187.

59. Katz, *Life and Times*, 420–421; French, *A Peaceful and Working People*, 152.

60. Knight, *The Mexican Revolution*, 2:178–179; Andrew Grant Wood, *Revolution in the Street: Women, Workers, and Urban Protest in Veracruz* (Wilmington, DE: Scholarly Resources, 2001), 22.

61. *Estadísticas Históricas de Mexico* (Aguascalientes: INEGI, 2000), Cuadro 1.4.2, 20. Information on gender differences is based on census information from the *Censo general de habitantes. 30 de noviembre de 1921* for the Federal District and taken from Ann Blum, "Cleaning the Revolutionary Household: Domestic Servants and Public Welfare in Mexico City, 1900–1935," in *Journal of Women's History* 15:4 (Winter 2004), 77.

62. Linda Hall and Don Coerver, *Revolution on the Border: The United States and Mexico, 1910–1920* (Albuquerque: University of New Mexico Press, 1988), 126–127.

63. Hall and Coerver, *Revolution on the Border*, 128–129; Martín Valadez, "Migration: To the United States, 1876–1940," in Werner, *Encyclopedia of Mexico*, 891–892.

64. Myron Gutmann, Robert McCaa, Rodolfo Gutiérrez-Montes, and Brian Gratton, "Los efectos demográficos de la revolución Mexicana en Estados Unidos," *Historia Mexicana* 50:1 (July–September 2000), 145–165.

65. Hall and Coerver, *Revolution on the Border*, 136; Manuel Gamio, *Mexican Immigration to the United States* (Chicago, University of Chicago Press, 1930), 2.

EIGHT

Reading Revolution from Below: Cuba 1933

Gillian McGillivray

Revolutions often begin as middle-class movements for demo-cratic reform, but the participation of "the masses"—workers, farmers, and marginalized people—turn such political move-ments into social revolutions. This statement accurately describes the course of the 1933 and 1959 Cuban Revolutions, and yet much historical scholarship prioritizes the first group of "revolution-aries" over the second. The role of middle-class groups such as students, intellectuals, and politicians is easier to document be-cause these individuals were literate and they wrote about their experiences. There is no denying that these groups functioned as important catalysts for change, but one cannot ignore the impact of mass mobilizations during and after the two insurrections: "the masses" pushed through fundamental transformations in the Cuban state.

The tumultuous events of 1933, as an astute United States ob-server noted, should "not be confused with the usual recurrent Latin American political upheavals." He was referring to the small-scale revolts that arose over struggles for power across the region since the early nineteenth century. The 1933 insurrection in Cuba, he insisted, "is made of sterner stuff. It goes far deeper. It has in it the essence of the last Mexican Revolution or the Russian Revolution."[1] The mass mobilizations across the island demanding social rights were the "stuff" the observer was referring to, and they constitute the focus of this essay. In the case of 1933 Cuba, a vast majority of civilians became revolutionaries both in the cities and in the countryside; "the daily lives of civilians" thus becomes, in this essay, "the daily lives of revolutionaries." Sugar mill workers are a primary focus here, because sugar made up 80 percent of exports, dominating the Cuban economy. Most Cubans grew, cut, or benefited from the sale of sugar in some way.

Reconstructing the activities of Cuba's urban and rural poor is difficult because most workers and farmers were illiterate, and hence they did not leave much of a written record of their early-twentieth-century lives. Even so, this chapter attempts to "read" the actions of the masses during Cuba's Revolution of 1933 to better understand the daily lives of the working-class and marginalized people of the cities and countryside. It argues that the so-called riots of the "mobs" in 1933 Havana represented a clear and dignified rejection of the system of rule based on U.S. power, Cuban political corruption, and economic inequality. The actions of their counterparts in sugar mills across the countryside represented an equally clear rejection of the local system of rule based on control, unpredictable philanthropy, and repression. Both groups achieved certain reforms, but sugar workers in particular precipitated a fundamental change in the Cuban state after 1933, as they would do again in 1959.

THE CONTEXT: U.S. POWER, GERARDO MACHADO, AND THE GREAT DEPRESSION

The palace group is talking loudly about running Cuba without American interference. How stupid! Cuba will always be under the influence of the United States. Her strategic position in relation to the Panama Canal and the Gulf of Mexico forces such a relationship upon Cuba. Furthermore, a billion and a half dollars of American capital are invested here. (U.S. resident of Cuba, Ruby Hart Phillips, diary entry, August 1933)[2]

During the first two decades of the twentieth century the United States exercised formidable economic, political, and military power over many Latin American countries. U.S. capital integrated them into the world economic system through investments, exports, and imports, and American Marines stood ready to protect U.S. investments whenever political chaos threatened. But the 1929 Great Depression ushered in a significant change whereby many countries, including the United States, began a period of inward-looking nationalism. President Franklin D. Roosevelt's New Deal closed off the United States economically while his Good Neighbor foreign policy promised that U.S. troops would remain at home. The combination of economic crisis and political space gave rise to a series of populist, nationalist experiments across the region that included the regimes of Lázaro Cárdenas in Mexico and Getúlio Vargas in Brazil.

As the above quote by Ruby Hart Phillips reveals, the United States adopted a somewhat different attitude towards Cuba, which remained more or less its political and economic colony. After helping the island gain independence from Spain in 1898, U.S. troops left Cuba four years later, but not before U.S. officials embedded two key principles in the Cuban political-economic system. The first, the Platt Amendment to the Cuban constitution, distorted independent political development by calling for U.S. intervention whenever large-scale political struggle threatened order on the island. Based on this justification, U.S. Marines occupied the island during or after the contested elections of 1906, 1912, 1917, and 1921. The second, the Reciprocity Treaty, made Cuba's economy increasingly dependent on exporting one product—unrefined sugar—to one market—the United States—while entrenching low tariffs for nearly all imports from the same market. The competition from mass-produced U.S. goods inhibited the development of domestic industries in the newly independent nation.

From 1900 to 1920 U.S. investment in Cuba's sugar economy grew exponentially, making Cuba more of a monoculture economy than it had ever been; sugar made up roughly 80 percent of exports in this period. Many middle-class and elite Cubans expressed gratitude to American capitalists for bringing progress through the modern sugar plantations that they established on the island. Philanthropic plantation owners tended to provide parks, housing, medical clinics, and schooling for workers, cane farmers (*colonos*), and their families on an ad-hoc basis, favoring upper-level employees and varying benefits according to year-to-year profit levels. When sugar sold at high prices, as it did during World War I from 1917 to 1919, Cubans in the cities and in the countryside benefited from a booming economy. Thus, they tolerated the high level of U.S. investment and interference in the economic and political sphere. But the worldwide over-production of sugar and consequent crash in sugar prices that began in 1920 and extended into the 1930s sparked increasing nationalism and popular mobilization for change across the island.

American policymakers breathed a sigh of relief when Cubans elected Gerardo Machado as president in 1924 on a popular, but moderate, platform based on support for national industrial development and public works. At least in its early years, the Machado regime sought to contain worker and *colono* mobilization with the populist combination of repression and co-option. The president might send in the Rural Guard (Cuba's soldiers) to end a strike on one occasion, but on another he might ask a mediator to convince workers to end the strike in exchange for a few, minimal reforms. Machado certainly horded money for himself and his cronies, but he also funneled at least some of the export taxes, payoffs from capitalists seeking contracts, and extremely large loans from Wall Street banks into public works programs such as a national highway system and a new capital building in Havana.

Machado's populist position became increasingly untenable as sugar prices dropped from an average 2.96 cents per pound in 1927 to 1.47 in 1930. That same year the U.S. Congress passed into law the Hawley-Smoot Tariff, which hurt the Cuban economy even more by favoring the producers of beet sugar in the western United States and cane sugar in Hawaii, Puerto Rico, and the Philippines. Cuban intellectual Herminio Portell Vilá assessed the effect of such protectionism in a language that eloquently reflected Cuban nationalist sentiment: "A difference of half a cent in the tariff . . . represents the difference between a national tragedy in which everything is cut, from the nation's budget to the . . . alms handed to a beggar, and a so-called state of prosperity, whose benefits never reach the people as a whole or profit Cuba as a nation."[3] The Machado regime cut back on public works projects and introduced strict cane quotas to limit the total production of sugar, hoping that a smaller supply would increase the price. Other countries simply increased production, offsetting Cuba's painful efforts to curb the world supply. Prices resumed a downward spiral, and by 1930 the crop restriction was hurting the planters almost as much as workers and cane farmers. Since less sugar was being sold at lower prices, workers lost jobs, cane farmers lost income, and plantation owners lost profits.

Machado had prolonged his presidential term in 1928 in the name of political and economic stability, but his incumbency deprived Cubans of a political avenue for protest. As a result, almost everyone on the island began to resent Cuba's combined state of depression and dictatorship. Veterans of the 1895–1898 War for Independence tried to overthrow the government in 1931, but Machado's army repressed the movement. Students and middle-class professionals organized "ABC" secret cells that responded to Machado's repression with terrorism, and Communist leaders (who followed directives from Joseph Stalin's Russia) or Trotskyst leaders (who believed in the principles espoused by Leon Trotsky, the former Russian Bolshevik and Leninist revolutionary) organized workers clandestinely.[4] Machado's well-funded police force and army targeted them all.

Machado lost his populist balance when he abandoned co-option for extreme repression. He increasingly relied upon U.S. funds, the secret police, and Rural Guard soldiers to put down the mounting opposition in the cities and countryside. Use of the *ley de fuga* became a common tactic in the cities: secret service or policemen would round up suspects for interrogation, set them free, and then claim that they had to shoot them because the suspects were trying to run away. Soldiers in the countryside were equally brutal with any workers or professionals suspected of organizing unions or opposition groups: the Rural Guard would expel them from their homes, put them into prison, and sometimes torture them or hang them from trees. A critical April 19, 1933 editorial in the *Nation* correctly asserted that "Machado has been maintained in office against the obvious will of the Cuban people by the financial support of our great corporations. More heavily loaded with per capita debt charges than any other Latin American country, Cuba . . . has been unable to revolt or default. Machado would doubtless have fallen in 1930 but for the $50,000,000 lent him by the Chase bank."

The interpretation is powerfully expressed in an cartoon image on page 208.

"Wall Street" strings hold up a machine-gun-toting Machado puppet that stands over a chained *"Cuba Libre."* Cuban presidents since 1902 practiced graft and repression to varying degrees, but none before Machado had engaged in corruption under such dire economic conditions or employed such extensive state terrorism that included the murder of middle-class journalists, students, and political activists.

DEPRESSION AND DICTATORSHIP IN THE COUNTRYSIDE

Populist politics could not survive the Great Depression, nor could philanthropic social control in the sugar plantations across the island. Large U.S. corporations like the Cuban-American Sugar Company and the Cuba Company, which had managed to weather the 1920s without deficits, began to lose money in 1930. Manuel

Rionda, owner of the Tuinucú Sugar Mill, among others, wrote to Administrator Oliver Doty in 1929: "Fortunately, the sales last summer show a profit of $194,000.00 [. . .] but even this does not permit us to continue paying dividends, so then: (1) out with the idea of paying the [cane farmers] but just what they are entitled to; (2) we must cut down expenses; (3) we must cut down our staff. . . . Tuinucú must change its methods, or stop paying dividends, which alternative shall it be?"[5] Rionda posed this as a rhetorical question because he obviously considered philanthropic rule a luxury. Among other things, Tuinucú stopped paying pensions in 1932, and reduced the monthly salaries of the most fortunate employees (those with jobs during the "dead season" between harvests) by 82 percent.

Field workers suffered the worst cutbacks during the Depression. In December 1930 Rionda advised Doty that the extremely

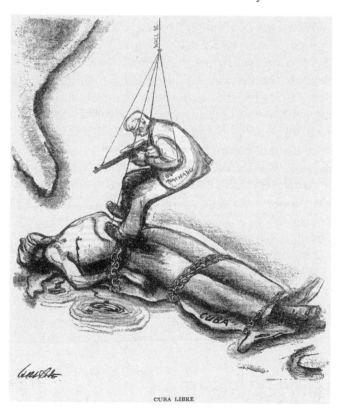

CUBA LIBRE

Cuba Libre. (© *The Nation*, vol. 136, p. 492. Reprinted with permission from the May 3, 1933 issue of *The Nation*. For subscription information, call 1-800-333-8536. Portions of each week's *Nation* magazine can be accessed at http://www. thenation.com.

difficult jobs of cutting, lifting, and hauling a days' work worth of cane ought not to cost more than 80 cents—50 cents for cutting and lifting and 30 cents for hauling. "I am sorry to have to reduce the wages of those poor laborers," Rionda wrote, "but I can not see how it can be done otherwise."[6] When Doty did as he was told, Rionda responded with what can only, in retrospect, be read as extreme naïveté: "[Y]ou have done well in reducing [the budget] to such an extreme as to make us wonder how much can be done when things are bad. Cuba has great facilities to expand and contract."[7]

Mills across the island made similar reductions. A September 1932 report from Oriente Province's Punta Alegre Sugar Company observed that "the average daily pay for 1932 was 40 percent less than the averages back in 1910, and some 30 percent less than the seven-year period from 1910–1917."[8] The British Embassy in Havana asserted one year later that wages had been steadily declining since 1929, adding that it was "probably no exaggeration to say that field workers are worse off in some respects today than in the days of slavery. They are expected to work 10 or 11 hours a day for 25 cents, with seldom more than 100 days' work in the year."[9] Most mills espoused a strategy of shortening the milling season: from an average of almost five months a year in 1925, the harvest declined to just over two months in 1933. Some mills had to close altogether: there were 163 mills active in 1929, but only 125 in 1933.[10]

Besides cutting jobs, salaries, and the milling season, mills across the island slashed the budgets for schools, medical services, light, and power. The educational expenses at the Cuban-American Sugar Company's massive Chaparra and Delicias plantations fell from the 1929–1930 level of $41,690 to $9,050 by 1933–1934. The company gave fewer discounts for medical services, and stopped paying for doctors and teachers in more rural areas. Rural Cubans thus suddenly found themselves unable to remain in their communities. The Cuban-American Sugar Company archives are full of letters and petitions to General Manager R. B. Wood from workers and cane farmers pleading for the return of schools, teachers, and doctors to their communities in the cane farm towns or mill towns. Workers and small farmers also asked for land because they were literally starving. For example, Cándido Fernández wrote in July 1932: "Will you please ... give me a piece of land on the former 'Campo Sport' [to] cultivate corn, sweet potatoes, beans etc. I am an old employee of the Analysis Department Central Office, and have

six small children to give food."[11] Other letters in the same file reveal the incredible contrast between the lives of men like Cándido
and the administrators. While one new administrator at the mill
(H. M. Hicks) requested a list of luxury furniture to be shipped from
the United States and his dog "couriered" from his former place of
employment, another (R. B. Wood, the "President" of the Chaparra
Yacht Club) was called to a meeting in Havana to discuss prepara-
tions for the National Sailing Regatta.

Workers and farmers lost jobs, a place to mill their cane, and their
health and education services in one blow. Unwilling to tolerate
such harsh conditions and extreme inequality any longer, small
farmers and field and factory worker representatives from 32 sugar
mills across the island met in Santa Clara in December 1932 to constitute the National Union of Sugar Industry Workers—Sindicato
Nacional de Obreros de la Industria Azucarera (SNOIA). They did
so despite—and in reaction to—the extreme levels of military repression under Machado. By the second meeting of SNOIA, held
the following May at Camagüey, the number of mills represented
had grown to 102.

Sugar worker manifestos from 1932 and 1933 demonstrate how
much labor leaders learned from an earlier strike wave that had
taken place in 1925. The proclamations emphasize the need to do
solidarity work among workers of the sectors related to sugar, especially railroad and dock workers, but also among soldiers, small
and medium cane-farmers, and farmers of other products in the
region. Railroad workers could refuse to run trains that might otherwise bring soldiers to repress a strike. Dockworkers could refuse
to load sugar made by strikebreakers while soldiers might decline
to repress workers. Cane farmers could complete a production
blockade against a company by joining striking workers, and merchants, farmers, and other residents near the mills could provide
sustenance for striking workers. The manifestos also recognized
the participation of women and immigrant workers in the first
strikes. They encouraged mill workers and agricultural workers to
form strike committees together, coordinating mill and field strikes,
and they included a special request to women, urging them to form
"Aid Committees" to provide for basic needs, and "Anti-Eviction
Committees" to protect strikers and their families.[12]

Although a significant number of unions were represented, only
a small minority of workers within each mill participated in this
early unionization movement. Few individuals wanted to join a
union in those years because, as one former Chaparra worker put

it, "[that] meant losing one's job, and the majority of workers had families with no alternative means of support."[13] With the help of the Rural Guard or private security forces, companies would expel anyone accused of organizing a union from their homes, together with their families. This was an effective way to use the apparent worker benefit of housing as a means of control.

When companies barred workers from the legal avenue for protest (unions), after having cut salaries, jobs, and the already minimal social services, many workers took to sabotage. Crime reports from Chaparra and Delicias reveal that such acts proliferated during 1932 and 1933. Workers stole or destroyed telephone wires, wood, bridges, and other materials. They placed obstacles in the way of company trains, left the doors open on cane trains so that cane would fall out as the train moved, and they burned, among other things, the private security force barracks, a cane train bridge, and the slaughterhouse. In March 1933 someone even made an attempt on the life of General Manager Wood.

The most common and highest-profile worker strategy was to set the cane fields on fire. American press sources reported in March 1933 that 200 million pounds of cane had been torched in the eastern province of Oriente alone.[14] Cubans came up with ingenious ways to light the fires clandestinely, thereby protecting themselves from punishment and conviction. One example was the burning rag method, whereby a rag was soaked in gas, placed at the center of a clearing under a pile of cane leaves, and then set ablaze. It took a while for the fire to reach the rows of cane stalks, allowing the arsonist time to leave the area without a trace. Another approach was to slip into the cane fields at night and scatter balls of phosphorus covered with wax. The next day, the sun would melt the wax and light the phosphorus on fire, with the arsonist long gone. Two other methods were to wire a brand to the tail of a snake and let it dash in agony through the cane fields, or to soak a large tree rat in oil and release it with its fur on fire.[15]

Sabotage may have given workers some moral satisfaction, but it could not relieve their hunger. Many workers had to abandon the countryside to avoid repression and starvation. The Spanish Ambassador in Havana described the consequent "caravans of hunger" that came streaming to the cities in search of jobs, food, and a place to settle their families.[16] But companies in the cities were also cutting back on jobs and salaries. Given that sugar was the base of the Cuban economy, the sale of most goods and services depended on Cubans gaining wages and profits from sugar;

the Great Depression thus devastated the entire Cuban economy. Estimated national revenue fell from 708 million pesos in 1925 to only 294 in 1933.[17] In city and countryside, Cubans responded with strikes and unemployment marches.

REVOLUTION IN THE CITY: THE FALL OF MACHADO

Workers across the country staged a general strike on August 5, 1933, to demonstrate their sympathy to the Havana bus-drivers who refused to pay Machado's transportation taxes. Two days after the strike began, a false rumor spread across Havana that Machado had left the island, and many ecstatic Cubans rushed to the National Palace to celebrate. Policemen and soldiers surrounded the unarmed civilians and shot at them. Such a large, open confrontation between police and civilians was unprecedented in Cuba, and Cubans renewed the general strike to rid the island of Machado's dictatorship.

The masses paralyzed the Cuban economy, and they should be credited for the fall of Machado. But before the strike could achieve its ultimate goal of ousting Machado *and* his congress and army, on August 12 several officers from that very army escorted him to the airport and named an upper class Cuban, Carlos Manuel de Céspedes, as his successor. The officers acted upon the advice of a U.S. mediator, Secretary of State Sumner Welles, and their appointment of a new president left Machado's congress intact along with much of his army. Despite the mass participation in the strike, the events of early August resembled more a palace coup than a revolutionary change for Cuba.

Workers and middle-class Cubans nevertheless seized the opportunity to flood the streets and celebrate Machado's departure. Contemporary descriptions in the U.S. press allow for a historian's analysis of the moral economy of the Havana crowds; in other words, by looking at what they did one can learn a little bit about what they felt. The throngs were quick to target and attack the most notorious elite supporters of the dictatorship as well as its foot soldiers: the *porra* or secret police. Impoverished and hungry Cubans also used the celebrations to take food and goods from the rich associated with the dictatorship. Finally, workers and students renewed strikes and protests when they realized that there had not been a significant change in the government.

Middle-class Cuban mobs began by attacking symbols of the dictatorship. Students tore down street signs reading *Avenida del*

Presidente Machado and replaced them with new ones that bore the name of a student who had fallen victim to the *machadato*. Groups of literate citizens stole typewriters and destroyed the headquarters of the Machado newspaper, the *Heraldo de Cuba*. According to one U.S. analyst, the paper had done much of Machado's work for him. "If reputations were to be destroyed, *Heraldo* was given the job. If propaganda was to be spread, *Heraldo* did it."[18] Informed groups of Cubans also attacked the barbershop where Machado had his hair cut because its owner ran a string of pornographic theaters for him.

Thousands of lower and middle-class Cubans then descended upon the presidential palace and the houses of 28 notorious Machado supporters. The crowd, according to the same U.S. observer, "was not chiefly interested in looting. Time and time again, when someone started to carry away a piece of furniture which was intact, he would be met with the cry, 'no, no, it is dirty, dirty,' and the axe would fall upon it." Cubans forced their way into the lower floor of the palace, smashed furniture, and tore up trees and plants in the garden. Someone hung a "For Rent" sign on the main entrance. At the Machado supporters' homes, the crowds destroyed furniture and china. They threw oranges and mangoes at paintings, tossed books out the windows, broke down doors, and threw débris into the street. These actions reveal that at least middle-class *Habaneros* (residents of Havana) mainly desired to expose and destroy the lies, luxurious excesses, and corruption of the rich few.

Besides this rejection of corruption and excess, two other motivations of the crowds became evident, the first shared by most, and the second most prominent among lower-class residents of the city: revenge and hunger. The officers of Machado's army were not objects of revenge, because they had rejected their unpopular leader, but there were many "mob reprisals" against leaders of the *porra*, Machado's strong-armed killing squad. Someone described as "one of the oldest American residents of Havana" wrote a colorful description of this type of revenge for the *Philadelphia Saturday Evening Post*: "The relief felt by a long-suffering people expressed itself in blood . . . Of course, the *porristas* had it coming to them. They had murdered wantonly . . . laughed if they happened to kill the wrong man and jested when they disemboweled boys . . . It was enough for any man to yell 'There's one!' and point: and then there would be one less! . . . the crowd tallied a hit at the top of their voices; and after each hit, human eyes turned to look for more bull's eyes."[19]

What the mobs did to the *porristas'* bodies once they were killed reveals elements of revenge, humor, and disdain. According to an

August 28, 1933 report in *Time*, someone placed a cigar between the teeth of Former Police Chief Antonio Ainciart's corpse as jubilant individuals hung it by the neck from an arc light. The crowds made a bonfire beneath the corpse, and danced around it as the rope burned through. When an ambulance arrived to take away the corpse, the crowds shouted "Dump Ainciart into the sea! He is not fit to be buried in the cemetery with human beings." This is reminiscent of the statements that the crowds made about the items in *Machadista* homes: evidently Cubans rejected the excessive violence, power, and luxury of the few as "dirty" in the context of depression and political dictatorship.

The "hunger" motivation shows up most clearly in Hudson Strode's article for the progressive U.S. journal, the *New Republic*. He noticed that while middle-class Cubans waved palm fronds stolen from the presidential garden at the American Embassy, thanking Sumner Welles for helping to rid the island of Machado, another "more grimly ecstatic" group looted the palace and *Machadista* houses for food. They lugged off a prize hog not *pour le sport* (for the fun of it). "It was butchered into small pieces and distributed among hungry bystanders, who rushed off with bloody joints and hunks of meat into the side streets to seek . . . charcoal fires for the cooking." Poor Cubans may, in fact, have been genuinely interested in taking some of the furniture and goods that middle-class Cubans had the luxury of destroying with the statement, "No, it is dirty." At least in one case, a poor Afro-Cuban woman had the wherewithal to justify taking something in terms that middle-class protesters could accept. She took Machado's linens from the National Palace and waved them to the crowd, declaring that "she deserved them because she was a taxpayer."[20]

THE REVOLUTION SHIFTS LEFTWARD:
GRAU SAN MARTÍN'S "100 DAYS OF REFORM"

President de Céspedes did not bring any immediate relief to the extreme poverty, nor did he significantly reform the political or military underpinnings of the Machado dictatorship. As the palm frond wavers mentioned above suggest, many Cubans believed that his government had come into office largely as the result of Welles' mediation. According to a popular saying, de Céspedes bore a "Made in the U.S.A." label. Therefore, the popular classes continued to use strikes and protests through August to demand speedy justice, revenge, and a more equitable distribution of goods. Riding on this popular wave of protest, Sergeant Fulgencio Batista, other soldiers, and a group of radical students, professors, and journalists led a bloodless coup—the so-called Sergeants' Revolt—against ex-*machadista* officers and President de Céspedes on September 5, 1933. This motley group represented the first nationalist-populist coalition in Cuba not recognized by U.S. power. Professor Ramón Grau San Martín became provisional president and Sergeant Batista began his meteoric rise to power in the background. (Batista would stage a far less popular coup in 1952, ruling for 7 years until Fidel Castro seized power on January 1, 1959.)

Grau and his co-conspirators—the University Student Directorate and the sergeants—broadcast an English-language message to Americans in the *New York Times* on October 8, 1933, explaining that they wanted to give Cuba a "New Deal" like the one Roosevelt was implementing in the United States. "We can no longer tolerate puppet governments born of monopolies and concessions," Grau declared, because they make Cuba merely "a sweatshop for the privileged few . . . Our success will mean a new Cuba, born of new ideals. . . . We are called radicals because we are closely following the tracks of your own National Recovery Act; we are called Communist because we endeavor to return the buying power of the Cuban people." The Student Directorate's speech was far more threatening, proclaiming the revolutionary goal to "conquer economic and political freedom."[21]

Although this development distressed U.S. policymakers, they did not want to jeopardize the new Good Neighbor image. The Roosevelt administration therefore assembled the Latin American ambassadors in Washington, told them that there would be no "intervention," but then proceeded to announce that the United States would not recognize the Grau regime until it proved its popularity and ability to maintain order. "Just in case," the United States sent 29 ships to surround Cuba's shores. The overbearing challenge that the United States thus created for Cubans who wanted significant nationalist change is captured in the two cartoons from *The Nation* that appear on pages 216 and 217.

The Grau regime introduced a series of reforms that responded directly to the popular demands of the mobilized masses: it repealed the Platt Amendment, gave women the vote, lowered utility and interest rates (nearly all were run by U.S. companies), and gave autonomy to the universities.[22] The government also sponsored the inauguration of a National *Colono* Association and a program of land reform that guaranteed cane farmers the permanent right

The Shadow

The Shadow. (© *The Nation,* vol. 137, p. 315. Reprinted with
permission from the September 20, 1933 issue of *The Nation*.
For subscription information, call 1-800-333-8536. Portions
of each week's *Nation* magazine can be accessed at http://
www.thenation.com.

to stay on the land they cultivated.[23] This was significant because
most cane farmers were Cuban, and many of the sugar mill owners who rented land to them were American. The Cubans did not
gain full ownership of the land, but at least they had more security
because landowners could not evict them.

For workers, the regime established a Labor Ministry to arbitrate
strikes, workers' compensation, a minimum wage, an 8-hour work-
day, and a 48-hour workweek. The reforms symbolized a great deal
to laborers. For the first time the state had pledged to intervene

"No sir! We're not through yet!"

No Sir, We're Not Through Yet. (© *The Nation*, vol. 137, p. 232. Reprinted with permission from the August 30, 1933 issue of *The Nation*. For subscription information, call 1-800-333-8536. Portions of each week's *Nation* magazine can be accessed at http://www.thenation.com.

in more than an ad-hoc or repressive way between capitalists and labor. The 8-hour day meant an end to the brutal 12-hour work regime whereby men and women had to work one 6-hour shift, lose up to an hour walking home to eat and sleep for 4 hours, and then trek back to work before the bell rang to signal the start of another 6-hour shift.

The Grau regime also approved a Nationalization of Labor decree that required Cuban nationality for 50 percent of all employees and 50 percent of total salaries in industry, commerce, and agriculture. This extremely popular piece of legislation promised to end the practice whereby foreigners' family members or foreign professionals got positions that Cubans could fill, leaving only the worst paid and most difficult jobs for nationals. Great numbers of Cubans, many of them Afro-Cubans (who suffered the worst discrimination), staged demonstrations to support the law and to demand that the ratio be increased from 50 to 80 percent. Companion legislation ruled that only Cubans could lead unions on the island, not foreign citizens. Working-class Cubans participated enthusiastically in the effort to rid the island of foreigners, whom they perceived as competition for scarce jobs. This confounded Communist and Trotskyist union organizers. Many were Spanish citizens themselves, and all hoped to forge class solidarity across national and ethnic barriers. When these unions published manifestos and newspaper articles condemning the laws as a fascist effort to divide the working classes, mobs stormed the newspapers and targeted their union headquarters.[24]

Despite the regime's efforts to satisfy popular aspirations, forces on both ends of the political spectrum threatened its existence. The above-mentioned leftist unions, the Communist National Congress of Cuban Workers (CNOC) and the Trotskyst Federation of Havana Workers (FOH), perceived the regime as middle-class, nationalist, and fascist, along the lines of Adolph Hitler's Germany, and there were certainly elements of truth to their interpretation. While historians have attributed the Grau regime's most concrete social reforms to the radical Minister of the Interior Antonio Guiteras, many members of the original Grau coalition neither enforced nor supported the reforms. As the administration neared its 100th day in power, then-Army Chief Fulgencio Batista, his U.S. allies, and traditional Cuban *políticos* put it at risk from the Right. Batista posed the chief threat. He had consolidated his control over the armed forces, and soldiers consequently no longer fraternized with workers and students but instead repressed them.[25]

REVOLUTION IN THE COUNTRYSIDE:
MILL OCCUPATIONS AND "SOVIETS"

Despite its internal divisions, the 1933 revolution provided a populist moment with far more potential for worker protest than Machado's short-lived populism. At least for a brief interregnum, the armed forces and state leaders pledged their allegiance to the popular classes and the Cuban nation to a greater extent than any previous regime. Workers certainly rose to the occasion. Sugar workers across the island had already participated in the June, July, and August strikes that forced Machado to leave; some of them were members of the Communist sugar workers' union mentioned above (SNOIA). Machado's departure on August 12 elicited outbursts in smaller cities and mill towns across the island similar to those in Havana, combining jubilation, looting, and destruction of newspapers and notorious *machadista* homes. But most sugar mills did not erupt into full-scale revolutionary mobilization until Batista led the Sergeants' Revolt in September. Only then could workers take advantage of the break in the power of the forces of repression—the Rural Guard.

A revolutionary avalanche took place at sugar mills across the country after Machado's exile. Workers forced management to leave many mills, and then different political groups competed to organize and lead the mobilized sugar workers: one, the "Guiterista" students and new labor ministry officials who supported the left wing of the Grau San Martín regime; two, the Trotskyst Federation of Havana Workers (FOH); and three, the Communist National Congress of Cuban Workers (CNOC). Despite the manifesto wars generated by these parties, workers on the ground at most mills appeared to maintain the unity necessary to win their demands.

In general, like their poor and working-class counterparts in the cities, sugar workers sometimes reacted violently and with vengeance against the extreme repression they had faced. Revolutionary arson persisted after Machado's fall but it did not reach the extent of 1895–1898 or 1952–1959 because only a small minority advocated the strategy. More often than not, workers reacted with irony, humor, and dignity against the planters' and administrators' control. Workers at the Tacajó sugar mill devised a most creative act of vengeance; they installed a loudspeaker that rang a bell on the street corner near an administrator's house so that he could feel what it was like to be sleep-deprived.[26]

Inspired by examples from the 1917 Russian Revolution, field and factory workers, and small cane farmers on a few mills, organized worker *soviets* to take over, protect, and run the mills from September 1933 through January 1934. These *soviets* constituted elaborate experiments in political, juridical, and economic life. Strike committees took over crude and refined sugar stocks and sold them to pay workers' salaries, to purchase food for families living at the mills, and to stock up on rifles for armed self-defense groups. In the case of Mabay, committees distributed tools, machinery, and over 250 acres of land to peasants and workers. Workers operated the mill without upper-management oversight, opened schools, and established a Justice Tribunal.[27] A remarkable feature of this revolutionary occupation of sugar mills is that one of the primary goals of strike committees and worker "red guards" was to protect the mills from any form of destruction or sabotage. It seemed that they wanted to prove that they were not savages, but rather Cuban citizens, worthy of a larger share of sugar profits. They used the fall months of September to December to prepare the fields and mills for the January harvest.

Those not needed for work at the mills marched in flying brigades from mill to mill to support their counterparts to gain demands from other mills. For example, over 3,000 workers and farmers armed with sticks, machetes, and a few small arms marched from the Tacajó and Baguanos mills to Santa Lucía to free the workers from the company-Rural Guard tyranny in that eastern Cuban enclave. Upon meeting a group of marchers, a Rural Guard sergeant advised them to elect a 15-person committee to go and speak to the mill administrators. The leader said that "he would have to wait for the rest" to see if they would agree. When the sergeant climbed a tree and saw men as far as the eye could see, he stepped aside and allowed them to destroy the sentry post and to break the entry gate chains that symbolized the company's extreme control over its residents. Workers from all three mills marched through the town, raising the Cuban flag and the international workers' symbol from Russia: the Red flag. They also sang the national anthem and the Communist "Internationale."[28]

Like the workers of Santa Lucía, Tacajó, and Baguanos, workers at the mills owned by Manuel Rionda broke the system of company control in more subtle ways. They wanted to make administrators know how it felt to be a worker, and made them live without servants, eat humble food, and ask permission for just about everything. On September 12, 1933, one of Rionda's nephews reported that workers at Francisco, Elia, Tuinucú, Céspedes, and "all of the other mills of Cuba" had completely frozen all activity in the mill towns and cane farm towns. At Francisco they had gone "to the extreme" of cutting off all electricity and refusing to allow anyone to leave without permission from the strike committee. Workers allowed water and electricity to flow at Tuinucú, but only between 6 P.M. and 6 A.M. The strike committees ordered office employees to leave their jobs. These employees and their families complained that their lives were made "almost impossible" when the workers denied them the domestic servants who normally washed their clothes and cooked their meals. Workers at Tuinucú imprisoned interim administrator Earl Hine in his home, letting him and his wife leave the mill only under the promise that Hine would present their demands to the shareholders in Havana and New York.

Workers at Tuinucú also categorically rejected their philanthropic matron, Isidora Rionda, and the system of dependence and charity that she represented. "The strike committee ordered Isidora to leave her Tuinucú," Manuel Rionda wrote to his nephew, "and because she did not want to do so, they took away her servants, leaving only her oldest maid Teofila, and her sister Concha. Upon hearing this, we offered to raise daily wages of less than $1.00 by 30 percent and over $1.00 by 20 percent."[29] Another nephew, Silvestre, went to the mill to try to get Isidora and Concha to leave because of the family's concern that it was too dangerous for the elderly sisters. But, as nephew Higinio Fanjul wrote on September 14, "Isidora would die before abandoning her beloved Tuinucú." He added that "one cannot help but admire her: 87 years old! The saddest part is that some of the people she has protected since their births are among the vanguard of the strike movement. I refused to believe that these movements would make it to mills like Tuinucú and Francisco, but to live is to learn."[30]

Fanjul complained about the "wave of communism," but stated that the most important thing was to "sprinkle some cash around" because the fundamental cause of the problems was hunger, and "no one deserve[d] the blame more than [U.S. President Herbert] Hoover and Smoot [of the Hawley-Smoot Tariff]." Manuel Rionda shared Fanjul's opinion that a little money could eliminate the movement. He sent a telegram to the strike committee at Tuinucú that read:

[W]e are sorry that you have taken this approach. We consider it unnecessary because as soon as the sugar situation improves, and the price of sugar increases, we will be the first to ameliorate the lives of all of those employed at our beloved Tuinucú. In order to avoid misery and sickness, we have authorized Doñas Isidora and Concha to distribute up to $1,000.00 a week during the rest of the month to those faithful, old employees who have found themselves without work for no fault of their own.[31]

But the workers, in a remarkable gesture given the context of extreme poverty and hunger, rejected the funds.

In late September, Manuel wrote his nephew in London that matters "in the interior and in Cuban plantations" were "pretty well muddled." Tuinucú was "in the hands of the working men—very friendly but no work." Manuel preferred to keep American administrators away since "their presence might precipitate trouble."[32] He was right: as another nephew noted, the mills that were having the least hard time were those where workers had no one to argue with. "In all the mills," Higinio Fanjul wrote, "including Tuinucú, all of the pigs, chickens, and provisions are running out."[33] Most mills had strike committees who set up soup kitchens to distribute such food equitably to all residents who remained on the occupied mills.[34] The redistribution of food and goods, though short-lived, constituted a very revolutionary effort to create a more equitable system of rule.

Rionda adopted the attitude that the companies might as well concede whichever demands his nephews considered reasonable in order to avoid any damage. He wrote his nephew José on September 28 that as far as he was concerned none of the contracts were worth the paper they were written on "until Cuba has a strong government."[35] Two days later, José reported back on a meeting at the new Labor Ministry office in Havana with Tuinucú strike representatives Agustín Valdivia, Donato Arcia, and Hernández Díaz. The powerful letter captures the radical change that the 1933 revolution brought to the island:

They were much harsher than I thought they would be, and one can say that the "feeling [*sentimiento*]" of the old Tuinucú has disappeared. This is a changed Cuba. The workers are perfectly organized and united, everywhere, and marked by communist tendencies. The Government is weak, and can give only minimal guarantees to capital and property. It has placed itself on labor's side to get their support, and that is why the workers feel so strong, ruling the roost, and imposing conditions.

José reported that the hardest condition to swallow was the workers' insistence that worker delegates be recognized to ensure that the company fulfilled those commitments made in the agreement. The Tuinucú managers, he asserted, had always acted in good faith, and he took offence at the implication that they would not. José was incensed when Hernández Díaz referred to the company as *esta gente* (these people) when talking to government representative Loret de Mola: "and these are the children of those who worked with us in harmony, and who received so many favors from Tuinucú."[36]

Favors no longer sufficed. Workers wanted contracts and government legislation that established fixed social and economic rights, and the 1933 revolution provided them with the opportunity to win these. According to Agustín Valdivia, Interior Minister Guiteras told him at a meeting in Holguín to "press these people [*apriete a esta gente*]"; *esta gente* meaning the Rionda family interests on the island, which were very large at the time.[37] Precisely to avoid this kind of grouping—workers from all the Rionda mills versus the companies—Manuel advised his nephews to schedule the meetings in Havana with workers from the various mills for different days. Even though they were kept apart, the workers from all of the mills nevertheless succeeded in winning most of their demands, including higher salaries than the minimum wage later established by President Carlos Mendieta in January 1934. He set it at $1.00 per day in the cities and sugar mills, and Tuinucú paid $1.20.[38]

THE REVOLUTION AT CHAPARRA AND DELICIAS

The Cuban-American Sugar Company could not maintain any such division between their two massive mills in Puerto Padre, Chaparra and Delicias. Rank-and-file workers at Chaparra, Delicias, and the private Cuban-American port of Juan Claro managed to forge a new union across ideological and sectoral barriers during the fall of 1933 through meetings, assemblies, and popular demonstrations. This can be understood as a sort of oppositional politics whereby residents were willing to unite against the company in the context of depression despite their ideological, class, and ethnic differences.

In early September dockworkers declared a strike and Chaparra and Delicias workers followed suit, demanding an 8-hour day, a 25 percent salary increase, free rent and utilities, and recognition of their union. About 1,000 sugar, dock, and rail workers met at the port and then marched to the Rural Guard's barracks at Delicias, where Mr. Wood and his assistant were hiding. A guard named "Tamayo," already infamous for killing an old man, shot at the workers and killed two. One of the workers entered the barracks, grabbed Tamayo and hit him with his revolver. More workers arrived and beat Tamayo to death. In a move reminiscent of the action of the mobs against the *porra* in Havana, they then tied the guard to a horse's tail, paraded him through the mill town, and burned him. General Manager Wood and his assistant H. M. Hicks managed to escape and took refuge on a British merchant ship docked at the port.[39]

The strikers created worker militias to maintain order at the mill and in the surrounding areas; reports suggested that over 450 workers armed themselves at Delicias. At the Juan Claro port, workers formed 13 "Auxiliary Committees" and strategically placed a "Red

Guard" made up of 80 armed sentinels in a fort at the town's entrance. Self-defense (*"Estaca"*) committees surrounded the town to keep soldiers or strikebreakers from entering. Many members of the company's armed guard supported the strike.[40] This is not surprising, given that many of the 1932–1933 letters requesting access to credit, land, housing, and electricity came from the company guards.

U.S. Navy officers, upon inspecting the Puerto Padre district in October 1933, remarked that the workers maintained "unusually good organization," "allow[ed] no depredation or unauthorized visiting," and "continue[d] to be efficient." The same sources remarked that strikers were delivering water by truck and train to areas in need, and that they extended "courtesies to citizens like permitting funeral processions to operate on the railroads." The Navy officers also stated that Guiterista university students, one of the popular support bases of the Grau regime, were administering the revolutionary militias, "a well-organized group in each locality having as leaders several men educated in the U.S."[41]

The worker manifestos that remain in the Santiago de Cuba Provincial archives suggest that many political factions competed for leadership. CNOC-affiliated communist SNOIA led the union at Delicias and the Juan Claro port, while the FOH-affiliated Trotskyst "Partido Bolchevique-Leninista" led workers at Chaparra and Puerto Padre. The Cuban Communist Party (PCC) maintained an extremely sectarian stance, attacking the Grau-Guiteras-Batista regime as "bourgeois" and the Trotskyites as divisive opportunists. On the other hand, the FOH manifestos spoke more of events in Havana and Europe than Puerto Padre; they criticized the PCC and CNOC for attacking the 50 percent law only through manifestos, not through strikes. Despite their differences, the manifesto battles between the CNOC and FOH concretely indicate that the two organizations completely rejected the Grau regime's populist reforms.

Meanwhile, workers on the ground had to decide whether to negotiate with the company and the state during the Grau interregnum. The Guiteristas, whom Navy officers seemed to think led the workers at Puerto Padre, were the only organization that supported the populist regime and advocated using the space created by it. The radical Minister of the Interior, Guiteras, worked hard to try to establish more links with Cuban workers to counter Batista's growing power, but the CNOC rejected his requests for support. The FOH toned down its attack on the regime only after its Spanish leaders were exiled and replaced with Cubans, according to the demands of Grau's new labor law.

It is understandable that neither Communists nor Trotskysts recognized Guiteras's sincerity: every pro-worker act he carried through might be reversed by one of Batista's counter-acts. Guiteras, for example, would set workers free from jail only to have Batista put them back. In late 1933, while Guiteras' newly created, pro-worker Ministry of Labor engaged in strike mediation and helped workers form militias to defend themselves and their government, Batista and his soldiers toured the country breaking strikes on U.S.-owned plantations to win the support of Ambassador Welles.[42]

Whoever its leaders, the strike at Puerto Padre continued throughout the fall months, but the company determined that it would grant no reforms and would pay the same wages in 1933–1934 as it had in 1932–1933 despite national minimum wage decrees to the contrary. On December 19, the company stated that it would be unable to mill in the 1933–1934 season. It closed the hospital, bakery, butcher shop, and other food shops. Department heads were told to leave their posts, and telegraph, telephone, hospital, and other public services were closed. Workers responded by issuing a manifesto calling for solidarity for the locked-out workers of Chaparra and Delicias, and a boycott of the Chaparra Light and Power Company, which continued to operate through the strike. The same manifesto explicitly called on the Grau regime to fulfill its rhetoric: "You will be our real defender when you do not allow us workers to be trampled, as we are now."[43]

Interior Minister Guiteras stepped up to the challenge. On December 22, 1933, he ordered the mayor and local authorities at Puerto Padre to take possession of the power plant, hospital, and commercial departments at Chaparra and Delicias. This included the general stores, slaughterhouse, ice plant, butcher shops, and bakeries. A U.S. diplomat communicated the Cuban Department of Agriculture's message that they were taken over "on the ground of public need, *since they were the only plants existing on the lands of this Company, from which from 40,000 to 60,000 people could secure service and products suitable to their needs.*"[44] He had sent a letter two days earlier reporting that "Doctor Carlos Hevia, Secretary of Agriculture of de facto Government, . . . said in effect: 'If they do not grind and we do not do anything about it, you can easily understand that the one hundred thousand inhabitants of the district will take matters into their own hands.'" A January 11, 1934, confidential follow-up report stated point-blank: "The recent difficulties at Chaparra and Delicias . . . arise from the fact that the Company can pay average field wages of only about fifteen cents a day."[45]

British reports provide a broader picture of company-state relations under the Grau regime that help clarify Guiteras' December intervention. A November 1, 1933, report stated that many companies had stopped paying taxes, assuming that the regime would soon fall without U.S. recognition. These companies refused to accept Grau's pro-worker decrees, and waited in expectation for a counter-revolution. The report's astute conclusion was that "the sugar crop is the supreme test of the administration."[46] A December memorandum indicated that the administration might triumph. Guiteras' action at Chaparra, it explained, "has caused other sugar mill owners to modify their attitude towards the Government[;] some of them [had been] about to issue an ultimatum to the effect that they would be compelled to close down unless the Workmen's Insurance Law was satisfactorily amended." Guiteras' intervention at Chaparra sent a strong message to these mill owners: reform or lose your company.

THE REACTION BEGINS: JANUARY 15, 1934

An early January report from the American Consul at Antilla reveals that he had not figured out what the British author of the October memo had: namely, that social and political struggle in Cuba tended to fit around the sugar harvest. "Nominally," the report reads, "the various strikes which have occurred throughout the sugar mills all over the country have resulted in a higher scale of wages, which have not been put into effect as the crop of 1934 has not yet begun. It is believed, at this writing, that the majority of sugar mills will not operate this year not only on account of the wage demands being made by unionized labor but, also, on account of the political and economic chaos at present existing in Cuba."[47] Cuba depended too heavily on sugar to let this prophecy come true. Batista and his soldiers were willing to stand by and watch, even join sugar workers in September and October, but they opted for repression as the harvest approached in November and December.

Perhaps to preclude U.S. invasion, perhaps in response to Cuban and U.S. capitalists' entreaties for order and peace on the island, but certainly to allow mills to begin the sugar harvest, Batista shifted his support from Grau San Martín to Carlos Mendieta on January 15. U.S.

policymakers responded almost immediately: they granted recognition to the new conservative president (and Batista), and officially recognized the annulment of the Platt Amendment. Middle-class nationalists thus got their way, but workers had a harder time. Immediately upon taking power, the Mendieta-Batista regime began to repress workers both physically and legally under the motto: "*Habrá zafra o habrá sangre* [there will be harvest, or there will be blood]." One of the new regime's first decrees returned Chaparra and Delicias to the Cuban-American Sugar Company. The army and Rural Guard stormed union headquarters at Puerto Padre and throughout the island, took papers and furniture, jailed or evicted labor leaders from sugar mills, and declared unions illegal.

Nevertheless, because of the massive popular mobilization that had taken place during the 1933 Revolution, even these repressive measures had to be carried through legislation, disguised as "compromises" between capital and labor. For example, Decree #3, passed on February 7, 1934, allowed workers to strike, but required them to give eight days' notice before they did so. The law took away the element of spontaneity that made strikes effective. It also gave the companies time to rally together strikebreakers and to evict or exile the leaders of the strike before it began. Communists, Trotskysts, and Guiteristas all advocated the rejection of this controlling social legislation, but they had no choice but to modify their stance after the failure of a general strike in March 1935. The government repressed the walkout with extreme force, and shortly thereafter the SNOIA began to advocate working from within the system to avoid more violence. SNOIA issued circulars explaining how to make unions legal, and trained unions to combat the legalese that companies were using to get around legislation.

The Mendieta-Batista government passed a series of decrees to save cane farmers, including an August 17, 1934 moratorium to help them pay off their debts. The directives were complemented by a series of minimum wage laws introduced for workers in agriculture and industry. Finally, the 1937 "Law of Sugar Coordination" permanently established a new system: protection for tenant cane farmers on the land they worked and profit sharing between workers, cane farmers, and mill owners according to a sliding scale that moved with the price of sugar.

In the end, workers and cane farmers managed to use the nationalist, social reformist movements of the 1930s and 1940s to create a new Cuba; the break with tradition is demonstrated at both the national political level and at the local mill community level. The state, which included the president and his cabinet, judges, prosecutors, the military, and the new ministry of labor, became mediators who tried to ensure that workers, cane farmers, and sugar-mill owners got their fair share of sugar industry profits. At the national level, each group created an association to lobby for spoils, and locally the representatives of these associations, or unions in the workers' case, went to the state mediators (lawyers, judges, ministry of labor representatives, and governors). The state thus entered the sugar mills on an unprecedented level, and Batista's soldiers, at least until his 1952 coup, were not merely oppressive forces. They became key players on the local scene, soliciting bribes, marrying into local families, and teaching at schools, among other activities.

A participant in the Fidel Castro-led 1959 revolution wrote that "revolution in Cuba means burning sugar cane—it did in 1868, 1895, and 1930–33, and it did for us."[48] In February 2000 I asked two former field workers at Tuinucú if they had ever burned cane fields. The 92-year-old Rafael Gutiérrez Rodríguez and Armando Cruz García, roughly 20 years his junior, began to shake their heads, but then their friend and local historian Eladio Santiago pushed them: "You *never* burned cane?" At that point, Cruz took me aside and told me they did burn cane at Tuinucú. He said that cutters occasionally did so to get more work if the quota was too little, and during the 1950s workers did so extensively as a form of sabotage. Cruz left Tuinucú to join guerrilla leader Ernesto "Che" Guevara in the Escambray mountains near Santa Clara in the late 1950s, but other revolutionary workers, including Eladio Santiago and Arquímedes Valdivia, remained at the mill where they collected funds and supplies for the guerrilla army and organized clandestinely to commit cane burnings, Molotov cocktail bombings, and other forms of sabotage.

This essay is not about the 1959 Revolution; the Cruz anecdote highlights the need for further studies on the 1948–1958 period before accepting the dominant version of the "Castro Revolution" that attributes its success to guerrilla leaders in the mountains and radical students and professionals in the cities. Given the workers' track record for protest and political participation, it would be surprising to find them as quiescent in the 1950s as many studies suggest. Ramón Eduardo Ruiz, for example, has argued that "labor remained aloof from the Revolution; only the upheaval of 1933 had drawn the worker into its vortex. . . . In 1933 . . . jobless and hungry men had been driven to extreme measures but no such motivation existed in 1958. . . . Not once did organized labor heed Castro's call for a general strike."[49] What Ruiz misses is that "organized labor" was then under the leadership of government-controlled unions. Interviews and anecdotal evidence suggests that workers (including sugar workers) did, in fact, protest on their own and support the revolution outside of their official unions.

The extensive cane burnings of the late 1950s, like those of 1895 and 1933, were an attack on the political, social, and economic systems that underwrote sugar production in Cuba. Revolutionaries did not necessarily want to abolish sugar production from the island, but they did not agree with a *status quo* that prioritized it above any other political, social, or economic aspect of life. Participants in the sugar economy—cane farmers and workers—wanted a larger share of the profits, and the middle classes—students, industrialists, and professionals—sought a more diverse national economy. Overall, those who fought in the revolutions wanted greater access to political and economic power, and the 1933 revolution did indeed bring more profound popular nationalist reform. The revolution, in combination with the populist alliance between President Batista, cane farmers, and Cuban communist workers in the late 1930s, significantly altered political, social, and economic structures. Organized labor and cane-farmers finally won a place in the Cuban political arena alongside military men and Cuban and U.S. capitalists and politicians.

The positive worker legislation passed in the late 1930s and early 1940s demonstrates this triumph. The change is also reflected in the fact that the most influential labor confederation switched from advocating rejection of Cuban state institutions to promoting engagement and negotiation from within. This very change reveals the transformation that mass popular mobilization provoked in the Cuban state: from openly repressive dictatorship in 1932 to "populist" regimes from 1933 to 1952. The quotation marks around *populist* are there because the inclusion of popular groups varied immensely during the period. The early years included top-down labor legislation combined with extreme repression. The far more significant inclusion of popular groups came during the 1937–1944 period. Finally, the *Auténtico* party that ruled from 1944 to 1952 introduced a highly insidious form of populism that divided labor unions from within and undermined some of the power that workers had accumulated.

At the local level in the countryside, paternalism and minimal capitalist welfare lasted only as long as the profits were good. Mill owners and managers overestimated the number of cutbacks mill residents would accept. When the fragility of company welfare became exposed in the context of the Great Depression, workers and cane farmers in Cuba, like their lower-and middle-class counterparts elsewhere in the western hemisphere, demanded more formal, lasting reform and protection from the state. The transition from the company welfare programs to legislated welfare under the populist governments of the 1930s and 1940s was rocky, but Cuba was not alone. The island fits into the larger Latin American pattern more than most studies recognize. To understand the 1959 revolution, then, one needs to look more closely at the 1947–1959 Cold War era that preceded it.

This essay has emphasized the important changes that Cubans initiated during and after the 1933 revolution, but the U.S. role in precluding more extensive national reform should not be ignored. One can read with historical irony the 1934 *Literary Digest* summary of the mainstream U.S. press's take on Batista:

There is nothing in the little brown man's character to justify appellations of "Little Napoleon" or "Emperor Batista." He is smart but has none of the makings of a dictator so far as political ambition is concerned. . . . Long experience in close contact with army leaders taught him . . . the danger of rising too high in a Latin-American republic. He is of the people and his inclination is to support the Government which will do the most for the masses.[50]

In contrast, the *Foreign Policy Review* consistently got it right. *Foreign Policy* associate Charles A. Thomson first forecast the army overthrow of President de Céspedes, and then foresaw with prophetic accuracy the rise of the "Batista Dictatorship." (In an impressive analytical coup, he came up with this label almost 20 years before it became common shorthand in the political discourse of Cuba.) Thomson's January 1936 retrospective observed that nonrecognition had been a powerful instrument in the hands of the Roosevelt administration. Refusal to recognize the Grau regime, he argued, "helped to doom, as it now appears, the most promising opportunity for a constructive solution of the Cuban problem. . . . The forces of protest have been driven underground . . . but whether to disappear or to reappear in more aggressive form, the future alone will decide."[51] They did reappear, with a vengeance, in 1959. Upon the triumph of that revolution, which also largely began as a middle-class movement, workers carried out extensive land reform and nationalization. As in 1933, their actions preceded and made essential the reformist legislation that followed.

NOTES

The author gratefully acknowledges support from the Social Sciences and Humanities Research Council of Canada, the Georgetown University History Department, and the Brock University Humanities Research Institute for the research and writing of this article. She also thanks John Tutino, Alison Games, Thomas Klubock, Pedro Santoni, and the Brock History Department professors who offered comments and editing suggestions.

1. Cognosco, "Selections from *The Machadato*," *North American Review* 236 (November 1933): 398.

2. *Cuba: Island of Paradox* (New York: McDowell, Obelensky, 1959), 65.

3. In "By Way of Prologue" to the book by Fernando Ortiz, *Cuban Counterpoint: Tobacco and Sugar* (New York: A. A. Knopf, 1947), xix. Spanish edition: *Contrapunteo cubano del tabaco y el azúcar* (Havana: Jesús Montero, 1940).

4. The "ABC" organization was made up of cells with about 10 members each. The cells operated independently of the others so that if Machado's police caught one, those remaining would not be detected. The leading cell was "A."

5. Manuel Rionda to Oliver Doty, January 31, 1929. Braga Brothers Collection, Special Collections, Smathers Library, University of Florida, Gainesville (hereafter BBC), Record Group (RG) 2, Series (S.) 10, file: Tuinucú, Colonos—A&L.

6. Rionda to Doty, December 27, 1930, BBC, RG 2, S. 10, file: Tuinucú, Doty, Correspondence 1931.

7. Rionda to Doty, January 14, 1931, BBC, RG 2, S. 10, file: Tuinucú, Doty, Correspondence 1931.

8. Punta Alegre Sugar Company to R. B. Wood, September 15, 1932, Provincial Archives of Las Tunas, Cuban American Sugar Company Collection (hereafter APLT, CASC), legajo 7, expediente 77.

9. Public Records Office, Foreign Office, London (hereafter PRO, FO) 371/16575, Document #304.

10. Barry Carr, "Mill Occupations and Soviets: The Mobilisation of Sugar Workers in Cuba 1917–1933," *Journal of Latin American Studies* 28 (1996): 132.

11. Original letter is in broken English. Chaparra, Cándido Fernández to Mr. H. M. Hicks, Auxiliary General Manager, July 20, 1932, Chaparra, APLT, CASC, leg. 50, exp. 558.

12. "SNOIA: Proyecto de Resolución para la II Conferencia Nacional," June 16, 1933, Instituto de Historia, Fondo: 1er Partido Marxista-Leninista y otros, leg.: Organización de los Trabajadores Sindicales Nacionales, exp.: SNOIA (hereafter IH, SNOIA), document 1/8:87/3.1/1–6.

13. Luis Merconchini, interview by Víctor Marrero, Delicias, August 21, 1990. Audiotaped interview is at the Office of the Historian of Las Tunas (hereafter OHLT).

14. Workers adopted the very same strategies of sabotage during the Second War for Independence (1895–1898) and the struggle against Fulgencio Batista's dictatorship (1952–1959). Charles W. Hackett, side note on Cuba in his article on "Mexican Constitutional Changes" in *Current History* (May 1933): 214.

15. The three methods are described, respectively, in: Secret Police Agent Francisco Micó Urrutia's "Informe" about the cane burnings at Chaparra and Delicias forwarded by Rafael Balart Perera, Chief of Secret Police, Santiago to Governor of Santiago, forwarding, March 22, 1936, Santiago de Cuba, Provincial Archives, leg. 312, exp. 16; The Mapos Sugar Co. Case #121 in Department of Justice, *Special Report of William E. Fuller*, 47; George Atkinson Braga, "A Bundle of Relations," Typed Manuscript, BBC, RG 4, S. 24 (Additional), page 47.

16. Carr, "Mill Occupations," 133.

17. *Les Années Trente A Cuba: Actes du colloque international organise a Paris en novembre 1980 par le Centre Interuniversitaire d'études Cubaines et L'Université de la Sorbonne-Nouvelle, Paris III* (Paris: Editions L'Harmattan, 1982), 34.

18. Hubert Herring, "The Downfall of Machado," *Current History* (October 1933): 17–18.

19. Edwin Lefevre, "Soldier and Student Control in Cuba," *Philadelphia Saturday Evening Post*, January 6, 1934, 36.

20. Hudson Strode, "Behind the Cuban Revolt," *New Republic*, October 4, 1933, 204–207.

21. Cited in Muriel McAvoy, *Sugar Baron: Manuel Rionda and the Fortunes of Pre-Castro Cuba* (Gainesville: University of Florida Press, 2003), 256.

22. For more on the impressively strong student and women's movements see Lynn Stoner, *From the House to the Streets: The Cuban Woman's Movement for Legal Reform, 1898–1940* (Durham, NC: Duke University Press, 1991).

23. Louis A. Pérez, Jr., *Cuba: Between Reform and Revolution*, 2nd ed. (New York: Oxford University Press, 1995), 268.

24. The same law produced injustices and violence in the countryside as well. The targets there were the large number of workers from the English, French, and Dutch Caribbean who had come to Cuba during boom times to cut cane and had remained settled there with their families in the 1930s. The Rural Guard practiced raids along with bounty hunters, who tracked down foreigners and deported them, often without their belongings and wages. Barry Carr, "Identity, Class, and Nation: Black Immigrant Workers, Cuban Communism, and the Sugar Insurgency 1925–1934," *Hispanic American Historical Review* 78:1 (1998), 103–109.

25. Robert Whitney, *State and Revolution in Cuba: Mass Mobilization and Political Change, 1920–1940* (Chapel Hill: University of North Carolina Press, 2001), 105–107.

26. Octaviano Portuondo Moret, *El soviet de Tacajó: experiencias de un estudiante de los 30* (Santiago de Cuba: Editorial Oriente, 1979), 69, cited in Carr, "Mill Occupations," 153.

27. Carr, "Mill Occupations," 155.

28. Carr, "Mill Occupations," 139–158; Jacobo Urbino Ochoa, Gabriel Milord Ricardo, Dionisio Estévez Arenas, *Datos para la historia. Movimiento Obrero y Comunista, Holguín 1918–1935* (Holguín: Ediciones Holguín, 1983), 120–137.

29. Rionda to Bernardo Braga, London, September 15, 1933, BBC, RG 2, S. 4, Vol. 3.

30. Fanjul to Aurelio Portuondo, September 14, 1933, BBC, RG 2, S. 11, file: Correspondencia con Higinio Fanjul, Manuel Rasco y Cuban Trading Co., Havana.

31. Rionda, President, Tuinucú Sugar Company to Tuinucú [Comité Central], September 11, 1933, BBC, RG 2, S. 4, Vol. 3.

32. Rionda to Bernardo Braga, London, September 26, 1933, BBC, S. 4, vol. 3.

33. Higinio Fanjul to Aurelio Portuondo, September 25, 1933, BBC, RG 2, S. 11.

34. Former Tacajó worker Ursinio Rojas remembered strikers making administrators and upper level employees eat humble food. One can almost feel his smirk as he wrote: "Sr. Hernández lost quite a bit of weight because he didn't like the *'rancho'* that the union made in the soup kitchen." Ursinio Rojas, *Las Luchas Obreras en el Central Tacajó* (Havana: Editora Política, 1979), 83. Also see PRO, FO 371. A 7120/255/14. Grant Watson to Foreign Office, London, enclosing letter from A. Hopton Jones, dated September 16, 1933, cited in Carr, "Mill Occupations,"153.

35. Manuel Rionda, New York to José Rionda, Havana, September 18, 1933, BBC, S. 2, vol. 78.

36. José Rionda to Manuel Rionda, September 30, 1933, BBC, RG 2, S. 10, file: Tuinucú, Labor Troubles.

37. Arquímedes Valdivia Hernández, interview by author, February 1, 2000, Tuinucú.

38. Oliver Doty to Sindicato de Obreros y Empleados de la Industria Azucarera, Sección del Central Tuinucú, Tuinucú, January 11, 1935, BBC, RG 2, S. 10, file: Tuinucú, Labor Troubles.

39. Luis Merconchini, interview by Victor Marrero, Delicias, August 21, 1990, OHLT; Artemio and Antonio Fernández, Comisión de Historia Partido Comunista de Cuba Municipal, "Historia del Movimiento Obrero del Central Antonio Guiteras (antes Delicias)," Typed Manuscript, Library, IH.

40. "SNOIA Report on the Provincial Conference of Oriente, 17–18 September 1933," published September 19, 1933, IH, SNOIA, document 1/8:87/15.1/1–10.

41. United States National Archives (hereafter USNA), RG 84 Cuba Embassy Post Records. Part 12 800 Cuba 1933—Reports from Ships.

Commanding Officer USS *Dupont,* October 8, 1933, to Commander, Special Service Squadron. Subject: Station File at Puerto Padre, Entry for September 30, 1933, cited in Carr, "Mill Occupations," 156.

42. José Tabares del Real, *Guiteras* (Havana: Editorial de Ciencias Sociales, 1973), 197, 282–283.

43. "Chaparra" Chapter of SNOIA manifesto, no date, Santiago de Cuba, Provincial Archives, "Tribunal de Defensa Nacional. Juicios establecidos por propaganda subversiva."

44. (Emphasis mine). U.S. Chargé D'Affaires Samuel S. Dickson to Secretary of State, December 30, 1933, USNA, RG 59, Stack 250, Row 26, Decimal file 1900–1939, Box 1339, 337.115 SM/665 to 37.1153 CU [Re: 1933 nationalization of Cuban-American sugar mills].

45. The diplomat received this information from an American newspaper correspondent who had obtained it confidentially from one of the company's accountants. Jefferson Caffery to Secretary of State, January 11, 1934. USNA, RG 59, Stack 250, Row 26, Decimal file 1900–1939, Box 1339, 337.115 SM/665 to 37.1153 CU.

46. Mr. Grant Watson to Sir John Simon, PRO, FO 371/16575 and surrounding documents.

47. "Current Wages in the Antilla Consular District," January 8, 1934, in USNA, RG 59, 837.5041/63.

48. Carlos Franqui, *Family Portrait with Fidel: A Memoir,* trans. Alfred MacAdam (New York: Vintage, 1985), 163. Thanks to Marc McLeod for sending me this citation.

49. Ramón Eduardo Ruiz, *Cuba: The Making of a Revolution* (New York: Norton, 1968), 14.

50. "Cuba's Procession of Presidents," *Literary Digest,* January 27, 1934, 14.

51. Charles A. Thomson, "The Cuban Revolution: Reform and Reaction," *Foreign Policy Reports,* January 1, 1936, 276.

NINE

Repression and Resistance, Hatred and Hope: Civilian Life during the Military Dictatorships in the Southern Cone, 1964–1990

Margaret Power

"Didn't you hear him? Start taking off your clothes or I'll rip them off you." I only managed to say, "I'm tied up." They untied my hands. "Are you gonna get undressed or not? Look, I don't like it when bitches get smart." They tore off my blouse, while another pulled down my pants. I tried to avoid it but soon I was naked and I heard someone saying, "Search her." They began to interrogate me. They tortured me over and over. Several times I thought I would get lucky and break my back when the electric current arched my body. I didn't die. I regained consciousness over and over again. I assumed that I was still alive and I tried to be conscious of the days and hours to know when to stop that torture and tell them my name.[1]

In March 1974 Luz Arce, a member of Chile's Socialist Party and a supporter of the Popular Unity government that ruled that country from 1970 to 1973, paid a heavy price for her political beliefs. That month agents of the Chilean military arrested Arce and subjected her to brutal torture, a small part of which she describes above. The treatment meted out to her was not unique. Arce's experience represents an all-too-common story of what people in Latin America's Southern Cone—Argentina, Brazil, Chile, and Uruguay—experienced under the military regimes that seized and held power between 1964 and 1990.

During this 25-year span the Southern Cone militaries tortured, murdered, and disappeared several thousand of their fellow citizens. This essay explores why these military dictatorships came to power and employed such barbaric behavior against the citizens of the nation they had pledged to defend. It argues that national elites, in conjunction with the United States government, imposed military dictatorships to repress the popular and prosocialist movements that threatened their economic interests and political power. To understand what impact military rule had on civilians, the essay focuses on people's lives and daily experiences in Chile during the Augusto Pinochet regime (1973–1990). It also illustrates that people's experiences of life under dictatorship and their relationship to military rule varied widely, usually as a result of their political beliefs, moral values, and economic situation. While some individuals detested and resisted military rule, and suffered both directly and indirectly from it, others supported the armed forces and benefited from their rule. This chapter offers the stories of some of these people and their lives.

THE SEIZURE OF POWER

Military dictatorships came to power in response to political changes that swept the Southern Cone during the 1960s and early 1970s. At that time popular organizations, leftist political parties, progressive Catholic groups, trade unions, peasant organizations, and revolutionary movements emerged or grew stronger in the region. These groups and their members demanded housing for the homeless, struggled for workers' rights, and supported peasants' demands for land reform and their right to own and farm their own land. They also attempted to democratize their societies by expanding voting rights, by encouraging people to become politically active, and by interpreting Catholic teachings as a call for solidarity with the oppressed. The new associations also held their governments accountable for the abuses they had committed against their people, and criticized foreign, principally U.S., control of their economies and political systems.

Politics within these countries reflected the growing popular demand for change. In 1960 Brazilians elected Jânio Quadros as president and João Goulart as vice president. When Quadros resigned in 1961, Goulart became chief executive. Hoping to improve the Brazilians' quality of life, Goulart encouraged development of the Northeast (the poorest part of the country), democratization of the armed forces, land redistribution to peasants, increased wages, and reform of the tax system as a way to reduce the highly un- equal distribution of income. Goulart's reforms both reflected the demands of social movements and stimulated their development. Peasant Leagues in the Northeast demanded land for the landless, and when landowners refused to hand it over to them they took over the estates. Students radicalized (as they did throughout Latin America in the 1960s) and called for more rights and social justice, and workers went on strike to demand higher wages.[2]

Brazil was not the only Southern Cone nation where an increas- ingly radicalized population demanded reforms. In the late 1960s and early 1970s a political and economic decline that had begun a little over a decade earlier engulfed Uruguay. The government's concomitant failure to provide the population with the benefits to which it had been accustomed since the early twentieth century, when President José Battle established a welfare state, compounded the crisis and exacerbated people's feelings of anger and despair. Hoping both to replicate the successful guerrilla experience of the July 26th Movement in Cuba—in which Fidel Castro overthrew the Fulgencio Batista regime and took power—and bring about sub- stantial political and economic changes in the country, a group of mainly middle-class youth founded the *Tupamaros* in 1963. This urban guerrilla organization carried out armed actions to achieve their goals, including the 1970 kidnapping of U.S. Agency for Inter- national Development (AID) advisor Dan Mitrione. The *Tupamaros* accused Mitrione of training the Uruguayan police in methods of torture and demanded the freedom of political prisoners held in Uruguayan jails in exchange for his release.[3]

Many Chileans also sought far-reaching transformations of their country, but unlike the Tupamaros they hoped to achieve their goals through peaceful means. In 1970 the Chilean people voted for so- cialist Salvador Allende as president. For the first time in history a nation had democratically elected a Marxist to serve as its leader. In an attempt to improve the standard of living of most Chileans, the Allende government nationalized U.S. copper holdings in Chile, broke up many large agricultural estates and distributed the land to the peasants, increased workers' salaries, established health care programs and clinics in poor neighborhoods, and made it clear that the government would prioritize the needs of the workers, peas- ants, and the poor, not those of the wealthy.[4]

A different political scenario unfolded in Argentina when Juan Domingo Perón came back to power in 1973. Even though the

Argentine military had toppled Perón from the presidency in 1955, after which he went into exile for 18 years, the military invited him to return in the hope that his reappearance would quell growing labor unrest and eliminate the guerrilla organizations that were carrying out armed actions to achieve greater rights for workers and minimize foreign domination of the Argentine economy. For example, in 1972 the *Ejército Revolucionario del Pueblo* (Revolutionary Army of the People) kidnapped the manager of a British firm in the city of Rosario that had fired 4,000 workers without severance pay. They demanded, and got, publicity about the workers' situation and within one week the company rehired the workers and spent $50,000 to distribute food to poor communities in Rosario.[5] Perón's return and subsequent election as president, however, did not achieve the desired results. The leftist guerrilla organizations realized that Perón would not advance their goals of creating a socialist society, and the paramilitary right and the military called for and carried out more repression against the guerrilla organizations and the progressive movement. Fighting between the Right and the Left intensified, particularly after Perón died in 1974. His wife, Isabel, became president, and José López Rega, Perón's former secretary and a leader of the paramilitary Argentine Anti-Communist Alliance, heavily influenced her rule. He encouraged a sharp increase in attacks against the Left, and such policies set the stage for the military's brutal crusade against the Argentine people that occurred after the armed forces seized power in 1976.

In response to the increased democratization and the growing popularity of reformist and revolutionary movements and governments, the elites (both national and U.S.) that ran the Southern Cone countries allied themselves with the armed forces to overthrow their respective governments and install the military in power. This process began when the Brazilian military overthrew Goulart in 1964 and subsequently swept the region. Nine years later the Uruguayan military declared a state of siege, banned Congress, outlawed leftist parties, and instituted what one author has characterized as "an authoritarian state based on fear."[6] In 1973 the Chilean armed forces also seized power, an assault that led to Allende's death and ended decades of democratic rule. Three years later, the Argentine military staged a coup d'etat and initiated what has come to be known as the "Dirty War" against the civilian population.

Contrary to its claims that it upheld democracy, the U.S. government supported the military's seizure of power in all four Southern Cone nations. It did so partly for geopolitical reasons. Following the 1959 Cuban Revolution, U.S. officials feverishly tried to prevent another successful revolution from erupting in Latin America and urged governments to institute political and economic reforms. President John F. Kennedy established the Alliance for Progress and earmarked U.S. $20 billion to finance a number of socioeconomic reforms and incorporate more people into the electoral system throughout the region.[7]

At the same time, the U.S. government beefed up its counterinsurgency training program so that it could effectively confront any political or military threat that revolutionary forces posed to it in the region. Members of the Argentine, Brazilian, Chilean, and Uruguayan military and police received training in the School of the Americas in Panama and the U.S. police academy in Washington, D.C. As part of their curriculum, Latin American military officers learned the Doctrine of National Security.[8] It stated that the armed forces' principal enemy was internal: subversive elements that threatened the Western, capitalist order that the military had sworn to defend. These "subversives" need not just pose a military challenge; they could also represent an ideological one, or so the doctrine taught the armed forces to believe. General Jorge Rafael Videla, the leading member and main ideologue of the Argentine military government, said as much in 1978: "A terrorist is not just someone with a gun or a bomb, but also someone who spreads ideas that are contrary to Western civilization."[9] Likewise, General Pinochet of Chile declared that Marxists were "intrinsically perverse" in order to justify any and all measures of repression employed against them.

The U.S. government also supported the Southern Cone's militaries to protect the massive economic investments of U.S. companies in the region. For most of the twentieth century U.S. banks and companies had invested in—and extracted substantial profits from—key areas of economic activity in the area. In 1965 close to 14 percent of all U.S. overseas sales came from Latin America, as did 17 percent of its purchases. In that same year, 19 percent of all U.S. direct investment abroad was in Latin America, primarily in the most productive and profitable sectors of the economy.[10] In the 1970s nearly three-quarters of all foreign investment in Latin America came from the United States.[11] Chile offers a clear example of the extent to which U.S. economic interests penetrated the Southern Cone nations. Two U.S. companies, Anaconda and Kennecott, controlled the Chilean copper industry. According to the 1972 speech that President Allende gave to the United Nations, in 1967 Kennecott obtained profits of 106 percent; and two years later the number had almost doubled to 205 percent. Between 1955 and 1970 Anaconda made a profit of 21.5 percent over its book value, while Kennecott accrued an astounding 52.8 percent profit during those same years. These enormous rates of profit garnered an overall gain of $4,000 million on an initial investment of $30 million. As Allende noted, "only a small part of this amount would assure proteins for all the children in my country once and for all."[12]

During the 1960s and 1970s, nationalist forces in the region criticized the extent of U.S. control of their economies and proposed acquiring ownership for their countries. After Allende and the Popular Unity government came to power in 1970 they nationalized U.S. corporate holdings such as Anaconda and Kennecott (with the unanimous support of the Chilean Congress) and the International Telegraph and Telephone Company. Both U.S. companies and the U.S. government opposed these actions and wanted to prevent other countries from following Chile's example. Protection of U.S. economic interests in the region prompted the U.S. government—in this case, the Richard Nixon administration—to oppose those regimes it considered a threat, even if doing so meant supporting the overthrow of a democratic government and backing a military dictatorship. President Nixon and the Chilean upper classes opposed the Allende government because it upheld democracy, not because it opposed it.

THE OPERATIONS OF A MILITARY DICTATORSHIP

After seizing power, the armed forces in Argentina, Brazil, Chile, and Uruguay took control of public affairs in their country. Government censorship of the media prevailed to such an extent that many people internalized the restrictive policies and censored themselves. Newspapers in Uruguay could not report that parliament was closed or make any statement critical of the armed forces. Threats from the military to close newspapers or torture journalists who defied their orders effectively discouraged defiance of these commands.[13] The Uruguayan military forced the nation's key literary figures, writers such as Mario Benedetti, Eduardo Galeano, and Juan Carlos Onetti, into exile.[14] In 1967 the Brazilian regime passed a law to regulate the liberty of expression, thought, and information. The stated goal was to prevent any news that could favor the forces of "subversion." It declared that nothing could be published that provided "false information, or true information that has been cut short or distorted, about public disturbance." Another decree issued by the Brazilian armed forces declared it illegal to "divulge news, information, manifestos, or interviews which reveal the political attitudes of the clergy [since many of them opposed the repression], or third parties, which could create tensions or conflicts of a religious nature."[15] The Argentine military not only censored the news, it also prevented the playing or selling of music that it found immoral or subversive. By 1981 the prohibition had affected some 242 songs, including a number of classic tangos from Carlos Gardel, the genre's foremost musician in Argentina.[16]

In order to gain or maintain power the armed forces frequently imposed a curfew, which enabled the military to further control both interactions among and the mobility of the civilian population by decreeing the times of day people could and could not be outside. The actions of the Chilean military were typical of policies implemented by the armed forces throughout the region. They did not allow people to leave their houses at all in the first three days that followed their seizure of power. By 1977, people had to remain indoors between midnight and five A.M. The military arrogated to itself the right to arrest or shoot anyone caught violating the curfew during these hours, a time when witnesses were less likely to observe the crimes committed by the repressive forces.[17]

The military dictatorships also attempted to eliminate any opposition to their authority. To achieve this goal they abolished any and all political activity that they considered a threat and implemented a wide range of repressive policies against those individuals and organizations they believed did or could pose a danger to their rule. They replaced the established political institutions, elected officials, and constitutional and legal norms with themselves or their supporters. They declared a state of siege, closed or greatly reduced the democratic functioning of Congress, and restricted, if not completely eliminated, the rights of civilians; the powers of military courts superseded those of civilian courts. Military regimes abolished elections and proscribed political parties—except for those they controlled—and targeted elected officials as potential or actual challengers to their power. The Chilean military published lists of key political officials and requested that they turn themselves in. When some of them naïvely acquiesced, the military occasionally let them go, but more commonly either jailed and tortured or killed them outright. In its zeal to destroy the trade union movement in

Chile, the armed forces turned the full force of its repressive apparatus against the workers and their representatives. Many union leaders were arrested, tortured, and disappeared. Members of the intelligence branch of the military went to some factories, and "interrogated the workers one by one, pressing them to inform on their coworkers, and especially on their leaders."[18] In addition to hunting down leftists and progressives, the Argentine armed forces made psychoanalysts a particular target of their wrath. They considered Sigmund Freud and Freudianism "the chief enemies of the Christian family, a school [of thought] dedicated to placing sex at the center of family life."[19] The military's belief that psychology was subversive and that most psychologists were leftists encouraged many psychologists to flee the country or cease practicing their profession.

The military dictatorships employed brutal repression to generate fear, silence dissent, and quell opposition. Drawing on their own knowledge and the training offered them by experts in torture from both the French and U.S. military, armed forces in the Southern Cone rounded up, imprisoned, tortured, murdered, and disappeared tens of thousands of people in the years they were in power.[20] They subjected their captives to a variety of brutal forms of torture. Military personnel applied electric shock to the most sensitive parts of people's bodies, suspended prisoners in painful positions for lengthy periods of time, deprived people of food, water, and sleep; they also extracted their nails, beat them mercilessly, raped them and committed other forms of sexual abuse on them, simulated executions, and tortured their loved ones— including children—in front of them.[21] The Argentine military also took some babies born in captivity to female political prisoners and sold or gave them to friendly families.[22]

Military regimes employed torture and the threat of torture for several reasons. They wanted to gain knowledge about people and organizations that opposed their rule or about activities that opponents of military rule planned to carry out. Since many people would not willingly incriminate others or share information with their captors, the military used physical and psychological torture to compel them to do so. The military understood that many individuals it detained were political activists, people who had dedicated their lives to ending social injustice, poverty, and inequality through membership in political parties, trade unions, church groups, or social movements. The armed forces knew that they needed to destroy the captured individual's sense of

A young boy cries as a police vehicle takes away his father in Santiago, Chile, September 14, 1983. The boy and his family claimed they were simply walking down the street near a religious protest outside an alleged secret police station when their father was taken into custody along with members of Santiago's religious community. (AP Photo).

commitment to society and, in many cases, the specific political organization to which she or he belonged, in order to break the detainee. The torturers wanted to obliterate the intimate link that existed between their captives' personal identity, their political and moral commitments, and the communities and organizations to which they belonged. They wanted to wipe out these people's belief in themselves and, as a result, the political projects of which they were a part. In addition, the armed forces wanted to inject fear into society at large to facilitate their control of the civilian population. They wanted people to know that resistance to military rule would likely result in torture, murder, and possibly disappearance. Indeed, disappearing people became one of the most chilling tactics used by military regimes in the Southern Cone. It was so horrifyingly common, especially in places like Argentina, that the words *desaparecer* (to disappear) or *desaparecido/a* (a disappeared person) acquired whole new meanings that evoked terror and suffering.

Recent research suggests that the first systematic disappearance of political activists took place in Guatemala in 1966. Following the guidance and training of U.S. security advisor John P. Longan, a special security squad kidnapped, tortured, and then disappeared

30 Guatemalans who supported peaceful, democratic elections and opposed the military that ruled their country.[23] The disappearance of people subsequently became a hauntingly frequent tactic employed by military regimes in the Southern Cone. Although the specific methods employed by the armed forces to make people disappear varied, similarities did exist. Military or police personnel, either in uniform or disguised as civilians, came to the target's house or place of work; they also picked them up on the street or while they were attending a meeting. Members of the military or police did not issue any formal arrest warrants or have judicial authorization to make the arrest. Instead, they captured those individuals or groups of people they sought and took them to a police station, military barracks, or torture center. There, members of the armed forces proceeded to torment their captives, using the methods described above. In some cases the military released the captives or incarcerated them with the other political prisoners, but it was far more common for the military to torture their victims to death or simply to execute them.

Disappearing people allowed the military regimes to disclaim any knowledge of or responsibility for the people they killed. No body, no crime, no guilty party, or so they thought. In some ways the disappearance of a family member, loved one, or good friend was worse than an outright killing. Not knowing what had happened to a loved one, not knowing whether they were alive or dead, imagining them sick, hungry, in pain or tortured, fearing the worst yet holding on to a shred of hope year after year can devastate those who yearn to know the fate of a family member, friend, or comrade. Such uncertainty is both scary and painful. To make someone disappear is to plunge them and their families into the unknown, and in countries ruled by military dictatorships the unknown easily became imagined as a place of terror, one's worst nightmares come to life. Thus, disappearances, like the omnipresent threat of torture, served to spread fear throughout those nations ruled by the military and intimidate public opposition to this barbarous practice.

CIVILIAN LIFE IN A MILITARY DICTATORSHIP

Fear is a powerful emotion and a potent weapon. It characterized and shaped many people's lives during the dictatorship. It affected their friendships, social networks, what they said and to whom they spoke, where they got a job, or if they got a job, how they dressed (in some of the countries the military made young men shave their beards and cut their hair), what books they read, what music they listened to, even what ideas they thought. The experience of an Argentine colleague of mine who was a college student when the military seized power and took over the university clearly illustrates this process. A few days after the 1976 coup she sat in a café with a friend waiting for her friend's boyfriend, who as a leftist was a target for the military. As they waited a group of soldiers, with weapons drawn, broke into the café and demanded to see everyone's identification papers. Luckily the boyfriend had not yet arrived. If he had, he and the two women would likely have been arrested, taken away, and perhaps never heard of again. My friend then withdrew from the university, retreated into her apartment, and cut off contacts with many of her friends. She subjected herself to an "internal exile." Years later, she told me, she realized that she had systematically ended her friendships with people associated with the Left given that they represented danger, and formed new ones with people not connected with those the military deemed the enemy.[24]

As military regimes extended their rule into many facets of the lives of the populace, they made a particular effort to influence how young people thought about them. For example, in an effort to both assert state power and create a positive attitude toward the military, many elementary and secondary schools throughout Chile changed their names to "*11 de Septiembre*" (September 11th), the day that the military toppled the Allende government. The Chilean dictatorship did not limit its control to state-run institutions; it also extended its tentacles into civic associations as well. Young men in Chile typically joined soccer clubs based on the political party they identified with. After the military coup, however, the regime banned soccer clubs affiliated with the Left and prohibited as well elections in all the clubs to extinguish the practice of democracy and the possibility that someone opposed to the military regime would be elected.[25] In a similar fashion, the Brazilian military censored news of elections in a São Paulo soccer club.[26]

For many Chileans, the repression was direct and brutal. Even when the military targeted individuals, the impact of its actions frequently extended beyond the one person it attacked, as illustrated by the case of Jorge Peña Hen. A member of Chile's Socialist Party as well as an artist, Peña Hen taught music in elementary schools in the northern city of La Serena; he also established and directed the first children's orchestra in South America. In October 1973 the infamous "Caravan of Death," commanded by General Sergio Arellano Stark and under orders from General Pinochet, traveled through northern Chile summarily assassinating supporters of the Popular Unity government. The campaign claimed Peña Hen's life. His immediate family and friends, as well as many parents of the children who had been in the orchestra he led, were so scared that they distanced themselves from any political involvement.[27]

Indeed, such were the severe psychological scars inflicted by the Pinochet dictatorship that many of the thousands of political prisoners arrested and tortured by the military seldom told their stories; they also rarely received public recognition for the ordeals they suffered. In an effort to partially right the many wrongs committed by the armed forces, the Lagos government (2000–2006) established the National Commission on Political Imprisonment and Torture. For the first time, thousands of former political prisoners recounted what had happened to them following their detention by the military. In November 2004, the Lagos regime further increased awareness of the magnitude of suffering the military dictatorship inflicted when it released the *Informe Valech,* which records the testimony and lists the names of the thousands of political prisoners arrested during the Pinochet dictatorship. After an exhaustive examination of the testimonies offered, the Chilean government concluded that the military had held 27,255 people as political prisoners. Although the amount of time they spent in prison and the conditions in which they were held varied considerably, 94 percent of political prisoners were tortured. Most of the 3,400 women who testified reported they had suffered sexual torture. The military did not refrain from detaining and mistreating children and pregnant women. Arrested along with their parents were 102 minors, and 11 babies were born in prison.[28]

Interestingly enough, some Chilean political prisoners were former members of the armed forces. They had opposed the coup and attempted to organize within the military to prevent the overthrow of the democratic government. In Chile, as in many countries, poor people joined the military because it offered them an education, economic sustenance, and the opportunity to improve their social standing. As a result, many enlisted members of the Chilean armed forces came from poor and working-class backgrounds; they supported the Allende government, as did some of the officers. Luis Torres offers a good example of those working-class members of the Chilean military who opposed the coup and suffered because he defended the constitutional order.

   Hailing from a lower middle class family, Torres became the sole support of his family when his father died in 1967. He then joined the Air Force, and in 1968 he traveled with other noncommissioned troops to Panama to receive training by the U.S. military. Before the trip Torres fervently admired the United States and its support for the democratic ideal it so frequently proclaimed, but what he saw in Panama raised doubts in his mind. He met a large number of U.S. veterans who had served in Vietnam. Scarred by their experiences there, many of them had become drug addicts. Even more troubling, however, was the marked difference in lifestyle between the North Americans and the Panamanian people. The U.S. military lived in comfortable and guarded communities, while a large number of Panamanians lived in squalor. When Torres returned to Chile, he further questioned the lack of democracy in the military and the feudalistic relationship between the officers and the troops. For example, officers could vote in national elections, but the troops could not. Officers had many privileges, such as better food, higher salaries, and the ability to issue arbitrary commands, all of which the troops lacked. For all of these reasons, and because he hoped that the standard of living of the Chilean people would improve, Torres supported Allende in the 1970 presidential elections.[29]

   Following the coup, however, Torres became yet another victim of the military. He was arrested and accused of treason along with close to 80 other members of the Air Force, including General Alberto Bachelet, who later died in prison from torture. After his arrest, members of the Air Force, including his superior officers whom he knew well, tortured Torres. They accused him of being a subversive when he had merely fulfilled his constitutional duty and defended the elected government. They put him on an airplane and, once the plane was in flight, repeatedly threatened to push him out the open door. Back on the base, they ran high-voltage electric current through his genitals and his teeth, pulled out his fingernails, beat him, and starved him.[30]

   Torres was subsequently incarcerated in the Penitentiary, a massive prison built in 1843 in Santiago, the capital of Chile, along with hundreds of other political prisoners, most of whom were civilians and had been active supporters of the Allende government. These individuals lived together in a special block that allowed them to maintain their identities as political prisoners and to operate more as a collective unit than as isolated individuals. This is not to say that life in prison was good; it was not. The prisoners were in jail because they had defended a democratically elected government, and for that "crime" they were paying a very heavy price. They lacked decent food, medical care, and, most of all, freedom. Nevertheless, they continued to function as human beings, concerned family members, and committed political activists.

The political prisoners took advantage of special visiting days to conduct political activities inside the Penitentiary. For example, on Mother's Day 1977 the prisoners recognized the women who had written them letters, brought them food, washed their clothes, visited them, worked for their release, offered them emotional support, given them hope, and helped them survive. On this occasion different prisoners stepped forward and thanked the women, and then they presented each female in the visiting room with a red carnation, the symbol of struggle. This spirit of resistance allowed

Luis Torres (on the left) in his cell at the Penitentiary in 1977. (Courtesy of Margaret Power).

the Chilean people to defy the dictatorship and also helped them, in 2000, to usher in a democratic government.

Civilian Support for the Dictatorship

One of the saddest aspects of dictatorships is that they do not govern by repression and fear alone. They also generate and rely on a base of support among the civilian population that welcomes their attacks on those sectors of the population that challenge their power, beliefs, or way of life. In other words, many citizens either applaud or acquiesce in the suppression of democracy and the repression of their fellow citizens. Without a doubt the armed forces were the predominant power during the dictatorships, and in many countries military officers filled the political, economic, media, and academic positions previously held by civilians. However, the military also had civilian supporters who had backed their overthrow of the established governments and applauded their repression of democracy. Although many people equate military dictatorships with men, women frequently played prominent public roles, first in calling on the military to intervene and then openly backing it once it had seized power.

This kind of mobilization first became apparent in 1964 when hundreds of thousands of Brazilians, led by conservative Catholic women, marched in 51 cities throughout the country. The protestors denounced the Goulart administration in a campaign called "March of the Family with God for Liberty." Brazilian women, joined by anticommunist men, continued to march even after the military had overthrown Goulart to demonstrate both their repudiation of the deposed government and their gratitude to the armed forces that had, in their minds, saved the nation from Goulart and communism.[31]

Upper- and middle-class Chilean women, as well as some from the working-class, also mobilized against the Allende government. They organized the first large demonstration against the regime, the March of the Empty Pots, on December 1, 1971, and continued to protest right up to the day the armed forces seized power. Women carried out nightly banging of pots and pans to demonstrate their displeasure with Allende, encouraged the military to overthrow the government by calling them sissies for their failure to intervene, and raised funds for striking workers to create economic disorder and undermine the government. Despite the supposed unity of these women, class distinctions defined their movement. Elite women sported gold pins, shaped like pots, made by Cartier, while poor women could only afford ones made of copper.[32]

Chilean women also expressed their support for the coup and the subsequent dictatorship. Some upper- and middle-class women uncorked bottles of champagne on September 11, 1973, and toasted the military's seizure of power. They welcomed an end to what for them had been the chaos and disorder of the Allende years, and viewed authoritarian rule as just what the country needed. Following the coup, many Chilean women became the military regime's most visible symbol of support. They contributed their jewelry to reconstruct the nation, joined volunteer organizations headed by Lucía Hiriart (General Pinochet's wife), participated in promilitary parades, and attended events in support of military rule. Some women even enthusiastically supported the curfew because it meant that their husbands would be more likely to be home with them, and not out with other women or drinking in a bar. They also did not mind that the military burned books because they believed that the texts contained incendiary ideas. Thus, many of the military's female supporters turned a blind eye to the death of democracy and the murder of their fellow citizens because they believed it was the only way to remove the danger that the Allende government represented to them.[33]

Conservative women continued to rally around Pinochet during and after the 1988 plebiscite on military rule. That ballot allowed Chileans to either vote *Sí* (yes) to affirm their support of continued military rule or *No* to indicate they opposed it. The dictatorship had promised it would hold the plebiscite and, perhaps deceived by its own propaganda, erroneously believed it would win the vote. Female backers of the armed forces, along with male supporters of the dictatorship, campaigned for Pinochet and urged their friends and neighbors to vote for him. Although Pinochet lost the plebiscite and military rule ended in 1990, conservative women remained devoted to him, often congregating outside his home to commemorate the September 11 overthrow of Allende. And when their beloved general found himself in trouble, as he did following his 1998 arrest in London, England on charges of terrorism, murder, and genocide, they continued to passionately support him. Some of Pinochet's devotees flew to London, while others in Santiago protested his arrest and held angry rallies outside the British and Spanish embassies (Spain issued the initial order for his arrest). When the British courts ruled against Spain's extradition order and sent Pinochet back to Chile, thousands of his admirers welcomed him back as if he were a returning hero. Unrepentant and undeterred by the charges lodged against him, they hailed the general as the man who had saved their country from communism.[34]

Opposition and Resistance to Dictatorship

While some people supported the dictatorships, many more throughout the region suffered widespread torture, imprisonment, murder, and disappearance at the hands of the military. These experiences, combined with the generalized absence of freedom and democracy, generated a courageous and determined human rights movement. Its members demanded an end to the repression, justice for victims of the dictatorship, and a return to democracy, and in many Southern Cone nations they were led by progressive, prodemocracy women. Gendered ideas about men and women help explain the prominent role that women played in this phenomenon. Despite some notable exceptions and the fact that gender roles had begun to change by the late 1960s and early 1970s, much of society still considered politics a largely masculine affair and believed that women should primarily concern themselves with the family and the home. As a result, a disproportionate amount of men numbered among the victims of the repression. Although some women active in the human rights movement had been politically active prior to the dictatorships, the torture, imprisonment, and murder of male family members, and in some cases political comrades, spurred many women to action.

Women initiated many of the human rights organizations that spearheaded opposition to the dictatorships. At a time when few dared to go into the streets to protest military rule, women gathered in small, then larger groups to demand the return of their disappeared loved ones or the release of their husbands, brothers, fathers, and in some cases daughters, sisters, and mothers. The best known of these associations is the *Madres de la Plaza de Mayo* (Mothers of the Plaza de Mayo) in Buenos Aires, Argentina. In many ways, they served as a prototype for the other organizations of mothers of the disappeared that sprang up in the region. Like other women missing their family members, the *Madres* first went to police stations and government offices trying to find their loved ones. After a while the faces of other women involved in the same activities became familiar, and the women realized that what had happened to them had also happened to others. That recognition of this sad truth was not instantly apparent reveals the horrible novelty of the crimes committed by the dictatorships. Mutual understanding that theirs was not an isolated case led the women to join together in 1977 and to develop one of the most effective political organizations in recent history. As Temma Kaplan writes, "out of terror and repression, a group of relatively inexperienced housewives and mothers became a social movement."[35]

Wearing black clothing to symbolize mourning, a white kerchief to symbolize hope and their children, and holding pictures of their disappeared family member, or members in some cases, these women gathered in the *Plaza de Mayo*, the traditional seat of government power in Argentina. Fueled by maternal love and righteous anger, they marched around the plaza, demanding the return of their disappeared family members. At a time when the vast majority of Argentines were too scared to defy the regime of terror, these women braved the military's wrath to go into the streets to expose and shame the criminals who ran the government and violated both basic standards of human decency and Argentine and international law.[36] Theirs was not an easy task. Not only did they confront the threats, and in some cases attacks, of the Argentine military, they also had to deal with the fear, indifference, and even hostility of other Argentines. They marched to convince their fellow citizens that the military government had systematically kidnapped, tortured, and murdered thousands of Argentines, most of

The Mothers of the Plaza de Mayo, a group made up of women whose children disappeared during the 1970s war against subversion, march in front of the Presidential Palace in Buenos Aires, December 12, 1985, to protest sentences given by a Federal Court to nine former military junta members accused of human rights abuses during the war. (AP Photo/Eduardo DiBaia).

them young people. They worked to convince people that this was a crime. And eventually they shook people out of the stupor of passivity and paralysis into which the military had induced them.

In Chile, progressive members of the Catholic Church worked with poor people to oppose the dictatorship in a variety of ways. The Catholic Church lent its protection and resources to those forces and individuals whom the armed forces persecuted or who suffered as a result of the Pinochet regime's neoliberal economic policies, which promoted the dismantling of tariffs and government support for national industry, the privatization of the economy, the production of goods for sale on the international market, and the cutback of social services. These policies led to the closure of national industries, thus to soaring unemployment rates and a decline in wages (which fell from "an index of 100 in 1970 to 47.9 in 1975"). They also produced tremendous shortages in basic necessities, and caused much hunger and despair among the poor, many of whom had supported the Allende government and had already become, as a result, targets of military repression.[37]

In order to maintain their identity as political people, to survive an economic situation that offered them little to nothing, and to work against the regime, impoverished and unemployed Chileans formed a variety of organizations that frequently found shelter in a church parish. One such organizational type was the *bolsas de cesantes*, or unemployed workers groups. Members of the *bolsas* met to discuss their situation and to develop ways to eke out a living. Since many of the participants had previously worked in industries, they learned new skills, such as working with leather goods. This allowed them to produce shoes and school bags for children, thus simultaneously offering affordable necessities to their communities and generating income for themselves.[38]

Just as unemployed workers creatively invented new sources of employment, the Chilean Left developed innovative ways—some clandestine, some semipublic—to conduct political events during the dictatorship. For example, May First celebrates International Workers' Day, an event that developed following the murder of protesting workers in Chicago, Illinois, in 1886. In Chile, May First commemorates the struggles of workers around the world to end their exploitative conditions and to achieve greater political and economic justice. During the dictatorship, the period leading up to May First usually featured heightened political activity by opponents of the regime, and increased surveillance and repression on the part of the military government. Leftist organizations clandestinely published and distributed leaflets decrying the high levels of unemployment, lack of food, attacks against the union movement and labor leaders, and the absence of democracy. Typed and mimeographed secretly in people's homes, courageous members of the resistance distributed these leaflets under people's doors during the night, putting themselves doubly at risk both for breaking the curfew and for distributing antigovernment literature. Military blockades patrolled traffic in and out of the poor neighborhoods, both to detect "suspicious" activity and to intimidate those who might consider undertaking any antimilitary actions.[39]

Other antidictatorship programs were less risky because many of them were conducted under the auspices of the Catholic Church. In May 1977 workers in Santiago, both those fortunate enough to have a job and the many more who were unemployed, cosponsored a program in conjunction with a Catholic parish in the western part of that city. The first speaker recounted the history of May Day. The archbishop then addressed the crowd, focusing on the role that the church could and would play in support of unemployed workers. Next, the president of the Construction Workers Union delivered a fiery speech that called on all workers, whether employed or not, to jointly consider themselves members of the working class. He also urged all the unemployed to join unions and union members to welcome the unemployed with open arms. The atmosphere was infused with calls for solidarity and an affirmation that despite the hardships many Chilean workers currently faced, they would continue to fight and not give up hope.[40]

THE LEGACY OF DICTATORSHIPS

The military regimes that ruled Chile, Argentina, Brazil, and Uruguay ended, in large part, due to popular protest and mass dissatisfaction with rule by the armed forces. The principal factors that stimulated wide-ranging opposition to military rule were the dictatorships' repressive policies and curtailment of democracy, the economic problems that beset these countries, international pressure, and, in the case of Argentina, the military's defeat in its attempts to regain control of the Malvinas (Falklands) Islands from the British. By the 1990s, democratically elected governments ruled where once military dictatorships had reigned.

Yet the return to democracy has been uneven and contested.[41] A crucial issue facing these Southern Cone nations has been whether to persecute those members of the military who abused human rights. To date most members of the armed forces have not been tried or sentenced for those crimes because, before stepping down, the military issued laws granting themselves amnesty. In 1978 the Chilean armed forces passed a decree to ensure that none of its members would be brought to trial for crimes they committed between 1973 and 1978. The Uruguayan military only agreed to relinquish power after it passed the 1986 Law of Nullity, which granted amnesty to the armed forces. Although impunity has been the order of the day, a number of recent changes—namely the election of presidents who were themselves victims of military repression, the ongoing demands for justice voiced by the domestic and international human rights movement, and internal changes in the armed forces—have altered the political climate in the Southern Cone.

One key event that encouraged this changing political dynamic was General Pinochet's aforementioned 1998 arrest. His detention also undermined the military's belief in its own invulnerability. Although the British courts ultimately ruled that Pinochet could not be extradited to Spain to stand trial, his arrest testified to the strength and unrelenting determination of the international human rights movement to obtain justice. Although his death in December 2006 brought to an end any attempts to bring him to trial, earlier that year the former dictator had been forced to witness the election of Michele Bachelet—whom the military had imprisoned and tortured, and who was the daughter of the aforementioned General Bachelet—as president of Chile. Her victory demonstrated, among other factors, a repudiation of the Pinochet dictatorship and the abuse of human rights it embodied.

The Uruguayan military, which has long escaped any accounting for its crimes, is under investigation as well. In March 2005 Uruguay elected as president Tabaré Vázquez, a medical doctor and community activist who has long advocated for better conditions for the poor. Members of his governing coalition range from former *Tupamaros* to communists to social democrats. He has pledged to ameliorate the problem of poverty and to confront directly the human rights abuses carried out during military rule. As a result of his stance, for the first time different government institutions are investigating the cases of past rulers who violated human rights. Authorities have begun to conduct excavations at military barracks where victims of military violence are likely to be buried and the government has charged Juan María Bordaberry, who was president during the years of the worst repression, with "aggravated homicide."[42]

Argentina and Brazil have also taken important steps to overcome the impunity that has prevailed in their countries. Néstor Kirchner, president of Argentina between 2003 and 2007, rejected the statute of limitations on crimes against humanity that the military has used to prevent charges being brought against it.[43] Reflecting the government's increased willingness to persecute those members of the military responsible for crimes, in July 2005 the Argentine Supreme Court "struck down two amnesty laws that prevent military officers from facing prosecution for human rights violations."[44] The Brazilian *Programa Nacional de Direitos Humanos* (National Human Rights Program) released its report in 1996 during the presidency of Fernando Henrique Cardoso. The account, approved by Cardoso's government, publicly acknowledged for the first time that the military dictatorship was responsible for the disappearances, torture, and killings committed by its agents during the dictatorship. In recognition of the crimes that the Brazilian state had committed against its own citizens, it paid indemnification to the families of 265 victims.[45]

For the civilians who lived through and suffered from the military dictatorships the push to prosecute those members of the armed forces who persecuted them is of invaluable importance, as it is to their respective societies as a whole. It establishes that they are both victims and survivors of horrendous crimes that members of their militaries committed against them. It converts the victims into heroes, and validates them as people who fought and suffered because they believed in a more just society for their fellow citizens. It condemns those who carried out these crimes and makes it clear that society will not tolerate such barbarity. It states to the world that human rights and democracy must be respected and promoted, and that *Nunca Más* (never again) will such brutal dictatorships be allowed to hold power in the Southern Cone.

A NORTH AMERICAN IN CHILE
DURING THE DICTATORSHIP

My sister and I arrived in Santiago in December 1976, three years after the military had seized power. Based on the stories that Chilean political refugees in the United States had told me about their lives after the overthrow of Allende, and my own images of what Nazi Germany was like, I entered the country expecting to be snatched up by the military at any moment. Instead, I stayed for six months and experienced what it was like to live in a dictatorship. Because the political refugees I had known in the United States had given me the addresses of their families in Chile, I was able to develop friendships with opponents of the military regime. They trusted me because I knew their sons; otherwise it is unlikely they would have opened up to a stranger from the United States. As a result, I entered the world of those Chileans who had suffered directly from military repression as well as those who actively resisted the dictatorship.

What most defined Chile for me at that time was the sense of dual realities: on one hand the façade of normality, the pervasive awareness of military rule, and the large number of people who apparently led their daily lives as if nothing had changed, and on the other the lives of the former supporters of the Popular Unity government, the political prisoners, the families of the disappeared, and members of the resistance who found it impossible to forget how much their lives and those of other Chileans had in fact been transformed as a result of the dictatorship. In some ways, life continued as it had before. Women shopped daily in the open-air markets for food. Families and friends socialized with each other for entertainment, since at that time the huge malls that would later entice Chileans into the world of consumption did not exist. On Sundays downtown Santiago was deserted, as people retreated to their homes for lengthy meals, to rest, or take care of chores they had been unable to do during the week.

Yet, on another level, the reality of living under military rule permeated people's everyday lives. Men and women planned their parties knowing that they had to leave by a certain hour; otherwise they had to stay all night in the host's house because the curfew would not allow them to venture out. Chileans rarely if ever spoke of politics with strangers, a practice I adopted. If I met someone for the first time, I would never voice any of my political beliefs unless I first knew what she or he thought, and even then I was circumspect. When I bumped into someone I knew on the bus, we made sure that our conversation was either innocuous or could not be overheard. Sometimes, we would just give each other smiles that indicated we knew we were on the same side; no more needed or could be said. Fear and mistrust influenced many people's social interactions because one just could not have confidence in the other person.

Still, despite the fear that permeated much of Chilean society, some Chileans were brave and resisted the military. On May 1, 1977, International Workers Day, a special mass was celebrated in the cathedral downtown. I attended the service, along with my sister and the family we were staying with, whose daughter the military had disappeared. The cathedral was filled with people who had suffered from and opposed the dictatorship. It was a

Table 9.1 Table of Repression

Country	Years of Dictatorship	Detained	Percent Tortured	Numbers Killed/ Disappeared
Argentina	1974–1983	9,000–30,000	Most/all	9,000–30,000[1]
Brazil	1964–1985			125–184[2]
Chile	1973–1990	27,255–200,000	94%	2,905–4,500[3]
Uruguay	1973–1985	1,000s[4]	Most/all	200+[5]

1. 9,000 is the "official" figure of the National Commission on the Disappeared, formed in 1983 by the Raúl Alfonsín government. The Mothers of the Disappeared, along with most of the human rights movement, asserts the figure is *at least* 30,000. Unlike in other countries, practically all those arrested in Argentina were killed and/or disappeared, so the figures in all three categories are roughly the same. Marguerite Bouvard, *Revolutionizing Motherhood: The Mothers of the Plaza de Mayo* (Wilmington, DE: Scholarly Resources, 1994), 31.
2. The lower number is from *Torture in Brazil: A Shocking Report on the Pervasive Use of Torture by Brazilian Military Governments, 1964–1979, Secretly Prepared by the Archdiocese of São Paulo*, ed. with a new preface by Joan Dassin, trans. Jaime Wright (Austin: University of Texas Press, 1998), 235–38. The higher number is from Movimiento Tortura Nunca Mais, www.torturanuncamais-rj.org.br/sa/M_D.asp?refresh=20080.
3. Again, there is no agreement as to the numbers. See Steve Stern, *Remembering Pinochet's Chile: On the Eve of London 1998* (Durham, NC: Duke University Press, 2004), xxi, 158–61; and the *Valech Report*, http://www.gobiernodechile.cl/comision_valech/index.asp#Map.
4. I have been unable to determine more exact figures. A number of sources, however, point out that in relation to the size of its population, Uruguay had the largest number of political prisoners and torture victims of any country in the world. See Diana Cariboni, "Rights—Uruguay: Uncovering the Truth, Three Decades On," http://ipsnews.net/print.asp?.idnews_35009.
5. *El Mostrador* (Santiago, Chile), December 27, 2006.

visible and powerful display of courage and solidarity. I remember a little boy whose father was disappeared. He delivered a moving message from the pulpit asking for the return of his *papá*. A woman whose husband was a political prisoner demanded his release. After the service ended, people left the cathedral singing Beethoven's "Song of Joy"; others shouted, "*Abajo con la dictadura fascista*" (Down with the fascist dictatorship), while others hushed them, telling them to be careful, there were spies in the crowd. When we walked outside, *carabineros* (Chilean police) with guns and fierce-looking dogs surrounded the exit. We stepped out of the safety of the cathedral, unsure of what would happen to us. Fortunately, no one was arrested and we all walked home safely.

As a U.S. citizen I was safer than most Chileans, but I still felt scared a lot of the time.[46] Since I was politically active—I visited the political prisoners, I worked with the resistance—I remained conscious of the fact that I could be a target of the dictatorship's agents. In fact, one day the military police came to the house where my sister and I were staying, and asked for us. We were not there and they did not come back. We were fortunate, but many Chileans were not.

NOTES

1. Luz Arce, *The Inferno: A Story of Terror and Survival in Chile* (Madison: University of Wisconsin Press, 2004), 39–40.

2. Thomas E. Skidmore, *Politics in Brazil: An Experiment in Democracy* (London: Oxford University Press, 1967), 187 302.

3. *Urban Guerrilla Warfare in Latin America,* eds. James Kohl and John Litt, (Cambridge, MA, and London, England: MIT Press, 1974), 184–188. When the Uruguayan government refused to meet the *Tupamaros'* demands, the group killed Mitrione. In 1973 Greek director Constantin Costa-Gavras directed the highly acclaimed film *State of Siege,* which portrays this episode in Uruguayan history.

4. Margaret Power, *Right-Wing Women in Chile: Feminine Power and the Struggle against Allende* (State College: Pennsylvania State University Press, 2002), 24–27.

5. *Urban Guerrilla Warfare,* 329.

6. Juan Rial, "Makers and Guardians of Fear: Controlled Terror in Uruguay," in *Fear at the Edge: State Terror and Resistance in Latin America,* eds. Juan E. Corradi, Patricia Weiss Fagen, and Manuel Antonio Garretón (Berkeley: University of California Press, 1992), 93.

7. Peter H. Smith, *Talons of the Eagle: Dynamics of U.S.-Latin American Relations* (New York: Oxford University Press, 1996), 149–150.

8. In 1962, "the peak year, the United States trained nearly 9,000 Latin American officers and enlisted personnel." The average during the 1960s, however, was 3,500 men per year. Stephen C. Rabe, *The Most Dangerous Area in the World: John F. Kennedy Confronts Communist Revolution in Latin America* (Chapel Hill: University of North Carolina Press, 1999), 130.

9. As quoted in Patricia Weiss Fagen, "Repression and State Security," in *Fear at the Edge,* 43.

10. Mark Falcoff, "Latin America Alone?" in *Neighborly Adversaries: Readings in U.S.-Latin American Relations,* eds. Michael LaRosa and Frank O. Mora (Lanham, MD: Rowman & Littlefield, 1999), 255.

11. Eduardo Galeano, *Open Veins of Latin America: Five Centuries of the Pillage of a Continent* (New York: Monthly Review Press, 1973), 225.

12. Salvador Allende, "Speech to the United Nations," December 4, 1972, http://www.rrojasdatabank.org/foh12.htm.

13. Such warnings could be delivered either as direct statements to the media or through legislation passed by the military. They could also be communicated more indirectly, through conversations at informal gatherings between military officers and prominent members of the media or business community. Both the murder of journalists and the censuring of the media clearly transmitted the idea that the publication or broadcasting of certain opinions or news items was risky. Ana María Kapelusz, personal communication, October 15, 2005.

14. Mercedes Rowinsky, "Uruguay," in *Censorship, A World Encyclopedia* (Chicago: Fitzroy Dearborn Publishers, 2001), 2545.

15. Lúcia Sá, "Brazil," in *Censorship, A World Encyclopedia*, 284–285.

16. Andrés Avellaneda, "Argentina," in *Censorship, A World Encyclopedia*, 91.

17. Margaret Power, personal observation, Santiago, January—July 1977.

18. Peter Winn, "The Pinochet Era," in *Victims of the Chilean Miracle*, ed. Peter Winn (Durham, NC: Duke University Press, 2004), 22.

19. Jacobo Timerman, *Prisoner without a Name, Cell without a Number* (New York: Vintage Books, 1988), 101.

20. For a powerful examination of the French military's role in training Latin American militaries see Marie-Monique Robin's 2003 film, *Death Squadrons: The French School.*

21. Temma Kaplan, *Taking Back the Streets: Women, Youth, and Direct Democracy* (Berkeley: University of California Press, 2003), 143, 152–153.

22. There are approximately 400 of these missing children, now adults. An organization called the Grandmothers of the Plaza de Mayo dedicates itself to finding the women's missing grandchildren. Kaplan, *Taking Back,* 130. A 1985 film by Argentine director Luis Puenzo, *The Official Story,* movingly tells the story of a woman who unknowingly adopts the child of a disappeared couple. In her search for the facts about her daughter's past, she learns the truth about her daughter's and Argentina's history, and meets the girl's likely grandmother.

23. Greg Grandin, *The Last Colonial Massacre: Latin America in the Cold War* (Chicago: University of Chicago Press, 2004), 11–12.

24. Anonymous, personal conversations, Chicago, September 1997.

25. Luis Torres, interview, Santiago, December 29, 1998.

26. Sá, "Brazil," 284.

27. In 1990, however, the restoration of democracy helped Chileans to overcome this fear and reestablished Peña Hen as both a great musician and a dedicated teacher. A film that honored his musical contributions and his work with Chilean children premiered in 2004 to positive reviews and public acclaim. Patricia Politzer, *Miedo en Chile* (Santiago: CESOC, 1985), 164; and "Estrenan documental Jorge Peña Hen: Su música y los niños," http://web.uchile.cl/facultades/artes/sala_zeqers/temporal/12agosto.

28. A copy of the report can be found at http://www.gobiernodechile.cl/comision_valech/index.asp#Map.

29. Luis Torres, Santiago, taped interview, May 19, 1999.

30. *Chile-America*, Rome, numbers 16, 17, and 18 (April–May 1976), 112–113; Luis Torres, Santiago, taped interview, May 18, 1999.

31. Carlos Fico, *Além do Golpe* (Rio de Janeiro: Record, 2004), 208–210.

32. Power, *Right-Wing Women*, 166, 189, 228–230.

33. Power, *Right-Wing Women*, 240–246.

34. Power, *Right-Wing Women*, 147–156, 259–260.

35. Kaplan, *Taking Back*, 110.

36. Kaplan, *Taking Back*, 110.

37. Phil O'Brien and Jackie Roddick, *Chile: The Pinochet Decade* (London: Latin American Bureau, 1983), 63.

38. Margaret Power, personal observations and diaries, December 1976–June 1977.

39. Margaret Power, personal observations and diaries, December 1976–June 1977.

40. Margaret Power, personal observations and diaries, December 1976–June 1977.

41. For a thoughtful discussion of the truth and reconciliation commissions set up in Guatemala, Argentina, and Chile following the end of military rule, see Greg Grandin, "The Instruction of Great Catastrophe: Truth Commissions, National History, and State Formation in Argentina, Chile, and Guatemala," *The American Historical Review* 110:1 (February 2005), 46–67.

42. Larry Rother, "Uruguay Tackles Old Rights Cases, Charging Ex-President," *The New York Times*, July 31, 2005.

43. Andrés Gaudin, "The Kirchner Factor," *NACLA, Report on the Americas* 38:4 (January–February 2005), 16–17.

44. Human Rights Watch, "Impact," July 2005, http://hrw.org/update/2005/07/#argentina.

45. Linda Rabben, "Human Rights in Cardoso's Brazil," paper presented at the Brazilian Studies Association Meeting, Recife, Brazil, June 2000.

46. Being a North American did not always guarantee safety in Pinochet's Chile. In 1973 the Chilean military killed two U.S. citizens, Charles Horman and Frank Terrugi. Director Costa-Gavras filmed their story in his 1985 movie *Missing*. That year the Chilean military also killed mathematics professor Boris Weisfeiler as he was hiking around *Colonia Dignidad*, a secret compound in southern Chile where the military tortured and killed its opponents.

TEN

And the Storm Raged On: The Daily Experience of Terror during the Central American Civil Wars, 1966–1996

Arturo Arias

The Central American civil wars of the 1980s were the last step of a long conflict whose immediate roots lie with the 1954 Central Intelligence Agency (CIA)-sponsored invasion of Guatemala that overthrew a legitimate, democratic government. The consequences of the 1954 assault engulfed the entire region in a vortex of violence that forever changed the daily lives of its denizens, even after the end of armed conflict following the signing of the Guatemala Peace Accord on December 29, 1996. This chapter, which chronicles the gross human rights violations that took place in Central America during this time, focuses on Guatemala as representative of the region because that country experienced both the longest civil war and the worst civilian atrocities. It includes personal and autobiographical data to show the depth of pain and the ravages that these conflicts generated on ordinary people. The essay is an exercise that feels as if I have spoken with the dead, a sentiment that evokes both the question of why I survived and the matter of how posterity will judge such egregious crimes.

THE POLITICAL BACKGROUND

To better understand the damage suffered by civilians during the Central American civil wars, one must first explain the politics that brought about the struggles in Nicaragua, El Salvador, and Guatemala. The origins of the Nicaraguan conflict rest in the United States' desire to build a canal across the Central American country's territory early in the twentieth century—construction of an inland waterway from which only U.S. corporations would profit. When President José Santos Zelaya objected to the scheme because Nicaragua would have lost much of its sovereignty, U.S. Marines landed in the nation's Caribbean coast in December 1909 and overthrew him to secure canal rights. The Marines' continued presence prompted Augusto César Sandino to take up arms in 1927, and for the next six years he fought a guerrilla war to expel the marines from Nicaraguan soil and establish a sovereign government. The inauguration of Franklin D. Roosevelt as U.S. president in 1932 made it easier for the contending factions to negotiate a peace treaty, after which elections were held and Sandino turned in his weapons. However, General Anastasio Somoza, who had become head of Nicaragua's National Guard with U.S. support, orchestrated Sandino's assassination in February 1934 and took over the presidency two years later. He and his two sons governed ruthlessly until 1979.

In El Salvador economic factors—the 1929 Great Depression and the ensuing collapse of coffee prices—laid the groundwork for civil war. Starving peasants launched a spontaneous insurrection in January 1932 to which the Salvadoran Communist Party, led by Farabundo Martí, latched on at the last minute. The rural masses, armed only with machetes, could not match the potency of the Salvadoran army. The military repressed the uprising with full force, killing an estimated 30,000 men, women, and children during that month alone. General Maximiliano Hernández Martínez seized power following his brutal suppression of rural resistance, and from that time until 1980 all but one Salvadoran president came from the ranks of the army. These authoritarian governments relied on political repression, mixed with limited social and economic reforms, to maintain power.

The foundation for Guatemala's civil war can be traced to the emergence in 1944 of a university student-led movement that represented all sectors of society and employed the rhetoric of U.S. President Roosevelt's "Four Freedoms" to protest against General Jorge Ubico's dictatorship. Although the United States had supported Ubico since 1931 to prevent another massive peasant uprising like El Salvador's, by 1944 American officials believed that he was obsolete. Consequently, the United States did not preempt the demonstrations and protests that toppled his regime that July.

As Guatemala's new government moved to approve eight-hour work days, paid vacations, and health provisions for all workers it clashed with the United Fruit Company (UFCO), the most powerful U.S. corporation in the Caribbean basin, a situation that grew more tense in 1952 when President Jacobo Arbenz put into action a land reform program modeled on the one implemented by the United States in Japan at the end of World War II. The plan targeted UFCO's possessions, so the company moved to denounce Arbenz' government as "communist." The administration of U.S. President Dwight Eisenhower heard these cries and moved to protect UFCO's interests, but it also desired to take a stand against communism and enhance global stability. It thus ordered the aforementioned 1954 CIA intervention that toppled Arbenz, an operation that many believe insured the rule of oppressive military regimes until the mid-1980s.

These short summaries help explain why the small guerrilla groups that turned up in Central America during the 1970s gained the sympathy and allegiance of nationalist individuals and many others who resented U.S. meddling in the sovereign affairs of their country. The ruthlessness of the region's dictatorships, the rise of peasant movements organized by radicalized Catholic priests and nuns, and the Maya struggle against racism in Guatemala further strengthened the guerrillas. Members of these groups eventually linked forces with the insurgents, and their combined strength gave them sufficient political clout to build broad-based mass movements that usually attracted middle-of-the road sectors. Events in Nicaragua proved the power of such movements. On July 19, 1979, the Sandinista National Liberation Front (FSLN), an organization that had taken its name from Sandino, toppled the last surviving member of the Somoza dynasty, Anastasio Somoza, Jr., and ended the family's rule once and for all.

Ronald Reagan, however, did not believe in Central American self-empowerment. In March 1979, when he ran for the Republican party's presidential nomination, the future U.S. chief executive asserted that most Sandinistas were "Cuban-trained, Cuban-armed, and dedicated to creating another Communist country in this hemisphere."[1] His administration, likewise, refused to acknowledge the nationalist and modernizing aspirations of the region's citizens. President Reagan and his advisors saw the Central American wars as part of an East-West conflict, and to the degree that the Soviet Union—or, as Reagan called it, the "Evil Empire"—was brought down, insurrection would disappear in Central America.

Consequently, the Reagan administration instituted policies that helped escalate the region's civil wars. It sent military aid and military advisors to prop up military governments in El Salvador and Guatemala, or, in the case of Nicaragua, where the Sandinistas held power and were perceived as foes of U.S. interests, it provided financial and military support to armed groups known as the *contras* (from the Spanish term *contrarrevolucionario*, or counter-revolutionary). In the end, and despite President Reagan's efforts, the collapse of the Berlin wall in 1989 and the disintegration of the Soviet Union the following year made it easier for the United States to acknowledge its erstwhile opposition and negotiate peace processes between opposing factions in all Central American countries. Hostilities in the region finally ceased in 1996.

DAILY LIVES IN THE 1960S AND 1970S: THE CALM BEFORE THE STORM

The 1954 CIA invasion of Guatemala brought to power Carlos Castillo Armas, who viewed the civilian population with suspicion and labeled them an "internal enemy."[2] This attitude, combined with the fact that the Castillo Armas' administration was only accountable to the U.S. government, made the regime nonchalant about the welfare of the population and cynical regarding their safety. As a result, the Castillo Armas government quickly moved to incarcerate—without warrant or trial—those peasants who had received land titles from the Arbenz government. The regime then assassinated union members and peasant activists, prompting many urban Guatemalans to seek shelter in foreign embassies and go into exile.[3] The terror implanted by the Castillo Armas government made ordinary citizens fearful of venting their political opinions, even in private. Many believed that *orejas* (or "ears") were everywhere,[4] so people kept their views to themselves. This attitude not only shut down potential dialogue and earnest public discussion, but also introspective reflection by scores of citizens. The inability to articulate questions, doubts, or feelings about the events around them kept people from bouncing ideas off each other, and Guatemalans thus behaved as if they had been placed under a bell jar. The increased alienation was partly responsible for the stunted emotional growth that facilitated an unimpeded reign of terror, which lasted until the 1996 peace treaty, an experience vividly illustrated in Luis Argueta's 1994 film, *The Silence of Neto*.

Despite the overall silencing of the population, the Castillo Armas regime did not deal in the same way with all sectors of society. Fearful that future opposition to the government's record of human rights violations would come from the ranks of high school and university students, the government, instead of annihilating them as it had done with labor and peasant unions, often expelled students from their schools for expressing a hostile attitude toward the CIA invasion. This was the case in 1955 with then-13-year-old César Montes,[5] the son of a Mormon pastor who went on to become a guerrilla leader in the 1960s. But even individuals who did not fit the profile of a troublemaker, such as my cousin Arnoldo Fernández, who migrated to the United States in 1960 to avoid political problems at home, recounted how policemen chased him and his older brother Rafael inside the Central Institute for Boys, Guatemala's best-known public secondary school, for yelling anti-Castillo Armas slogans in 1957. They were lucky to climb a high wall and escape.[6] Miguel Angel Sandoval, another future leader of the revolutionary opposition, remembers that in 1962 policemen caught him on the same grounds, severely beat him, and cut off his hair. As his locks fell to the floor, Sandoval swore to himself that he would become a stalwart enemy of the regime, a promise he has kept to this day.[7]

The triumph of the 1959 Cuban Revolution greatly contributed to the increased repression and violence in Guatemala. After the failed United States-led Bay of Pigs invasion in 1961, Fidel Castro openly declared his communist sympathies, turning Cuba into a key player in the Soviet Union and U.S. global power struggle during the Cold War. In addition, Castro's foreign policy included support for guerrilla forces in many Latin American countries, and both factors generated a hysterical reaction in Guatemala, especially because a November 13, 1960, young officers' uprising had led to the formation of the country's first guerrilla group. Fearing the worst, successive regimes declared a state of siege. As a result, government agents could arrest anyone without a warrant and they did not have to account for that person's arrest within 24 hours, as stipulated by law. The state of siege also meant that group meetings could not take place because the government might label them as subversive activities. Consequently, many families had to suspend ordinary events so crucial to Central American social behavior as birthday celebrations, baptisms, and church weddings. Likewise, the government's decision to impose an 8:00 P.M. curfew—after which time anyone caught outside their home without a permit was subject to arrest—also curtailed social activities like restaurant dinners, soccer games at local stadiums, evening movies, teenage partying and dating, as well as added to problems involving more critical doings such as sudden health emergencies, childbirths, and deaths in the family.

In addition, the stage of siege led the army to place checkpoints at all crucial points in the capital city and major highways, where soldiers commonly stopped civilians during the most routine outing. When this happened, troops pointed their weapons at the occupants of each vehicle, demanded identity papers from all, and searched the car, especially the trunk and glove compartment, to verify whether the occupants carried weapons or "subversive propaganda." As a child who lived through many such checkpoints, I can attest to the unforgettable fear of having a soldier point a gun at both yourself and your parents. One's sense of impotence, and the fear manifested by one's parents, is a trauma that never fades away. In no way can people get used to the menacing presence of soldiers or any other uniformed authority figure. Many works of literature subsequently reproduced the soldiers' deadly gaze and the victims' fear. The following scene from a prize-winning short story by Dante Liano, one of contemporary Guatemala's leading cultural figures, became tragically common:

The night before, Ricardo's brother was returning home late from a party. Some patrol officers signaled for him to pull over. He stopped his car and waited for the officers. The police asked him for his papers. When he reached into his coat pocket for his wallet, the officers fired, believing—that's what they stated, before disappearing into anonymity—that he was taking out a gun. Harsh times had set in, and the government had decreed a state of siege in an attempt to cover up the fact that it had caused nineteen union members to be assassinated.[8]

While fictional, the incident became emblematic of the Guatemalans' daily suffering and turned Liano into one of his country's most recognized writers.

The escalating political crisis also resulted in news censorship, both of newspapers and radio stations. The government forced the latter to be *en cadena*, in other words, to air the programming of the official government radio station, which became the sole source of news for the entire country (television, introduced only in 1956, did not assume that role until the 1970s). Individuals thus lacked information about current events, a situation made all the more serious because in those days the expense of long-distance telephone calls made them a rarity. As a result all kinds of rumors circulated that grossly exaggerated whatever figments of truth they had, if any. Such tales intensified the anxiety or panic with which ordinary citizens lived their daily lives, and became sources of great stress and even mental breakdowns.

The daily lives of Guatemalans, however, took a qualitative turn for the worse on the eve of the March 1966 presidential elections. Until then, students, young professionals, and those individuals likely to oppose dictatorship—from benign name-calling to more radical means—were routinely sent to prison where they were often beaten, frequently tortured, and kept illegally for weeks or even months at a time, until their eventual release. Often they built a small amount of trust or camaraderie with their jailers, who became conduits for messages and goods. As a result, families or political organizations could find out the whereabouts of given prisoners, ascertain the status of their health, and send them food and clothing for the duration of their incarceration. When released, government officials drove many prisoners to the Mexican border, abandoned them on the Mexican side with a few dollars, and warned them that things would be worse for them if they returned. Some never did, others spent a few years in Mexico, while still others came back as soon as they could. What remained constant, regardless of the beatings or violations of their human/civil rights, was that former prisoners remained alive and able to function as constructive human beings following their ordeal.

With presidential elections drawing near, however, the practice of holding political prisoners came to an end. In early March 1966 police surrounded a house where 26 communists, or communist sympathizers, were meeting. Those arrested included the Secretary General of the *Partido Guatemalteco del Trabajo* (PGT), Víctor Manuel Gutiérrez, as well as the secretary-general of the National Peasants Federation, Leonardo Castillo Flores.[9] The two men had the dubious honor of being Latin America's first *desaparecidos*.[10] After them, many individuals arrested by the army or police simply disappeared, never to be seen again. One year later, the assassination of Rogelia Cruz Martínez, an architecture student who in 1959 had represented the country at the Miss Universe Pageant, further traumatized Guatemalans. Renowned for her beauty and seen in many national publications, Cruz Martínez became a target because she had a left-wing boyfriend. Just before Christmas 1967, the *Mano Blanca* (White Hand), a death squad run by Colonel Carlos Arana Osorio and integrated by soldiers dressed as civilians, captured her, tortured her in a most grotesque fashion, and scattered pieces of her body on the banks of the Motagua River.[11] The combination of her fame, her beauty, the monstrous nature of the crime, and the fact that she was the first distinguished citizen known to have been publicly raped (which implied that women were no longer safe) haunted middle-class denizens and transformed Cruz Martínez into both an icon and a phantasm of Guatemalan terror. Even the country's conservative Catholic archbishop, Monsignor Mario Casariego, was not safe from these developments, as in 1968 a right-wing death squad kidnapped the cleric and held him in a secret location. The army then sealed off Guatemala City and searched its every block looking for his whereabouts. I distinctly remember being alone with my 13-year old sister after school on a weekday (both my parents worked) when someone knocked at the door. When I opened it, a fully-armed patrol stood outside in single file. The sergeant in charge informed me that they had orders to go inside the house and look for the archbishop. I stood flat against the wall, holding my sister's hand, while they entered the house and searched under the beds, inside the closets, and in any conceivable space where a man could be hidden. As they trotted out of the house, the sergeant gave me a military salute, "informed" me that the archbishop had not been found in the premises, and left. The terror of that experience lingers to this day, nearly 40 years later.

The early 1970s, however, seemed more bearable for ordinary Central Americans than the previous decade due to the emergence of mostly legal, unarmed, and generally democratic mass organizations of peasants, students, urban workers, and women whose members were able to proselytize without fear of being abducted. Those years also witnessed the appearance of Christian Base Communities (CBCs)—the grassroots organizations that materialized in Latin America in the wake of the Second Vatican Council (1962–1965), a meeting of high-ranking Catholic Church leaders that put the plight of the world's poor at the center of the church's agenda. These communities consisted of small groups of lay men and women that met with the poor to read the Bible, pray, or discuss social problems. Nevertheless, the commitment to the poor by all these groups insured that local elites would view them suspicion (of engaging in Communist activities), resentment, and even fear. As a result, government authorities soon unleashed a wave of violence that set the stage for the civil wars of the 1980s.

The following case involving the Ixil Mayas who lived in the northern region of Guatemala's Quiché department illustrates the perceived threat posed by such newly emergent associations, as well as the impact of the intensified repression of the 1960s. By the end of the decade, authorities in Guatemala had developed a more sophisticated military intelligence network (labeled "the Black Box" by the army's secretive intelligence officials) that had begun to draw up blacklists, both in Guatemala City and the indigenous countryside. Individuals could also add names to blacklists for reasons—personal enmities, rivalry over a well-paid job, or a love affair that ended badly—that had nothing to do with politics. People lived in terror of turning up on such listings, as that always meant exile—if one had the time and means to leave the country in time—or death if one did not take the list seriously or if one moved too slowly after finding one's name on it.

Individuals in northern Quiché lived under more backward material conditions, at a much greater distance from the departmental capital, and very close to the Ixcán jungle, where the clandestine Guerrilla Army of the Poor (*Ejército Guerrillero de los Pobres*, EGP) had operated since early 1972. The region's remote location, furthermore, had facilitated the efforts of CBCs to organize and raise the consciousness of the area's inhabitants. The situation prompted Sebastián Guzmán, Ixil leader of the town of Nebaj, and 11 other members of the town council, to write General Carlos Arana Osorio (then president of Guatemala) in January 1973, and request his direct intervention because "there is now among us a bad seed, the communists, who are fighting against us with cooperatives and other idiocies."[12] Because Arana Osorio did not respond, the influence of CBCs continued to grow. The appearance two years later in the Quiché region of the Committee for Peasant Unity (*Comité de Unidad Campesina*, CUC) further alarmed Guzmán, who in November sent his request directly to the army commander of the Santa Cruz del Quiché zone. The letter apparently had the desired effect, as in January 1976 Maya leaders drew up the first blacklist in Guzmán's home, which included names, personal data, characteristics, and photos. The assassinations or kidnappings of Christians, leaders of cooperatives, directors of development committees, and popular organizations began in mid-March.

Two years later a new phenomenon—massacres of entire villages—appeared on the Central American scene with the slaughter of 150 Kekchí Mayas from the village of Panzós on May 29, 1978. After this incident, inhabitants of all Central American villages knew that the possibility of the army marching into their village, razing it, and killing all of its inhabitants, was real. Such massacres were especially brutal for women, children, and old people. Not only were most women raped prior to being tortured and killed,[13] but also they often had to first witness the murder of their own children, while pregnant women had fetuses pulled from their bodies while still alive. Female children were also raped prior to being assassinated in grotesque fashion, such as having their skulls smashed by rocks in front of their parents. The army deliberately killed old people because it knew about the Mayas' reliance on oral tradition, and it knew that village elders passed on knowledge to their grandchildren. The military's efforts to disrupt this cycle and end the continuity of Maya culture led the United Nations (UN) to label their campaign as "genocidal": an attempt to exterminate an entire group of people. Indeed, international human rights agencies define genocide as the systematic killing of substantial numbers of people on the basis of ethnicity, religion, political opinion, social status, or other particularity, with the intent to destroy the social identity of a given people. This process would repeat itself in the 1980s.

THE STORM ERUPTS: THE 1980S

The July 1979 victory of the Sandinista Liberation Front in Nicaragua shocked the governing army and ruling elites in Guatemala and El Salvador. They believed that opposition groups in their countries would launch an all-out effort to gain political power as the Sandinistas had, and their apprehensions were not unwarranted. Through 1979 more and more Indians in Guatemala joined not only the EGP but also a second guerrilla group, the Organization of the People in Arms (ORPA, *Organización Revolucionaria del Pueblo en Armas*). On October 15 in El Salvador, meanwhile, reform-minded junior military officers staged a coup in an attempt to implement a broad land reform program and curtail the privileges of the wealthy. These developments convinced elites that they had to take strong measures to forestall a transfer of power, but those actions led to an all-out intensification of civil wars in both countries.

The key event in Guatemala took place in late January 1980, when 39 Maya protesters occupied the Spanish embassy in Guatemala City. The demonstrators wanted to hold a press conference to denounce the burning of their villages in the Quiché department, and the Spanish ambassador granted them permission to do so. Nevertheless, Guatemalan president General Romeo Lucas García violated international law—which holds that embassies are sovereign grounds of the country in question—and ordered the police to storm the embassy. They burnt it down with all its occupants. The incident isolated the Guatemalan government, as a nauseated population could not quite believe that the regime would resort to such violence. Meanwhile, the junior army officers who had staged the October 15, 1979 coup in El Salvador could not consolidate their hold on power and bring about the desired reforms. Their failure led to the emergence of a new guerrilla group that named itself after Martí, the Farabundo Martí National Liberation Front (FMLN), which fought the U.S.-trained Salvadoran army to a standstill for the next decade.

The assassination of El Salvador's Archbishop Oscar Arnulfo Romero polarized the situation even more. An outspoken defender of human rights, one day before his death Romero had given his usual Sunday homily at the Cathedral when he often reviewed the "events of the week" that official news sources failed to report on. In that speech he named the army as the perpetrator of human rights violations and ordered it to "stop the repression."[14] The discourse, however, coincided with the Salvadoran government's decreasing tolerance for dissent and led to his assassination. On March 24, 1980,

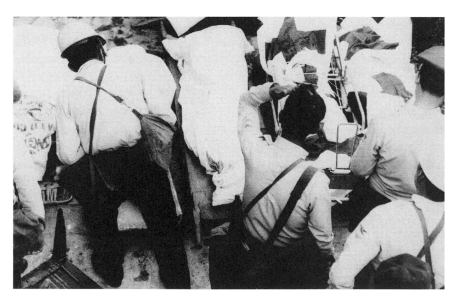

Red Cross workers look over stretchers outside the Spanish embassy in Guatemala after 39 people were killed when a blaze started by police and state security agents engulfed the building on January 31, 1980. (AP Photo).

at 6:25 p.m. in the chapel of the Divine Providence Cancer Hospital, in San Salvador, a gunman fired a bullet that went through Romero's heart and killed him. Despite the scandal that the assassination of an archbishop entailed, pressure from the Vatican, and international condemnation of the episode, the government failed to arrest anyone for the heinous crime. This is particularly disturbing given that Major Roberto D'Aubuisson, head of Military Intelligence at the time of the assassination, and described as a "pathological killer" by former U.S. Ambassador Robert White, was accused in 1989 of ordering Romero's murder. D'Aubuisson, however, never came to trial and died a natural death a few years later.[15]

The assassination of other prominent nuns and priests followed that of Archbishop Romero, which served to highlight the Salvadoran army's conviction that the clerics were the brains behind guerrilla activity. Consequently, in October 1980 the Salvadoran military launched an offensive against guerrillas in the eastern province of Morazán. Much to their surprise, resistance was strong and they failed to capture very many guerrillas. The fiasco led the army to switch tactics; instead of concentrating on the capture of insurgents it began a campaign of massive civilian assassinations. Two months later, members of the National Guard brutally raped, tortured, and murdered four American Roman Catholic churchwomen—Dorothy Kazel, Ita Ford, and Maura Clarke, who were nuns, and Jean Donovan, a lay missionary. Their deaths illustrated the military's new, "take no prisoners" approach. Then, in mid-December 1981, the army carried out a massacre of horrendous proportions over a period of several days in the towns of El Mozote, La Joya, Cerro Pando, Ranchería, Los Toriles, and Jocote Amarillo. Nearly 10 years later, in November 1991, *Tutela Legal*, the archdiocesan human rights office, charged the U.S.-trained and armed Atlacatl Battalion, which had been created as a special task force to "clean the countryside" and whose members called themselves "the little angels from Hell," with responsibility for most of the slaughter. Although the precise death toll at El Mozote will never be known, forensic investigators who in 1982 exhumed the corpses believe that more than 1,000 people may have been murdered in the aforementioned villages. They further determined that "approximately 85 per cent of the 117 victims killed in the main square of El Mozote were children under 12 years of age," and indicated that a more precise estimate of the victims' ages would be made in the laboratory. In the end, the skeletal remains of 143 bodies were identified, including 131 children under

12 years old, 5 adolescents, and 7 adults. The experts further noted that children's average age "was approximately 6 years."[16]

The Guatemalan army followed the burning of the Spanish embassy with an all-out assault against the Catholic Church, just as in El Salvador. Unknown members of a death squad kidnapped Father Conrado de la Cruz in broad daylight in Guatemala City with some of his parishioners and his sacristan on May 1, 1980. Shortly afterwards, another death squad "disappeared" the two daughters of Archbishop Casariego's personal secretary, both of whom worked in Catholic charity houses. Their father, a politically conservative man, relied on his relationship with the archbishop to arrange for a personal meeting with then-president General Lucas García, but the visit never took place as the father disappeared shortly afterwards. Similar events began to take place in the countryside as well. When the army began to assassinate priests in Quiché department in July 1980, its bishop, Juan Gerardi, ordered all priests to abandon the diocese. By 1981 the growing list of murdered or disappeared priests and nuns had left Guatemalans bereft, lacking spiritual guidance

Marta Arcadia Ramírez Portillo, 61, waits for remains of four family members—who were executed by the Salvadoran army in December 1981—to be exhumed from El Mozote. In 2003 a group of Argentine forensic anthropologists hosted by the Roman Catholic Church renewed the search for victims of the massacre. (AP Photo/Luis Romero).

when it was most needed, and feeling like hopeless prisoners inside their own country. Even the thought of attending mass paralyzed ordinary citizens. Some priests went underground and began to celebrate mass in secret places, but the risks for ordinary citizens were enormous. In the words of an American Catholic nun who worked in the country, "no one has good reason to think he or she is being sought, and yet no one has any reason to feel safe, either."[17]

The army's terror apparatus also manhandled universities and educational institutions. While academic journals have amply documented the army's occupation and destruction of Guatemala's San Carlos University as well as that of the National University of El Salvador (which led to their closure for several years), a lesser-known fact is that professors and students were shot and killed. The experience of Rolando Medina, a professor of literary theory at San Carlos, is typical of the horror lived by academics in Central America. He and his wife had finished teaching at the School of Humanities, and were heading for their car to go home for dinner. A student suddenly stopped Mrs. Medina in the corridor to request an appointment. Professor Medina continued on his way, and as he stepped outside the building four heavily armed men grabbed him. His wife saw how they dragged him to a jeep with tinted windows, and forced him into the back seat. She immediately called my home in Mexico City, and flew in the next day. With tears in her eyes, she described his last gaze, his eyes fixed on her, while his head was shoved inside the car and the door was closed. She never heard from him again.

In addition, labor unions and all kinds of grassroots community organizations became victims of repression and random terror. On September 23, 1980, a platoon of soldiers assassinated Andrés Avelino Zapeta y Zapeta, the mayor of Santa Cruz del Quiché, the most important indigenous town in Guatemala's northwestern highlands.[18] A moderate K'iché Maya, that is, someone who sympathized neither with the military dictatorship nor with guerrillas and a firm believer in the democratic process, Zapeta's death came to symbolize the impossibility of exercising legal political office for Mayas, who comprised 60 percent of the country's population.

Whereas some observers noted that Zapeta's death was unfortunate but inevitable because he governed one of the country's most conflictive towns, Stanford anthropologist Benjamin Paul's chronicle about the tourist town of San Pedro La Laguna reveals that what happened to Zapeta was an all-too-common occurrence. Paul's account also illustrates the manner in which death squads operated throughout the region, and their effect on the daily lives of ordinary citizens. According to Paul, at 11 P.M. on September 29, 1980, a baker named Francisco "heard someone knock on the door. He thought it was a harmless drunk. When he opened the door, he was seized by armed men dressed as soldiers and wearing masks." Francisco was not the mayor of his town, and people did not even know why he had been kidnapped. Everyone had different theories, but he was not involved in politics.[19] Stories like that of Francisco repeated themselves in most Guatemalan and Salvadoran villages and towns during the first half of the 1980s. Army death squads did not observe legal niceties when taking someone into custody. Those hauled away were tortured, and their anguished families remained convinced that their relatives would never reappear. Indeed, most never returned unless the army wanted to use their corpses as an object lesson for others by abandoning the mutilated, badly tortured bodies on the sides of roads.

But it was ordinary Mayas who suffered the worst during the 1980s largely due to the Guatemalan army's so-called "Victory [19]82" campaign. This scorched-earth operation made no distinction between guerrilla combatants and the Maya civilian population in the targeted areas, inducing widespread terror. Mayas suffered mass killings and atrocities. The army later acknowledged destroying over 455 villages and killing at least 150,000 people out of a total population of 10 million. The 1999 release of the U.N.-sponsored Report of the Commission for Historical Clarification raised those numbers to 626 razed villages and more than 200,000 documented dead or disappeared.[20] In addition, the report blamed the Guatemalan army for 93 percent of the human rights violations. The army also created as many as one million internal refugees, that is, people who fled from the army to the jungle, surviving from whatever they could collect there. On top of this, close to a quarter million Guatemalans, most of them Maya, migrated to Mexico.[21] In short, the "Victory 82" campaign became the bloodiest in Guatemala's history since the invasion of the country by the Spanish in 1524.

Other organizations bore responsibility for the killings and disappearances of Mayas in Guatemala, including the "civil self-defense patrols" known as PACs *(Patrullas de Autodefensa Civil)*. Initiated by Efraín Rios Montt's government in 1982 and designed to keep control over the countryside and isolate guerrilla columns, the patrols became an important part of the military's counterinsurgency strategy. Organized at the village level throughout Guatemala's rural areas, PACs consisted of male villagers forced to serve, without pay or remuneration, under the command of a local military officer. Members had to check on their neighbors, and to participate in kidnappings and/or murders. They also served as a human shield for the army's military columns in case of a guerrilla attack. Men who refused to join them were disappeared or murdered. According to the Guatemalan Minister of Defense, approximately 537,000 villagers served in PACs before their dissolution in 1996.[22]

Both individual assassinations and village massacres gradually became common in northern Nicaragua approximately four years after President Reagan signed the top secret November 1981 National Security Decision Directive 17 (NSDD-17), an order that gave the CIA the authority to recruit and support the *contras* (the counter-revolutionaries) by appropriating $19 million in military aid. By the mid-1980s the *contras* had begun to enter that territory from the Honduran border, and their incursions caused extensive damage to crops and farming cooperatives, and demolished farmhouses and machinery. *Contras* also destroyed roads and bridges to prevent peasants from moving produce. Furthermore, the *contras'* activities came with a high human cost because people caught in their assaults were often tortured and killed in gruesome ways. For example, one survivor of a raid in Jinotega province, which borders on Honduras, noted that

Rosa had her breasts cut off. Then they cut into her chest and took out her heart. The men had their arms broken, their testicles cut off, and their eyes poked out. They were killed by slitting their throats and pulling the tongue out through the slit.[23]

Indeed, the human rights group Americas Watch noted that the *contras* engaged in "violent abuses . . . so prevalent that these may be said to be their principal means of waging war."[24]

While violence on such a grand scale is probably hard to imagine, it might be harder to believe that one group of human beings did this to another. Some scholars have argued that in Guatemala "conservative interests blamed every undesirable event on the guerrillas and extended that association to anyone whom they found threatening. Indians, who were inherently threatening anyway, now became specific targets."[25] Many maintain that indigenous subjects were not the only ones who became specific targets. Enough stories have been compiled by Central America's Truth Commissions to certify that a whole array of social groups—university students, writers and artists, liberal professionals, members of liberal political parties such as the Christian Democrats or

Social Democrats—were equally targeted. Indeed, even innocent bystanders were at risk, as the following stories illustrate.

Civilians reacted to the persecution either with abject fear and paranoia, or they exaggerated their sense of not being at risk because they had done nothing wrong. The experience of the aforementioned writer Dante Liano, who visited his friend Franz Galich while he waited for a safe-conduct out of Guatemala at the Costa Rican embassy, illustrates this state of affairs. Because he had never had any political participation, Liano felt he had every right to visit his friend, bring him news of his family as well as presents, and cheer him up. Afterwards, however, he also began to be followed. Liano eventually left the country and settled in Italy, the land of his ancestors. Another individual convinced of his innocence, Carmelo López Santos, mayor of San Antonio Aguas Calientes, suffered a worse fate than Liano. He arrested the son of a mixed-blood (*ladino*) landowner for firing an automatic rifle against the local villagers. The landowner had arranged with the town's police chief to take advantage of the chaotic situation and illegally seize the lands of indigenous peoples, claiming them as his own. Because López Santos tried to prevent such an injustice he had been "repeatedly warned" that he was a marked man. His family and friends urged him to flee, but he refused. A few weeks after the arrest, when he was returning to San Antonio from a business meeting in the capital, armed men in civilian clothing pulled over the bus he was riding in. The men entered the vehicle, demanded each passenger's papers, and ordered López Santos off the bus after spotting him. His badly mutilated body appeared in the coffee bushes just outside town a few days later.[26]

Roberto Obregón, a well-known Guatemalan actor living in Paris, France, lived through a similar experience when he returned home for a visit in 1982. Totally apolitical, he attended a nephew's baptism on a Sunday afternoon, after which he walked with a cousin (while it was still daylight), to a bus stop. Seeing an army barrier as they turned a corner, Roberto's cousin panicked and ran away in the opposite direction. The soldiers shot at him but missed. Roberto, paralyzed by the suddenness of the events, froze on the sidewalk, and was immediately arrested. Soldiers took him to a clandestine prison with his hands tied behind his back, where a man wearing only shorts would simultaneously caress him, lick him, and then deliver horrific punches and kicks to his body and head. Roberto's cousin, who was able to escape from the area of the arrest, recovered his composure, and immediately called the French ambassador. He, in turn, contacted the French government, which firmly demanded Roberto Obregón's immediate release. Although the soldiers let him go within 24 hours, he had severe bruises, a broken eardrum that has left him half-deaf to this day, and severe head trauma that led to months of hospitalization and years of treatment that brought his theatrical career in Europe to a standstill. Obregón never returned to Guatemala.[27]

A story from my own family—itself divided by political preferences and wealth, like many other urban Central America folks— provides the final illustration of this process. The tale concerns the August 1981 birthday of an 8-year-old boy who invited his classmates, including my nephew, to an after-school party at his house on the south side of Guatemala City. Fearful of the political tension, most mothers decided to attend the gathering along with their children. In the midst of the party, while the children playfully smashed the *piñata*—a bright, papier-mâché candy-filled container in the shape of a popular figure suspended from a rope that children take turns breaking so as to collect the candy that falls to the floor—explosions and machine-gun fire rattled the neighborhood. Everyone lay down on the ground while gunfire and explosions continued for about a half-hour. When the blasts subsided, guests quickly gathered their children and attempted to drive home, only to discover that the army had surrounded the area. It turned out that the military had found a guerrilla safe house in that upper middle-class neighborhood. The guests and their mothers had to stay in the birthday boy's house until their fathers could pick them up in the very late evening when the general public was allowed to enter the area. My nephew, now a young adult, still suffers physiological and psychological problems as a result of this experience.

In the end, the army's brutal campaign against Guatemala's civilian population earned international condemnation and most nations withheld all economic aid. The military regime had little choice but to call for elections following the approval of a new constitution in 1985. International observers verified the fairness of the March 1986 ballot, which brought to power the country's first civilian president since 1950, Vinicio Cerezo Arévalo. Although the new chief executive stated that he controlled only 20 percent of power because the army had retained 80 percent for themselves, the election nevertheless signaled the return to nominal democracy. These circumstances, coupled with a truce arranged by Costa Rica's president Oscar Arias, began long and protracted negotiations between the government and the guerrillas that culminated in the 1996 peace accord.

During this same period, the human rights record in El Salvador continued to be plagued by a terror campaign. The UN Truth Commission on El Salvador, for instance, refers to the years 1980–1983 as "the institutionalization of violence." During that time "violence became systematic and terror and distrust reigned among the civilian population. The fragmentation of any opposition or dissident movement by means of arbitrary arrests, murders and selective and indiscriminate disappearances of leaders became common practice. Repression in the cities targeted political organizations, trade unions and organized sectors of Salvadorian society . . . murders of political leaders and attacks on human rights bodies."[28] Another human rights group, the Inter-American Commission on Human Rights (IACHR), received and processed charges of cruel, inhuman, or degrading treatment to which almost all persons of both sexes held by Salvadoran authorities had been subjected. The general consensus is that at least 100,000 people suffered such handling over the course of the decade.

The campaign of terror put pressure on both the government and the FMLN to find a quicker, negotiated solution to what appeared in 1989 as a never-ending conflict. Aware of these pressures—and of what they implied in terms of U.S. aid for the Salvadoran military—the FMLN decided to make a show of force to prove that they were neither defeated, nor losing the war, as both the Salvadoran army and the United States claimed. In November 1989 all-out urban war erupted in the capital city of San Salvador when the FMLN launched its so-called "final offensive" against the government. According to the UN Truth Commission on El Salvador, the offensive was "one of the most violent episodes of the war."[29] As guerrilla forces took cover in densely populated areas they became the targets of indiscriminate aerial bombardment. While hundreds of noncombatant civilians were also arrested, tortured, murdered and disappeared, the best-known civilian casualties involved Jesuit priests at El Salvador's Universidad Centroamericana José Simeón Cañas. Panicked by the spread of combat in urban areas and convinced that Jesuit priests were FMLN ideologues, 16 soldiers killed Father Ignacio Ellacuría, a professor and rector at the university, 5 other clerics, their housekeeper, and her daughter. While these high-profile assassinations confirmed the need of a negotiated solution as the only possible outcome for the civil war,[30] the high body count of lesser-known participants during the "final offensive"—446 soldiers dead and 1,228 wounded, and 1,902 guerrillas killed and 1,109 wounded—also influenced the push for negotiations that culminated with a peace treaty in 1992 and the FMLN becoming an opposition political party.[31]

Although Nicaragua's *contra* war did not result in as high a number of civilian deaths as the conflict in El Salvador, by 1988 the

The caskets of six slain Jesuits priests are carried to the graveyard on November 19, 1989, in San Salvador, El Salvador. The six clerics, comprising the leadership of the prestigious University of Central America in San Salvador, were found murdered and mutilated, together with their housekeeper and her daughter. (AP Photo).

struggle had worn down the Nicaraguan people. Citizens feared that the *contras* and the United States would never relent in their campaign to overthrow the Sandinistas. "We can't take any more war. All we have had is war, war, war, war," said Samuel Reina, a driver for the presidential election monitoring team of former U.S. President Jimmy Carter on February 25, 1990. Many families as well feared that their sons would be drafted into the Sandinista armed forces and die fighting in a never-ending struggle; in some cases one son fought for the Sandinistas and another had joined the *contras*, thus tearing families apart.[32] These sentiments greatly contributed to the Nicaraguans voting the Sandinistas out of power, bringing the *contra* war to an end.

LASTING EFFECTS OF CIVIL WAR

The violence inflicted on civilians during the Central American civil wars is not the kind of experience that individuals can leave behind. The trauma of war on everyday lives had permanent effects. Most survivors could not make peace with memories from the massacres or from having had relatives kidnapped in front of their eyes. Millions were humiliated, tortured, and forced to witness unspeakable brutality. Even people who left the country could not escape the mental anguish and trauma, a situation vividly illustrated by Antonio Bernal, the main character in Héctor Tobar's novel, *The Tattooed Soldier.* Formerly a middle-class government worker in Guatemala, in 1992 Bernal found himself in Los Angeles, California, electrified by the possibility of avenging his loved ones. Seven years before, Bernal had missed the death squad that came for him but instead killed his wife Elena and 2-year-old son. The murderer, Guillermo Longoria, an ex-Guatemalan soldier, was now in Los Angeles as well. Bernal's thoughts did not stray too far from the minds of many victims' family members.

Bernal also typifies the countless Central Americans who immigrated, in many cases illegally, to the United States in the 1980s so as to flee from the daily terror and the violence caused by their countries' civil wars. By 1990, according to the U.S. census, approximately 2,359,432 Central Americans lived in the United States (roughly 10 percent of the region's population of 20 million).[33] This mass exodus created a model that has made Central Americans different "from many other immigrant groups . . . in that they are neither strictly economic migrants nor accepted as refugees, but have the characteristics of both."[34] They were not accepted as official refugees, as Vietnamese and Cambodians were in the 1970s, because, in the Central American case, the U.S. government supported those dictatorships that Central Americans fled from. This detail tainted immigrants in three ways: Americans perceived them as both illegal and communist; they saw themselves as less than the Mexicans; and these perceptions, external and internal, made them hide their identity, as the case of Marlon Morales, a Salvadoran born in 1974 who migrated to the United States when he was a year old, illustrates. On his first day in fourth grade a boy asked him where he was from, to which Morales responded:

"Mmmm," I started. "Mmmm," I continued looking him in the eyes. I was going to say Mexico. I'm supposed to say Mexico, add "but born here" and leave it at that. My mom said I'm supposed to say this all the time, even at Union Avenue Elementary School. Anything Salvadoran like *pupusas, pacaya, flor de izote* and Spanish was left at home, never in public.[35]

The mixture of all these elements has intensified burdens already familiar to all immigrant groups, such as learning a new language and a new culture, separation from loved ones, as well as the resentment of a hostile population, which in this particular case includes Latinos from other national groups who arrived in the United States prior to them. Central Americans do not build on their victimization to create an identity in this country or to obtain any recognition or privileges. They try to transcend this victimization while pretending that it never happened. Accordingly, Americans of Central American heritage end up denying their own roots.

Diane Nelson wrote that Guatemalans speak of their nation as "a wounded body," and defines their notion of *body* as one "scarred and wounded by violence."[36] When used in the latter sense, this metaphor would be just as apt to address the situation in El Salvador or Nicaragua. What is more, nations are not the only "wounded bodies." All citizens from these countries—whether living in their countries of origin, in the United States, in Canada, or elsewhere—are also "wounded bodies." In the words of Victoria Sanford,

(*La Violencia*) represents more than . . . a historical marker. . . . It represents the continuum of lived experience. It represents not only the actual violent events . . . but also the experience of that violence and its effects. . . .The term "*La Violencia*" is also used as a demarcation between the violence of the past and a contemporary, ongoing contestation of that violence.[37]

In some cases, survivors are wounded physically, but in all cases they are wounded psychically. They have invisible scars that mark them for life that pass on what one author has called a sense of "being incomplete, vulnerable, and never completely fixed."[38]

While it will certainly prove difficult to remove those invisible scars from many individuals, a number of recent developments bode well for Central America's future. In March 1999, for example, U.S. President Bill Clinton visited the region and expressed deep regret for the U.S. support of military dictators during the Cold War. He noted that it had been a mistake to link the region's nationalist aspirations and yearning for modernity with terrorism. Then, after Hurricane Stan ravaged Central America in October 2005, Guatemala's president Oscar Berger (2004–2008) requested that the army not enter the Santiago Atitlán region on rescue missions because the past war experiences of the population still scarred their memories. His administration, instead, sent international rescue missions into spots that had been scenarios of past army massacres. His decision showed that the government had at last gained a bit more of both wisdom and humanity, and also served as a potential marker that augurs healing for the people of Central America. Thus, although Central America's story is tragic, as with all historical tragedies one can only hope that it is remembered. Whereas the recuperation of this memory remains a vital task for those concerned with the abject horror of human rights violations of this magnitude, it is of the utmost importance that this memory inspire humans all over the world not only to recoil in horror, but also to assess their present and future behavior from the perspective of the lessons of these infamous experiences so as to collectively help build a better world for all.

NOTES

1. *The Nation*, April 19, 1986, quoted in E. Bradford Burns, *At War in Nicaragua: The Reagan Doctrine and the Politics of Nostalgia* (New York: Harper & Row, 1987), 22.

2. Commission for Historical Clarification, *Guatemala, Memory of Silence*, 12 vols. (Guatemala City: Commission for Historical Clarification, 1999), 5:24.

3. Greg Grandin, *The Blood of Guatemala: A History of Race and Nation* (Durham, NC: Duke University Press, 2000), especially the subsection of chapter 8 titled "Strange Fruit." He documents arrests and assassinations on 215.

4. *Orejas* literally means "ears." This popular expression refers to government spies suspected of overhearing all conversations that took place in the country.

5. Richard Gott, *Guerrilla Movements in Latin America* (Garden City, NY: Doubleday Anchor, 1972), 98.

6. Arnoldo Fernández, personal communication, May 22, 2005.

7. Miguel Angel Sandoval, personal communication, August 12, 2003.

8. Dante Liano, "An Indolence of Feelings," in *Contemporary Short Stories From Central America*, eds. Enrique Jaramillo Levi and Leland H. Chambers (Austin: University of Texas Press, 1994), 25.

9. Gott, *Guerrilla Movements*, 91.

10. Americas Watch, *Guatemala: A Nation of Prisoners* (New York: Americas Watch Committee, 1984), 16.

11. Gott, *Guerrilla Movements*, 99–100, and 112.

12. "Sebastián Guzmán, principal de principales." This document is an anonymous mimeograph that circulated among militants of the Guatemalan Revolutionary Movement and its supporters in June 1982. I obtained a copy in Mexico City at that time.

13. Commission for Historical Clarification, *Guatemala, Memory of Silence*, 5:28.

14. "Archbishop Romero: The Last Sermon (March 1980)," in *The Central American Crisis Reader*, eds. Robert S. Leiken and Barry Rubin (New York: Summit Books, 1987), 380.

15. Walter La Feber, *Inevitable Revolutions: The United States in Central America*, 2nd edition, revised and expanded (New York: Norton, 1993), 250, 358; and Cynthia J. Arnson, *Crossroads: Congress, the Reagan Administration, and Central America* (New York: Pantheon Books, 1989), 40-41, 90-91.

16. Raymond Bonner, *Weakness and Deceit: U.S. Policy and El Salvador* (New York: Times Books, 1984), 138.

17. Bernice Kita, *What Prize Awaits Us: Letters from Guatemala* (New York: Orbis Books, 1988), 209.

18. Robert M. Carmack, "The Story of Santa Cruz Quiché," in *Harvest of Violence: The Maya Indians and the Guatemalan Crisis*, ed. Robert M. Carmack (Norman: University of Oklahoma Press, 1988), 39–69.

19. Benjamin D. Paul and William J. Demarest, "The Operation of a Death Squad," in Carmack, *Harvest of Violence*, 121–123.

20. Commission for Historical Clarification, *Guatemala, Memory of Silence*, 5:24.

21. See www.disappearances.org/news/mainfile.php/doc/68/, and Manuel Ángel Castillo, "Mexico: Caught Between the United States and

Central America" (April 2006), in www.migrationinformation.org/fea
ture/display.cfm?ID=389

22. Commission for Historical Clarification, *Guatemala, Memory of Silence*, 1:227.

23. The quote appears in William Blum, *Killing Hope: U.S. Military and CIA Interventions since World War II* (Monroe, ME: Common Courage Press, 1995), 127.

24. Reed Brody, *Contra Terror in Nicaragua: Report of a Fact-Finding Mission: September1984–January 1985* (Boston: South End Press, 1985), 23. In 1996 Gary Webb, a reporter for the *San Jose Mercury News*, wrote a three-part series entitled "Dark Alliance." The articles disclosed that the CIA had prepared an instruction manual for its clients which, among other things, encouraged the use of violence against civilians. U.S. congressional intelligence committees learned from the CIA, present and former *contra* leaders, and from other witnesses that the *contras* had indeed raped, tortured, and killed unarmed civilians, and that groups of women and children had been burnt, dismembered, blinded and beheaded. In the wake of the furor that the exposé caused in the U.S. Congress, the State Department had little choice but to publicly condemn the *contras'* terrorist activities.

25. Richard N. Adams, "Conclusions: What Can We Know About the Harvest of Violence?" in Carmack, *Harvest of Violence*, 286.

26. Sheldon Annis, "Story From a Peaceful Town: San Antonio Aguas Calientes," in Carmack, *Harvest of Violence*, 163–167.

27. Roberto Obregón, personal communication, March 23, 1982.

28. *From Madness to Hope: The 12-Year War in El Salvador/Report of the Commission on the Truth for El Salvador* (New York: United Nations, 1993), 27.

29. *From Madness to Hope*, 39.

30. Personal communication. Third Secretary of U.S. Embassy in El Salvador, 1986–1992.

31. *From Madness to Hope*, 40. Interestingly enough, the report does not mention civilian casualties nor the destruction and terror suffered by them. Their numbers, however, were likely higher than the army's and FMLN's losses. To this day, bullet holes, cracked walls, rubble, and other signs of destruction still scar the various neighborhoods where the November 1989 combats took place.

32. Blum, *Killing Hope*, 210.

33. Census figures might not accurately reflect the actual numbers, however, because undocumented persons probably were undercounted.

34. Nora Hamilton and Norma Stoltz Chinchilla, *Seeking Community in a Global City: Guatemalans and Salvadorans in Los Angeles* (Philadelphia: Temple University Press, 2001), 2.

35. Marlon Morales, "The Voice of Marlon Morales," in *Izote Vos: A Collection of Salvadoran American Writing and Visual Art*, eds. Katherine Cowy Kim and Alfonso Serrano F. (San Francisco: Pacific News Service, 2000), 66.

36. Diane M. Nelson, *A Finger in the Wound: Body Politics in Quincentennial Guatemala* (Berkeley: University of California Press, 1999), 1–2.

37. Victoria Sanford, *Buried Secrets: Truth and Human Rights in Guatemala* (New York: Palgrave Macmillan, 2003), 15.

38. Nelson, *A Finger in the Wound,* 371.

Glossary

1917 Immigration Act. This piece of legislation imposed a literacy test as well as a head tax of $8.00 on Mexicans who legally migrated to the United States. Under pressure from employers in the U.S. Southwest, who needed agricultural workers in the midst of World War I, the Woodrow Wilson administration loosened the law for Mexican immigrants, with the stipulation that they could only toil in agriculture.

"ABC" Organization. Founded in 1931, this revolutionary organization became the first in Cuba to develop a large mass following. With its supporters coming largely from the middle-class youth, the "ABC" tried to organize a mass insurrectionary movement that cut across class lines. It played a significant role in the struggle against Gerardo Machado.

Allende, Salvador. 1908–1973. A medical doctor, Allende made unsuccessful bids for the Chilean presidency in 1952, 1958, and 1964. Six years later his Popular Unity coalition won the elections and Allende became the world's first democratically elected Marxist. His efforts to improve the standard of living of most Chileans, however, earned him the animosity of both elites and the U.S. government, and on September 11, 1973, the military staged a coup to depose him. A 2004 documentary by the well-known Chilean director Patricio Guzmán suggests that Allende shot himself, fighting to the end, at the presidential palace of *La Moneda.*

Arango y Escandón, Alejandro. 1821–1883. Prominent Conservative party member who also achieved fame in Mexican literary circles. After the War of the Reform he was a member of the Junta of Conservative Notables who in 1863 offered Maximilian, the Hapsburg Archduke of Austria, the crown of Mexico.

Arbenz, Jacobo. 1913–1971. The military hero of Guatemala's Revolution of 1944, which deposed dictator Jorge Ubico, Arbenz was elected president of Guatemala in 1951. His administration instituted agrarian reforms, mobilized the peasantry, and welcomed members of the Communist Party into the government. His expropriation of the holdings of the United Fruit Company prompted the United States to overthrow him in 1954. Arbenz then went into exile, and died in his bathroom (some do not consider his demise an accident) in Mexico in 1971.

Arellano Stark, Sergio. (birth year unknown)–present. Acting under orders from General Augusto Pinochet in Chile, Brigadier General Arellano Stark led a military commission that visited several cities in northern and southern Chile between September 30 and October 22, 1973. Known as the "Caravan of Death," Arellano Stark's mission resulted in the deaths of nearly 100 civilians and succeeded in implanting terror among residents of Chile.

Bachelet, Michelle. 1951–present. A medical doctor and a life-long Socialist, Bachelet suffered greatly during the Pinochet dictatorship in Chile. Her father, General Alberto Bachelet, was among the regime's victims, and she was interrogated and tortured at Villa Grimaldi, one of Chile's most infamous detention centers. Bachelet then spent nearly four years in exile before returning to Chile. At that time she became involved in politics, and in 2006 became her country's first female chief executive.

Batista, Fulgencio. 1901–1973. A sergeant in the Cuban army, Batista entered the national political stage when he and others staged the so-called Sergeants' Revolt in September 1933. He became Cuba's dominant political figure for the next quarter century, twice serving as president (1940–1944, and 1952–1959). During his first term he made the transition from a military strongman to populist leader who acknowledged the power of the masses, but he staged a coup to come to office in 1952, and thereon operated as a dictator.

Bolívar, Simón. 1783–1830. A romantic and controversial patriotic political and military leader, Bolívar remains the symbol and hero of the wars of independence in northern South America, where he liberated six countries from Spanish rule. He also sought, but failed, to establish a permanent coalition of Spanish American nations to face the rest of the world.

Bourbon Reforms. When the Bourbon family assumed the Spanish throne in the early 1700s it moved to tighten control of its colonies in Spanish America and extract greater profits through measures that included higher taxes. The reforms provoked much unrest and are widely considered a precursor to independence.

Cáceres, Andrés Avelino. 1833–1923. Perhaps inspired by Mexican resistance to the French intervention in Mexico (1862–1867), this Peruvian general led guerrilla resistance in central Peru against Chile during the War of the Pacific. He capitalized on his wartime heroics to become Peru's president in 1886, and dominated public affairs in that country for the next decade.

Cádiz constitution. Also known as the constitution of 1812, this charter—Spain's first—restructured the relationship between Spain and its American colonies by providing for, among other things, greater popular participation in public affairs. Creole elites hoped it would provide them with an unprecedented level of political power and autonomy.

Carranza, Venustiano. 1859–1920. A wealthy landowner from Coahuila, Mexico, in 1913 Carranza assumed command of the "Constitutionalist" movement in the 1910 Mexican Revolution. A staunch nationalist, Carranza triumphed in the civil war that followed the fall of Victoriano Huerta partly because he expanded his movement's political base to include urban workers and peasants. Carranza also convoked (albeit reluctantly) the constitutional congress that gave Mexico the 1917 Constitution. He was elected president that same year, but his efforts to appoint his successor three years later provoked a rebellion that cost him his life.

Casa del Obrero Mundial. Founded in Mexico City in 1912, this anarchist-inspired working-class organization gave workers a place to meet and exchange views. Patrons intended for it to be a center for the study of modern labor and economic ideas, and also to build labor unions and organize strikes in order for workers to improve their lives. The Casa struck an alliance with the "Constitutionalist" movement in 1915; the deal included mobilization of the so-called Red Battalions that fought against Pancho Villa and Emiliano Zapata.

Casariego, Mario. 1909–1983. Born in Castropol, Spain, Casariego was appointed Archbishop of Guatemala in 1964, and he served in that position until his death. He also became the first clergyman in Central America elevated to the rank of Cardinal. A zealous supporter of the country's military rulers, his conservative ideas notwithstanding failed to prevent his kidnapping in 1968 by a right-wing death squad.

Castillo Armas, Carlos. 1914–1957. A graduate of Guatemala's national military academy, Castillo Armas was selected by the Central Intelligence Agency to lead the 1954 covert operation that overthrew the Jacobo Arbenz regime. After becoming president of Guatemala that September he rolled back the reforms implemented by Arbenz. A palace guard murdered him in 1957.

Caxias, Marquis de. 1808–1880. Luís Alves de Lima e Silva (his real name) emerged as the outstanding military figure in Brazil in the latter part of the nineteenth century because of his efforts in the War of the Triple Alliance. Caxias' popularity created much tension with Pedro II, and the friction led to a political crisis in 1868 that weakened the Brazilian monarchy.

Cerezo Arévalo, Vinicio. Born 1942. He took office as president of Guatemala in 1986 after winning a landslide election, and became Guatemala's first civilian chief executive in two decades. Although he promised to curtail the influence of right-wing elements in public affairs, Cerezo Arévalo could do little in this regard. His administration, nonetheless, began discussions with the guerrillas that culminated in the 1996 peace accords.

Céspedes, Carlos Manuel de. 1871–1939. A personal friend of U.S. ambassador Sumner Welles, Céspedes emerged as the compromise choice to replace President Gerardo Machado as provisional president of Cuba in August 1933. But the perception that the United States had imposed Céspedes on the Cuban people prevented his regime from gaining any kind of popular support. He was overthrown in the so-called Sergeants' Revolt of September 5, 1933, which brought to power Ramón Grau San Martín.

Creole. Individuals of Spanish descent born in Spanish America.

D'Aubuisson, Roberto. 1944–1992. After training during the mid-1970s at the International Police Academy in Washington, D.C., D'Aubuisson ascended to the rank of major in the Salvadoran army and intelligence chief of the Salvadoran National Guard. He also created the White Warriors, a death squad in El Salvador, and is widely believed to have masterminded the murder of Archbishop Romero. He also became involved in politics, and founded the right-wing party ARENA (*Alianza Republicana Nacionalista*) in 1980. D'Aubuisson died from cancer in 1992.

Daza, Hilarión. 1840–1894. A barely literate individual, Daza moved up the ranks of the Bolivian army and used his power within that institution to seize control of the presidency of Bolivia in 1876. Two years later, in a clear breach of an 1874 agreement, he increased taxes on nitrate exports by a Chilean-British company that operated in the Bolivian port of Antofagasta, a decision that helped bring on the War of the Pacific. Daza misjudged the military strength of Bolivia and its ally Peru, and committed a number of blunders in the field that led his own troops to unseat him. He went into exile in France in 1879, and was assassinated when he returned to Bolivia 15 years later.

Díaz, Porfirio. 1830–1915. As president of Mexico (1876–1880, 1884–1911), Díaz provided the nation with unprecedented political stability and significant economic growth. His continued reelection, as well as the problems engendered by the economic changes he introduced, bred numerous contradictions that brought on the 1910 Revolution. After being ousted from power in 1911, Díaz went into exile in France, where he died four years later. His remains are in the Parisian cemetery of Montparnasse.

Dundonald, Thomas Lord Cochrane. 1775–1860. In 1818 this socially ambitious former English naval officer assumed command of the Chilean
naval squadron that subsequently transported José de San Martín's
Army of the Andes to liberate Peru from Spain. Cochrane's fleet prevented Spanish reinforcements from reaching Lima and successfully
blockaded the Peruvian coast, thus facilitating San Martín's task. A subsequent dispute between the two men, however, led Cochrane to seize
the entire bullion reserve of the San Martín government in September
1821, and jeopardized San Martín's ability to rule.

Ferdinand VII. 1784–1833. Son of Charles IV, he and his father were forced
by Napoleon Bonaparte to abdicate the Spanish crown in 1808. He became the object of popular affection, which earned him the moniker of
El Deseado (the Desired One). Upon returning to the throne in 1814, and
until 1820, he ruled in an absolutist manner and demanded that Spanish America return to the royal fold.

García, Romeo Lucas. 1924–2006. After being elected to the presidency of
Guatemala in 1979, General García violated human rights at an alarm-
ingly high rate. Perhaps the most noteworthy such violation was the
police raid on the Spanish embassy—which had been occupied by
demonstrators—in the Guatemalan capital, Guatemala City, late in
January 1980. This illegal raid left 39 people dead. García was deposed
by the army in 1982, and went into exile in Venezuela in 1994. Eleven
years later the Venezuelan Supreme Court did not allow his extradition
to Spain to answer charges for his role in the 1980 raid, claiming insufficient evidence.

García Calderón, Francisco. 1834–1905. With Chilean support, this at-
torney and politician from Arequipa was elected provisional president
of Peru late in February 1881, and permanent president three months
later. García Calderón then began discussions with Chile to end the War
of the Pacific, but support from the U.S. government encouraged him to
oppose making territorial concessions. Chilean general Patricio Lynch
arrested García Calderón and his family that November, and banished
them to Chile.

Goulart, João. 1918–1976. A protégé of former Brazilian President Getu-
lio Vargas, who was widely popular among the poor, Goulart became
president of Brazil in 1961 and moved to empower labor unions and the
rural poor. His efforts provoked widespread resistance among elites,
and led to the 1964 military coup. As the takeover unfolded, high-ranking U.S. officials in Brazil kept in touch with then U.S. President Lyndon
Baines Johnson, who had authorized support for the military plotters.

Grau San Martín, Ramón. 1887–1969. A popular university professor,
Grau San Martín became provisional president of Cuba in September
1933 (following the Sergeants' Revolt). His regime enacted a number
of measures that responded to the wishes of the masses as well as to

the growing sense of nationalism in the island, but these proved controversial and eroded the support that the regime had from right-wing civilian and military elements, as well as from the United States. This loose coalition succeeded in deposing Grau San Martín early in January 1934.

Guatemala Peace Accords. These 1996 agreements officially put an end to the country's 34-year civil war. Its provisions included demobilization of the guerrillas, a reduction in the size of the army, promotion of indigenous rights, and increased social spending. Opposition to the accords, in the form of the military as well as some elites and international actors, have prevented their full implementation.

Guiteras, Antonio. 1906–1935. Cuban Minister of the Interior under the Grau San Martín government. Widely sympathetic to the demands of urban workers, Guiteras moved to institute a number of social reforms that met their needs. After the 1933 Revolution and until his death at the hands of the army, Guiteras headed an underground radical group, *Joven Cuba,* to resist Fulgencio Batista's regime.

Hidalgo y Costilla, Miguel. 1753–1811. Regarded by many as the father of Mexican independence, in 1810 this Creole parish priest from the town of Dolores put himself at the head of a mass-based military rebellion that quickly spread throughout central Mexico. Captured and imprisoned by Spanish troops in March 1811, he was subsequently tried and executed that July.

Huerta, Victoriano. 1854–1916. Rose to the rank of general in the Mexican army by the early 1900s. In 1913 Huerta headed the conspiracy that ousted President Francisco Madero, and to this day many hold him responsible for his murder. Huerta subsequently took the reins of power and tried to consolidate a militarized regime. This attempt earned him the enmity of the U.S. government and incited further popular rebellion, and the combination of both forces ended his presidency in mid-1914.

Iglesias, Miguel. 1830–1901. Peruvian general who in 1882, with Chilean support, emerged in northern Peru claiming to be the true head of state. Eager to end the conflict like other prominent Peruvians, he engaged in diplomatic talks with Chile. Chilean forces defeated his rival, Andrés Avelino Cáceres, at the July 10, 1883 Battle of Huamachucho, and Iglesias was finally able to sign a peace treaty three months later.

Iquique, Battle of. On May 21, 1879, Chilean Captain Arturo Prat faced Peru's most powerful vessels off the coast of Iquique while commanding the *Esmeralda,* the most wretched wooden ship in his country's navy. Although Prat died in a hopeless attempt to board the enemy vessel, after which the *Esmeralda* sank, his bravery elevated him to the pantheon of Chile's military heroes.

Iturbide, Agustín de. 1783–1824. A Creole officer in the Spanish army in Mexico, he conspired to separate Mexico from Spain and authored the Plan of Iguala in 1821. One year later he became Mexico's first constitutional emperor (Agustín I), but he was overthrown and exiled in 1823, and executed upon his return to Mexico the following year.

Jarauta, Celedonio. 1814–1848. This Spanish-born priest arrived in the city of Veracruz, Mexico, in 1844, where his sermons and demeanor in the confessional made him a popular figure. Jarauta became a resourceful guerrilla fighter in Veracruz state in 1847, and that September he led poor residents of Mexico City in the street fighting that followed the U.S. occupation of the Mexican capital. In June 1848 he joined an uprising led by General Mariano Paredes y Arrillaga to protest the peace treaty with the United States, but he was captured by government forces. Jarauta then received a summary court-martial and was executed.

Kendall, George Wilkins. 1809–1867. Kendall, who cofounded in 1837 the New Orleans *Picayune*, became perhaps the most prominent of all U.S.-Mexican War correspondents. Shortly after the commencement of hostilities, Kendall joined General Zachary Taylor's Army of Occupation, and in 1847 he traveled with General Winfield Scott's army from Veracruz to Mexico City. His reports provided readers in the United States coverage of military activities, as well as his own criticisms of some of his government's policies.

Liano, Dante. 1948–present. A native of Guatemala and a graduate of that country's University of San Carlos, Liano is one of present-day Guatemala's most prominent writers. His novels explore various aspects of his country's recent history. In *El hombre de Montserrat* (1995), Liano tells the tale of an army lieutenant charged with developing programs to fight the guerrillas, while his *El misterio de San Andrés* (1997) covers the October 1944 Patzicia massacre. Fearing for his life, Liano decided to move to Italy in 1980, where he continues to reside to this day.

Lynch, Patricio. 1825–1886. Born in the Chilean port city of Valparaíso, and known as the "Red Prince," in 1880 this Chilean naval officer led a punitive expedition against Peru's northern coast and also commanded an army division in the final assault on Lima. In May of the following year he became commander-in-chief of his country's expeditionary forces and held administrative responsibilities over Peru. He then checked Peruvian President Francisco García Calderón's efforts to pursue policy independent of Chile's wishes, and deported him to Chile late in 1881.

Martí, Agustín Farabundo. 1893–1932. The heart and soul of the radical left in El Salvador, this college-educated Salvadorian steadfastly held to Marxist-Leninist principles, and in 1930 helped mobilize peasants and university students. Two years later he organized a massive insurrection that the government crushed ruthlessly. Although he was publicly executed on February 1, 1932, nearly 50 years later other Salvadoran rebels would take his name to legitimize their struggle against the government.

Machado, Gerardo. 1871–1939. Machado served as president of Cuba between 1925 and 1933. Although his regime was well-liked at first, the impact of the 1929 Depression, coupled with his reliance on unconstitutional means to remain in power for another six years, made his government extremely unpopular. He was removed from power in 1933.

Madero, Francisco. 1873–1913. In 1910 this landowner from the northeastern state of Coahuila challenged Porfirio Díaz for the Mexican presidency, but his bid grew so powerful that Díaz had him arrested. Madero escaped to San Antonio, Texas, from where he organized the movement that resulted in the 1910 Revolution and ousted Díaz. Elected to the presidency in 1911, he could not meet the demands for social and economic change advocated by the lower classes, nor could he restore stability. General Victoriano Huerta, with the connivance of the U.S. ambassador, had Madero arrested and murdered in 1913.

Miramón, Miguel. 1832–1867. As a young cadet in 1847 Miramón helped defend Chapultepec Castle against U.S. forces in the U.S.-Mexican War. He later became a leading conservative general (and president) in the War of the Reform, and championed as well the cause of Emperor Maximilian, with whom he was executed in June 1867. Official Mexican historical discourse has hence turned him into a villain.

Montes, César. 1942–present. This university-educated man, who trained as an elementary school teacher, played a leading role in two of Guatemala's most important guerrilla groups. He cofounded the November 13th Movement of the Rebel Armed Forces (*Fuerzas Armadas Rebeldes, FAR*) in 1962, and later became the leader of the Guerrilla Army of the Poor (EGP, or *Ejército Guerrillero de los Pobres*). He returned to Guatemala in 1996 to take part in the discussions that led to the peace accords.

Morillo, Pablo. 1775–1837. Spanish general who arrived in Venezuela in 1815 at the head of an expeditionary force of 10,500 intended to reconquer the viceroyalty of New Granada. Within two years, however, tropical disease and increased patriot resistance weakened Morillo's troops; the restoration of the Cádiz constitution in 1820 deprived Morillo of reinforcements and forced him to sign an armistice with the patriots.

Morelos, José María. 1765–1815. *Mestizo* (mixed-blood) parish priest from what is now the state of Michoacán who took up the struggle for Mexican independence following Miguel Hidalgo's death. Unlike Hidalgo, he articulated a clear set of goals for the movement to attract Creole support. Spanish troops captured and executed him in 1815.

Obregón, Alvaro. 1880–1928. Born in the northwestern state of Sonora, Mexico, Obregón joined the "Constitutionalist" movement and became its greatest general. His military acumen allowed him to defeat Pancho Villa in the 1915 battles that sealed the victory of the Constitutionalists and allowed them to mold the Revolution's outcome. In 1920 he led a movement against his erstwhile ally, Venustiano Carranza. His presidential term (1920–1924) helped reestablish unified, stable government in the country.

Otero, Mariano. 1817–1850. One of the leading *moderado* politicians in Mexico, Otero wrote for one of Mexico City's most prominent newspapers, *El Siglo XIX,* and became an influential member of Congress during the war with the United States. Many scholars believe he authored the pamphlet *Consideraciones sobre la situación política y social de la república mexicana en el año de 1847,* which attempted to address the causes of the military debacle of 1846–1848. Otero died in a cholera epidemic in 1850.

Páez, José Antonio. 1790–1873. Venezuelan *llanero* (cowboy, or plainsman) chieftain who allied himself with Simón Bolívar in 1816, and provided him with military support in the struggle to liberate that territory from Spain. Páez brokered the separation of Venezuela from Gran Colombia in the mid-1820s, during which time he severed ties with Bolívar. Páez held a prominent role in Venezuela's public affairs for the next three decades.

Panzós Massacre. On May 29, 1978, between 500 to 700 Q'equchi'-Mayan women, men, and children gathered in the town of Panzós, Guatemala, to present a letter to city authorities that detailed their complaints against local landowners. Guatemalan government soldiers opened up fire on them. The exact number of victims remains in dispute, but survivors insist that the dead numbered in the hundreds. The massacre began a pattern of increased repression against rural Mayans that culminated during the Efraín Ríos Montt regime.

Paredes y Arrillaga, Mariano. 1797–1846. A brigadier general in the Mexican army by 1832, Paredes y Arrillaga participated in many of Mexico's domestic political conflicts. Late in 1845 Paredes y Arrillaga deposed the government because, so he argued, it was attempting to peacefully settle its differences with the United States. Paredes then served as president from January 4 to July 28, 1846, during which he pursued a belligerent policy against the United States. Paredes's military failures doomed the efforts of Mexican Conservatives and the Spanish ambassador in Mexico to install a European monarch as the country's ruler.

Pedro II. 1826–1891. Second (and last) constitutional emperor of Brazil. He ascended to the throne in 1840 and remained in power until 1889, at which time a civilian-military coup forced him to abdicate. His relatively peaceful reign held Brazil together for nearly 50 years and helped consolidate it as a nation-state.

Perón, Isabel. 1931–present. A nightclub dancer in her youth, she met Argentine president Juan Domingo Perón during his exile and became both his personal secretary and second wife. Isabel Perón served as his vice-president between October 1973 and July 1974, and became chief executive of Argentina upon her late husband's death. She granted the military liberty of action against those regarded as subversives, a policy that set the groundwork for the atrocities of the "Dirty War." Early in 2007 an Argentine judge ordered her arrest over these actions.

Perón, Juan Domingo. 1895–1974. One of Argentina's most controversial politicians, the populist leader served twice as president (1946–1955, and 1973–1974). During his first term Perón largely pursued policies friendly to urban labor. Ousted by the military in a 1955 coup, Perón spent 18 years in exile. In 1973 leaders of the armed forces allowed him to return in the hope that he could restore calm in the country. Although Perón won the presidential elections later that year, he proved unable to mediate the growing tensions between right-and left-wing factions of his movement. He died of a heart attack on July 1, 1974.

Pezuela, Joaquín de la. 1761–1830. He assumed his duties as viceroy of Peru in the summer of 1816, but lost much political capital when he failed to anticipate José de San Martín's campaign to cross the Andes and liberate Chile. His position weakened further in 1820 when the Riego revolt forced Ferdinand VII to restore the Cádiz constitution, and in late January 1821 royalist army officers forced him to abdicate his office

Piérola, Nicolás. 1839–1912. A prominent Peruvian politician, in 1879 he returned from exile and late that December capitalized on the incumbent president's absence (Mario Ignacio Prado had left for Europe, supposedly to purchase armaments), and proclaimed himself supreme commander-in-chief. His efforts to repel Chilean forces during the War of the Pacific proved unsuccessful, and in November 1881, after the fall of Lima, he was forced to resign. Piérola again served as president from 1895 to 1899. At that time he ousted Cáceres and began to professionalize the Peruvian military.

Pinochet, Augusto. 1915–2006. A controversial political leader in Chile, General Pinochet joined the 1973 military conspiracy against democratically elected Marxist Chilean President Salvador Allende, and following the September 11 coup he ruled the nation until 1990. Supporters claim his regime brought about unparalleled economic growth to Chile, while opponents denounce his human rights record. Although his December 2006 funeral demonstrated Chileans remain deeply divided over what Pinochet meant to his country's history, a more recent development (the discovery of a private library worth millions of dollars) suggests that Pinochet was also exceedingly corrupt.

Platt Amendment. The brainchild of U.S. Senator Orville H. Platt, this amendment to the 1901 Cuban constitution gave the United States authority to intervene militarily in the island's affairs whenever order was threatened. For all intents and purposes, the amendment truncated

Cuba's political sovereignty and turned the island into a protectorate. Although the amendment was repealed in 1934, U.S. power continued to limit Cuba's freedom of action.

Political parties (Brazil). The two major political groups in nineteenth-century Brazil were the Conservative and Liberal parties. Although centered in different parts of the country, both were organized in the 1830s and had the same general constituency (they represented broad factions within the landowning elite). Few ideological differences existed between them.

Polkos Revolt. Led by *moderado* Mexican politicians, senior army chiefs, and high-ranking clerical leaders, this rebellion, which erupted on February 27, 1847, sought to oust *puro* leader and acting chief executive Valentín Gómez Farías, who had issued a decree that authorized the government to raise 15 million pesos by mortgaging or selling ecclesiastical property in order to finance Mexico's war against the United States. The principal weapon at the conspirators' disposal was the aristocratic national guard, whose battalions had been organized during the fall of 1846. Members of these battalions came to be known as the *"polkos"* after the polka, the most popular dance of elite society. Their revolt weakened the total war effort, as it prevented the Mexican government from assisting Veracruz (which surrendered on March 29), and strengthening the city of Puebla and the fortifications near the coast.

Prado, Mario Ignacio. 1826–1901. Twice president of Peru (1865–1868, and 1876–1879), this general retired from politics in 1868. Eight years later civilians urged him to return to public affairs, and he did so as a candidate for Peru's *Civilista* party. Prado presided over a deeply divided nation, and lost confidence in his ruling abilities as Peru began to fare poorly in the war against Chile. He then departed for European exile.

Próspero Pérez, Francisco. (birthdate unknown)–1848. A *puro* partisan, by the mid-1840s Próspero Pérez had become a key political broker for Mexico City's urban poor. He emerged as one of the leaders of the capital's masses as they rebelled against General Winfield Scott in mid-September 1847. Próspero Pérez died sometime in January 1848, a victim of a street battle between residents of some poor neighborhoods in Mexico City and U.S. soldiers.

Reciprocity Treaty. This 1903 accord between Cuba and the United States conceded a 20 percent concession to Cuban agricultural products that entered the United States in exchange for a 20 to 40 percent reduction on U.S. imports. While the treaty breathed new life into the sugar industry, it also restrained the development of domestic industries in the newly independent nation.

Ríos Montt, General Efraín. 1926–present. A born-again evangelical Protestant who held the presidency of Guatemala between 1982 and 1983, Ríos Montt implemented a civic action program known as *"fusiles y* *frijoles"* (guns and beans) whereby the army herded thousands of rural Guatemalans into model villages across the country to watch over suspected guerrillas and their supporters. His tenure as chief executive, however, was also the bloodiest in the country's history, with an estimated 70,000 civilians having been killed or disappeared. Although he faced criminal charges in 2000, these were later dismissed. Ríos Montt made an unsuccessful bid for the presidency in 2003.

Romero, Oscar Arnulfo. 1917–1980. A soft-spoken priest who became El Salvador's archbishop in 1977, Romero slowly changed from an apolitical member of the clergy to a staunch advocate of liberation theology and of the poor's struggle for social justice. Romero criticized the death squads and the increasing number of human rights violations on the part of the Salvadoran government, and thus became a major threat to the government of El Salvador. A right-wing group (probably under orders from Roberto D'Aubuisson) had him murdered on March 24, 1980, as he said mass in the chapel of a church-run hospital.

San Martín, José de. 1778–1850. Born in Argentina, San Martín spent much of his youth in Spain, where he started his military career. He returned to his homeland in 1812, received command of the Army of the Andes, and gained independence for Chile and Peru. Following the so-called 1822 Guayaquil conference with Simón Bolívar, San Martín resigned his command and went into a self-imposed exile in Europe until his death.

Sandino, Augusto César. 1895–1934. The illegitimate son of a mid-size coffee plantation owner and a poor peasant woman, from 1927 to 1933 Sandino waged a guerrilla war in his homeland to force the U.S. government to withdraw its troops from Nicaragua. Although Sandino achieved this goal, the founder of the dynasty who would rule Nicaragua for most of the twentieth century—Anastasio Somoza—had Sandino murdered. Sandino then became a symbol of resistance to those who opposed Somoza's rule, and in 1960 young university students created an organization that bore Sandino's name, and which seized power in 1979.

Santa Anna, Antonio López de. 1794–1876. Santa Anna was Mexico's preeminent military and political leader during the first half of the nineteenth century. Although official Mexican history has long demonized him as responsible for many of the troubles that befell the early republic, including deliberately losing the war against the United States, Santa Anna was more of a poor general than a traitor. He also did not desire dictatorial powers throughout his political career; in fact, he only became a dictator during his last presidential term (1853–1855). Following his ouster from office in 1855, Santa Anna went into exile. He returned in 1874 and died two years later.

Solano López, Francisco. 1826–1870. Assumed the presidency of Paraguay in 1862 after the death of his father. Emboldened by his country's military strength to take a more active role in the affairs of the River Plate region, his actions helped precipitate the War of the Triple Alliance. Rebuffed by Brazil, Argentina, and Uruguay in his efforts to negotiate an armistice after the conflict began, Solano López kept up a dramatic (some may say hopeless) resistance until Brazilian troops surrounded and killed him in 1870.

Somoza, Anastasio. 1898–1956. Born to a lower-lower middle-class Liberal family in Nicaragua, and educated in the United States, Somoza was named by Nicaraguan authorities in 1932 to head the National Guard, the force that would be responsible for maintaining peace in his country after U.S. troops had departed. He ordered Sandino's murder and ruled Nicaragua (either as president or from behind the scenes) between 1936 and his assassination in 1956. His two sons, Luis and Anastasio, Jr., held power until the 1979 Nicaraguan Revolution.

Suárez Iriarte, Francisco. (birthdate unknown)–1851. Born in Toluca, Mexico, this former cabinet member and legislator came to head the *puro*-controlled Mexico City town council in late 1847. After the war his political enemies accused him of trying to annex Mexico to the United States, and he was brought to trial in 1850. Although he defended himself ably, Suárez Iriarte had to spend a few months in jail, during which he became ill. The government then released him, but he died shortly thereafter.

Republican Party. This offshoot of Brazil's Liberal Party came to life in 1870. Its leaders hoped to abolish the monarchy and set up a more open political system in the form of a federal republic.

Robles Pezuela, Manuel. 1817–1862. Conservative Mexican army general who, after overthrowing Félix Zuloaga, briefly held the presidency (December 23, 1858-January 21, 1859) during the War of the Reform. He was killed by Liberal forces in March 1862 as he attempted to join the troops from France, Great Britain, and Spain that had landed in Mexico to begin the so-called French Intervention.

Taunay, Alfredo d'Escragnolle. 1843–1899. A veteran of the War of the Triple Alliance, this prominent Brazilian author penned in 1871 that country's best-known firsthand account of that conflict, *A retirada da Laguna*. He also joined the Conservative party, but abandoned politics following the fall of the Brazilian empire in 1889.

Urban guerrillas. Following the 1967 death of Ernesto "Che" Guevara, who had advocated guerrilla warfare (based in the countryside) as a means to export revolution throughout the hemisphere, the focus of the revolutionary struggle shifted to the cities. Several urban guerrilla groups emerged in Latin America, including Uruguay's *Tupamaros*, Argentina's *Montoneros* and *Ejército Revolucionario del Pueblo* (Revolutionary Army of the People), and Brazil's Action for National Liberation. Their efforts to bring about a popular insurrection through armed actions that would discredit the national governments, however, failed.

Urrea, General José. 1797–1849. Urrea rose through the ranks of the Mexican army and earned a promotion to brigadier general in 1835. During the war with the United States, Urrea commanded guerrillas in the northern state of Tamaulipas, and his forces inflicted significant damages and casualties on U.S. troops and convoys. He happened to be in Durango when a cholera epidemic swept through the city in 1849, and the disease claimed him as one of its victims.

Videla, General Jorge Rafael. 1925–present. Videla led the March 1976 coup that deposed Isabel Perón and set up Argentina's military dictatorship. He formally took power as chief executive within a few days of the coup, and then proceeded to launch an unprecedented campaign against so-called subversives known as the "Dirty War." Videla handed over power to another general in 1981, and from that time he has been subjected to various efforts to bring him to justice for human rights violations.

Villa, Francisco. 1877–1923. A native of the northern Mexican state of Chihuahua, Villa led an assorted group of rebels into the 1910 Mexican Revolution and eventually came to lead the largest revolutionary army ever produced in Latin America, the 10,000-man *División del Norte*. An idealistic man, Villa pursued agrarian reform and urban social welfare programs in those areas he controlled until his military fortunes collapsed in 1915. He then fought a guerrilla war in Chihuahua against Venustiano Carranza, and eventually cut a deal with federal authorities to end that struggle. Nonetheless, his former rival Alvaro Obregón still viewed him as a potential threat, and some scholars assert that Obregón instigated Villa's 1923 assassination.

Virgin of Guadalupe. Mexico's patron saint, this dark-skinned virgin supposedly appeared to an Indian named Juan Diego in the outskirts of modern-day Mexico City in 1531. Creole intellectuals made use of her story in the late 1700s to promote a sense of national identity among residents of Mexico. The rebellion led Miguel Hidalgo y Costilla to utilize her image to rally the indigenous masses against Spain.

Welles, Sumner. 1892–1961. Welles, who held the post of Assistant U.S. Secretary of State, was appointed ambassador to Cuba in May 1933 with orders to mediate the growing struggle between President Gerardo Machado and the opposition. He played a key role in forcing out Machado later that year, and in 1934 abetted Fulgencio Batista's bid to seize power.

Wilson, Woodrow. 1856–1924. Elected president of the United States in 1912, the highly moralistic Wilson twice sent troops to Mexico in an effort to shape the outcome of the 1910 Revolution. He first ordered the U.S. Marines into Veracruz in 1914 in order to pressure General Victoriano Huerta to resign, and two years later, in 1916, he authorized General John Pershing's so-called "Punitive Expedition" to march into northern Mexico as retaliation for Pancho Villa's raid on Columbus, New Mexico.

Zapata, Emiliano. 1879–1919. An official (as well as a popular) national hero, this peasant leader from the southern state of Morelos joined the 1910 Revolution in the hopes of recovering the communal property (*ejidos*) that villages had lost in the preceding decades. Zapata broke ties with Madero in November 1911 and issued his own plan for agrarian reform. In 1919 Venustiano Carranza devised a plan to entrap and kill Zapata, but the assassination transformed Zapata into a triumphant figure who stands for the ability and willingness of the rural poor to fight in order to maintain their dignity.

Zuloaga, Félix. 1813–1898. Mexican army general who, as commander of the Mexico City garrison, proved instrumental in bringing the Conservatives to power in December 1857. He served as chief executive three times, though his most important and extensive term occurred during the War of the Reform (January 22, 1858–January 24, 1859). In 1861 Congress declared him (and others) an outlaw for his involvement in the assassination of Liberal leader Melchor Ocampo.

Bibliography

SUGGESTIONS FOR FURTHER READING

Chapter One. Two Centuries of War in Latin America: An Overview

Braun, Herbert. *Our Guerrillas, Our Sidewalks: A Journey into the Violence of Colombia*, 2nd ed. (Lanham, MD: Rowman & Littlefield, 2004).
  The author, a professor of history at the University of Virginia, details his efforts to free his brother-in-law, a Texas oilman whom guerillas kidnapped in 1988. In doing so he sheds light on the issues that since 1948 have shaped the relationship between the Colombian government and the guerillas.

García Márquez, Gabriel. *News of a Kidnapping* (New York: Penguin Books, 1996).
  This account tells the story of the abduction late in 1990 of ten individuals by Pablo Escobar, the head of the Medellín drug cartel. The story exemplifies the way that narcotics have penetrated nearly all aspects of Colombian society and exacerbated its immense problems.

Marston, Joshua. *Maria Full of Grace* (2003).
  This feature film illustrates how impoverished Colombians have become involved in the international narcotics trade. Colombian actress Catalina Sandino Moreno portrays a 17-year old girl from a poor family who becomes a drug mule. She swallows heroin pellets to smuggle them into the United States.

Molano, Alfredo. *The Dispossessed: Chronicles of the Desterrados of Colombia*, trans. Aviva Chomsky (Chicago: Haymarket Books, 2005).
     Molano, a renowned Colombian sociologist and journalist, tells the story of those individuals who have been displaced from their homes since the mid-1980s by the violence that has afflicted his nation. In so doing he also sheds light on how United States' policy has contributed to their plight.

Restrepo, Laura. *Leopard in the Sun* (New York: Vintage 2000).
     A novel by one of contemporary Colombia's most renowned writers about a feud between two families involved in the drug trade.

Walker III, William O., ed. *Drugs in the Western Hemisphere: An Odyssey of Cultures in Conflict* (Wilmington, DE: Scholarly Resources, 1996).
     Through this collection of 46 documents and articles, the author aims to shed light on the historical and cultural roots of the struggle over drugs in the Americas.

Chapter Two. Death, Destiny, and the Daily Chores: Everyday Life in Spanish America during the Wars of Independence, 1808–1826

Andrien, Kenneth J., and Lyman L. Johnson, eds. *The Political Economy of Spanish America in the Age of Revolution, 1750–1850* (Albuquerque: University of New Mexico Press, 1994).
     This collection of essays by important historians deals with commercial, financial, and mercantile issues in the independence era.

Archer, Christon I., ed. *The Wars of Independence in Spanish America* (Wilmington, DE: Scholarly Resources, 2000).
     A compilation of articles by major historians that focuses on the military aspects of independence. The book also includes some primary source documents.

Chasteen, John Charles. *Americanos: Latin America's Struggle for Independence* (New York: Oxford University Press, 2008).
     The most recent publication to examine the conflicts that resulted in the creation of 19 independent republics in the region.

Kinsbruner, Jay. *Independence in Spanish America: Civil Wars, Revolutions, and Underdevelopment* (Albuquerque: University of New Mexico Press, 1994).
     This general history emphasizes the concepts of an active citizenry and an exploitative economic structure, and argues that the wars were, in fact, revolutionary.

Lynch, John. *The Spanish American Revolutions 1808–1826* (New York: Norton, 1986).
     Still the best general history of the independence era, this book offers a clear, concise, elegant account of the complicated events throughout the continent.

Rodríguez O, Jaime. *The Independence of Spanish America* (Cambridge: Cambridge University Press, 1998).

> A general history that casts the wars for independence more as a civil war within the Hispanic world through an emphasis on the innovations of the liberal constitution produced by the 1812 Cortes of Cádiz.

Uribe-Uran, Víctor, ed. *State and Society in Spanish America during the Age of Revolution* (Wilmington, DE: Scholarly Resources, 2001).

> A collection of articles that offer insight into the lives and activities of various sectors of Spanish American society during a turbulent era, including essays on: bureaucrats, import-export businesses, marriage patterns, female-headed households, architecture, and dance.

Voss, Stuart F. *Latin America in the Middle Period, 1750–1929* (Wilmington, DE: Scholarly Resources, 2002).

> A broad survey that attempts to extend the issues and patterns of the early 1800s well into the next century by focusing on the issue of modernization.

Chapter Three. The Civilian Experience in Mexico during the War with the United States, 1846–1848

Foos, Paul. *A Short, Offhand, Killing Affair: Soldiers and Social Conflict during the Mexican-American War* (Chapel Hill: University of North Carolina Press, 2002).

> The book focuses on the experience of enlisted soldiers in the U.S. army during the war with Mexico, and analyzes the atrocities— which included instances of rape and stealing, as well as large-scale massacres—committed by U.S. soldiers against Mexican civilians.

Gayón Córdova, María, comp. *La ocupación yanqui de la ciudad de México, 1847–1848* (Mexico City: Instituto Nacional de Antropología e Historia, 1997).

> This book brings together a variety of primary sources (in Spanish) that shed much light on everyday life in Mexico City during the time the U.S. army occupied the Mexican capital.

Granados, Luis Fernando. *Sueñan las piedras: Alzamiento ocurrido en la ciudad de México, 14, 15, y 16 de septiembre de 1847* (Mexico City: Ediciones Era, 2003).

> Examines the three-day September 1847 riot by Mexico City's so-called "masses" against General Winfield Scott and the United States expeditionary army, and demonstrates that the urban popular classes were key historical actors during the turbulent decades that followed independence.

Hool, Lance. *One Man's Hero* (1999).

> One of the few feature films about the U.S.-Mexican War, this production tells the story of the San Patricio Battalion, a unit of U.S.

soldiers—many of Irish extraction—who deserted the U.S. army to fight for Mexico.

Levinson, Irving W. *Wars within War: Mexican Guerrillas, Domestic Elites, and the United States of America, 1846–1848* (Fort Worth: Texas Christian University Press, 2005).
> Analyzes the guerrilla war led by irregular Mexican troops that frustrated the efforts of both the U.S. and the Mexican governments to fight each other and negotiate a peace.

Libura, Krystina M., Luis Gerardo Morales Moreno, and Jesús Velasco Márquez. *Echoes of the Mexican-American War,* trans. Mark Fried. (Toronto: Groundwood Books, 2005).
> This book offers a compilation of images and excerpts from primary sources that illustrate both the U.S. and Mexican perspectives on the conflict.

"U.S.-Mexican War, 1846–1848." www.pbs.org/kera/usmexicanwar.
> Maintained by the Public Broadcasting Service, this comprehensive Web site includes biographies of the war's most important personalities, a timeline, and resources for educators.

Chapter Four. Civilians and Civil War in Nineteenth-Century Mexico: Mexico City and the War of the Reform, 1858–1861

Craib, Raymond B. *Cartographic Mexico: A History of State Fixations and Fugitive Landscapes* (Durham, NC: Duke University Press, 2004).
> This book analyzes the intersection of geography and national identity in nineteenth-century Mexico. It helps illustrate the symbolic meaning of Mexico City, as both a place and a space, to the leadership of the Conservative regime during the War of the Reform.

Hamnett, Brian R. *Juárez* (London and New York: Longman, 1994).
> This biography of Benito Juárez, the nineteenth-century statesman who headed the Liberal regime in the War of the Reform, helps situate the experience of Mexico City during the War of the Reform in a broader social and political context.

Pani, Erika. "Dreaming of a Mexican Empire: The Political Projects of the 'Imperialistas.'" *Hispanic American Historical Review* 82:1 (February 2002), 1–31.
> Explores Conservative efforts to refine their political vision following their defeat in the War of the Reform. The essay invites comparison with the political projects of the Conservative leadership of Mexico City during that conflict.

Staples, Anne. "*Policía y Buen Gobierno:* Municipal Efforts to Regulate Public Behavior, 1821–1857," in *Rituals of Rule, Rituals of Resistance: Public Celebrations and Popular Culture in Mexico,* eds. William H. Beezley, Cheryl English Martin, and William E. French (Wilmington, DE: Scholarly Resources, 1994).

This essay provides a useful introduction to the ideas and practices that defined law enforcement in Mexico after independence.

Wasserman, Mark. *Everyday Life and Politics in Nineteenth-Century Mexico: Men, Women, and War* (Albuquerque: University of New Mexico Press, 2000).
    A synthesis of recent historical literature that provides a useful overview of everyday life in nineteenth-century Mexico.

Chapter Five. The Brazilian Home Front during the War of the Triple Alliance, 1864–1870

Leuchars, Chris. *To the Bitter End: Paraguay and the War of the Triple Alliance* (Westport, CT: Greenwood, 2002).
    Although based almost exclusively on secondary sources, this work provides a valuable general introduction to this destructive conflict.

Kray, Hendrik, and Thomas L. Whigham, eds. *I Die with My Country: Perspectives on the Paraguayan War, 1864–1870* (Lincoln: University of Nebraska Press, 2004).
    This compilation of essays by prominent historians sheds light on the everyday experiences of war rather than on military, political, and diplomatic affairs.

Saeger, James Schofield. *Francisco Solano López and the Ruination of Paraguay: Honor and Egocentrism* (Lanham, MD: Rowman & Littlefield, 2007).
    Tells the story of the Paraguayan ruler who mobilized the entire population of his country in the War of the Triple Alliance, and whose actions earned him heroic status following his death on the battlefield.

Tuck, Lily. *The News from Paraguay: A Novel* (New York: Harper Perennial, 2004).
    A vivid fictional account of the romance between Francisco Solano López and his Irish mistress Ella Lynch. The novel, which illustrates Paraguay's development and demise, as well as Solano López's political ambitions, won the National Book Award in 2004.

Whigham, Thomas L. *The Paraguayan War: Volume 1, Causes and Early Conduct* (Lincoln: University of Nebraska Press, 2002).
    This discussion of the factors that led to the war emphasizes the contending nationalisms among the nations of the River Plate region during the 1800s.

www.geocities.com/ulysses_costa/.
    This Web site, which is part of the South American Military History Web page, has accounts of the war's origins and of its most important battles; statistics; and original photographs.

Chapter Six. Civilians and the War of the Pacific, 1879–1884

Farcau, Bruce. *The Ten Cents' War: Chile, Peru and Bolivia and the War of the Pacific* (Westport, CT: Greenwood, 2000).
    A short, narrative history of the conflict and its background aimed at the general reader.

Querejazu Calvo, Roberto. *Guano, Salitre y Sangre* (La Paz: Editorial Los Amigos del Libro, 1973).
    Written in Spanish, this volume offers a highly readable narrative history of the war and its political background. The book is written from the Bolivian perspective, but the author is not gentle with his own country's performance in the war.

Sater, William F. *Andean Tragedy: Fighting the War of the Pacific, 1879–1884* (Lincoln: University of Nebraska Press, 2007).
    This fresh publication provides a detailed examination of the war's military and naval campaigns.

Scheina, Robert L. *Latin America's Wars*, vol. 2, *The Age of the Professional Soldier 1990–2001* (New York: Brassey's, 2003).
    This survey of the major wars in Latin American history, while perhaps somewhat superficial for the serious scholar, will prove useful for the general reader; the author's approach contextualizes each conflict historically.

Skuban, William E. *Lines in the Sand: Nationalism and Identity on the Peruvian-Chilean Frontier* (Albuquerque: University of New Mexico Press, 2007).
    The book analyzes the processes of nationalism and national identity formation in the territories that Chile gained in the conflict with its neighbors.

www.laguerradelpacifico.cl/
    Maintained by Mauricio Pelayo González, this Web site (in Spanish) has original photographs, documents, and computer animations.

Chapter Seven. "¡*No Vamos a la Revolución!*" Civilians as *Revolucionarios* and *Revolucionados* in the 1910 Mexican Revolution

Brunk, Samuel. *Emiliano Zapata!: Revolution and Betrayal in Mexico* (Albuquerque: University of New Mexico Press, 1995).
    Brunk focuses on Zapata the man as much as the movement, pays particular attention to his relationship to urban intellectuals, and examines the often rocky relations between Zapatista troops and civilian *pacíficos.*

de Fuentes, Fernando. "*Vámonos con Pancho Villa*" (1936).
    This film, the third of a trilogy about the 1910 Mexican Revolution, closely follows the actions of six men—the so-called "Leones de San Pablo"—who joined Pancho Villa's army in northern Mexico.

González y González, Luis. *San José de Gracia: Mexican Village in Transition* (Austin: University of Texas Press, 1974).

This book helped define a generation of "microhistories" of the Mexican Revolution. Writing about his own rural town in the state of Michoácan, González finds the Revolution a largely foreign and hostile phenomenon in which locals were more *revolucionados* than *revolucionarios*.

Hall, Linda, and Don Coerver. *Revolution on the Border: The United States and Mexico, 1910–1920* (Albuquerque: University of New Mexico Press, 1988).

This study of the border area includes much discussion of and data on refugees and migration.

Hart, John M. *Revolutionary Mexico: The Coming and Process of the Mexican Revolution* (Berkeley: University of California Press, 1987).

This important study of the Revolution encompasses a broad array of unarmed mobilization efforts by workers and peasants.

Katz, Friedrich. *The Life and Times of Pancho Villa* (Stanford: Stanford University Press, 1998).

An exhaustive study of Pancho Villa that pays considerable attention to the supportive and conflictive relations between Villa's troops and the civilian population.

Knight, Alan. *The Mexican Revolution*. 2 vols. (Lincoln: University of Nebraska Press, 1990).

Knight's masterful account remains the definitive history of the Revolution. It is relatively short on military aspects of mobilization and long on the social changes that underlie them.

Lear, John. *Workers, Neighbors, and Citizens: The Revolution in Mexico City* (Lincoln: University of Nebraska Press, 2001).

Given the limited fighting in Mexico City, this book pays attention to civilian mobilization, particularly among poor and working citizens, and their relations with revolutionary leaders.

Womack, John, Jr. *Zapata and the Mexican Revolution* (New York: Knopf, 1969).

This classic study of the Zapatista movement emphasizes the solidarity of the Morelos communities as the source of Zapatista cohesion.

www.latinamericanstudies.org/mex-revolution.htm.

This Web site has photographs of the many of the events that comprised the Revolution, and links to several of the most important documents issued during the 1910 decade.

Chapter Eight. Reading Revolution from Below: Cuba 1933

Bronfman, Alejandra. *Measures of Equality: Social Science, Citizenship, and Race in Cuba, 1902–1940* (Chapel Hill: University of North Carolina Press, 2005).

An impressive examination of the ways that ideas about race and citizenship changed over the course of time in twentieth-century Cuba.

de la Fuente, Alejandro. _A Nation for All: Race, Inequality, and Politics in Twentieth Century Cuba_ (Chapel Hill: University of North Carolina Press, 2001).
The author traces in exemplary detail how race relations changed from Cuba's inception as a nation in 1902 through to the contemporary socialist regime. His discussion of the 1933 Cuban Revolution is particularly thorough.

Domínguez, Jorge. _Cuba: Order and Revolution_ (Cambridge: Belknap Press of Harvard University Press, 1978).
Written by a political scientist, this study provides important statistical data and identifies patterns of economic and political change.

Guerra, Lillian. _The Myth of José Martí: Conflicting Nationalisms in Early Twentieth-Century Cuba_ (Chapel Hill: University of North Carolina Press, 2005).
Analyzes how the ideas espoused by José Martí, one of the key organizers and principal ideologues of the movement for independence who died in 1895, produced competing interpretations about the nature of the postindependence Cuban state.

Pérez Stable, Marifeli. _The Cuban Revolution: Origins, Course, and Legacy_, 2nd ed. (New York: Oxford University Press, 1993).
A reassessment of the triumphs and failures of the 1959 Cuban Revolution. The book traces the political, social, and economic history of Cuba beginning in 1902.

Román, Reinaldo. _Governing Spirits: Religion, Miracles, and Spectacles in Cuba and Puerto Rico, 1898–1956_ (Chapel Hill: University of North Carolina Press, 2007).
Looks into the emergence of popular religions like Spiritism and others that came from Africa, and the way they impacted notions of citizenship and race.

Solas, Humberto. _Lucía_ (1972).
Divided in three parts, all of which are centered on a woman named Lucía, the middle section of this film is set during and after the fall of Gerardo Machado in 1933.

Thompson, E. P. "The Moral Economy of the English Crowd in the Eighteenth Century." _Past and Present_ 50 (1971), 76–136.
This article helps readers understand why people (the so-called popular classes) rebel.

www.latinamericanstudies.org/1933-revolution.htm.
This Web site has photographs of the events of the Revolution, and links to U.S. State Department dispatches for 1933 and 1934, as well as to two scholarly articles.

Chapter Nine. Repression and Resistance, Hatred and Hope: Civilian Life during the Military Dictatorships in the Southern Cone, 1964–1990

Constable, Pamela, and Arturo Valenzuela. *A Nation of Enemies: Chile under Pinochet* (New York: Norton, 1991).

> Drawing on interviews with a wide range of Chileans, both those who supported and benefited from the Augusto Pinochet dictatorship as well as those who opposed and suffered from it, this book explores a variety of attitudes toward and experiences of life during military rule. It also depicts events on the day of the 1973 coup, the military regime's economic policies, and the various ways in which people struggled against the dictatorship.

Corradi, Juan E., Patricia Weiss Fagen, and Manuel Antonio Garretón, eds. *Fear at the Edge: State Terror and Resistance in Latin America* (Berkeley: University of California Press, 1992).

> Written by distinguished Latin American scholars, this book explores the Southern Cone military dictatorships' use of fear to subdue and terrorize people, explains how citizens of these countries responded to these policies, and details the influence these regimes continue to have in the region.

McSherry, Patrice J. *Predatory States: Operation Condor and Covert War in Latin America* (Lanham, MD: Rowman and Littlefield, 2005).

> The book offers a comprehensive look into the inner workings of Operation Condor, the covert alliance among Southern Cone militaries. Through a careful analysis of diverse materials, McSherry reveals how the military forces worked together to locate, arrest, torture, and disappear those citizens they deemed a threat.

Power, Margaret. *Right-Wing Women in Chile: Feminine Power and the Struggle against Allende, 1964–1973* (University Park: Pennsylvania State University Press, 2002).

> This book explores why a high number of Chilean women opposed the Popular Unity government of Salvador Allende and supported the military dictatorship of Augusto Pinochet. Using a gendered analysis and historical data, it draws on interviews with both women and men to explain why the majority of women worked to overthrow Allende.

Puenzo, Luis. *The Official Story* (1985).

> An award-winning Argentine film set in the early 1980s when the military dictatorship was beginning to collapse. It tells the story of Alicia, a high-school history teacher who comes to realize the horrors of the Dirty War as she begins to ask questions about how she and her husband adopted their daughter.

Robin, Marie-Monique. *Death Squadrons: The French School* (2003).

This French documentary explores the connections between the French military and the military dictatorships that ruled in South America between the 1960s and the 1980s. It contains interviews with members of the military who participated in the Dirty Wars, those who refused to participate in them, and some of the victims. It also discusses Operation Condor and the U.S. government's involvement in the Dirty Wars.

www.casahistoria.net/allendepinochet.htm

This Web site has links to the history of Chile, Salvador Allende, the U.S. role in the September 11, 1973 military coup, and the Augusto Pinochet regime. It also has links to posters of the time, and to information about movies and documentaries that shed light on the period.

Chapter Ten. And the Storm Raged On: The Daily Experience of Terror during the Central American Civil Wars, 1966–1996

Bencastro, Mario. *Odyssey to the North*. Susan Giersbach Rascon, trans. (Houston: Arte Público Press, 1998).

An accessible novel to all readers, it documents decades of civil war in El Salvador, coupled with the need for manpower in the United States, to explain immigrants' lives in this country and their struggles to survive.

Blum, William. *Killing Hope: US Military and C.I.A. Interventions Since World War II* (Monroe, ME: Common Courage Press, 1995).

One of the most useful summaries of the history of the Central Intelligence Agency from its creation through the 1990s. It describes how U.S. military interventions affected civilians in various countries, including Guatemala and El Salvador.

Bonner, Raymond. *Weakness and Deceit: U.S. Policy and El Salvador* (New York: Times Books, 1984).

The author describes the major players in U.S.-El Salvador relations during the 1980s. He does an excellent job of contrasting the propaganda from the Ronald Reagan administration, which sought to deceive the American public about what truly happened in El Salvador at that time, with the horrors that he witnessed while living there as a reporter for *The New York Times*.

Brody, Reed. *Contra Terror in Nicaragua: Report of a Fact-Finding Mission: September 1984–January 1985* (Boston: South End Press, 1985).

This book is a telling indictment of how U.S. policy destabilized the government of Nicaragua through a campaign of terror directed at its people. It collects testimonies of the victims of the attacks by the U.S.-supported *contras*, and exposes the policy of torture, murder, rape, kidnapping, and random violence these troops employed against ordinary Nicaraguans who were not politically active.

Carmack, Robert M., ed. *Harvest of Violence: The Maya Indians and the Guatemalan Crisis* (Norman: University of Oklahoma Press, 1988).

This book compiles firsthand accounts by anthropologists with long experience in Guatemala. After the worst of the civil war was over, they returned to the area where they had previously done field research to interview those who survived and were willing to tell about the abuses suffered by themselves, their friends, or their neighbors during the conflict.

Kita, Bernice. *What Prize Awaits Us: Letters from Guatemala* (New York: Orbis Books, 1988).

This collection of letters written by a Catholic nun who lived and worked in the village of San Jerónimo between 1977 and 1983 details the hardships of daily life in a remote outpost, and the persecution that the Guatemalan military, the government, and various right-wing elements meted out to native Indians, as well as to the Catholic Church and its priests.

Stone, Oliver. *Salvador* (1985).

This film by the controversial U.S. director tells the story of the major historical events of El Salvador from early 1980 through the first two months of 1981, and sheds insight on U.S. policy in that country.

Tobar, Héctor. *The Tattooed Soldier* (New York: Penguin USA, 2000).

The fates of Guatemalan death-squad veteran Guillermo Longoria and peasant Antonio Bernal are entwined in this thrilling novel. Obsessed by memories of his wife and son, whom Longoria killed in the early 1980s, and also by the mental picture of the assassin with a yellow jaguar tattooed on his forearm, Bernal flees Guatemala and ends up in Los Angeles, California, as a homeless person. Exhilarated by the possibility of avenging his loved ones thanks to a chance sighting of Longoria, Bernal's opportunity finally comes during the 1992 Los Angeles riots.

www.pbs.org/pov/pov2003/discoveringdominga.

This Web site tells the story of Denese Becker, a 27-year-old housewife in Iowa (when the accompanying documentary was released in 2003) who visited Guatemala hoping to discover lost relatives and the life she left behind in the early 1980s. Back then, as a 9-year-old named Dominga, she was orphaned when Guatemalan soldiers slaughtered her family and other Mayans in the Río Negro region. Adopted by a U.S. Baptist minister and his wife, Dominga became Denese and adapted to life in the United States. Yet, despite her efforts at burying the past, events forced Denese to confront the truth. The Web site includes links to related sources on Guatemala, U.S. involvement in that country, and the Maya.

Index

About the Editor and Contributors

EDITOR

Pedro Santoni is professor of history and department chair at California State University, San Bernardino. His research interests lie in the political, military, and cultural history of nineteenth-century Mexico, and his publications include *Mexican at Arms: Puro Federalists and the Politics of War, 1845–1848,* and "Where Did the Other Heroes Go? Exalting the *Polko* National Guard Battalions in Nineteenth-Century Mexico." He has also served as president of the Southwestern Historical Association, and as a consultant for historical research projects sponsored by the Ford Foundation and the Texas Parks and Wildlife Department.

CONTRIBUTORS

Arturo Arias is professor of Latin American literature at the University of Texas at Austin. The author of six novels in Spanish, he also cowrote the 1984 feature film *El Norte.* His other publications include *Taking their Word: Literature and the Signs of Central America, The Rigoberta Menchú Controversy, The Identity of the Word,* and *Ceremonial Gestures,* as well as a critical edition of Miguel Angel Asturias' *Mulata.* Between 2001 and 2003 Professor Arias served as president of the Latin American Studies Association (LASA), the world's largest professional association dedicated to the study of Latin America

Peter M. Beattie is associate professor of history and the acting director of the Center for Latin American and Caribbean Studies at Michigan State University. He is coeditor of the *Luso-Brazilian Review* for the fields of history and social science. Currently, he is researching Brazil's penal justice system in the second half of the nineteenth century. A recent publication related to this project is "The Disputed Sale of the Slave Silvestre: Mental Health, Sexuality, Corporal Punishment and 'Vices' in Recife, Brazil, 1869–1878."

Bruce Farcau lectures in international relations at the University of Central Florida. He spent 25 years in the United States Foreign Service, mostly in Latin America, before retiring in 2001. He has published several books related to Latin American military history in addition to half a dozen novels.

Daniel S. Haworth is assistant professor of history at the University of Houston-Clear Lake. His contribution to this volume arises from an ongoing study of the interplay of civil war and national consolidation in nineteenth-century Mexico.

Vitor Izecksohn teaches Latin American history at the Universidade Federal do Rio de Janeiro in Brazil. He has written extensively about Brazil's national guard and the War of the Triple Alliance.

John Lear is professor of history and Latin American studies at the University of Puget Sound. He has written various articles as well as the books *Chile's Free-Market Miracle: A Second Look*, and *Workers, Neighbors, and Citizens: The Revolution in Mexico City*. He is currently working on a history of the relationship of artists and the working class in postrevolutionary Mexico.

Gillian McGillivray is assistant professor of Latin American history at York University's Glendon College in Toronto. She recently completed a book entitled *Blazing Cane: Sugar Communities, Class, and State-Formation in Cuba, 1868–1959* (forthcoming, Duke University Press), and is currently pursuing comparative research on sugar and power in early twentieth-century Cuba, Mexico, and Brazil. Her most recent publication is "Revolution in the Cuban Countryside: The Blazing Cane of Las Villas, 1895–1898."

Margaret Power is associate professor of history at the Illinois Institute of Technology. She is author of *Right-Wing Women in Chile: Feminine Power and the Struggle against Allende, 1964–1973* and coeditor of *Right-Wing Women around the World: From Conservatives to Extremists*. She has also published in various journals and contributed chapters to several books. Her current research involves the Puerto Rican Nationalist Party and members of the Chilean military who supported Salvador Allende.

Karen Racine is associate professor of history at the University of Guelph in Canada. She is the author of *Francisco de Miranda: A Transatlantic Life in the Age of Revolution, 1750–1816,* and coedited (with Ingrid Fey) *Strange Pilgrimages: Travel, Exile, and National Identity in Latin America.* She has completed a book on Spanish American independence leaders who lived in London, and her current research focuses on patriotic culture in the independence era.